Convictions

Convictions

A PROSECUTOR'S BATTLES AGAINST
MAFIA KILLERS, DRUG KINGPINS,
AND ENRON THIEVES

John Kroger

[signature]

JAN, 28, 2010

FARRAR, STRAUS AND GIROUX
NEW YORK

FARRAR, STRAUS AND GIROUX
18 West 18th Street, New York 10011

Copyright © 2008 by John Kroger
All rights reserved
Distributed in Canada by Douglas & McIntyre Ltd.
Printed in the United States of America
First edition, 2008

Library of Congress Cataloging-in-Publication Data
Kroger, John.
Convictions : a prosecutor's battles against Mafia killers, drug
kingpins, and Enron thieves / by John Kroger.
    p.   cm.
ISBN-13: 978-0-374-10015-5 (hardcover : alk. paper)
ISBN-10: 0-374-10015-2 (hardcover : alk. paper)
1. Kroger, John.   2. Public prosecutors—United States—Biography.
3. Mafia trials—United States.   4. Enron Corp.—Trials, litigation, etc.
I. Title.

KF373.K76A3   2008
345.73'01—dc22
[B]

                                                      2008002350

Designed by Gretchen Achilles

www.fsgbooks.com

1   3   5   7   9   10   8   6   4   2

THIS BOOK IS DEDICATED TO MY PARENTS

We tell ourselves stories in order to live.

—JOAN DIDION, *The White Album*

Contents

PROLOGUE: Waiting for a Verdict   3

I. ROOKIE

1. The Making of a Prosecutor   11
2. The Code of Silence Murders   22
3. The Teddy Bear Burglary   42
4. Operation Badfellas   69
5. The Human Factor   103

II. MAFIA PROSECUTOR

6. The Scarpa Crew and the FBI   127
7. Hitmen   156
8. A Mafia Murder Trial   174
9. How We Beat the Mob   210

III. THE WAR ON DRUGS

10. Wiretaps   237
11. Bushwick   252
12. Hunting "The Puma"   273
13. The Dark Side   306
14. How to Win a War on Drugs   327
15. 9/11: Emergency Response   341

IV. ENRON: WHITE-COLLAR CRIME

16. The Enron Debacle   369
17. The Broadband Scam   386
18. Getting Away with Fraud   418
19. The Fastow Dilemma   434

EPILOGUE: New Beginnings   451

Sources   455
Acknowledgments   465

Convictions

Waiting for a Verdict

S al "The Hammerhead" Cardaci was a small-time Brooklyn car thief. Back in the 1980s, his head was blown off by a .357 fired at point-blank range. Years later we dug up his bones in a Brooklyn basement, where they had been buried under a rough concrete slab. For the last six months those bones have been in my office, sitting on my desk in a cardboard box. Today they are in evidence, back in the jury room. I am a federal mafia prosecutor, and I am waiting for a verdict.

My defendant is Gregory Scarpa, Jr., mafia capo and hitman. Before his arrest Scarpa controlled a big swath of working-class Brooklyn and Staten Island. Over the course of his career in organized crime he killed more than a dozen victims. Now he is charged with some forty federal crimes: racketeering, conspiracy, loansharking, illegal sports betting, numbers running, tax evasion. My indictment also charges Scarpa with five gruesome murders, the ones I believe we can prove beyond a reasonable doubt.

For fifteen years Scarpa was a major target of the FBI. Today, on this crisp fall afternoon, he finally faces justice. Scarpa sits huddled at a long oak table with his three criminal defense lawyers. A few feet away I sit with my trial partner, veteran mob prosecutor Sung-Hee Suh. For the past six months Sung-Hee and I have worked eighteen hours a day, seven days a week, preparing and trying this case. Together we presented more than a thousand pieces of evidence, each one painstakingly gathered from homicide crime scenes, surveillance operations, wiretaps, garbage pulls, autopsies, and raids on mafia clubs and gambling dens. We also presented testimony from three of Scarpa's underlings, all mafia hitmen, now in the witness protection program.*

Late in the trial Scarpa took the stand and told the jury that the United States government had authorized his life of crime: that the FBI was corrupt, that he and his hitman father had been on the government informant payroll for years, and that he had worked as an FBI antiterrorism spy, complete with a miniature camera. When I cross-examined Scarpa, I ignored these stories completely, hoping the jury would conclude they were bizarre and irrelevant fantasies. Actually, many of Scarpa's allegations were true.

The trial lasted more than a month. Now the jury is out, deliberating. For a federal prosecutor like me, waiting for a jury to decide a case is the hardest part of the job. As an Assistant United States Attorney, or AUSA, I wield considerable power. I run investigations, authorize arrests, and shape my own trial strategy. Control is second nature. Once, however, the jury gets a case, my fate—and that of my defendants—is out of my hands. All I can do is wait.

At 11:40 a.m., Jimmy, the court security officer, scuttles into the courtroom and hands a note to Eileen Levine, Judge Raggi's courtroom deputy. Jimmy is not supposed to disclose the contents of the note to the attorneys, but he and I have a personal connection: he used to be an Army Ranger, and I was in the Marines. He looks over at me, our eyes make contact, and he silently mouths the word "verdict." Jimmy and Eileen exit the courtroom by the back door, leading to Judge Raggi's chambers. Two minutes later, just long enough for the judge to put on her black judicial robe, they both return. Jimmy bangs loudly on the courtroom's solid oak door and calls out, "All rise." Scarpa, the attorneys, and the courtroom spectators all get to their feet.

Judge Reena Raggi sweeps into the courtroom. Tall and elegant, Raggi is known for her brains and her temper. Once she got so mad at one of my colleagues he fainted right in the courtroom. Not surprisingly, I tend to treat her gingerly, like a bomb that might explode at any minute. The lawyers approach the bench and stand respectfully at their podiums. Scarpa stays seated in his chair, watched closely by U.S. Marshals. The atmosphere, quite relaxed just a few minutes before, is now

---

*The correct title for this program is the Witness Security Program. People in law enforcement call it WITSEC.

electric with tension. Eileen states for the court reporter: "Case on trial, United States versus Gregory Scarpa, Junior."

Judge Raggi silently reads the note from the jury. Then she looks up and says, in her controlled, precise patrician voice, "Good morning, ladies and gentlemen. In the case on trial, I have received a note from the jury, which I have marked court exhibit ten. It says: 'Judge Raggi, we, the jury, have reached a verdict.' I will bring them in and take the verdict from them."

Sung-Hee and I return to our seats at the long wooden counsel's table directly in front of the jury box. My body is trembling slightly, from both nervousness and lack of sleep. This is my first big mafia trial, and after months of constant work and immense pressure, I am physically and spiritually exhausted. As the jury files in, only a few feet away, I try to judge their demeanor. Conventional trial lawyer wisdom says that if a jury makes eye contact with the defendant, it is bad for the government. Several jurors, I note, are looking right at Scarpa as they take their seats.

In tense moments I tend to smile. I fight that inclination now. I look back over my shoulder into the courtroom gallery. It is packed with spectators: newspaper reporters, fellow prosecutors, defense attorneys, a few judges. This is the big case in the courthouse right now. I take off my glasses, place my palms flat on the tabletop, and look straight down, focused on nothing. With my glasses off, the world is a gray haze.

I pray only when I'm in a tough bind. Now I silently beg, "God, please, let me have a guilty verdict." My desire to win this case is driven by mixed motives. Scarpa is evil personified. The FBI and the Justice Department have worked for more than fifteen years to nail him. I am 100 percent certain he is guilty. The idea that he might escape—that we might get an unjust verdict—makes me sick to my stomach. At the same time, my will to win, like that of all prosecutors, is personal and selfish. Sung-Hee and I have staked our careers on this case. If we win, we will be heroes. If we lose, no one will ever trust us with a big case again.

In television shows about cops and prosecutors, the dramatic moments are always loud: cops yelling at criminals; judges yelling at lawyers; the defendant's family yelling at the cops. In the real world, drama walks more softly. I hear Judge Raggi talking to the jury. She is explaining the procedure by which it will deliver its verdict. I barely listen.

I hear her words as if from a great distance or like a man submerged underwater. I do not refocus until I hear Judge Raggi's voice change tone and she says, with great formality: "Madam Foreperson, I understand that you, the jury, have reached agreement on the verdict. Is that correct?"

The foreperson stands. To protect the jury from mafia violence, the jurors' identities and backgrounds have been kept secret from both Scarpa and us. As a result, I know virtually nothing about her. Now, however, this anonymous woman is the most important person in the courtroom. She looks at Raggi and replies, "Yes."

Raggi: "All right. I am going to be using the verdict form as a guide. Let me begin with Racketeering Act Number One. As to part 'A,' have you found the charge of murder not proved or proved?"

The foreperson pauses, and I wait, listening for the simple words that mean success or failure, justice or defeat. I can hear the blood pounding in my ears. Will Scarpa go to jail for the rest of his life, or will he go home to murder again?

FEDERAL PROSECUTORS TOIL in obscurity. Most Americans know nothing about our work. None of us is on television, and none of us is a household name. If you ask the average American what an AUSA, or Assistant United States Attorney, does for a living, he will probably draw a complete blank. Even my own mother has a hard time getting it right. She always tells my relatives that I was a "district attorney," the common title for state and local prosecutors who combat most street crime. To most AUSAs, who pride themselves on their unique role, fighting the country's most dangerous criminals, that confusion is maddening.

The fact that no one in America knows anything about federal prosecutors is troubling, for in the United States today few people possess more power. As early as 1940 Supreme Court Justice Robert Jackson remarked that a federal prosecutor has "more control over life, liberty and reputation than any other person in America." Since Jackson's day, that power has only increased. In the words of federal judge (and former AUSA) Gerald Lynch, "Congress has cast the federal prosecutor in the role of God." Hyperbole? Certainly—but a revealing comment nevertheless.

Federal prosecutors have not always had so much influence. Traditionally, crime was the responsibility of state and local governments.

Federal criminal law was a sleepy and unimportant backwater. Starting in the 1950s, however, Congress passed a series of landmark crime bills that radically expanded the United States government's role in combating crime. These bills gave federal prosecutors, for the first time in our nation's history, the legal tools they needed to combat the nation's most serious criminal threats: the mafia, corrupt corporate executives, gangs, and drug dealers. As a result, the federal government is now deeply involved in law enforcement in your community.

During the exact same period, Congress, the Justice Department, and the federal courts quietly revolutionized law enforcement in a second, more subtle way. Back in the old days the federal government observed a strict division of labor: agents investigated crimes, and then prosecutors handled cases in court once those investigations were completed. Today that is no longer true. Disturbed by revelations of domestic political spying by J. Edgar Hoover's FBI and believing, rightly or wrongly, that lawyers would respect civil liberties more carefully than would gumshoe agents, America's lawmakers gradually shifted investigative power from law enforcement agencies like the FBI to federal prosecutors. As a result of this transfer of power, federal agents today cannot obtain a wiretap, a search warrant, an arrest warrant, an immunity order, or most subpoenas—the basic investigative tools required in every major case—without cooperation and prior approval from an AUSA. This gives AUSAs a virtual veto over most federal investigations. In some parts of the country federal prosecutors use this leverage lightly, and agents still run the show. But in most big cities and in all the most important federal cases AUSAs tell agents politely but firmly, "Investigate the case my way, or you won't investigate at all." As a result, AUSAs today are not just courtroom attorneys; they have become our nation's chief criminal investigators.

FROM 1997 TO 2003 I served as an Assistant United States Attorney. I supervised dozens of covert investigations, using wiretaps, searches, stings, and surveillance to bring sophisticated criminals to bay. Once these investigations were finished and my defendants were under arrest, I battled some of the nation's most talented defense lawyers in high-stakes jury trials.

Most federal prosecutors specialize in one kind of crime or another. They prosecute gangs, or drugs, or fraud. I was never a specialist. I won a very big trial as a rookie, and from that moment on, the Department of Justice moved me from one major case to the next. I prosecuted mafia killers, drug kingpins, and crooked Enron executives. Along with a team of agents, cops, and fellow prosecutors, I helped clean up one of New York's most dangerous neighborhoods. In September 2001 I worked briefly on the emergency response to the 9/11 terror attacks. As a result, I became an expert in almost every area of crime the Justice Department prosecutes.

I am very proud of my work as an AUSA. I know that without my efforts, and those of thousands of prosecutors and agents like me, the world would be a more dangerous place. This book is not, however, a simple celebration of the Justice Department's work. There is also a darker side.

When I first reported for work as an AUSA, I felt totally light-hearted. What, I thought, could be more morally straightforward, more socially beneficial than prosecuting dangerous criminals? This view proved naive. Over the next few years, to my surprise, I learned that my job was an ethical obstacle course. Like most prosecutors, I tried very hard to do the right thing. Sometimes, however, I discovered that the way we fight criminals is counterproductive, encouraging crime instead of preventing it. I also learned that on occasion the best solution to a legal problem turns out to feel pretty awful. By 2003 I had become a very good prosecutor. I had also concluded, to my deep regret, that sometimes it is impossible to be both a great prosecutor and a good human being.

PART I

Rookie

CHAPTER ONE

The Making of a Prosecutor

I n June 1996, at the age of thirty, I graduated from law school. That winter I applied to be a federal prosecutor. In my first interview a grizzled Justice Department veteran named Peter Norling asked, "Why do you want to be an AUSA?" I mumbled in reply that I possessed a "deep commitment to public service." This answer was true but incomplete. If you asked me today, I would say, "I got caught stealing hubcaps."

It was spring of 1983, my senior year in high school. My brother Bill was a sophomore at the University of Texas, and he invited me and a friend named Bob to Roundup, a big fraternity party. The morning of the party Bob and I loaded up his battered Ford Mustang in Houston with a case of Budweiser and a plastic jug of vodka screwdrivers, and we barreled down Highway 290 to Austin, drinking along the way. Bob drove fast, and we got to Austin by 3:00 p.m., already totally buzzed. We met my brother and his friends at the UT student union bowling alley, where we split several pitchers of beer. Then, to kill some time before the night's main event, Bob and I decided to drive around the city, finishing off the screwdrivers in the process. The alcohol proved our undoing. When we drove past the majestic State Capitol building, Bob saw another old Mustang sitting in the shadow of the pink granite dome with something Bob's car lacked—authentic Ford hubcaps. I don't recall what happened next. Did we discuss our next move, or was it instinctive? All I recall is that we jumped out of the car, and within seconds we had three hubcaps pried off with a crowbar. We were working hard on the fourth when the Austin police showed up. The car belonged to a state senator. Bob got charged with attempted theft. I got lucky. Because I was still sixteen and doing more watching than pulling, the cops decided to release me.

When I got home to Houston on Sunday, I was sober and scared, and that's where I made my mistake. In the criminal world it is always an error to talk about your crimes. When my parents asked me about my trip, I should have clammed up. Instead, I told them exactly what happened. My confession set off a firestorm.

My relationship with my father was already very strained. Like most family disputes, this one was neither his fault nor mine, but the product of mutual mistrust and misunderstanding. My father grew up in a tough Chicago neighborhood during the Depression and World War II, the son of hardworking German immigrants. His childhood left him with a stern worldview, with life conceived as a battle. He wanted sons built in his own image, football players who understood that "when the going gets tough, the tough get going," one of his favorite sayings. Tragically, we never saw eye to eye. From an early age I fell far short of his ideal: poor at sports, an intellectual, my head always buried in a book, good at school but decidedly lazy. My personality seemed to infuriate my father. To him, I seemed weak, "a dreamer," likely to fail.

Alcohol made things worse. For my family, heavy drinking was a normal daily ritual. In my case, it got out of control, resulting in chaos.

I had my first beer when I was five, as a "reward" for a good kindergarten report card. By the time I was fifteen, I was a total mess, drunk several times a week, staying out late and sneaking back home after my parents were asleep, barely paying attention in school. My parents recognized what was happening, and they were understandably upset. By the time I was in high school, we were barely on speaking terms.

The hubcap debacle was the last blow. When I told my parents what happened, my father exploded: "I will not have a thief living under my roof!" Fortunately, he did not kick me out that day. I was scheduled to graduate from high school in six or seven weeks. My father told me, "After you get that diploma, I want you out of here within forty-eight hours."

I was sixteen and on my own. I had little money, no job, and no prospects. I had no way to pay for college, and working at a gas station or convenience store seemed like a dead end. So I did what any red-blooded Texas boy would do. On my seventeenth birthday I went down to the local mall and enlisted in the United States Marine Corps. To make my enlistment legal, my parents had to sign the papers, since I was still underage. Thankfully, they did so, for they hoped the Marines would straighten me out. After that day I had almost no contact with my family for the next ten years.

When I enlisted, I thought I was striking off on an independent path. Today I can see that I was really trying to prove to my father that I was tough after all.

I SPENT THREE YEARS in the Marine Corps, stationed in California, in Panama, on the submarine USS *Blueback*, and on an assault carrier in the Pacific. In boot camp I learned to march in a straight line, fire an M-16, walk a post, and hump a seventy-pound rucksack. At infantry training school I was taught to read a map and use a compass, shoot heavy weaponry, operate a radio, and blow things up. I did none of these things particularly well, but I had high IQ scores, was a fast runner, and knew how to swim. Apparently, these skills were rare, at least in combination. To my total surprise, I was selected to join Recon, the Marine Corps's elite intelligence and special operations unit. Our motto: Swift, Silent, Deadly.

In Recon, my military skills deepened. I learned to travel on foot quietly and quickly, to swim long distances in the ocean at night, to rappel out of helicopters and climb up cliffs, to operate small boats and to service and repair their outboard engines, and to fire my rifle with a Zen-like assurance, hitting bull's-eyes repeatedly at five hundred yards.

The Marines taught me a lot about myself. When I enlisted, I worried deep inside that I was a coward and that in the ultimate tests of life, I would fail, a fear inculcated, in equal parts, by critical parents and a notparticularly profound reading of the later Hemingway novels. After three years in the Marines this fear had disappeared. Put in tough and stressful situations, often in physical pain, I discovered that I was neither the most nor the least courageous of men. I feared the cold but could handle heavy ocean surf with aplomb. Hated heights but enjoyed the dark. Could hike farther than most men, run faster than most, shoot better than almost anyone, but would never excel in hand-to-hand combat, for I simply did not like hitting people. Above all, I learned that physical courage is an overrated virtue, rooted more often than not in a lack of imagination.

My three years in the Marine Corps had a profound impact on the way I viewed the world. Before I enlisted, I had no particular ethical orientation. I wanted to be cool, like Jim Morrison of the Doors, or Sean Penn's perpetually stoned surfer character Jeff Spicoli in *Fast Times at Ridgemont High.* I wore cutoff jeans and Rolling Stones T-shirts riddled with holes, skipped school to drink beer at an abandoned skateboard park, and managed to get kicked out of advanced placement math. If you had asked me to articulate my values, I would have been struck dumb. At best, I might have quoted Spicoli: "All I need are some tasty waves, a cool buzz, and I'm fine."

The Marines destroyed my prior character and rebuilt me in their own image. The impact was profound. I enlisted for very selfish reasons: to travel, to have some adventures, and to get away from Houston. The idea of service to country was far from my mind. The Marines changed all that. Day in and day out, they taught me to believe that my country and my Corps were a higher priority than my own personal well-being and that some things are so important they are worth dying for.

I was never put to that test. When the Marine Barracks in Beirut was destroyed by terrorists in 1983, killing 241, the bomb wiped out an entire Recon platoon. My unit volunteered to take its place, but President Reagan pulled the troops out instead. That was as close to combat as I got. Still, my intense training in the value of patriotism permanently influenced my values. Today I still think like a Marine. To me, the primary purpose of life is to serve others, not yourself, and to work to make the nation a better place. That commitment ultimately led me to become a federal prosecutor. In retrospect, trying to steal those hubcaps was probably the smartest thing I ever did.

IN SEPTEMBER 1986 my Marine Corps enlistment came to an end, and I enrolled in college at Yale University, the only veteran in a class of thirteen hundred. Life at Yale came as a very pleasant shock. In the Marines I shared a tin Quonset hut with a dozen other enlisted men. Our "hooch" had a rough cement floor and was heated by a kerosene stove. At night I had to move my bed into the center of the squad bay to avoid an agile rat—a former Marine pet that had reverted to the wild—that frequently climbed the grooved metal walls and got into my bed. There was pornography everywhere; paying prostitutes for sex was common, particularly overseas; and disputes were resolved with fists. Punishment for disobedience was swift: fifty push-ups, while your NCO kicked you in the gut with his jump boots.

Yale, in contrast, was cushy. I had my own bedroom in Vanderbilt Hall, spare and clean as a monk's cell, with oak floors and built-in book-shelves, looking out over the shady Old Campus. My hours were my own to spend as I wished, and I passed most of my time reading—novels, history, poetry. I had expected to struggle to keep up with the other freshmen, but I quickly discovered that I could hold my own intellec-tually, for I had a good memory for facts and could write clear, precise prose. Even the food was good—at least compared with Marine Corps chow. But all these positives paled when compared with Yale's greatest gift, philosophy.

The Marines had left me ethically at sea. They had wiped out most of the rudimentary values I had been raised with—probably a good thing—and replaced them with a completely new set. This experience taught me a valuable lesson: that our moral orientation is not fixed but can change and thus should ultimately be a matter of rational choice. Unfortunately, many of the values taught by the Marines were clearly inappropriate back in the civilian world. Patriotism was fine. So was courage. But fistfights, sexism, drunken brawls, and bottle smashing were out. I needed to find a new way to live.

In the fall of my freshman year I enrolled in a course in classical Greek philosophy with Professor Nancy Sherman, a noted Aristotle scholar. My first assignment was to read Plato's *Meno*. In this brief dia-logue, Plato suggested that we can learn to be good people if we devote ourselves to rigorous philosophical self-analysis, submitting our actions and beliefs to close and careful scrutiny. I recall being shocked as I read this simple piece. My abrupt transition from the Houston suburbs to the Marines had taught me that values are mutable but not how to choose the right ones. Plato argued that not all values are of equal worth: some choices are good, some bad, and bad choices have bad consequences.

Discerning between good and bad is not easy. If, however, we apply ourselves and choose to be self-critical, we can learn to be moral—to live a good life.

Elated, curious, I devoted myself to philosophy for the next four years. When I graduated, I had a master's degree. Most of my work was highly technical, dense papers filled with what now appears to me to be almost incomprehensible philosophical jargon. But for me, philosophy was never just a course of study. I passionately believed in what the *New Yorker* writer Adam Gopnik calls "the sunny optimism of humanism," the conviction that if I read the right books and applied what I learned, I could lead a more perfect life.

In the 1980s Yale's philosophy department, headquartered in red-brick colonial Connecticut Hall, had no particular ideological focus, and this diffuse approach to the field seemed to rub off on me. I never adopted one single philosophical point of view. On the contrary, I borrowed bits and pieces of wisdom from a broad variety of thinkers: from Aristotle, the importance of forming good habits, of keeping one's life in balance, of friendship and the life of the mind; from Kant, the value of honesty, a virtue I lacked as a child; from Nietzsche, the importance of rigorous, independent critical thinking; from Aquinas, the value of analytic clarity. I revered these thinkers, but one influence stood out above them all: the great nineteenth-century British utilitarian philosophers Jeremy Bentham and John Stuart Mill.

Bentham and Mill were concerned with a very basic but critical question: What makes an action "good"? They answered that a person's actions should be judged by their social consequences. An action is good if it tends to maximize overall human happiness and bad if it leads to increased suffering. To give a simple example, donating two hundred dollars to a fund for hungry children is more virtuous than spending that money on a fancy pair of shoes, for the first choice will do more to alleviate human pain.

When I was first exposed to utilitarianism, I thought it a bit simplistic, but over time I found the utilitarian ideal increasingly compelling. As a child I had been extremely unhappy, so the idea that our goal in life should be to decrease human suffering resonated powerfully with me. I also liked the emphasis on selflessness. In the Marines I had been taught to place the safety of others before my own well-being. Now the utilitarians provided an ethical justification for that viewpoint. Looking back, I can see that I was not really doing much independent thinking—I was influenced primarily by philosophers who could explain and rationalize my own ethical intuitions. At the time, however, I felt as if I were making a great voyage of intellectual discovery.

My new utilitarian beliefs influenced many of my life decisions, both serious and trivial. When I bought my first car, I got a Honda Civic. From a utilitarian perspective, the high gas mileage, cheap price, and ultralow emissions seemed hard to beat, even though I secretly yearned for an SUV. The same kind of analysis shaped my career. When utilitarians make life decisions, they weigh the social consequences of their potential choices. As a college senior I asked: What job can I do to help decrease human pain? I considered becoming a philosophy professor or a high school teacher. In the end, however, I concluded that in a democracy the most direct way to improve human conditions is to get involved in politics. In May 1990, when I graduated from college, I packed up a U-Haul and moved to Washington, D.C.

DURING JUNE 1990 I walked the halls of Congress, handing out résumés. Within three weeks I had a job as a legislative correspondent with Representative (now Senator) Charles Schumer of Brooklyn. Every week Chuck received more than five hundred letters from his constituents. My job was to draft his responses. The first week I received my first lesson in practical politics. When Chuck reviewed my efforts, he told me, "In every one of our responses, we have to say that I agree with the writer. So read every one of their letters closely, and find something in it with which we can agree. Then emphasize that in your response."

I thought about this for a moment and then asked, "What if we disagree with every single policy position the person wrote about?"

Chuck paused and stared at me, a quizzical expression on his face, as if the answer were obvious. "Then tell them we agree that the issues are important."

From my time with Chuck, I learned that democracy actually works. Chuck paid very close attention to his constituents. He was also willing to fight to protect them. One morning, in a misguided effort to save money, the Bush administration's Department of Veterans Affairs canceled without prior warning the minivan rides that severely disabled veterans relied upon to get to their VA medical centers. Within hours Schumer's office was bombarded with telephone calls from panicking veterans who could not get to their hospitals for essential care like dialysis. As a veteran I thought the department's action was outrageous. I talked to Chuck, and he agreed we had to take action. We immediately drafted a tough letter to the administration demanding it restore this service. He and I then worked the phones, calling other Democratic congressional offices, lining up support. When we had gathered twenty signatures from Chuck's closest allies in the House of Representatives, we faxed the letter off to the VA—and to every major newspaper in the country. Faced with this political heat, the administration quickly backed off, and the rides for vets were restored.

Every day Chuck's congressional mail contained a giant stack of public policy magazines and think tank position papers dealing with the entire spectrum of national issues: foreign relations, national security, crime, health care, education, the economy. When I was hired, I discovered that most of this material went into the garbage. I put it into a box instead. Every night I carted the box home and stayed up late, reading, trying to learn my new trade.

One night, while skimming a trade journal titled *Space News*, I stumbled on an intriguing proposal to reform NASA's wasteful contracting procedures, an idea that could save taxpayers hundreds of millions of dollars. I wrote a brief policy memo summarizing the idea, and then I nervously handed it to Chuck the next day. Chuck looked at me skeptically at first—a natural reaction, for who wants policy advice from the "mail guy"? To his credit, he gave me a chance and read the memo. Within a few months Chuck's NASA Contracting Reform Act had passed the U.S. House of Representatives, and it was ultimately signed into law.

Over the next year several more of my ideas, on issues ranging from defense policy to telecommunications regulation, were passed by the House of Representatives, a tribute to Chuck's legislative skill.* Chuck gave me a raise and a promotion, but I was ambitious, and I wanted to

---

*I should make clear that in every one of these cases, Chuck took my initial idea and made it much better. These were his bills, not mine, and they reflected his own very deep command of public policy.

try my hand in a larger sphere. After a short stint working for Speaker of the House Tom Foley,* advising him on economic and education policy, I signed on in the fall of 1991 as a deputy policy director with the campaign of a newly declared presidential candidate, Arkansas governor Bill Clinton.

———

BILL CLINTON WAS A POLICY ADVISER'S DREAM, for he had a voracious appetite for new ideas. Almost every day I faxed him at least one memo on some aspect of domestic or foreign policy from my office in Little Rock—some two hundred in all over the course of the 1992 campaign. Sometimes he rejected my ideas outright. I once suggested tinkering with the operation of the Federal Reserve Board, the secretive group of bankers and economists that sets monetary policy. Clinton wisely sent the memo back, the relevant paragraphs crossed out with a black marking pen. If, however, he liked an idea, he would incorporate it into his stump speech that very day or save it for a major policy address. Over time I quietly made a significant contribution to his policy agenda, helping craft his proposals for deficit reduction, hiring one hundred thousand new cops, and "reinventing government" to improve efficiency and cut waste.

When I look back at these events today, I find them astounding. Why would anyone like Bill Clinton take advice from an inexperienced twenty-six-year-old? At the time, however, I thought it was natural. My ego inflated to absurd proportions, and I began to believe I was entitled to help set national policy. Instead of keeping my mouth shut and trying to learn from others, I pressed my own agenda. I harangued Governor Clinton about the importance of deficit reduction, argued with Senator Gore over carbon taxes, and vetoed several of Hillary Clinton's pet domestic policy ideas. When I disagreed with recognized experts like Harvard economist Robert Reich, I sent Clinton blistering memos criticizing their work. At the time I thought I was just doing my job, fighting for good public policy. Now, however, I know I must have looked absurd, an arrogant kid who was in way over his head. The press eventually

*The Speaker was a very good man, but he was more interested in being Speaker than in using his power for good. We had no agenda, no goals, and no plan. I found myself being a policy adviser to a man uninterested in public policy.

picked up on this. When, after the 1992 election, I found myself in a job as a "senior policy analyst" at the ripe old age of twenty-six, the conservative *Washington Times* had a field day. "How old would that make a 'junior policy analyst'?" the paper asked. "Fourteen?" At the time I was offended. Now it makes me laugh. The *Times* editors were right, of course. In life, experience matters, and I did not have any.

My time working with Clinton was priceless because I got to learn about American politics at the side of a master. Watching him work a crowd, I saw firsthand the source of his power, a matchless ability to forge an instant emotional bond with each person in a cheering crowd, using just a wink, a smile, a wave, or a silently mouthed "thank you" as he looked in his or her eyes. Later, when I found myself in front of juries, I found these lessons invaluable. By 1993, however, I was ready to leave. Part of this was personal pique. After every successful presidential campaign, some advisers get shoved aside in the inevitable scramble for power, and I, because of my abrasiveness, was one of the victims, relegated to a backwater at the U.S. Treasury Department. But it also reflected two larger concerns.

My first job with Chuck Schumer was unimpressive at first glance: negligible pay, cramped little cubicle, no prestige. I spent the vast majority of my time drafting letters to angry Brooklyn constituents. But though my job was unimportant, I found it personally rewarding because the results were real and concrete. When veterans lost their hospital transportation, we got them relief almost immediately, and when we found a problem that needed correcting, Chuck introduced legislation. For a person with a deep utilitarian desire to reduce pain and suffering, that kind of direct action and measurable progress was very satisfying.

When I worked for President Clinton, in contrast, progress was less easy to see. I certainly had an enviable job. I got to know Clinton and Gore pretty well, and I was on a first-name basis with the government's top officials. *The Washington Post* reported my "beep-me-at-home access to George Stephanopoulos, James Carville and the rest of the Little Rock stars." But it felt incredibly hollow. I attended endless staff meetings, shuffled huge stacks of papers, and wrote memos crafting "themes" for Clinton to articulate, but I never saw any real measurable results. The higher my position, it seemed, the less it had to do with helping real people, the more with manipulating voters and the press. I found myself hungering to do something more practical, to find a job with positive real-world results.

I was also troubled by the atmosphere of moral and political compromise. Clinton was a political shape shifter, constantly modifying his positions in response to the immediate political context. In the campaign, for example, we began the primaries by opposing federal gay rights legislation in a calculated effort to distinguish ourselves from our more liberal opponents. When, however, we found ourselves in a three-way battle against both President George H. W. Bush and the billionaire Ross Perot, desperate for support from our liberal base, we shifted 180 degrees. The same thing happened with deficit reduction. One day we were deficit hawks, and the next we were sending Congress a pork-inflated "stimulus package" that even Congress did not want.

At the time this constant changing of position seemed disastrous to me, for it sacrificed the president's long-term political and moral credibility in exchange for fleeting short-term advantage. But it also depressed me personally. I had gone to Washington to help fight for good policies. Now I found myself trapped in a cynical game in which public policy was a bargaining chip. Our goal, it seemed, was not to make the country stronger but to make a president more popular.

During the campaign Clinton had promised to streamline government by eliminating one hundred thousand government bureaucrats. That struck me as a good goal. So, in the fall of 1993, I decided to start with myself. I resigned from the Treasury and enrolled at Harvard Law School. My goals at the time were simple. I wanted to remain in public service, but in a job that offered concrete, measurable results and moral clarity, a job where at the end of the day I would know I had done something useful and ethical. I was not certain, but I thought I had identified that job: prosecutor.

CHAPTER TWO

The Code of Silence Murders

D uring the summer of 1994, after my first year of law school, I worked as a law clerk for the U.S. Department of Justice in Boston. My first day on the job, to my surprise, I was assigned to the biggest case in the office, the Charlestown Code of Silence Murders.

Charlestown is a small Boston neighborhood of some fifteen thousand residents, famed for its historic landmarks, Bunker Hill and "Old Ironsides," the USS *Constitution*. To Bostonians in the early 1990s, however, Charlestown was known primarily for violence. Between 1975 and 1994 more than fifty-five people were murdered in the neighborhood. According to news reports, the police and Charlestown residents knew who committed nearly all the murders, for there were often eyewitnesses. Unfortunately, no one in the community was willing to step forward and testify against the killers, for Charlestown was ruled by the Irish Mob, and it enforced a strict code of silence: "townies" did not talk with the police, on pain of death. In the United States, roughly 60 percent of murders are eventually solved by the police. Because of the code of silence, that figure in Charlestown was less than 25 percent.

Most law enforcement officials believed the Charlestown killers would never be brought to justice. On March 6, 1992, however, the Boston police received a major break. That day the police executed a search warrant in the Charlestown apartment of George Sargent, a local cocaine dealer, and busted Sargent with his stash. Caught red-handed, Sargent flipped—that is, began to cooperate with law enforcement. That evening he told police detectives that he worked as a street distributor for two major drug traffickers, Michael Fitzgerald and John Houlihan, who ruled the Charlestown neighborhood and enforced the code of silence. Sargent told the cops that "Fitzie" and Houlihan were experienced killers who had recently executed several drug dealers trying to move in on their turf. He also warned that if word leaked out that he was cooperating, Houlihan would try to kill him. Weeks later the cops met with Sargent again and recorded his statements on audiotape. This precaution turned out to be prescient. On the night of June 28, 1992, George Sargent was shot twice in the chest while walking down Bunker Hill Street, Charlestown's main thoroughfare. A crowd gathered around the body of the dying informant, and an anonymous voice hissed, "Shut your mouths and don't be a squealer."

Nothing motivates federal prosecutors and agents more than the murder of a witness. Armed with the leads Sargent provided before he died, AUSA Paul Kelly and a team of Drug Enforcement Administration (DEA) agents went after the Fitzgerald-Houlihan gang. Ultimately, they hit pay dirt in the form of Bud Sweeney. Sweeney was a former cocaine distributor for Fitzgerald and Houlihan who had the temerity to go into business for himself. In 1993 Houlihan tried to kill Sweeney on three separate occasions. In the last attempt Sweeney was shot seven times, and though he was paralyzed, he maintained a tenuous hold on life. Sweeney recognized that at the rate he was going, he would be dead before the year was out, and so he made a fateful decision: he contacted the DEA, agreed to testify against his former bosses, and disappeared into the Witness Security Program. Armed with Sweeney's cooperation, Paul Kelly had enough information to indict the Fitzgerald-Houlihan gang. That's when I showed up.

On my first day as an intern Karen Green, the Deputy U.S. Attorney, told me I would be working with Paul on the Code of Silence case. As she walked me to his office, she said, very casually, "I hope you'll check in with me every once in a while, to let me know how the case is going." At that moment the remark seemed innocuous. I soon learned otherwise. In many U.S. Attorney's offices, there is tension between the "front office"— the senior managers—and the frontline grunt prosecutors. In Boston that tension was palpable, even to a clueless intern. Karen was well known as an excellent attorney, a leader of the Massachusetts bar, but her prior stint as an AUSA had been in the Civil Division, representing the government in environmental and tax disputes, and she did not always trust the "cowboy prosecutors" on the criminal side of the office. Criminal prosecutors in turn thought a civil attorney like Karen simply did not understand law enforcement.

This fault line surfaced in my first five minutes on the Code of Silence case. As soon as I sat down in Paul's office, in one of his decrepit Naugahyde chairs, he remarked with a tired smile, "So, is the front office sending you down here to spy?" I was so stunned I didn't know what to say.

After stuttering for a few moments, I told Paul that Karen had asked me to keep her up-to-date but that I wasn't going to do anything behind his back. "I just want to learn how to be a prosecutor. Anything I tell her, I'll tell you first."

Paul looked at me for a moment, studying my face, and then he smiled. "Good. Let's get to work." Paul was not a petty man.

That morning I got my first assignment. Paul handed me a copy of the federal criminal statute book and a thick cardboard redwell folder filled with DEA investigative reports, grand jury transcripts, search warrant returns, and drug lab reports—all the evidence in the Code of Silence case. He also printed out a draft indictment charging Fitzgerald, Houlihan, hitman Joseph Nardone, and a dozen underlings with forty federal offenses: murders, armed robbery, drug trafficking, racketeering. "Take this stuff and read it," he barked, gruffly but kindly, with a touch of Boston accent in his voice. "Then write me a memo. For every crime charged in the indictment, make sure we've got enough evidence to indict. Also, if you can think of any additional crimes I should charge, put that in too." As I packed up my book bag, Paul gave me one more piece of advice: "Don't leave this stuff lying around. It could get someone killed." I walked out of the office a few minutes later with a very tight grip on my bag.

That afternoon I took the train back across the river to Cambridge and went to the Harvard Law School library, to my customary seat in the main reading room. When I dug into the redwell, the first thing I found was a DEA six, as DEA investigative reports are called, summarizing a debriefing session with Sweeney, the paralyzed informant. I began to read it, and within five minutes I was mesmerized.

If you are a law-abiding citizen in the United States, life is pretty orderly. People go to work, pay their taxes, raise their children, cut their lawns. Sometimes we catch a glimpse of another, more sinister world that exists alongside our own, a parallel universe of crime and violence, but we almost never encounter it, except on television or in movies. Now, however, I discovered that this criminal underworld was not just a fantasy, the creation of Hollywood directors, but was quietly bubbling all around me, a separate moral universe with its own values, its own rules, and its own heroes and villains. Every day, I learned, desperate men toting M-16s were knocking off armored cars, selling kilos of cocaine in back-alley meetings, and delivering beatings and hits to keep rival dealers off their turf. In this world nothing was what it seemed. Kerrigan's, an innocuous Charlestown flower shop, was actually a secret command post for the Irish Mob, and a run-down bar just a few blocks from my apartment was not just a hangout for rummies but the office of hitman Joseph Nardone. Nardone bragged that he was a "headache specialist": "you got a headache, I will take care of it." Bring five thousand dollars to the bar in a shoebox, and you could have your enemies killed.

Over the next week I wrote Paul a memo carefully analyzing his case. For each criminal charge listed in the indictment, I identified the "essential elements" that the government would have to prove in order to convict and then listed all the evidence that satisfied those elements. I did not find any holes, but I did discover an important point that Paul had apparently overlooked. The Fitzgerald-Houlihan gang had sold a large amount of cocaine. As I flipped through the federal statute book, I realized that its leaders were criminally liable under the government's drug kingpin statute, the continuing criminal enterprise, or CCE, law. In the memo I carefully explained why CCE might be added to the indictment. Later that week I handed my work in to Paul. He read it silently for ten minutes while I nervously fidgeted, and when he got to the CCE section, he laughed. "It's good you caught this, but it isn't an error; it's a strategy. I've already charged RICO, an incredibly complicated statute.* The jury's gonna have enough problems with that as it is. If we add CCE, we run the risk that they will get totally confused. So we're gonna keep it simple."

Paul complimented me on my work and asked me for a copy on

---

*Paul was referring to the Racketeer Influenced and Corrupt Organizations Act, a notoriously abstruse but very powerful statute that makes it a crime to participate in an organized criminal enterprise. I discuss RICO in more detail in Part II.

disk. Then he cut and pasted my entire memorandum into his own official prosecution memo, asking the front office for approval to indict. I was glad he liked my work and felt I had passed a test.

A few days later Paul told me that Karen Green had insisted that he put a CCE charge into the indictment. When I heard this information, I raised both my hands shoulder high, palms out, in a classic defensive gesture, and blurted, as quickly as I could, "It wasn't my fault!" Paul just laughed. One week later Paul indicted the Fitzgerald-Houlihan gang. The vast majority of indictments are matters of public record. On any business day you can go down to your local courthouse and find out who got charged with a crime. Paul, however, put this indictment under seal, so it would remain secret.

———

IN EVERY MAJOR FEDERAL CASE with multiple defendants, agents and prosecutors plan and execute carefully coordinated simultaneous arrests, an event known as a takedown. The goal is to pick up every single target at once, before word hits the street and the defendants have time to flee.

A few days after securing the indictment, Paul and I walked over to DEA Headquarters to attend the final takedown planning session. At the main security post, we flashed our IDs, signed into a logbook, and then were escorted upstairs to a large open-floor squad room filled with desks and filing cabinets, where dozens of agents were waiting. These were the first federal agents I had ever seen, and I took a close look. Almost all white, almost all men, many of them abnormally big, suggesting they spent some serious time in the weight room. Most of the agents had 9 mm pistols strapped to their bodies in shoulder holsters. Others had small black or nickel-plated revolvers in ankle holsters peeking out from under the cuffs of their trousers. As soon as we got through the door, we—or, rather, Paul—got a hero's welcome. Many of the agents shouted, not exactly "hooray," but something close, a deep, rumbling "haaaaaaayyyyy." Some clapped. The agents all got up and crowded around Paul, shaking his hand, pounding him on the back, congratulating him on the indictment. That was the moment I realized, for the first time, how important this case truly was. A few minutes later the meeting was called to order.

I had assumed, up to this point, that Paul would play a small role at the takedown meeting. Paul was just a lawyer, after all. Arrests, I thought, were certainly the responsibility of the DEA agents on the case. I was surprised, then, when Paul got up to run the meeting. He reviewed the indictment with the assembled team and went through the list of defendants, one by one.

"Who wants Billy Herd?" he called out.* A couple of agents looked at each other wordlessly and then raised their hands.

"Who wants Kevin Haugh?" A couple of agents chuckled.

A grizzled veteran said, "We'll take him, Paul."

Someone immediately shouted, "Don't forget your body armor!" and everyone laughed.

Another team volunteered to pick up an informant who was going to be placed in the Witness Security Program. An agent called out boisterously, "You guys gonna take life insurance out on her?" and again everyone laughed.

Paul ran through the rest of the defendants, reviewed the time schedule, and told the agents to get the defendants down to the courthouse for arraignment as quickly as they could. A few minutes later we were back out on the street. The next day, after clockwork arrests, every single defendant was in custody.

IN MANY DISTRICTS a major case like Code of Silence would not go to trial for years. In Boston, however, Judge William Young put the case on a fast track, with the trial scheduled just a few months away, in November. For Paul, that meant he had no time to waste. A few days after the takedown, we began to prep for trial. Though we felt rushed, the quick timetable was probably wise. Right after the takedown, three of our witnesses had their cars firebombed, and we were forced to relocate or provide protection to more than a dozen people, at an ultimate cost of more than a million dollars. Getting the case over as rapidly as possible was probably best for their safety.

---

*Herd was later acquitted at trial of all charges.

Paul possessed some pretty good evidence in the Code of Silence case. Sweeney was a powerful witness, and Nardone's girlfriend had also flipped—agreed to testify—giving us another inside look at the gang. We bolstered their testimony with damning forensic evidence. Acting on an informant's tip, we pulled a snub-nosed .38-caliber pistol—a murder weapon—out of the polluted Mystic River behind the Bunker Hill projects. We also matched a microscopic DNA sample from the lip of a beer bottle abandoned at a murder scene with the DNA of one of our defendants. Despite this proof, Paul was still worried about the relative weakness of the case, for it relied too much on circumstantial evidence.

One morning Paul took me aside and gave me my next assignment. "Our best evidence," he said, "is the tape of Sargent's confession. The problem is, I don't think we can use it." Paul explained that under the Constitution every criminal defendant has a right to confront and cross-examine hostile witnesses in person. As a result, the government cannot simply give the jury tape recordings of statements witnesses have made to the police; it must call those witnesses to testify in person. That was of course impossible in this case, for Sargent was dead. Paul, however, did not want to give up on the tape. Instead, he handed me a transcript of Sargent's confession and gave me a mission: "Go away and figure out how to get this thing in." I packed up my book bag—I still didn't have a briefcase—and headed back again to the law school library. That afternoon I began to research my first legal brief.

At first blush, it seemed clear that Sargent's detailed confession could not be used at trial, for it was a classic example of inadmissible hearsay, a factual statement made out of court by someone who was not going to testify in person at the trial. Fortunately, Paul had given me one helpful clue: a photocopy of a Supreme Court case, *Reynolds v. United States.* In *Reynolds*, the Court held that a defendant in Utah who physically prevented a witness from testifying at trial could not object if the government used the missing witness's prior hearsay statements in lieu of live testimony. That was good for us, since Houlihan and Fitzgerald were responsible for Sargent's death. Unfortunately, there was a catch. The *Reynolds* case was decided way back in 1878, when Utah was not even a state. Since that time the Court had declared that confrontation of witnesses is "a fundamental right." To make matters worse, the facts in *Reynolds*, involving a

Mormon defendant in a bigamy case hiding his second wife, were absurd. Would a modern court think this strange old case relevant?

Today, as an experienced attorney with Internet access and a Westlaw* account, I could research this question online in about thirty minutes. In 1994, however, I had never written a brief before, the Internet was still in its infancy, and I had been trained to research "by the book." For the next several days I leafed through hundreds of pages of the relevant federal digests, large books printed on cheap newsprint paper containing tiny blurbs describing the holdings of hundreds of thousands of cases. Whenever I found something that was potentially relevant, I would go to the shelves of Federal Reporters, find the listed case, and see whether it helped us out. By the end of the week, I was hard at work on my second legal memo, telling Paul what I had discovered.

The news was mixed. Several modern courts had ruled that if a defendant kills or threatens a witness to prevent that witness from testifying, the defendant waives his right to insist on person-to-person confrontation. These cases were useful but not definitive. The United States is broken up into thirteen separate federal circuits, each with its own court of appeals. Though circuits in the South and West had addressed this witness tampering question, our First Circuit, covering most of New England, had never considered the issue before. As a result, our legal argument would raise a "question of first impression" in Massachusetts, which Judge Young would be free to decide however he wanted. Moreover, all of the recent cases involved defendants who killed or threatened witnesses right on the eve of trial. In our case, in contrast, Sargent had been killed years before the case was even indicted. That fact might make it hard to prove that he had been killed to prevent him from testifying and not for some unrelated reason.

After Paul had digested the memo, he asked me to turn it into a motion in limine, a pretrial motion asking the court to rule on the admissibility of a key piece of evidence. I did my best, and then Paul gave my draft to Robert Peabody, another prosecutor on the case, who edited my work and honed my arguments. Holding our breaths, we filed the brief

---

*Westlaw is a commercial legal database containing searchable texts of every single reported federal and state legal case.

with Judge Young. I was hoping Young would rule on our motion quickly. Instead, he commented in court that he had "never heard of such a request" and stuck our motion in his desk drawer. Paul was forced to open the trial without knowing whether he could play the Sargent tape or not.

The Code of Silence trial began in November 1994 and lasted for more than two months, in what the court of appeals later called "a seventy-day saga of nonstop violence." I played no role in the case; the summer was over, and I was back in school full-time. Nevertheless, Paul kept me up-to-date on his progress. One afternoon I got home and saw my telephone message light blinking. It was Paul, telling me to look in the paper the next morning. There, in the front section, I read, CODE JUDGE'S RULING RAISES EYEBROWS. In a decision *The Boston Globe* deemed "unusual" and "groundbreaking," Young had granted our motion. The next day I hustled over to the courthouse to watch Paul play the tape. The scene was breathtaking. The jurors were hunched over, their eyes focused intensely on empty space as they listened to Sargent's raspy, almost ghostly voice—a voice speaking from the grave—describe his life in the violent Fitzgerald-Houlihan gang. After eleven nerve-racking days of jury deliberations, Houlihan, Nardone, and Fitzgerald were convicted, and they are now in prison for life.

———

DURING MY STINT on the Code of Silence Murders case, I fell in love with federal law enforcement. Many lawyers lead professional lives of deep and stultifying dullness, waging paper wars for petty stakes, squabbling over money. As an AUSA I thought I might escape all that. To me the U.S. Attorney's Office seemed to possess an almost magical, albeit roughshod, glamour. I admired Paul Kelly, sitting at his battered oak desk with his sleeves rolled up, methodically plotting his case, drawing an investigative noose, day by day, tighter around the necks of his targets. I liked the easy camaraderie of the gun-toting federal agents, who turned death and violence into jokes in order to deal with the dangers that came with their jobs. I was fascinated too, truth be told, by the criminals, who chose to rob and kill as a way of life rather than pursue safer, more humdrum existences. After this brief, voyeuristic brush with the criminal underworld, I concluded that if I chose law enforcement as a career, I would see America, and perhaps even human nature, in a whole new light.

MY ROMANTIC STREAK RUNS DEEP, but I can be coldly rational as well. Ultimately, it was a lesson learned in the classroom, not the courtroom, that confirmed my desire to be a federal prosecutor.

In the United States every law student is required to take a course in professional ethics. Because of my intellectual training in philosophy, I looked forward to this class. I expected a substantive discussion of the morality of law and lawyering, things that would help me learn how to be a good lawyer and a good human being at the same time. Instead, to my surprise, I learned that these two goals are often in tension.

In American legal ethics, a lawyer owes a duty of zealousness to his or her client. This duty requires a lawyer to make every legal or factual argument he or she can think of that favors the client, as long as it is not frivolous, a very low threshold. This rule makes some sense. A person who hires a lawyer wants to know for certain that that lawyer is professionally committed to doing everything he can to help him or her win the case. The rule also has a plausible policy justification. Under our traditional adversarial legal system, we have long assumed that the best way to discover the truth about a dispute is for both sides to present their versions of the facts as aggressively as they can and then let a neutral jury sort out the facts from the spin.

The problem is, the duty of zealousness leads to almost constant abuse. Under the rule, lawyers have a duty, in the words of Yale law professor Daniel Markovits, to "present colorable versions of the facts that they do not themselves believe and make colorable legal arguments that they reject." As a result, modern American trial lawyers spend most of their time trying to mislead juries. As one top attorney recently commented, "too many lawyers rely on their duty to be a zealous advocate to subvert our adversary system into a mechanism for distorting truth, subverting justice, and treating others with incivility."

Placing a broad duty of zealousness on all attorneys has had two dire results. First, it has destroyed the reputation of the legal profession. Today the public believes that lawyers are untrustworthy hacks, lower than pond scum. In a 2006 Gallup Poll, for example, only 18 percent of respondents had a "high" or "very high" opinion of the honesty and ethical standards of lawyers, compared with 84 percent for nurses and 69 percent for medical doctors. We just barely beat out insurance salesmen (13 percent), HMO managers (12 percent), and members of Congress (14 percent). One reason for this low public estimation of our honesty is that we are constantly making arguments in and out of court that we ourselves do not believe and that no one with any common sense would believe. What we call zealous representation, most folks call lying.

The zealousness requirement also comes with a serious personal cost. Eric Corngold, my first supervisor as a federal prosecutor, summarized the problem succinctly. Over time, Corngold told me, "a person who constantly makes counterfactual arguments loses their reverence for the truth." As a law student I could not have explained this problem so eloquently, but I already understood, intuitively, that a life spent trying to spin the socks off a jury could not be ethically satisfying and might even be ethically harmful. Indeed, the rule regarding zealous representation made me wonder if I could ever practice as a lawyer. Respect for the truth seemed too important a virtue to discard.

Fortunately, I discovered there was a loophole. Although the vast majority of lawyers have to conform to the duty of zealousness and live with its pernicious ethical side effects, one group of lawyers is exempt: prosecutors. The United States Supreme Court has stated that "the ethical bar is set higher for the prosecutor than the criminal defense lawyer," because a prosecutor is "under an ethical obligation, not only to win and zealously to advocate for his client but also to serve the cause of justice." This idea received its classic expression in 1935, in the landmark case of *Berger v. United States*. There Justice George Sutherland said:

> *The United States Attorney is the representative not of an ordinary party to a controversy, but of a sovereignty whose obligation to govern impartially is as compelling as its obligation to govern at all; and whose interest, therefore, in a criminal prosecution is not that it shall win a case, but that justice shall be done. As such, he is in a peculiar and very definite sense the servant of the law, the twofold aim of which is that guilt shall not escape or innocence suffer. He may prosecute with earnestness and vigor—indeed, he should do so. But, while he may strike hard blows, he is not at liberty to strike foul ones. It is as much his duty to refrain from*

improper methods calculated to produce a wrongful conviction as
it is to use every legitimate means to bring about a just one.

Justice William O. Douglas put it more bluntly: "The function of the prosecutor under the Federal Constitution is not to tack as many skins of victims as possible to the wall. His function is to vindicate the right of people as expressed in the laws and give those accused of crime a fair trial."

The notion that a prosecutor's duty of zealousness must always be tempered by a commitment to fairness and justice really struck a chord with me. Criminal defense lawyers are required to try to convince the jury that guilty men are innocent, that night is day, and that black is white whether they personally believe these things or not. But when, I asked myself, would justice and fairness ever require a prosecutor to say anything other than the absolute truth? Never, I think, making prosecution one of the only legal jobs commensurate with my own personal beliefs.

IN THE SUMMER OF 1996 I graduated from law school and began a one-year clerkship with a federal judge. That fall I began to hunt for a permanent job as a prosecuting attorney. At the outset I faced a basic career choice. In the United States there are two very different types of prosecutors. State prosecutors, typically called Assistant District Attorneys or ADAs, prosecute violations of laws passed by one of the fifty states. These laws cover the gamut of criminal conduct, from minor public disturbances to rape, child abuse, and murder. Federal prosecutors, in contrast, pursue only violations of federal laws, passed by Congress and signed by the president. These federal laws tend to focus on crimes of interstate or international significance: drug trafficking, large-scale fraud, immigration violations, environmental crimes, and violence committed by members of organized criminal groups, like gangs and the mafia.

In some ways the choice between state and federal prosecution was a coin flip. Both jobs are very challenging, and both types of prosecutors provide an invaluable public service. Moreover, each job has unique advantages the other one lacks. Federal AUSAs get to supervise criminal investigations and typically work on bigger, more complex cases. State district attorneys, however, prosecute more homicides, and they go to trial much more frequently. In a typical year, an average ADA might conduct dozens of jury trials, while a senior AUSA might try only one or two. For someone who aspired to be a trial lawyer, battling it out in the courtroom, the sheer volume of trial work available at the state level was appealing.

In the end, however, I gravitated toward federal work. My decision was in part pragmatic. AUSAs make more money, and the job carries more professional prestige. There are only forty-three hundred criminal AUSAs in the United States, compared with some twenty-seven thousand state prosecutors. AUSAs get to handle big cases early in their careers, while state prosecutors often spend years paying their dues handling misdemeanors and minor felonies. And of course I wanted to be like Paul Kelly.

My decision was also influenced by advice from Karen Green. When I talked to Karen about my options, she was blunt: "Don't become an ADA if you can avoid it. You'll get into bad habits." Her reasoning was simple. ADAs, she told me, tend to have bone-crushing caseloads, often carrying as many as three hundred cases at a time. These heavy dockets come with a severe professional cost. Because of time pressure, ADAs must learn to shoot from the hip. They put witnesses on the stand whom they have never met or debriefed, and their cross-examinations are often made up on the spot, with the defendant sitting in the witness chair. Closing arguments are not carefully plotted and practiced but delivered spontaneously, and legal motions are argued orally, not in carefully researched briefs.

Federal prosecution is very different. AUSAs carry lighter caseloads, and they are trained to research and prepare their cases carefully. Before the Code of Silence trial, for example, Paul Kelly met with every witness several times, to ensure he knew precisely what each would say on the stand, on both direct and cross-examination. He began to prepare for his own cross of potential defense witnesses months ahead of time and had all his questions worked out on paper. Kelly's approach was not unusual; federal prosecutors tend to be cautious, deliberate, and precise.

This difference in practice norms can have a huge impact on your legal career. AUSAs are known in the legal profession for their painstaking and meticulous style because they have the time to practice law that way. As a result, they are always in high demand in the legal marketplace. Karen was clear on this point: "If you decide to bail out of criminal law, a law firm would always be eager to hire a former AUSA. A former state prosecutor might not be so lucky."

THE UNITED STATES DEPARTMENT OF JUSTICE is headquartered in Washington, D.C., in a giant building occupied by thousands of political appointees and bureaucrats. Employees at "Main Justice" like to think they are running the show, and they do have some important functions: setting policy, collecting statistics, approving wiretap applications, and working with foreign law enforcement agencies. Alas, life is very dull there. One friend calls it the Tomb of the Unknown Lawyer. Most of the real work, and all the real action, take place in the DOJ's local branches, the United States Attorney's Offices.

The United States and its territories are divided into ninety-three separate federal judicial districts that stretch from Maine to the Marianas Islands, far off in the Pacific.* In each federal district the president appoints (and the Senate confirms) one lawyer to supervise all of the Justice Department's legal work within its borders, the United States Attorney. The U.S. Attorney is assisted by his or her Assistant United States Attorneys or AUSAs. Some of these lawyers are civil assistants, representing the United States in civil lawsuits. If a mail truck runs over your dog, you could sue the United States government, and a civil AUSA would defend the case. But most AUSAs are criminal prosecutors, responsible for investigating, indicting, and convicting people who violate federal criminal laws. Criminal AUSAs handle more than 90 percent of the federal prosecutions in the United States, with the rest, mainly in specialty areas like antitrust and civil rights, falling to prosecutors back

---

*Each district has its own courthouse, its own judges, and sole jurisdiction over the federal legal cases, both civil and criminal, occurring within its boundaries. Most states with small populations have just one district covering the entire state. Big states, however, usually have multiple districts. In California, for example, there are four: the Northern (San Francisco), Eastern (Sacramento), Central (Los Angeles), and Southern (San Diego). Even some relatively small states get several districts. Alabama, Louisiana, and Georgia, for example, are all divided into thirds. These states do not need three different federal judicial districts, but back in the days when the Senate was controlled by long-serving southern Democrats, these powerful senators demanded this division, to bring multiple courthouse construction projects to their states and increased political patronage to themselves.

at Main Justice. AUSAs live and work on the front lines of the fight against crime, and thus they have come to be called line assistants.

When I got out of law school, I did not want to be a Washington, D.C., bureaucrat, I wanted to be a line assistant in a U.S. Attorney's Office. Unfortunately, the odds of getting hired as an AUSA right out of law school were extremely bad—so bad, in fact, that the career services office at Harvard told me not to waste my postage stamps. In small cites like Charlestown, West Virginia, or Cheyenne, Wyoming, an AUSA's pay is comparable with or better than what most lawyers can make in private practice. Even in places like New York, however, where big firm lawyers easily earn five or ten times more money than an AUSA, experience in a U.S. Attorney's Office is a very good career investment. In many big law firms, work as an AUSA makes it easier to become a partner and is thus a ticket to personal wealth. For this reason, AUSA positions are highly desired plums. In most U.S. Attorney's Offices throughout the nation, there are five hundred to a thousand applicants for every available slot. Like me, most applicants are graduates of good law schools, but they also typically have something I lacked in 1996: three to ten years of experience litigating at a top firm or prosecuting as a state-level Assistant District Attorney. That made my job prospects look bleak.

Despite the bad odds, I decided to persevere. I was already thirty, a fine age to apply, and I had unique work experiences as a Marine, judicial clerk, and political aide that might, I hoped, make up for my lack of legal training. I also had strong recommendations from Karen Green and Paul Kelly, my supervisors back in the U.S. Attorney's Office in Boston. Besides, what did I have to lose?

Early in my judicial clerkship, I mailed off thirty résumés to U.S. Attorney's Offices from Portland, Maine, to Portland, Oregon. Within weeks, I had collected twenty-eight rejections. To my joy, however, two offices decided to offer me interviews. Interestingly, both were in New York City: the Southern and Eastern Districts of New York.

———

ONE COLD AND RAINY DAY in the early spring of 1997 I took the train into New York and went for my first AUSA interview. The Southern District of New York, covering Manhattan, the Bronx, and most of New York City's wealthy northern suburbs, is, as its own website insists, "one of the nation's premier legal institutions," long considered the Justice Department's crown jewel. Over the past century some of the nation's greatest lawyers and public servants have served in the district: Supreme Court Justice Felix Frankfurter, Secretaries of State Elihu Root and Henry Stimson, Governor Tom Dewey, Mayor Rudy Giuliani. When I went to my interview, I was aware of that tradition as well as the office's reputation for professional excellence.

I spent a whole day at the SDNY, meeting with three different AUSAs. I was impressed by their brains and obvious legal talent. Nevertheless, the atmosphere rubbed me the wrong way. All three prosecutors I met had gone to Ivy League law schools and had worked at elite Manhattan law firms. They were exceedingly polite, polished, well dressed, and a bit condescending. They exuded an unmistakable aura of privilege and self-satisfaction, more like members of an exclusive club than a prosecutor's office. As I rode the train home that evening, I thought, the SDNY may be the best office in the country, but they shouldn't be so smug about it.

The following week I went to the Eastern District of New York. Unlike the SDNY, which covers bastions of wealth and privilege like Wall Street, Tribeca, and the Upper East Side, the EDNY's turf is really gritty: the tough working-class boroughs of Brooklyn, Queens, and Staten Island, plus the sprawling middle-class suburbs of Long Island. Somehow, that geographical difference seemed to rub off on the district's prosecutors, who gave off a totally different vibe from their Southern District counterparts. Of the four AUSAs I met that day, one had gone to Harvard and another to Yale, but the others had gone to Fordham and Brooklyn Law. Several were former ADAs, not corporate lawyers. No one seemed to be temporarily warming a chair, waiting to return to private practice. Instead, they all seemed committed to working in law enforcement. Even their voices were different. In the SDNY, people spoke in quiet, serious, neutral tones, like Manhattan corporate lawyers. In the EDNY, however, I heard several broad New York accents, and people cracked jokes about cases they had screwed up when they were rookies.

In both districts, job applicants go through three rounds of interviews. Shortly after my initial rounds, I received calls from both offices. The EDNY call was straightforward; it wanted me back for a second interview as soon as possible. The SDNY call was more problematic. The

SDNY wanted to conduct a second round, but it also told me that it could not guarantee me a slot as a criminal prosecutor. If I wanted to continue the interviews, I had to agree to accept a position as either a criminal or a civil AUSA, regardless of which was offered. I had no interest in civil work—I wanted to prosecute criminals—so I scheduled my second EDNY interview immediately and put the SDNY on hold.

My first round at the EDNY had been relatively easy, mostly a discussion of my résumé, plus the oft-repeated question, Why do you want to be a prosecutor? The next two rounds were, I heard, going to be much more difficult. In the EDNY, job candidates were given complex hypothetical situations and asked to describe how they would respond as AUSAs. These "hypos" often put the putative AUSA in a totally untenable position, with no good resolution, just to see how the job candidate would deal with the pressure. I was very nervous. Fortunately, I got a little help.

Two days before my second interview an AUSA from the Eastern District I will call "Jim Washington" telephoned out of the blue. Jim had clerked for the same judge as I had, and now he was offering assistance. "In our interviews," Jim said, "we tend to use the same hypotheticals over and over. In your second round you will probably get a typical drug courier case. A person arrives at the airport from Colombia. During routine screening a customs agent finds drugs in her suitcase. The person claims she did not know the drugs were there. To indict, you have to be able to prove that the courier knew she was transporting drugs. How would you prove that?"

I paused for a moment, my mind totally blank, and then said, quite honestly, "I don't have the slightest idea."

Jim waited for a moment, to see if I could do better, and then he said, somewhat sheepishly, "Look, it is kind of traditional to, uh, get some help on these things. Proving a drug courier's knowledge is a classic problem in criminal law, something you will see over and over in the General Crimes unit. If you have no direct evidence of intent, you have to make your case circumstantially. Tourists come for weeks, not days, so check to see when the courier is flying back to Colombia. If the return ticket is for a flight forty-eight hours later, that might show guilt. Figure out how the ticket was bought. Tourists buy tickets weeks or months in advance, to get cheap fares, while couriers buy at the last minute in cash, so the transaction cannot be traced. See if the target travels back and forth to Colombia all the time; that might suggest she's a professional courier. Examine her luggage: Did she come for a vacation, with guidebooks and vacation clothes, or does it look like she is just delivering drugs? Finally, consider the defendant's demeanor when she was interviewed by Customs. Did the target seem nervous or relaxed? Did she have good answers to routine questions, or did her answers seem weak? These are some of the signs you would look for."

While Jim talked, I scribbled everything down on a legal pad as quickly as I could. Two days later my panel interview with three senior AUSAs concluded with a hypothetical, the precise one Jim had explained to me on the phone. I listened to the problem, gulped, and then spit back about half the information Jim had told me, all I could remember at the moment. When I concluded, one AUSA raised her eyebrows a bit, another smirked, and I thought: Maybe I answered that too well. I am sure I fooled no one. The next morning, however, I had a phone message: please call to schedule your third round.

The final interview at the EDNY was supposed to be the most challenging. When I arrived, I discovered that the interviewers included U.S. Attorney Zachary Carter himself, the top lawyer in the district, plus all of his senior staff. The first part of the interview was routine. By this time I had been asked why I wanted to be a prosecutor so many times my answer came out by rote: "I really believe in public service blah blah blah."

Near the end of the interview Mr. Carter gave me a hypothetical: "You are in the middle of a suppression hearing in court. Here are the facts. Agents searched an apartment and found drugs. The agents did not have a search warrant, but they claimed that they had received consent to search from the defendant, who spoke halting but reasonably proficient English. After the arrest the defendant's attorney filed a suppression motion. He claims that the agents are lying: that his client does not speak any English at all, that he did not understand what the agents said to him, and that he never gave consent to the search. When you prepared your response, the agents told you that the defendant was lying. Five minutes ago, at the opening of the hearing, your lead agent testified under oath that the defendant spoke good English. Now, however, one of the junior agents pulls you aside and says that maybe the defendant did not really speak English after all. What do you do?"

For a moment I panicked. I had no idea where to begin, and this time no one was going to bail me out. After ten seconds I said, haltingly, "Well, my first step would be to call my supervisor and ask him what I should do."

Everyone laughed, and someone said, "Okay, your supervisor says it is up to you. Now what do you do?"

"Well," I said tentatively, "I would ask the court for a brief adjournment in the hearing, so I could interview the agents and see if I could determine what had truly happened."

This proposal got batted away as well. "Motion denied. What now?"

At this precise moment, as I was struggling to determine my next step, something dreadful happened. One of my interviewers was a woman who I will call Connie Blackstone. Connie was in her late forties, and—how can I say this?—extremely odd-looking, like a clumsy male actor in drag, stuffed into a baggy, shapeless cotton dress. Connie, I later discovered, had enjoyed an extremely distinguished legal career. She was also remarkably absentminded. One day she came to work with her dress inside out, and no one bothered to tell her. Sunk deep in a comfy leather armchair, Connie was sitting right in front of me during the interview. At first she was sitting quite normally, but as I gathered my thoughts during the hypothetical, she restlessly shifted her position, sliding her butt forward and hooking one leg over the arm of the chair. Unfortunately, her dress did not shift with her. It got bunched up around her thighs, so that when she spread her legs, I got, for one brief but stunning moment, a very full look up her dress, long enough to determine that she wore giant white cotton underwear. I snapped my shoulders around so that I was facing in a different direction, and then I blushed. I was supposed to be analyzing a hypothetical ethical quandary, and my future career was on the line, but all I could think was: Wow, those are some underpants.

Would a veteran federal prosecutor veto a job candidate because he looked up her dress? I had no time to answer that question. I had to regain my composure and focus. I faced away from Connie and tried desperately to come up with a coherent response. The clock ticking, my mind blank, I simply gave up. "If the judge denied my motion to adjourn, then I guess I would disclose what the agent told me to the judge and defense counsel and see how they responded. Presumably, defense counsel would file some sort of motion, maybe to reexamine my witnesses."

Everyone nodded silently, and Zach Carter said, "And . . . ?"

"Then I'd ask for another adjournment."

Carter laughed, and everyone laughed with him. Apparently the hypothetical was over.

As the interview concluded, I had a sinking feeling in my stomach. An experienced ADA or corporate litigator, I thought, would have known how to deal with this problem. As everyone began to get up, however, Zach asked me one more question: "I know you are interviewing with the Southern District as well. If you get offers from both offices, which would you accept?"

I had five seconds to formulate a reply. I thought: This is no time to mess around. I looked at Zach and said, as confidently as I could: "Whoever makes the first offer."

The next day I got a call from Zach at my judge's chambers, offering me a job as an AUSA. He asked me if I needed a day to consider. "No, sir, I accept." He laughed and hung up.

Later I learned that when all hell breaks loose in a criminal case and you learn about potentially unethical conduct by one of your witnesses, your best response is immediately to disclose the facts to the judge and your opponent. I had passed the test.

I HAVE SAID THAT WHEN I BECAME AN AUSA, I felt totally lighthearted. What, I thought, could be more morally straightforward, more rewarding, more socially beneficial, than prosecuting dangerous criminals? Alas, this was naive. I should have paid more attention to the warning signs that were clearly evident in my interviews. If being an AUSA was ethically simple, then why, I should have wondered, was the major test I had to pass an ethically complex hypothetical in which federal agents—the good guys, right?—had apparently committed perjury? And wasn't it a little bit odd that I began my career as an AUSA by cheating on an interview question? Or that this cheating was "traditional"?

Years later I told a senior AUSA in my office what had happened, and he just laughed. "That's Jim. Pretty results-oriented. Likes to cut some corners." I must have looked unsatisfied, for he made an additional remark that has stayed with me all these years: "Look, if you aren't smart enough to steal the answers, we probably don't want you as an AUSA anyway."

CHAPTER THREE

The Teddy Bear Burglary

I n September 1997, after months of background checks and a drug test, I began work as an AUSA in Brooklyn. That same month customs inspectors made a bizarre discovery that led to my first criminal trial.

ANGELO TUFFANO AND MICHAEL D'AMATO worked at the United States Customs Service's mail facility at John F. Kennedy Airport, in Queens, part of the Eastern District's turf. Their job was to examine mail coming to the United States on flights from foreign countries and intercept any contraband, such as illegal drugs or child pornography. On most nights Tuffano and D'Amato were extremely busy, putting thousands of boxes through an X-ray machine, looking for anything suspicious. On September 7, however, things were slow. Only one flight had come in, a Lufthansa 747 from Germany.

Today, after the 9/11 attack, most foreign parcels are inspected closely, but back in 1997 a more casual regime was in place. Inspectors focused on mail from so-called source countries such as Colombia, Thailand, and Mexico, since packages from these nations were more likely to contain drugs. Packages from Germany, in contrast, were typically ignored. On the evening of the seventh, however, Tuffano decided to give the German mail a hard look. He didn't expect to find anything; he was just setting a good example for D'Amato, a rookie he was supposed to train. Besides, there was nothing else to do.

Tuffano and D'Amato went down to the foreign mail receiving room, dumped several large canvas bags full of parcels on a dolly, and wheeled them back up to the inspection room. D'Amato opened the mailbags and began to place the packages on the X-ray machine's moving conveyor belt. Tuffano, the veteran, glued his eyes to the machine's glowing monitor. A few minutes into the examination Tuffano stopped the conveyor belt and called D'Amato over. On the screen D'Amato saw the ghostly gray and silver X-ray image of a large square box containing what appeared to be a giant stuffed animal, perhaps an oversize teddy bear, and several small triangular boxes. Tuffano had examined hundreds of stuffed animals during the course of his career, and he told D'Amato that when a stuffed animal is X-rayed, the interior usually appears almost transparent. Not this bear, however. Looking at the screen, the two men could see hidden inside the bear's stomach a large black rectangular brick, most likely a shipment of drugs.

D'Amato picked up a knife, sliced the box open, and started to lift a large plush purple teddy bear free from the packaging. He immediately realized this was no ordinary stuffed animal. It was really heavy, weighing some twenty-five pounds, and when he squeezed its middle, he felt something hard and bulky inside. D'Amato placed the bear facedown on the inspection table and made a short incision, five or six inches long, down the bear's back seam, just below the neck. He put his hand inside the incision and then pulled his hand back slightly in surprise. The object inside the bear did not feel like a package of drugs, more like a stack of textured paper. D'Amato got a grip on a part of the stack, pulled it out of the bear, and immediately saw that it was brightly colored foreign currency. A few minutes later his inspection table was covered with towering piles of money: German deutsche marks, Italian lire, Swiss francs, French francs, and Austrian schillings. D'Amato then opened the triangular boxes that had been packed underneath the bear. The box labels indicated that they contained jigsaw puzzles. Inside, however, there were no puzzle pieces, just more foreign currency.

It is not illegal to ship money by mail from one country to another. If you do so, however, you are required to declare that currency in your customs declaration. After emptying the bear, D'Amato and Tuffano examined the declaration attached to the side of the box. "Three boxes of puzzles, one teddy bear, three t-shirts, twenty chocolate bars," but not a word about stacks of foreign money. Obviously, someone—drug traffickers, perhaps, or maybe just a tax cheat—wanted to transfer money secretly from Germany to the United States without declaring it to the German and American governments. Tuffano and D'Amato loaded the money and the bear back into the box and carried it to the evidence detention room. There they counted the loot: 721,130 deutsche marks, 13,700 Austrian schillings, 5,446,000 Italian lire, 3,500 French francs, and 1,240 Swiss francs. They placed it and the false customs declaration into evidence bags and put everything in a safe for the night.

The next morning Herbert Almeida, a senior customs inspector, counted the money one more time to verify the amount. He then input the currency types and quantities into a desktop computer and converted it to U.S. dollars. The currency, he discovered, was worth almost $420,000. Once he was done, Almeida picked up the telephone and called his boss, Customs Special Agent Joe Leonti.

JOE LEONTI WAS A VERY EXPERIENCED FEDERAL AGENT. Educated as both an accountant and a lawyer, he had investigated nearly every kind of federal case during his career: tax fraud, white-collar crime, money laundering, drug trafficking. Now in his late forties, he was in charge of Customs' mail interdiction program at JFK. After receiving the call about the seizure, he drove over to the mail facility to inspect the bear and the money.

In every federal law enforcement case, one agent is designated the case agent, or lead investigator. Leonti considered assigning another agent to what quickly became known as the Teddy Bear Case, but ultimately he decided to keep it himself. The amount of money was not large; in New York seizures of hundreds of thousands of dollars are relatively common. Still, Leonti was intrigued by the case. South American drug traffickers often ship narcotics to Europe through the United States rather than directly to Berlin or London. Leonti thought this was probably a return payment. Properly investigated, this seizure might unravel a major drug trafficking cartel.

Leonti began his work that day by dusting the shipping box for fingerprints, but he had no luck; all the prints were smudged. He thought about dusting the money for prints as well but decided against it. The money had already been handled by too many customs agents, so any prints left by the shipper were likely to be ruined. Instead, Leonti moved on to the box's shipping labels. In cases involving mail parcels, Leonti tried to identify and locate the parcel's sender and intended recipient. According to the labels on the box, the teddy bear had been shipped by a person named Ange Lechmann, at 75 Rostocker Street in Berlin. Leonti contacted the Customs Service's attaché in Germany and asked him to run down the name and address. Not surprisingly, the attaché quickly reported that the name and address were fake. Leonti then turned to the address of the intended recipient, Antoinette St. Martin, living at 3029 Barnes Avenue, Apartment A, Bronx, New York. He called the U.S. Postal Service's law enforcement division, the Postal Inspectors, and asked it to check this information. Postal responded positively: real person, real address.

Armed with this lead, Leonti picked up the telephone and called Neil Ross, the intake chief for the U.S. Attorney's Office in Brooklyn. Leonti told Ross about the seizure and requested that an AUSA be assigned to his case. Ross consulted a list and told Leonti to meet with David Pitofsky, a young AUSA on arraignment duty. Leonti and Pitofsky sat down that afternoon, and together they came up with a plan.

To arrest the recipient of the teddy bear for involvement in smuggling, Pitofsky and Leonti needed to prove that the recipient knew that money had been hidden inside what appeared to be an ordinary teddy bear. To get this evidence, they planned to conduct one of the most basic law enforcement operations, a controlled delivery. Agents posing as postal workers would deliver the package to the St. Martin apartment and then carefully monitor the recipient's response, to see if her conduct indicated she knew about the contraband. This would not be easy, for the person who received the package was likely to open it indoors, where she could not be watched. To solve this problem, Leonti proposed a somewhat novel twist on the classic controlled delivery. What if, Leonti suggested, the bear contained a hidden transmitter that would send a secret signal to agents if, but only if, the bear were torn open by someone looking for the money? If this was possible, agents could wait until the transmitter was triggered, burst into the house, and catch the recipient red-handed, hunting for the smuggled loot.

To see if the plan was feasible, Pitofsky and Leonti called Alan Steinmark, a Customs Service technical expert. Steinmark was experienced in all sorts of high-tech law enforcement tricks: wiretaps, court-authorized break-ins, covert video and audio surveillance. Steinmark said that wiring up the bear would be easy. A few days later he got the bear from Leonti and installed a tiny black covert transmitting device inside the rip along the back seam where D'Amato had sliced it open. Then he took an almost microscopic trip wire, with a width of less than one-eighth of a human hair, and attached it to the transmitter. If the trip wire were broken, the transmitter would emit a high-pitched tone, inaudible to the human ear but audible to anyone with a radio receiver tuned to the proper frequency. Steinmark decided to sew the tiny trip wire down the bear's back seam. He did not, however, have any purple thread to match the vibrant color of the bear. Fortunately, his mother-in-law was a seamstress. He took the bear to her that night, and she was able to find purple thread that matched perfectly. Steinmark took the purple thread, coiled it around the trip wire, and then carefully sewed up the teddy bear's back seam, so that it looked as if it had never been touched.

While Steinmark worked on the bear, Pitofsky and Leonti took care of a critical legal task. Under the Fourth Amendment to the United States Constitution, law enforcement agents cannot simply burst into someone's house and arrest him; they need an arrest warrant from a judge. Most warrants are straightforward, listing the name and address of the person to be detained. Here, however, Pitofsky and Leonti did not know who was going to tear open the bear; it might be Antoinette St. Martin, but then again, it might not. Moreover, there would not be sufficient evidence to arrest anyone until that person ripped open the bear, displaying knowledge of the money hidden inside. To solve these problems, Pitofsky drafted (and a judge approved) a rare anticipatory warrant. The warrant authorized Leonti to enter the Barnes Avenue apartment and arrest *any* person who had ripped open the teddy bear, but only once the transmitter had been triggered, and not before. Pitofsky also got a search warrant authorizing the agents to conduct a search of the apartment for evidence of smuggling, but again, only if the beeper had been tripped. If the trip wire was never triggered—if no one ever ripped open the bear—the case would simply be over.

ON THE MORNING OF SEPTEMBER 22, 1997, a team of customs agents and New York City detectives took up security positions inside the Barnes Avenue apartment building. A second group of detectives parked one block up the street. These men had a radio receiver tuned to the bear's frequency. As soon as everyone was in place, Special Agent Angela Person drove up to the apartment building in a Postal Service van—with Leonti hidden in the back. Person was dressed in a blue and gray mail carrier's uniform. She got out of the truck, the boxed-up bear under her arm, walked up the steps, and rang the bell for Apartment A. A person quickly came to the door and opened it: a black male in his twenties, about five foot six inches, maybe 165 pounds. The man looked at Person, looked down at the box, and asked, "Is that for St. Martin?" Person said yes, handed the man the box, and asked him to sign for the package. The man did so, but when Person glanced at the signature, she saw that it was totally illegible, proof, perhaps, that he wanted to conceal his identity. The man went back inside, and Person walked back to the van. As she did so, she looked down at her watch: 9:50 a.m.

Person got back in the postal van, started the engine, and drove one block up the street. Just as she started to park, an excited voice blared out over the radio: *"The beeper's gone off! The beeper's gone off!"* Leonti immediately leaped out of the back of the postal van, sprinted back down the street, and knocked on the door of Apartment A. As soon as it opened a crack, he pushed his way in, gun drawn. Inside stood the man who had talked to Person at the door, looking very surprised. Leonti looked down around the man's feet. There was the teddy bear, lying on the floor. The bear's back had been ripped open, the stuffing pulled out.

Leonti asked the man his name and learned it was Ancel Elcock, Antoinette St. Martin's brother. Leonti handcuffed Elcock and told him he was under arrest. At the same time, agents fanned out and searched the apartment. They quickly discovered a purple suitcase, with Elcock's name on it, that had not yet been unpacked. Inside the suitcase they found two damning pieces of evidence. First, Elcock had ticket receipts showing that he had flown from Berlin to New York on August 31, 1997, the day after the bear had been mailed from Berlin. Second, the agents found a clear plastic bag containing a large number of jigsaw puzzle pieces. Leonti's eyes lit up when he saw this, for though most of the money had been smuggled into the United States inside the teddy bear, additional currency had been found stuffed in the empty jigsaw puzzle boxes. Here, then, was proof suggesting that Elcock had emptied the puzzle boxes, filled them and the bear with money, and then flown with the leftover puzzle pieces to New York. Only an idiot, Leonti thought, would have kept the incriminating puzzle pieces in his luggage, but as Leonti later reflected, most crooks are really dumb.

That afternoon Elcock was arraigned in Brooklyn on federal smuggling charges. He asked for bail, but because he was a citizen of Jamaica, not the United States, the judge thought he posed a flight risk. That night Elcock spent his first night in jail. After the arraignment David Pitofsky gathered all the paperwork relevant to the *Elcock* case and put it in one of the Justice Department's tan case file folders. He left the file on the desk of Eric Corngold, the Deputy Chief of the Eastern District's General Crimes Section, the rookie unit. The next morning Eric dumped the case file in my mailbox. *United States v. Ancel Elcock* was now my responsibility.

BY SEPTEMBER 22, 1997, the day of Elcock's arrest, I had been a federal prosecutor for roughly two weeks, and I had no idea what I was doing. When I became an AUSA, I expected to receive some formal training. I learned, to my surprise, that there was almost none; in the Eastern District new federal prosecutors learned on the job, asking questions and making mistakes. During my first few weeks I talked extensively with Corngold and other General Crimes prosecutors about how to handle a typical federal case. I took extensive notes, and then I distilled this received wisdom into a checklist of basic steps to take in every new case I was assigned. Eventually, following these steps became a matter of ingrained habit, but in late September 1997 I still needed my cheat sheet. On September 23, the day I received the *Elcock* case, I therefore referred to my list. Step one: "Call the case agent and arrange a meeting." Step two: "Meet with the case agent." Leonti's telephone number was listed on the front of the case file. I called him out at the airport, and he agreed to come down to the EDNY the next day.

At nine o'clock the next morning Leonti appeared in my office and parked himself in one of my chairs. At first glance, he looked pretty un-prepossessing. He was stocky, slow, a bit overweight, with a droopy brown mustache. He wore old brown polyester slacks and a cheap blue nylon Windbreaker with the Customs seal on the breast. I knew, how-ever, I was in very good hands as soon as he started talking. Leonti sum-marized the facts of the case quickly and clearly, and then he asked me politely what I thought the charges should be. I paused, blushed, and then said, "I really don't know yet. I haven't started to examine the case." I looked down at the case jacket. There, in black pen, Pitofsky had writ-ten "currency smuggling." I looked up at Leonti and said shyly, "Cur-rency smuggling, I guess."

Leonti stared at me closely, with a slight squint, as if he were only now focusing on me for the very first time. He had been an agent for twenty years, and he must have known I was brand-new, with a very weak command of the relevant federal laws. He did not, however, test my ignorance. Instead, he kindly suggested that in his opinion, Elcock was guilty of smuggling because he tried to sneak money into the country by filing a false customs declaration.

I nodded, and then I asked Leonti how we could prove that Elcock had mailed the package from Berlin himself. "We know Elcock did it," Leonti responded, "because his airline tickets say he was there, and the jigsaw puzzle pieces found in his luggage came from the triangular puz-zle boxes containing the money that were mailed from Berlin."

I interrupted: "How do you know that for sure?"

Leonti grinned. "Because I put one of the puzzles together last night. The puzzle makes a picture of a woman standing in a window. And the completed puzzle matches the picture printed on one of the boxes."

I kept a poker face, but in truth I was impressed; Leonti was clearly a pro. We arranged a time to present an indictment to the grand jury and shook hands. As Leonti left the office, I asked him one more question: "Do you know where the money came from?"

Leonti shook his head no but said it was probably drug money. "Don't worry. I'll work on it."

UNDER THE SPEEDY TRIAL ACT, which is designed to protect a defen-dant's constitutional right to a speedy and public trial, the government has to go to the grand jury and seek an indictment, a document formally charging a person with a crime, within thirty days of a defendant's arrest. If the prosecutor violates this rule, a defendant can have his case dismissed. This means that a prosecutor has thirty days to complete her investigation, write a prosecution memorandum for her boss summarizing the facts and legal issues raised by the case, type up an indictment, get approval to indict, and present the case to a grand jury. Normally a month is sufficient to get all this done, but if a prosecutor has a heavy caseload, he or she might ignore a case until right before the indictment deadline. This leads to a lot of last-minute panic. As a rookie prosecutor I was often in that boat, for after just two weeks on the job I was already responsible for fifteen cases, and I was working seven days a week, fourteen hours a day, trying to keep up. Fortunately, I started to work on the *Elcock* case right after the arrest, and that proved to be a lucky break. For when I began to examine the facts and the law, I discovered something shocking: that Elcock might not have committed a crime at all.

There are three federal smuggling statutes, one for drugs, one for money, and one for merchandise. To charge Elcock with smuggling, his conduct had to violate one of these three statutes. Leonti and I suspected Elcock's hidden money was from drug dealing, but we had no proof of that, so we could not charge him under a drug smuggling statute. That left the laws against smuggling money and merchandise.

At first I thought the money smuggling statute, referred to by agents and prosecutors as the inbound currency law, was directly "on point," as lawyers say, for the statute makes it a crime to bring ten thousand dollars or more into the United States without properly declaring it. I did some research, however, and I discovered that the fine print in the applicable Treasury Department regulations stipulates that if you receive money in the mail, you have ten days to report the money to Customs. That stopped me cold. If I charged Elcock with smuggling money, he and his lawyer could simply claim that Elcock had intended to declare the foreign currency after he received it but been prevented from doing so because he was already under arrest. Elcock, in short, had a "safe harbor," a perfect defense to the charge of smuggling money by mail. That left the merchandise smuggling statute.

Could I charge Elcock with smuggling "merchandise"? At first I thought the answer was clearly no. Money, after all, is what you use to purchase merchandise, but it is not merchandise itself. Nevertheless, I did not give up. I decided to examine the smuggling law more closely.

All the laws of the United States are contained in a set of books entitled the *United States Code*, which is divided up into separate titles. Most of the criminal statutes are in Title 18. The merchandise smuggling statute, for example, could be found in Title 18, Section 545. I started my legal work by reading Section 545 closely. Surprisingly, it failed to define the term "merchandise." That seemed to hurt my case, but I quickly decided that it wasn't a disaster. If the statute did not define the term, that meant that prior definitions of "merchandise" by federal courts would be relevant. I went online to a database of federal cases—I had learned to search electronically since the days of the Code of Silence case—and quickly struck pay dirt. In *United States v. Lozano*, the United States Court of Appeals for the Fifth Circuit held that gold coins were merchandise for the purposes of Section 545. Now, gold coins are not identical to deutsche marks and lire, but the analogy is close, for both are types of money. Unfortunately, *Lozano* was not binding precedent. The case was decided by the Fifth Circuit, which governs federal courts in Texas, Louisiana, and Mississippi. Thus a federal judge in New York was free to ignore the decision. Moreover, *Lozano* had been decided in 1927. I doubted that most judges would be impressed with a seventy-year-old case.

Because *Lozano* was a relatively weak precedent, I did not give up my research. I continued to think about the problem. From my work as a congressional aide, I knew that virtually every federal law defines the terms it uses. This made me wonder why Section 545 did not contain a definition of "merchandise." To answer that question, I decided to investigate the history of the statute. Originally, I soon learned, Section 545 had been in Title 19 of the *United States Code*, which deals with customs duties and tariffs. In 1940, however, Congress moved it to Title 18, where the other criminal statutes are located. I examined Title 19 and found, sure enough, a definition of "merchandise" that had originally applied to Section 545. According to this definition, merchandise includes "monetary instruments." That sounded good, but it raised another question: Was foreign currency a monetary instrument? Title 19, comically, told me to refer to the definition of "monetary instruments" contained in

Title 31, which is entitled "Money and Finance." There, buried in Section 5312(a)(3)(B), I learned that "monetary instruments" includes "foreign currency and coin," but only as prescribed by the Secretary of the Treasury. Thus I had to refer to the applicable Treasury Regulations to see if I was in luck. After a laborious search through hundreds of abstruse Treasury Regs, I found that some former Treasury Secretary, God bless him, had stipulated that all foreign legal tender qualified as monetary instruments. My paper chase through the *United States Code* and Treasury Regulations had led me to a simple conclusion: as long as the judge agreed that the Title 18 merchandise smuggling statute's terms were still defined by the original Title 19 definitions, Elcock was guilty of a crime.

I explained my convoluted legal analysis to Eric Corngold in a detailed prosecution memorandum. He agreed with my conclusion and authorized me to indict. On October 22, 1997, exactly one month after Elcock's arrest, a grand jury indicted him for smuggling merchandise. I had made the thirty-day indictment deadline on the very last day.

At this point, one might well ask, if it was not perfectly clear that Elcock had committed a crime, and if he was guilty only because of the existence of abstruse and highly technical Treasury Regulations that he could not possibly have known about, why was I working so hard to nail him? The answer was not simple. I knew in my heart something fishy was going on. Law-abiding people simply don't transfer their wealth inside stuffed animals. For this reason, it seemed like a mistake to walk away from the case. But I was also worried about my career. A prosecutor's reputation is made in his first year on the job. I worried that if I released Elcock right after his arrest, after weeks of effort to trap him, agents and fellow prosecutors might conclude I was "squishy," "weak," or incompetent. To avoid this judgment, I worked as hard as I could to find a criminal charge that would stick. Fortunately, this instinct proved to be sound.

AFTER I FILED MY INDICTMENT, Abraham Clott, Elcock's legal aid attorney, asked Judge David Trager to dismiss the case on the ground that money was not merchandise. Trager refused, for he concluded, after briefing, that my analysis of Title 19 and *Lozano* was correct. Despite my victory, this weakness in my case worried me. Under a long-standing principle of criminal law called the rule of lenity, ambiguous criminal statutes are always interpreted in favor of the defendant. Though Trager agreed with my legal conclusion, I was afraid the court of appeals might invoke the rule of lenity to let Elcock go. For this reason, I called Joe Leonti and asked him to increase his efforts to determine the source of Elcock's money. I figured that if we could prove Elcock was involved in drug trafficking, we could indict him for aiding and abetting drug distribution, a more solid charge.

Leonti went to down to Customs' evidence vault and removed the Elcock evidence. On the day of Elcock's arrest, Leonti had given Elcock's suitcase and other possessions a cursory inspection. Now Leonti spent an entire day examining all the evidence more closely, and he immediately found several critical clues. In Elcock's black leather wallet, he found a business card for "Claudia Pelz," an employee of the Köpenicker Bank in Berlin. Leonti then searched Elcock's address book. Tucked inside, where they had been overlooked, were a handwritten letter and a receipt showing that the letter had been faxed from New York to Germany. The letter read:

> Hello Claudia:
>
> How are you? I hope you are okay. I just want you to know that I love you so much and I will never do anything to change that. So how are they treating you? Just hold on, be strong, you know you didn't do anything, so please hold on for me. So why didn't they give you a court date? Why did they hold on to you, you are not the only one that worked in the bank. You are not the only one that got key [sic] to the bank. Forget all of that. Please tell me what's going on with you. If you need anything, just write to mom, unless she fax it to me [sic]. Claudia Conradus, I love you so much and I don't want to lose you. So when all this is over I hope soon and I want to marry you, Claudia. I don't want to write. I'm so sad over here, everything that happened. Well, on my side of the world, everything is okay so far, I'm just waiting for you . . . Claudia, be strong.

Suddenly, as he read the letter, Leonti understood: the foreign currency hidden in the bear was not from drugs after all, but the proceeds of a Berlin bank job. Leonti immediately called the Customs attaché in Germany and asked him to make some inquiries. Within forty-eight hours Berlin police confirmed that someone had broken into Berlin's Köpenicker Bank on August 30, 1997, and stolen more than four hundred thousand dollars' worth of European currency from the vault. As a security precaution, bank employees had recorded the serial numbers of some of the bills before they were placed in the vault that night, and now the bank supplied those serial numbers to Customs. Leonti compared the numbers, and sure enough, they matched those recorded on the bills hidden in Elcock's purple teddy bear.

Leonti and I immediately contacted the German police. They informed us that a bank cashier, one Claudia Pelz, also known as Claudia Conradus, had confessed to burglarizing the bank. The Germans gave a copy of this confession to Leonti and me, and it proved fascinating reading. According to Pelz, she had traveled to Jamaica in the spring of 1997 for a beach vacation. There she had met Ancel Elcock, who was hustling on the beach in front of her hotel. They began an affair, and soon she fell in love with him. When her vacation was over, Elcock returned with her to Berlin. At first they were happy, but as the summer dragged on, Elcock became restless. Pelz was supporting him financially, and she was doing the best she could, but Elcock kept pressuring her for more money. Finally, Elcock proposed that they rob the bank where Pelz worked. At first she resisted, but she loved Elcock and didn't want him to leave her. Pelz was a trusted Köpenicker employee, with keys to the bank and the combination to the vault. On the night of August 30, 1997, after the bank had closed, she and Elcock removed all the currency from the safe and took it home. They hid the money inside a teddy bear and some jigsaw puzzle boxes, placed those items in a box, and mailed the package to Elcock's sister in New York. Elcock flew to JFK the next day. Pelz was supposed to follow shortly thereafter but was arrested before she could leave Berlin. She was very sorry for what she had done. She was also, she said, pregnant with Elcock's child.

In every federal case, the government is allowed to change its indictment prior to trial by seeking what is called a superseding indictment. Through this process, the prosecutor can add new criminal charges, drop old ones, or change her description of the crimes. After I had reviewed the new evidence from Germany, I went to the grand jury and added two new criminal counts to Elcock's old indictment. Count One of the new indictment charged Elcock with transporting stolen property in August and September 1997. Count Two charged him with receiving and possessing stolen property on August 22, 1997, the day of the controlled delivery. Count Three was the old merchandise smuggling charge. I sent the new charges to Clott, along with a discovery letter describing the new evidence. A few days later, Clott called me and told me that Elcock wanted to plead guilty. I was elated by Clott's news. By now my caseload was up to sixty cases, and I was happy to get one off my desk. Here is where I made a big mistake.

Every experienced prosecutor knows that if a defendant wants to plead guilty, you should schedule the plea as soon as possible, before the defendant changes his mind. When I called Judge Trager's courtroom deputy, however, she suggested a date some two months away, in mid-March, only two weeks before Elcock's scheduled trial. I should have prodded her for an earlier date, but I was a rookie and let it go. I stopped working on the case, assuming that the plea would go off without a hitch. This negligence almost proved my undoing.

On March 14, 1998, I showed up in Trager's courtroom for Elcock's guilty plea. By this time I had been a prosecutor for six months, and I had already participated in twenty guilty pleas, so I was calm and relaxed, ready for a routine court appearance. When Trager took the bench, he asked Clott if his client was ready to plead guilty. I expected Clott to respond in the affirmative. Instead, he stammered, "Judge, my client and I are having some difficulties, and I think we need a little more time back in the pens." Trager stared at Clott for a moment over the top of his eyeglasses and then asked how much time was needed. Clott asked for an hour. The judge agreed and quickly left the bench. I started to ask Clott what was going on, but he refused to talk. He and Elcock quickly disappeared behind the heavy oak door separating the holding cells from the courtroom. I sat for the next hour on the hard wooden courtroom benches, a feeling of dread in my heart.

When Trager reappeared, Clott spoke clearly and confidently: "Judge, my client has decided not to plead guilty but to proceed to trial instead. We are requesting trial on the previously scheduled date, March 30."

Trager looked my way. "I assume," he asked, "the government can be ready by then?"

Though I was an inexperienced prosecutor, I knew that by custom, the Justice Department has only one answer to such a question: "Yes, Your Honor."

"Trial, then, on March 30," Trager huffed.

As soon as Trager was off the bench, I exploded. "What the hell!" I yelled at Clott. "You totally sandbagged me!"

Clott tried to calm me down. "Look, I advised him to plead, and I thought he was going to. But he changed his mind overnight. He's dead set on a trial. There's nothing I can do."

Clott walked away, and I followed him out of the courtroom. I felt sick to my stomach. My first trial was sixteen days away.

VIEWING THE PROBLEM OBJECTIVELY, I should have been thrilled that Elcock wanted to go to trial. In the Eastern District of New York, prosecutors cannot leave General Crimes, the rookie unit, until they have conducted three trials. After six months in the office I still had not had my first trial, and I was now long overdue. And to be frank, I could not have asked for a better first trial than Elcock. Prosecutors divide criminal cases into three categories. "Dogs" are tough cases with very weak evidence, ones that should not have been indicted in the first place. Even a great prosecutor can lose a dog. A "triable case," in contrast, has strengths and weaknesses. Given this equality of evidence, both the government and the defendant have a decent chance of winning. Finally, there are "slam dunks," which the defense calls "suicide missions." These are cases in which the government has such overwhelming evidence the defendant has no hope of escaping a guilty verdict. Given the evidence Leonti had uncovered, the *Elcock* case looked like a slam dunk. Nevertheless, I was extremely jittery.

My immediate concern was quite practical: I needed a witness from Germany. When a lawyer prepares for trial, the first thing he does is compile a list of his witnesses, persons with firsthand knowledge about the facts who can help you win. In the *Elcock* case, this task was easy. On my computer, I wrote:

1. D'Amato: describe the seizure.
2. Almeida: testify about the value of the money.

3. Person: recount the controlled delivery.
4. Leonti: talk about the arrest, authenticate the evidence seized in Elcock's apartment.

As soon as I was done, I realized that we had one serious gap in proof. To prove that Elcock's money had been stolen, I needed a witness from the Köpenicker Bank in Berlin to testify about the burglary. That was a problem.

Obtaining an American witness to testify in court is simple. The prosecutor fills out a one-page subpoena. Then the case agent finds the witness and "serves" him with this form, a process that legally obligates the witness to show up in court on the specified day. If the witness fails to appear, the agent gets an arrest warrant and drags him into court in handcuffs.

Unfortunately, this convenient (for prosecutors) process works only in America. "How," I asked Corngold, "do I get a witness to come from Germany?" His answer threw me into immediate panic. According to Corngold, I was not supposed to call any foreign witnesses directly. Instead, I had to contact the State Department in Washington and request that it ask German authorities to help. The State Department would weigh my request. If, after review, it agreed that German assistance was appropriate, State would contact the German Foreign Ministry and make a formal application for cooperation. Once our paperwork landed on the desk of a German diplomat, he or she would analyze our application and, after review, pass it on to the German police forces. The German police would locate a bank witness, interview her, convince her to testify, and fly her to the United States—as soon as it had the time. Corngold told me that this process worked well but that it would probably take six months. Of course I had only two weeks.*

Backed into a corner, I decided to ignore the red tape. Leonti had already spoken with the bank's lawyer, to inform her that we had its loot. Now I got the telephone number from him, called her, and asked her to send me a witness. I expected her to agree. To my surprise, she was not very helpful. The German police, the lawyer pointed out, had already arrested the bank clerk, and the stolen money was covered by insurance.

---

*Since the *Elcock* case, Germany and the United States have signed a mutual legal assistance treaty (MLAT), which simplifies and speeds this process.

What did they have to gain by cooperating? At first I had no answer to this question. A few days later, however, I saw an opportunity. The lawyer suggested that she might be able to provide a witness if we could return the stolen money right after the trial, avoiding the need for her to finish the insurance claim process. When she made this offer, I gulped. I had no idea if this was possible, given customs regulations on seized evidence, and I had no time to consult Leonti. My first trial was on the line, however: no time, I thought, to prevaricate. So I quickly responded, "Sure, that will be easy." The next day she left me a message: one bank witness was headed our way. A few days later, Joe told me, to my relief, that turning over the money would be no problem.

At the time I took pride in getting my witness and "cutting through bureaucratic bullshit." This, I thought, is what federal prosecutors are paid to do: solve problems and get results. Today I think differently. Years later, when I became involved in more serious international investigations, I learned that the rules I ignored were very important. Under a long-standing principle of international law called comity, all nations agree to respect one another's sovereignty. As part of that commitment, we don't conduct law enforcement operations in one another's countries. The Mexican police, for example, cannot conduct searches or interrogate witnesses here in the United States, and American police cannot do so in Mexico. The value of this rule is clear. We don't want foreign police violating our constitutional rights, and the same goes for them.

The principle of comity, I later learned, extends to contacting foreign witnesses. Foreign governments do not contact American witnesses directly but ask American police to do it for them, and vice versa. So when I reached out to the bank directly, hunting for a witness, I was not just "cutting through bullshit"; I was ignoring international law. Fortunately, no harm was done. We had not interviewed any Germans or conducted any operations on their soil, and we had always worked through the bank's lawyer, in a friendly and cooperative manner. But it was not my proudest moment, and I learned an important lesson: before you ignore the rules, ask why they exist.

―――――

AFTER I HAD SOLVED MY GERMAN WITNESS PROBLEM, I began to prepare for trial. Here I ran into a second serious roadblock, total igno-

rance. Most federal prosecutors are hired by the Justice Department after working for at least several years as state prosecutors or associates at
law firms, and they already know how to conduct a trial. In contrast, I
had no trial experience whatsoever. I had never selected a jury, delivered
an opening statement, examined a witness, or cross-examined a defendant. Now I had less than two weeks to learn what to do.

During the next two days I put myself through a crash course in trial
advocacy. When I joined the U.S. Attorney's Office, I had been given a
copy of Thomas Mauet's *Trial Techniques*, the bible of American trial
lawyers. I now took Mauet off the shelf and read it cover to cover. My office also maintained a library of videotaped lectures by famous prosecutors, many from the EDNY, offering advice on how to win a criminal
case. I moved a television into my office, closed the door, and watched
every relevant tape. These videos proved to be a godsend. One, for example, discussed opening statements, the brief introductions lawyers deliver to the jury at the start of a trial. Before I watched the tape, I had no
idea how to do an opening statement. The video stripped away the mys-
tery, recommending a five-part structure: brief introduction, statement
of the facts, summary of the charged crimes, review of how the expected
proof will prove the defendant committed those crimes, and request
that the jury find the defendant guilty. I took notes while I watched, and
shortly thereafter I was mumbling to myself in my office, trying out various opening lines. Ultimately I opted for simplicity: "This is a case
about stolen money and about the man who tried to smuggle that stolen
money out of Germany to the United States." Alas, hardly poetry.

Next, I began to identify the specific pieces of evidence I would need
to prove my case. Most of it was obvious: the bear, the stolen money, the
false customs declaration, the puzzle pieces. I could have asked Leonti to
bring just these critical items to my office. Instead, I told him to give me
every single piece of evidence he had seized in Elcock's apartment, so I
could examine all of it personally. This proved critical. Sometimes things
that don't look important to one person will jump out at someone else.
As I combed through Elcock's possessions, I discovered a receipt from
People's Foreign Exchange on West Forty-fourth Street in Manhattan.
According to the receipt, Elcock had exchanged 3,260 Swiss francs—
worth about $2,000—for U.S. dollars on September 16, 1997. I immedi-
ately got out copies of Leonti's reports describing the investigation.

According to the Köpenicker Bank, 4,500 Swiss francs were stolen. According to D'Amato and Almeida, 1,240 were inside the teddy bear. That left 3,260 Swiss francs unaccounted for, the precise amount Elcock had exchanged on the sixteenth! Here, then, was extraordinarily powerful proof that Elcock had been involved in the bank burglary. I immediately dispatched Leonti to People's Foreign Exchange to see if he could turn up any more evidence. The next day Leonti told me that one of the employees, a man named Driss Alami, had photocopied Elcock's driver's license during the transaction and put it in the company's records. Alami could confirm that Elcock had exchanged the Swiss francs in person that day, as well as the precise amount. I told Leonti to give Alami a subpoena and inform him that his testimony was needed at trial.

After reviewing all the evidence and marking it with identification stickers (GX 1, GX 2, and so on, with "GX" standing for "Government Exhibit"), Joe and I began witness prep, meeting with each witness to prepare his testimony. Prior to each meeting, I typed up a rough draft of my direct, the questions I intended to ask the witness at trial. Then, in my office, the witness and I ran through the questions together, practicing my questions and their answers. Most federal prosecutors meet with their witnesses at least once before trial, and many prosecutors think a single meeting is sufficient. I was nervous, however, and so I engaged in overkill, meeting with D'Amato, Person, and my other witnesses four or five times each in the ten days leading up to trial. My witnesses thought I was crazy, but there was method to my madness, for as I questioned my witnesses over and over, I discovered two important facts.

First, I found that if I altered the wording of a question even slightly, the witnesses responded in slightly different ways, sometimes giving a more vivid answer, sometimes a more boring one. Because I wanted to keep the jury interested in my case, I started to experiment, fine-tuning my questions so that I could elicit the most dramatic, compelling, and effective testimony possible. After a while I started to see myself as a director of a play, working with actors to make their presentations come alive.

I also learned that sometimes witnesses would disclose during the third or fourth prep session valuable new information for the first time, facts they had previously forgotten about or thought were irrelevant. For example, Alan Steinmark did not tell me that he had obtained the purple thread he used to sew up the bear from his seamstress mother-in-law until our last meeting, just before the trial. He thought this fact was triv-ial. I thought it would make Steinmark seem more human, more likable, and ultimately more believable.

After all the witnesses and evidence were ready, I went back to work on my opening statement. When I talked to experienced prosecutors, they advised me to write out my opening statement in full and then read it to the jury. This, they told me, prevents you from accidentally making a disastrous legal error or, even worse, forgetting your opening entirely, out of nervousness. When I watched attorneys at trial, however, I thought this method was incredibly ineffective, for they were constantly breaking eye contact with their jurors in order to look down at their notes. Decades ago, in a mandatory sixth-grade speech class, I had dis-covered that I could deliver speeches from memory after just a little practice, and I decided that I would do that now. Every night, when I walked home from work, I practiced my opening statement out loud, trying different phrases and gestures. People in Fort Greene, my gritty Brooklyn neighborhood, must have thought I was crazy, a white guy in a pinstripe suit mumbling and gesticulating to a nonexistent crowd. But it worked. Soon I had my opening speech down cold.

———

A FEW DAYS BEFORE TRIAL Clott and I appeared before Judge Trager to pick a jury. Eight hundred years ago, when English courts first began to use juries, the judges did not speak English in court, but Anglo-Norman French. In the law, change comes slowly. Today American lawyers still use the old French term for this process, *voir dire.*

In voir dire, lawyers examine potential jurors in person, looking them over closely and asking them questions. The goal of voir dire is to ensure that the jurors responsible for deciding a criminal case can be fair and impartial to both the government and the defendant. In state court the trial lawyers generally question prospective jurors directly, a process that can lead to grandstanding and gamesmanship. In federal court the judges typically ask the questions themselves. Judge Trager, for example, asked our jury panel members about their occupations, places of resi-dence, children, criminal records, whether they had any relatives who worked in law enforcement, whether they had ever been crime victims, and what newspapers, if any, they read on a regular basis. Finally he asked them whether they could be fair in a criminal trial. Trager eliminated a few jurors he thought might have trouble being impartial, and then he asked Clott and me to exercise our peremptory challenges, which we could use to knock anyone we wanted off the jury.

When rookie federal prosecutors try their first few cases, they are typically assigned a second seat, an experienced prosecutor they can turn to for advice. Mine was a gang prosecutor named Lisa Klem. That morning I asked Lisa how to pick a jury, and for ten or fifteen minutes she shared the Eastern District's conventional wisdom. Try, Lisa told me, to select solid middle-class jurors, people with stakes in the community: parents, homeowners, people with steady jobs. People with family ties to law enforcement—a sister or a cousin who is a cop, for example—are great. Avoid persons who might be sympathetic to Elcock: people with criminal records or who have been in disputes with the government in the past, over parking tickets or taxes. To convict, the jury has to reach a unanimous decision, and that means you want a jury that gets along well together, without arguments or disputes, so skip anyone who seems cranky or antisocial. Choose jurors from Long Island and Staten Island over those from Queens and Brooklyn: on average, they are tougher on crime. And if Trager asks about newspapers, pay close attention. You want readers of the *New York Post*, the simplistic conservative tabloid. If a juror reads *The New York Times*, she is probably a thoughtful liberal, and you should boot her off the panel.

Armed with this advice, I did the best I could. I eliminated all the well-read liberals from Brooklyn with tax problems. Clott, in turn, struck all the retired cops from Staten Island with *New York Post* subscriptions. In the end, neither of us was really happy with the jury panel, a pretty good sign that the process was fair.

The jury selection process held one surprise. Though lawyers can generally use their challenges to kick anyone off the jury, there is one important limit. In a landmark case called *Batson v. Kentucky*, the United States Supreme Court held that you cannot eliminate a person from a jury solely because of his or her race (a ruling later extended to gender). After I had used four or five of my challenges, striking several minority members in the process, Clott stood up and charged me with violating *Batson*. I have to say, I was outraged. I was raised in a suburb in Texas where racist comments were common, so I was highly conscious of discrimination. I had carefully monitored my challenges to ensure that race was not a factor. Judge Trager calmly asked me to justify my strikes, and after I provided my "racially neutral" explanations, Trager rejected the motion. He then noted that if anyone was violating *Batson*, it was Clott; while I had struck a racially diverse group from the panel, all his strikes had been aimed at white people. Later I asked Clott hotly if he really thought I was a racist. He sheepishly replied that he felt he had to make the motion to protect his client.

The Sunday night before trial, I couldn't sleep. Why, I kept asking myself, is Elcock going to trial? Clott is not stupid. There must be some trap, some secret defense that I've been too dumb to see. Finally, around four in the morning, I fell into a fitful sleep. The next day I drank several cups of coffee, put on my best gray suit, and went to the office early. Leonti and I put all our evidence on a cart, and together we wheeled it across the street to the courthouse. Elcock was already present in the courtroom, dressed that morning for trial in a bright purple suit. As soon as I saw him, I laughed out loud. The suit was the exact same color as the purple teddy bear! Clott had noticed the problem as well, and we delayed the start of the trial while he found his client a less flashy outfit.

———

THE TRIAL OF ANCEL ELCOCK BEGAN at nine-thirty on a cold gray Monday morning. Trager brought the jurors out and gave them some preliminary legal instructions, and then he asked me to deliver the government's opening statement. The courtroom deputy had placed a podium in front of the jury box for the attorneys to use. I now moved it to the side. I had my statement memorized, and I did not want a large wooden barrier between me and the jurors. I was tense as I began to talk, but this quickly faded. Ten minutes later I had finished my brief speech and was back in my chair. Lisa Klem leaned over and whispered, "Nice job."

Now it was the defense's turn. Clott's opening statement was written down, so before he could begin, he had to walk over to the podium, pick it up, and lug it back into place in front of the jury. This took a minute or two, and since the podium was heavy, Clott looked awkward as he muscled it back into place. I was amused, and I could see that some of the jurors were too. Indeed, that was part of the reason I had moved the podium in the first place. I wanted to call attention to a difference between us: my speaking from memory and apparently from conviction, while Clott read something off a piece of paper. This was bush-league psychological warfare, but I would do it again in a heartbeat.

I was a nervous wreck as Clott began his opening statement. During the prior night I had tortured myself, trying to imagine Clott's secret defense, the missing piece to the puzzle that would expose me to ridicule and set Elcock free. As soon as he started to speak, however, I began to relax, for Elcock's defense was preposterous. Elcock, Clott told the jury, was sitting at home one day when a package arrived from Germany. Since Elcock had recently traveled there, he assumed the package was for him, and so he decided to open it. When he did so, he found the bear. "You'll hear," Clott explained, "that it was not your usual teddy bear. It was probably the heaviest teddy bear, the most oddly-shaped teddy bear anyone would ever come across. It was obviously stuffed with something, obviously stuffed with something intended for the recipient. So Ancel Elcock did what any of us sitting here would do under the circumstances. He opened the teddy bear, and that, ladies and gentlemen, is the case, nothing more, nothing less."

As he spoke, I thought: If this is the defense, I've won the case. Clott assumed that when the package was delivered to Barnes Avenue, the bear inside the box was heavy and lumpy, filled with twenty pounds of currency, providing Elcock with an excuse to explain why he had ripped it open. In truth, however, all the money had been taken out prior to delivery, and the bear had been restuffed, so that it resembled an ordinary teddy bear in every respect. Clott's claim that "any of us" would rip open a giant purple teddy bear also seemed patently absurd. Clott had no explanation for the puzzle pieces found in his client's luggage or his exchange of the missing Swiss francs. As the jurors listened, I could see that some of them were trying not to laugh, and my confidence immediately improved. There was no missing trick. Elcock was simply in denial, on a suicide mission.

What does it feel like to conduct your first trial? For me, two things stood out. The first was the lack of surprises. Every one of my witnesses testified just as we had practiced, and I was not forced to adjust my trial strategy in any significant way. At the time I chalked this up to careful preparation, and this was true in part. Looking back, however, I now see it was also the result of the strength of my case, which left Clott with very little room to maneuver. In the future I would not be so lucky.

I also realized something bizarre. Inside the courtroom time does not flow the same way it does in the real world. When my witnesses were on the stand, I was more intellectually focused than I had ever been before in my life. As they answered my questions, I constantly monitored the jurors' facial expressions and body language, trying to see if they understood the testimony or were lost or bored. Then I made hundreds of microadjustments to the tone of my voice and the pace and contents of my questions or took short breaks to let them examine the physical evidence, in order to keep them engaged. Every few minutes I would look at my watch, and I would see in surprise that hours, not minutes, had passed. Trial work, I learned, is like surgery, totally absorbing. At the end of each day I was exhausted.

AFTER TWO TRIAL DAYS I RESTED MY CASE. Clott declined to offer any evidence—not surprising, under the circumstances, for there were no positive facts for him to present—and then we both gave short closing arguments. Late on Wednesday afternoon Trager sent the jury to deliberate. Here is where the trial got interesting.

When the jury left the courtroom, I was feeling great. I thought I had tried a good case, and Lisa agreed. "They'll be back this afternoon," she commented. Slam dunk, right? That afternoon, however, the jury sent the judge a note that immediately sent me into panic. It did not report that the jury had reached a verdict. Instead, it said, "We need to define what it means to 'receive' merchandise." After he read the note out loud, Trager snorted, choking back a laugh, and turned to me with a grin. "I think," he said, with a twinkle in his eye, "what they are concerned about is that you didn't leave any money in the teddy bear."

Did you see this problem coming? If you did, you are certainly smarter than I am. For Trager was right. When I sought my superseding indictment, I had made a fundamental charging error. Count Two of my indictment charged Elcock with receiving or possessing stolen property on September 22, 1997, the day of the controlled delivery. On that day, however, we had made an operational blunder. Instead of leaving some money in the bear, we delivered it totally empty. As a result, Elcock did not receive stolen property that day. He was innocent of Count Two.

At first I tried not to panic. After all, my error would not affect counts one and three, right? Unfortunately, the jurors finished the day without reaching a verdict, and the barrage of notes they sent out the following morning, about a host of technical legal issues, many of them irrelevant, suggested they might be confused about those two crimes as well. Was it possible that one fundamental error would infect the whole case? Would my mistake lead the jury to have "reasonable doubt" about the rest of the facts? I did not know. I lacked the experience to know what was going on. But it was clear to me by the second day of deliberations that the mood in the courtroom had changed. Clott and Elcock looked gleeful, Trager looked concerned, and Lisa was filled with pity. At one point she leaned over, patted me on the leg, and whispered, "Regardless of how this comes out, you should feel proud. You did a great job." I could tell she thought I might lose. As for me, I was simply in shock.

Waiting for a verdict is the hardest part of a trial. During the trial itself, there is a great deal of pressure, but you are so focused on the job at hand you have no time to be anxious. When, however, your work is done and the jury is out, all your worries catch up with you. You sit there at your table, physically drained, trying to imagine what the jury is thinking, and your emotions go on a roller-coaster ride, elated one moment, despondent the next. In your head, you replay every key moment of the trial. Could I have done that direct examination better? Should I have mentioned a particular fact in my closing? Should I have prepared more? For a rookie, all these anxieties are magnified by ignorance. By Thursday afternoon I was a wreck. Why, I kept asking myself, had I made such a stupid charging mistake?

Late Thursday afternoon the jury sent out another note: "Dear Judge Trager: We agreed on two counts but cannot agree on Count Two." I was afraid the jury was going to acquit on Counts One and Three, so I asked the judge tell the jury to continue deliberations. Trager, however, sensibly refused. "I'm not wasting any more time with this jury," he said quietly in disgust. You could tell Trager thought Elcock was guilty but might escape nevertheless. A few minutes later the jurors emerged from the jury room and took their seats back in the box. Elcock and Clott stood to hear Elcock's fate. I stayed in my chair, my stomach churning, fiddling with a pencil, trying to hide my nerves. Trager then addressed the foreperson.

"Madame Forelady, is this a partial verdict?"

"Yes, Your Honor."

"On Count One, how do you find the defendant, guilty or not guilty?"

"Guilty."

"On Count Three, how do you find the defendant, guilty or not guilty?"

"Guilty."

As I heard these words, I dropped my head toward the table and almost moaned in relief. My head was spinning and my hands trembled as Leonti and Lisa pounded me on the back, giving me their congratulations. As soon as the jury went back to the jury room, Trager complimented Clott. "You did a great job of turning nothing into something." Trager looked at me for a moment, but he did not say a word. He simply left the bench. I wondered if he thought I was an idiot.

———

A FEW MINUTES AFTER THE VERDICT Lisa and I went back to the jury room and talked to the jurors, who were packing up to go home. I told the jurors that it had been my first trial, and one of them laughed; they had been convinced, she told me, that I was an experienced trial lawyer. The foreperson—one of the "liberals from Brooklyn" I had not been able to eliminate—was very kind. "We kept trying to find some way to convict him for receiving the money, because we knew you wouldn't charge it unless there was some way to find him guilty, but we never could see what you were thinking." I smiled thinly and admitted, "I simply screwed up. You did a good job on Count Two."

Trager, it turned out, did not think I was an idiot. That afternoon he called Valerie Caproni, the chief of the EDNY's Criminal Division. Normally sparing of praise, Trager told her I had tried a very good case. Word got around. The next day David Pitofsky poked his head in my office door. "Hey, I heard you're the new star in the office," he said with a slight smirk. I could not have been more pleased.

The Elcock trial taught me an important lesson. My careless decision to charge Elcock with receiving stolen property, a crime he did not commit, almost lost me the case. Oddly, however, it also helped me win it. When Clott delivered his opening statement, he assumed the stolen money was still in the teddy bear at the time of delivery because I charged the case as if it had been. By the time he discovered my charging error, it was too late to change his client's defense; he had already told the jury that Elcock had ripped the bear open because he felt the heavy contents inside. In other words, my worst mistake also proved to be a major blessing.

When I discussed the case with some experienced trial lawyers, they said it proved that you can never really control what happens at trial. I drew a different lesson. Trial is a matter of controlling variables and limiting risk. When you make a mistake, you give up control, and though the resulting indeterminacy might ultimately work in your favor, out of pure luck, it might destroy your case as well. Even before the *Elcock* case, I was already a control freak. The *Elcock* result reinforced that tendency, for it showed me the risks of sloppiness. After the case I vowed never to make such a stupid error again.

And what about Ancel Elcock? When the jury brought back the verdict, he seemed stunned, confused, and a bit panicked. His mother was sitting in the courtroom gallery, and she immediately began to sob. Even then, in my triumph and relief, I felt an immense amount of pity for him as he was led away by the Marshals in handcuffs. Two months later Trager sentenced him to two and a half years in jail. After he had served his time in U.S. prison, Elcock was extradited to Germany to face bank burglary charges. For all I know, he is still in prison in Europe. Perhaps he and Claudia Pelz got married. But I doubt it.

A few days after the verdict Joe Leonti invited me to a ceremony at the Customs office at the World Trade Center to restore the $420,000 to the Köpenicker Bank, but I declined; I was simply too busy to get away from the office. I assumed the transfer went off without a hitch. Two weeks later, however, I got a voice message from the German attorney, who was screaming about a delay. I'm sorry to say I did not even bother to call her back. I was already focused on my next trial.

CHAPTER FOUR

Operation Badfellas

The Teddy Bear Burglary case was challenging for me because it was my very first trial, but at its heart, the case was legally and ethically simple. The defendant was clearly guilty, I possessed lots of reliable evidence, I trusted the case agent, the judge was fair, and the trial, despite my own errors, was relatively fast and painless. At the time I thought this would be typical of my experiences as a prosecutor. Though my cases might be stressful, they would also be straightforward. I soon learned otherwise.

Two weeks after the *Elcock* verdict, I received my next trial assignment. I was sitting in a magistrate's office, waiting for the judge to sign an arrest warrant, when I bumped into Gordon Mehler. Gordon was the chief of the Special Prosecutions Section, responsible for investigating and prosecuting corrupt public officials. Gordon and I chatted for a moment about the *Elcock* case, and then he made an offer: "John, I've got a problem, and I wonder if you can help me out. Seth Marvin's been doing this Badfellas case, with the crooked guards at the MDC. We have more trials scheduled than we can handle in Special Pros, so I wanted to see if you would try one of the cases for us, against Anthony Martinez. Martinez is a really bad guy, a senior manager who took a bunch of bribes. I think it's a very strong case, all on tape. It's a little more complicated than a General Crimes case, but I think you can handle it. I'll second seat you. What do you think?"

My immediate reaction was positive. Though *Elcock* had been a bumpy ride, I was eager to get to trial again, and all of my own General Crimes cases, mostly routine narcotics smuggling, immigration, and postal fraud matters, looked as if they were going to end in guilty pleas. I was also flattered that Gordon thought I could handle a complex trial of a "senior unit" case. Nevertheless, I declined to give Gordon an immediate answer. I told him that I would check with Eric Corngold, my supervisor in General Crimes, and get back to him. Later that day I talked with Corngold. He was pretty skeptical. "I hear those cases are screwed up. This may be a dump. Are you sure you want to do it?"

A dump occurs when a senior prosecutor gets rid of a messy trial with serious problems—a "dog" the government might easily lose—by getting the case reassigned to a naive junior prosecutor who can then be blamed for the loss. I told Corngold that Gordon believed the case was strong, but he only gave me a funny look. Sucker, I knew he was thinking. Corngold told me he would call Gordon to talk about the case. Later that day I poked my head in his door, and he gave me the okay. "Gordon promised me it is all on tape, and though the cooperator has lots of baggage, it should be all right."

At the time I thought Corngold's blessing—his conclusion that the *Martinez* case was all right—meant that it was not a dump but a good, safe opportunity to gain more trial experience. Months later I realized that his views were probably more complex. With ten years of experience as an AUSA, Corngold could probably foresee that the case might turn into a mess. However, his job as my General Crimes supervisor was not to protect me but to train me. He authorized me to work on the case not because it was unlikely to blow up but precisely because it might. Back in 1998, however, I was totally clueless, and I had no idea what I was getting into. That night I picked up the Martinez file from Seth Marvin, the lead prosecutor in the Badfellas investigation. Trial in *United States v. Anthony Martinez* was scheduled for May 20, 1998, one month away.

———

THE METROPOLITAN DETENTION CENTER, or MDC, is a very large federal prison located in Sunset Park, an economically depressed neighborhood on the rotting Brooklyn waterfront. From the outside the MDC looks like a giant concrete warehouse, not too different from the old freight and shipping warehouses lined up along the wharf. Inside, however, more than one thousand federal detainees are kept behind bars, most of them awaiting trial or appeal. These inmates are charged with the entire array of federal crimes: drug trafficking, armed robbery, credit card fraud, immigration violations, murder for hire. Many of the inmates are extremely dangerous career criminals, members of gangs, drug cartels, and robbery crews. On any given day the MDC also contains one or two dozen mafia members, New York City "wiseguys" caught up in the federal government's assault on organized crime.

Mafia inmates cause special problems for the Bureau of Prisons. Most senior mafia members consider luxury an entitlement, even when living behind bars. They also have lots of cash, which they have no way of spending while in jail. The inevitable result is bribery, with prison guards receiving almost constant offers of cash in return for special treatment or smuggled contraband.

Steve Grogan was a top federal agent with more than twenty years of law enforcement experience. He worked for the Justice Department's Office of the Inspector General in New York, responsible for, among other things, investigating corruption at federal prisons. In late 1995 Grogan began to hear rumors of widespread mafia bribery at the MDC. Some of the problems were relatively trivial. According to informants, mafia members were bribing guards to smuggle Italian delicacies into the prison from local Brooklyn delis: prosciutto, hot peppers, virgin olive oil, fresh Italian bread, olives, even caviar. Some got wine and scotch. Other information was more troubling. Guards, Grogan heard, were bringing drugs like heroin into the prison. They were even helping jailed mafia bosses run their crime families, sneaking mafia members into the prison for secret meetings with their incarcerated superiors. Clearly, the MDC was out of control. Grogan was assigned to investigate the rumors and opened up a formal inquiry. The case was soon dubbed Operation Badfellas, in homage to *Goodfellas*, the classic Scorsese mafia film.

From the start Grogan's investigation faced a serious obstacle. Typically, law enforcement agencies seeking to investigate ongoing crime insert an undercover officer into the picture to sniff things out covertly. That was impossible here. To appear as a credible inmate, an undercover agent would have to be imprisoned at the MDC for six months or more, perhaps even a year, way too heavy a burden to ask of anyone. The only alternative was to base the investigation on informants, actual prisoners secretly cooperating with law enforcement. Grogan had prison informants at the MDC, from whom he regularly received reports, but unfortunately, these snitches, as defense attorneys call them, were of little value to Grogan's investigation. None of them were mafia members or associates. As a result, they might see signs of mafia corruption at the MDC, but they had little opportunity to collect firsthand evidence of what the guards and mafia members were doing. What Grogan needed was a mafia informant, someone "connected" in the wiseguy world, but in the tight-lipped world of organized crime, where cooperation with the government is paid back by murder, mafia cooperators, as the government calls them, are hard to come by. That is, until Grogan met inmate Ray Saladino.

RAY SALADINO WAS A BIG towheaded guy in his mid-twenties, with a powerful physique pumped up by weight lifting and steroids. When he graduated from high school in the early 1990s, he could have gone to college, for he was smart and articulate. Instead, he decided to follow the path of his uncle, a wiseguy connected with the Gambino organized crime family. After graduation, Saladino got a "no show" job with the carpenters' union in Manhattan. Then he started a career in armed robbery.

In the early 1990s Saladino robbed dozens of jewelry stores and banks at gunpoint. These robberies often turned violent. In one incident, Saladino stripped a man naked and handcuffed him to a tree. Other people were pistol-whipped. Saladino told his victims that if they talked to the police, he would kill their families. When the law finally caught up with him, Saladino tried to obstruct justice. He convinced his mother to throw his guns into the Atlantic Ocean and his girlfriend to lie on his behalf, creating fake alibis. The perjury and destruction of evidence did not work. Faced with overwhelming proof of guilt, Saladino pleaded guilty to multiple counts of armed robbery and was sentenced to twenty years in federal prison. That was when he offered to cooperate.

Under federal law, a convicted felon can get a reduced sentence if he assists the government in law enforcement investigations and prosecutions. In these cases the defendant and the government sign a document called a cooperation agreement. The defendant agrees to be truthful with the government at all times about his own past crimes and the crimes committed by his accomplices. He also agrees to testify at trials if asked. The government in turn agrees that when the defendant's cooperation is completed, it will file a motion with the defendant's sentencing judge setting forth all the relevant facts about the defendant's assistance. The judge then decides if any reduction in sentence is warranted. The government typically takes no position on what reduction of sentence, if any, the defendant should receive; that decision is left to the individual judge. If the defendant's cooperation results in the arrest and conviction of many serious criminals, a big reduction may be in order. "Sammy the Bull" Gravano, for example, committed more than a dozen murders during his career as a Gambino Family henchman, and he faced life in prison as a result. Gravano cooperated, however, and helped bring Gambino boss John Gotti and some forty other mafia members to justice. In the end, Brooklyn Judge Leo Glasser sentenced Gravano to only five years in prison.

In cases like Gravano's, cooperation can be a defendant's ticket to freedom, the route to a second chance at life. Cooperation, however, can backfire. If the judge thinks the defendant has been dishonest or remains a serious risk to public safety, the judge may grant little or no reduction in sentence. Cooperators can also run afoul of their prosecutors. The government always retains the right to tear up its agreement with the cooperating defendant if he lies or commits new crimes. When this happens, the defendant may wind up serving an even bigger sentence than he or she started out with in the first place. This possibility gives cooperating witnesses a strong incentive to fly straight after they have signed their agreements.

Saladino's offer to cooperate was controversial at the Justice Department. In our office a prosecutor was not allowed to sign up a convicted defendant unless the defendant's original prosecutor, the person who knew the defendant best, agreed that cooperation was appropriate. In Saladino's case, that person was Cecilia Gardner, the AUSA on Long Island who had handled his robbery case. Gardner thought Saladino was such a dangerous guy he should serve his entire twenty-year sentence without the chance for a break. Grogan, however, badly needed a mafia cooperator inside the MDC, and he and AUSA Seth Marvin, the prosecutor assigned to the Badfellas case, convinced the office to ignore Gardner's warnings and sign Saladino up. In 1996, Saladino became a cooperating federal witness.

THE BADFELLAS INVESTIGATION BEGAN in earnest in November
1996. That month Grogan had Saladino assigned to the sixth floor of the
MDC. He instructed Saladino to ingratiate himself with the guards and
other mafia inmates and see what was going on. Saladino soon reported
that guards on the sixth floor were working for the mob, taking five-
hundred- and one-thousand-dollar bribes to sneak in contraband food,
cigars, vodka, and cologne. Saladino gathered evidence against several
guards and then was moved, at Grogan's instigation, down to the third
floor of the prison. There Saladino met Anthony Martinez, the supervisor of the third and fourth floors.

Martinez was in his mid-thirties, a high school graduate with a wife
and two kids. A New York native, Martinez joined the federal Bureau of
Prisons in 1986 as a low-level corrections officer, making sixteen thousand dollars a year. Over the years he worked in a number of different
federal pens, slowly rising in rank and receiving several minor awards. In
the spring of 1996 he was transferred to the MDC in Brooklyn. With ten
years of federal service under his belt, Martinez had a lot of seniority,
and he was quickly appointed one of the MDC's unit managers, in
charge of four hundred inmates. At first the warden was impressed with
Martinez's work, but after only a few months on the job, some Bureau of
Prisons employees noticed several disturbing signs. Most good corrections officers circulate freely among the inmates in their wards, to make
sure no trouble is brewing. Martinez, however, was often seen huddled
in his office with a group of senior mafia inmates, talking behind closed
doors. His clothing style had also changed. When Martinez arrived at the
MDC, he was a notoriously sloppy dresser. Now, however, Martinez
seemed to have undergone an extreme style makeover, with double-
breasted silk suits and slicked-back hair. He was trying to look, one inmate later told me, like a mafia don.

In early December 1996 Saladino reported that Martinez was taking
bribes from two of the most dangerous mafia leaders in the country,
Colombo Family boss Vic Orena and Lucchese Family consigliere Frank
"Frankie Bones" Papagni. Grogan ordered Saladino to offer Martinez a
bribe and see if he would take the bait.

One day Saladino was in Martinez's office with Orena and Papagni.

Orena was complaining about the food: "I'm losing weight here, I need to eat good. I need you to take care of me."

Martinez replied, "Anything you need."

Orena then vouched for Saladino, who had a reputation as a tough and loyal mafioso, a man willing to take a "twenty-year bid" rather than cooperate with the feds. Orena slapped Saladino on the back and gave Martinez a simple order: "I want you to take care of him."

Saladino told Martinez that his mother couldn't visit the prison during regularly scheduled visiting hours because she worked Monday through Saturday. He needed help arranging special visits for her on Sundays. Martinez said he would be glad to help, for a thousand dollars. Martinez told Saladino to have the money mailed to him, in cash. Saladino, following Grogan's instructions, asked Martinez instead if he could have the money dropped off in person by his brother. Martinez agreed. He gave Saladino the address of a house in Ozone Park, a quiet neighborhood in Queens, and said he would be there on December 15. Saladino then reported all this information back to Grogan. Grogan thought the address was interesting. Martinez, he knew, lived in a special Bureau of Prisons housing facility in Brooklyn. Apparently, Martinez thought that if he took a bribe at a BOP facility, which was wired with multiple security cameras, he might get caught. So he had arranged to have the bribe delivered to his in-laws' house in Queens instead.

———

ON DECEMBER 15, 1996, Grogan and a second Justice Department agent, Joe Lestrange, went to the house in Ozone Park to pay Martinez his bribe. They traveled in two separate cars. Lestrange, a short, wiry agent with somewhat swarthy features that just might pass for Italian, was posing as Saladino's brother. His job was to meet with Martinez and hand over the bribe. Lestrange was wearing a wire, a hidden tape recorder and transmitter. He also had a thousand dollars in cash. Lestrange walked slowly up the walkway to the front door. Grogan meanwhile had taken up his position half a block up the street, in a car with tinted windows. Through the dark windows, Grogan trained a video camera on the house, trying to get a visual recording of the meeting to go with Lestrange's audiotape. Grogan's main function, however, was not to gather evidence but to provide security. Undercover operations are inherently risky; you never know what might happen. Grogan had a radio receiver tuned to Lestrange's hidden transmitter, in order to follow the meeting. If it turned dangerous, Grogan was ready to intervene, with pistol fire if necessary.

As it turned out, the meeting went off without a hitch. Lestrange knocked on the door, and it was answered by Martinez's mother-in-law. Lestrange asked her for Martinez, and she replied that he was asleep. Lestrange politely asked her to wake him up and waited for several minutes. Finally Martinez appeared, looking very groggy.

LESTRANGE: I'm supposed to drop off some money from Ray.
MARTINEZ: Who?
LESTRANGE: Ray. Saladino. I got the wrong address?

For Anthony Martinez, this was the moment of truth. Did Martinez really want a bribe, or was he going to deny the whole thing and send Lestrange packing? Lestrange did not have to wait long for his answer. Lestrange asked Martinez if Saladino had told him that money would be dropped off, and Martinez replied, "Yeah."

Lestrange then handed Martinez a thick envelope stuffed with cash. As he did so, he told Martinez, "There's a thousand there."

Martinez looked down at the envelope in his hands, grunted, and then said, "All right, thanks."

The two men shook hands, and Martinez went back inside the house. The whole exchange took less than two minutes, but all of it was captured on video- and audiotape. A few days later Martinez filed the necessary paperwork granting Saladino special visits for his mother on Sundays.

In most undercover bribery investigations, federal agents will try to record several meetings with a target in order to ensure that the evidence is strong enough to withstand challenge at trial. In early 1997 Grogan authorized Saladino to ask Martinez for another bribe. Grogan had heard that guards were helping mafia members from "the street" to visit the MDC to conduct criminal business with their incarcerated bosses. To see if Martinez might be responsible, Grogan told Saladino to bribe Martinez to put men with criminal records on his visiting list, a practice prohibited by Bureau of Prisons regulations.

A few days later Saladino was hanging out in Martinez's office, using

Martinez's telephone.* After he hung up, he said to Martinez, "Listen, I just got off the phone with some friends of mine, and they need to come up and see me."

Martinez replied, "Sure, no problem. We'll put them on your visiting list."

Saladino interrupted. "No, no, no, that's a problem here. These are my boys on the street. They got records. I need to talk to them and conduct some business."

An honest corrections officer would have immediately refused and reported Saladino to the warden. Martinez took a different tack. He told Saladino that the illegal visits would be no problem but demanded four hundred bucks. Martinez told Saladino to send his brother back to the house in Ozone Park on the evening of January 6 to make the payment. Saladino agreed and reported this information back to Grogan.

On the night of January 6, 1997, Lestrange met with Martinez a second time in Queens. Once again the meeting was captured on tape. Lestrange knocked on the door, and Martinez answered. Lestrange quickly handed over an envelope, saying, "Ray wanted me to drop off the four hundred dollars he owes you."

Lestrange asked Martinez if he wanted to count the money, but Martinez enthusiastically replied, "No, no, you're good, man, you're good to go!"

Martinez and Lestrange then talked about Saladino. "You taking good care of him, or what?" Lestrange asked.

"Yes," Martinez replied, "he's a good kid."

The two exchanged a few more pleasantries, and then Lestrange left. A few days later Saladino gave Martinez the names of two persons with criminal records, one of them a convicted felon. These names were immediately added to Saladino's computerized visiting list. Before he added the names to the list, Martinez was supposed to conduct a criminal background check. Needless to say, no such check was done.

With two solid bribes on tape, Grogan decided to see how far Mar-

---

*Federal prisoners who want to place calls to the outside world are supposed to use special inmate telephones, which are constantly monitored and recorded in an effort to discourage crimes inside the prison, like smuggling drugs in through the waiting room. At the MDC, inmates were allowed to use a guard's unmonitored telephone on rare occasions to talk to their attorneys, but Martinez allowed favored mafia inmates to abuse this privilege, letting them make numerous calls to all sorts of persons on his personal phone so they could escape the monitoring system.

tinez was willing to go. Grogan heard reports that guards were smuggling drugs into the MDC. Grogan told Saladino to see if Martinez would agree to bring in heroin. A few days later Saladino went to Martinez and told him he had a problem: "I've gotten rid of some drugs here in the building, but my connection just went sour. I've got nothing anymore. Maybe you can help me out here and bring some heroin in for me so I can keep up the business."

Martinez agreed to help, in exchange for a thousand dollars. He also gave Saladino a friendly warning, ironic, under the circumstances. "Make sure you're careful," he told Saladino. "I don't want you getting into any trouble. There's lots of rats around here, you know, and these people talk."

On January 23, Lestrange returned to the Ozone Park house to pay Martinez a third bribe. The first two meetings had taken place on the house's doorstep. This time Martinez and Lestrange walked away from the house. Lestrange handed Martinez a Parliament cigarette pack containing a tiny plastic bag full of ten grams of sham heroin, a substance designed to look and feel like the real thing. As he did so, he showed Martinez the heroin and said, "I got the dope inside of here, so it looks less obvious. It's not going to be a problem getting this shit to him?"

Martinez replied, "No."

Lestrange then asked, "Is anyone going to search you?"

Martinez answered, "No, it's not gonna be a problem."

Lestrange then sprang a little surprise. Instead of paying Martinez the thousand dollars, he gave him only half. He told Martinez that he would return with the remainder as soon as he received word that Ray had received the heroin. Martinez urged Lestrange to come back the very next day; he had bills to pay.

In his first two meetings with Martinez, Lestrange had kept conversation to a minimum. This is standard procedure in undercover operations, for if the agent is extremely talkative and looks as if he is fishing for information, the investigation target might get suspicious. On this, their third meeting, Lestrange decided to try to get Martinez to open up a little. Lestrange asked Martinez how life was treating him. Martinez said he was content, but he had one major complaint about the MDC: "There is a lot of fucking rats." Martinez explained that with all the informants in prison, "these days, you can't talk." Lestrange nodded. "There's no 'stand-up' guys anymore." Martinez agreed. In life, he told Lestrange, you have to choose a side and stick with it. "Whatever life you choose, you choose. And you live it, and you learn as a man."

The next day Martinez handed the cigarette pack with the sham heroin to Saladino inside the MDC. Saladino in turn passed it to an associate warden working on the case with Grogan. Later the associate warden told me he was shocked. Martinez, a senior federal employee who had sworn to uphold the laws of the United States, was willing to traffic in drugs.

Later that night Lestrange met Martinez one final time in Queens. Tape rolling, Lestrange asked, "Did you get the shit in to him, no problem?"

Martinez coldly responded, "Yeah, everything went well."

Lestrange then handed over the remaining five hundred dollars. Business concluded, the two resumed their conversation from the day before—a conversation that resulted in the most astounding undercover tape I ever heard as an AUSA. Lestrange was in a suit that night, and Martinez commented that he "looked a little sharp." Lestrange replied that later that evening he had a sit-down, a mafia term for a significant criminal business meeting, usually to resolve a dispute. As soon as Lestrange mentioned the sit-down, Martinez became animated. Martinez told Lestrange he was interested in solidifying his ties to the mafia. Maybe, he suggested, he should change his name to Martino to fit in better. He also wanted to sit in on mafia meetings. "I'll just sit in there," he told Lestrange, "and say, 'Who we gonna whack next? Who's the next guy? What's up? What's the new line of work?'"

Lestrange laughed and told Martinez that his proposal was a good idea. Then he terminated the meeting, walked away, and turned off his tape recorder. That, Lestrange thought, finishes that guy off.

The investigation of Anthony Martinez came to an end that night, after the fourth and most devastating tape had been placed in the evidence vault. Whether Martinez's offer to join the mob was serious or not, Grogan knew his comments would look really bad in front of a jury. A few days later Grogan shifted Saladino to another floor of the MDC, and the agents focused their efforts on other prison guards.

For the next four months the covert investigation of the MDC quietly continued, with Saladino offering bribes and Grogan and Lestrange making tapes. Then, on May 24, 1997, Grogan struck. Teams of federal agents swept into the prison and arrested eleven MDC corrections officers at their posts, leading them in handcuffs off the prison floor and into waiting vans. One of the men arrested was Anthony Martinez. The next morning the Badfellas case was splashed on the front pages of all the New York City tabloids. It was, reporters noted, one of the most serious public corruption cases in American history.

In June 1997, five months before I joined the office, a federal grand jury in Brooklyn indicted all eleven MDC prison guards for taking bribes. After indictment, the Badfellas cases were assigned to federal district judge Frederic Block. During the next several months, eight of the guards quietly pleaded guilty. Three others, including Martinez, decided to go to trial. Here the case began to get tricky.

WHEN THE PRESIDENT APPOINTS a new federal trial judge, the last thing he wants is controversy. Most presidents choose safe, solid nominees, the kind that flies though the Senate approval process. The result, for better or worse, is a bench with a uniform, socially conservative outlook on life. The federal judges on the Eastern District bench, for example, tend to be pretty stodgy. Many are former prosecutors, and the rest typically practiced at large Manhattan corporate law firms. These judges may not always rule in the government's favor, but they understand and respect what the government prosecutors are trying to accomplish, and they usually give them a fair hearing. Many defense attorneys believe they have a pro-government bias.

Judge Fred Block was cut from a different cloth. Appointed to the federal bench in 1994 by President Clinton, Block had worked out on Long Island for his entire career, in solo practice and in very small firms. He was a lifetime member of the NAACP and had been active in various arts organizations. He had no prosecutorial background. He was often seen, friends told me, in Manhattan nightclubs, dressed in leather, drinking martinis.

As a rookie I had never appeared before Judge Block, but I had heard many rumors about him. Block, senior prosecutors told me, was anti-government, viewing many of the office's prosecutions with deep-seated skepticism. He also had a reputation for lawlessness. Instead of making decisions based on the *Federal Rules of Evidence* and the *Sentencing Guidelines*, he was often guided by his own sense of fairness and decency, turning court proceedings into unpredictable free-for-alls. I later concluded that these stories were exaggerated, but they overstated the case only to a degree. Block was not your typical federal judge.

From the outset, Judge Block thought the Badfellas cases were trivial. Under the *Sentencing Guidelines*, every Badfellas guard who had pleaded guilty was supposed to be sentenced to multiple years in prison. Block, however, refused to impose the sentences called for under the guidelines. Instead, he "departed downward," slapping the defendants on the wrist with probation or home detention. In his public statements, Block heaped scorn on the government for wasting so many resources on "guys smuggling salami." His comments led to angry replies from Seth Marvin, the lead Badfellas prosecutor, and their relationship quickly deteriorated.

In October 1997, the first of the remaining Badfellas cases, *United States v. Artis*, went to trial before Judge Block. The result was a total fiasco. Grogan's case against guard Willie Artis was weak because none of the alleged bribes was on tape. For that reason, Saladino's testimony was crucial to the case. Alas, Saladino was slaughtered on cross-examination. The evidence rules allow defense counsel to ask witnesses if they have committed crimes in the past, but not about the manner in which those crimes were committed. Seth Marvin tried to invoke these rules, to limit the questions the defense attorneys could ask, but Judge Block refused. Instead, Block let defense counsel ask Saladino hundreds of detailed questions about his past life of crime. As a result, all the horrible facts about Saladino's past came tumbling out before the jury. To make matters worse, these facts were revealed over Seth's strenuous and repeated objections, making it look as if Seth had something to hide. Since Artis's crimes had not been caught on tape, the jury could not convict unless it believed and trusted Saladino. It did not. The jury verdict was a disaster for the government: not guilty on all counts.

Gordon Mehler, Seth's boss, was very aware of these facts when he thought about staffing the next Badfellas case, the Anthony Martinez trial. Mehler was not too worried about *Martinez*. Unlike *Artis*, the three Martinez bribes were on tape, and those tapes were graphic and detailed. Mehler was concerned about Seth, however. By this point Seth's relationship with Block was so poor Mehler thought the case might suffer as a result. And so Mehler was looking around for someone to take Seth's place for the Martinez trial at the precise moment I stumbled into his path. Gordon was glad to find a replacement, even if it was only a member of General Crimes. As for me, I was blissfully ignorant of all these facts when I agreed to try Martinez in front of Judge Block. Had I known about the Artis acquittal or Block's negative attitude toward the case, I might have declined to do it.

DURING THE MONTH BEFORE THE MARTINEZ TRIAL, I did all the routine tasks I had learned from the *Elcock* case: identifying and marking evidence, interviewing witnesses, preparing direct examinations, planning my opening statement. These chores took up a lot of time, but they did not distract me from my biggest challenge, figuring out what to do with Saladino. I read his testimony from the Artis trial, and after that review it was clear to me that the government had lost the case because the defense lawyers made Saladino look like a lying, treacherous, conniving, cold-blooded psychopath. When I talked about what happened with Seth, he insisted that to win the Martinez case, I had to get Judge Block to limit Saladino's cross-examination. I tried to follow this advice, but Block denied my motion several weeks before trial. As a result, I was forced to take a different path. In *Artis*, Seth built his case around Saladino because he had very little other evidence. In contrast, I had four strong tapes showing Martinez's guilt. I decided to open the trial with Grogan, who could explain to the jury that he had kept Saladino on a short leash, under careful supervision. I would end the trial with Lestrange and the tapes, my most compelling evidence. And I would bury Saladino in the middle of the trial, keep his testimony as short as possible, and hope the jury ignored him.

In May 1997, when the Badfellas guards were arrested, Saladino had been whisked into the Witness Security Program, what television shows frequently, but erroneously, refer to as the "witness protection program." This was a necessary precaution. In an ordinary BOP facility, an informant who had ratted out his own guards would probably turn up dead. WITSEC, as the program is known, operates special prison facilities for at-risk witnesses who have not yet been released from custody. One of these secret prisons is in the New York metropolitan area, a few hours' drive from the city. One week after I took over the *Martinez* case, Grogan and I drove to this facility so I could meet Saladino face-to-face.

That morning I tried to act cool, but I was secretly very pumped up, excited to learn more about WITSEC, eager to meet my first real live mafia associate. In the Justice Department only very experienced prosecutors get a chance to handle WITSEC cases. To my delight, I had achieved this in my very first year on the job. This made me feel, I am now embarrassed to admit, like a big shot.

When we arrived at the prison gate, an armed guard in a pickup truck came racing up from inside the prison perimeter. The guard pulled up next to our car and asked to see our "creds," our law enforcement credentials. All federal law enforcement personnel carry slim black leather wallets containing identifying photographs and, for special agents, badges. Grogan whipped his out his creds and satisfied the guard. I was not so lucky. As a rookie prosecutor, still in my probationary period, I had not yet received my formal credentials. Embarrassed, for it showed how inexperienced I was, I gave the guard my temporary laminated Justice Department identification card. The guard radioed up to his headquarters to see if we were expected. A few minutes later we were standing in an austere entry room before a quiet and respectful guard, signing in to a green, cloth-bound logbook. As I signed my name, I looked to see who else had visited the WITSEC unit lately. I recognized many of the names. The log was a who's who of respected mafia and drug cartel prosecutors.

My first meeting with Saladino was also my first visit ever to a prison. Outside, it was bright and sunny, a beautiful spring day, but inside, it felt like a morgue. There was no natural light, and the halls were deathly quiet; all the prisoners, I learned later, were returned to their cells and put under lock when we arrived, to keep their identities hidden even from us. All the walls were painted dull yellow, the rooms lit with dim fluorescent lights, and everything—walls, furniture, even the Coke machine—was coated with a greasy film. There was almost no ventilation, and the air was stale and oppressive. I was almost overcome by the stench: heavy industrial disinfectant, human body stink, and a pungent smell I instantly remembered from my time in Marine Corps boot camp—the smell of human fear. Cameras monitored our every step. After passing through several heavy locked doors, opened automatically from a hidden control room, Grogan and I found ourselves in the "library," a decrepit room with out-of-date legal books, scores of tattered paperbacks, and a few battered board games. A few minutes later a guard ushered Ray Saladino into the room and left him with Grogan and me.

Grogan and Saladino greeted each other effusively, with hearty handshakes and pats on the back, as if they were old friends. This shocked me at the time. Saladino was on our side now, but he was still a violent armed robber. Had Grogan grown too close to our witness? I had no time to give this idea much thought; I had work to do. I looked Saladino in the eye. Quietly, cautiously, I shook his almost comically oversize hand. We then sat down at a table. I told Saladino that he would testify at trial within the next month against Anthony Martinez. I would try to get him on and off the stand as quickly as possible, but he should expect a repeat of the tough Artis cross. I also gave him a strict warning: "You are obligated to tell the truth at trial. You are going to be under oath. All I want from you is the truth and nothing more. I want to be perfectly clear. If I catch you lying to me or committing perjury at trial, I will rip up your cooperation agreement so fast it will make your head spin. Do you understand?"

Saladino assured me that he would always tell the truth. "I got a lot to lose here, you know," he said with great urgency. "I could have had a college scholarship. I could have made something of myself. I am trying to improve myself. I am trying to get a second chance." He seemed smart and, for an armed robber, fairly thoughtful. I could tell he wanted to make a good impression. When he talked about his lost opportunities, about needing a second chance in life, I sensed a strong note of anguish, of moral urgency, lying just below the surface. He looked me in the eye; he held out his hands, palms up, as if he were pleading for mercy; I thought he was sincere.

Over the next few weeks Saladino and I met once or twice a week for several hours at a time. At each meeting I followed a strict routine. At the beginning of our session, I repeated my warning: if Saladino lied to me or committed perjury, I would throw the book at him. I wanted him to understand that I meant business. I also wanted him to be able to say, on cross-examination, that every single time we met, I had instructed him to tell the truth and had threatened him with dire consequences if he lied. After my warning, Saladino and I worked on his direct. I found Saladino a very easy witness to prepare. He was a natural storyteller, and he conveyed his conversations with Martinez fluently and convincingly. At every session, he answered my questions consistently, providing the exact same information, a sign, I thought, that he was telling the truth.

Once his direct was ready, we practiced for his cross. I threw my hardest questions at Saladino, trying to rattle him, but he never got tripped up. As the trial grew closer, I felt confident he would do fine. I never got used to the jail, however. I found each visit incredibly depressing, and I was relieved every time Grogan and I brought our prep session to a close, and I could walk back out into the sunlight again.

THE TRIAL OF ANTHONY MARTINEZ began on May 20, 1998, and from the beginning it was very hard fought. In the Teddy Bear Case, my opponent, Abe Clott, was always soft-spoken and collegial. His cross-examinations were short, calm, and respectful toward my witnesses, and he never pulled any tricks, never tried anything unethical. Trial with Sam Schmidt, Martinez's lawyer, was a totally different ball game. Sam was in private practice, trying to build his reputation among the New York City defense bar, and several prosecutors had told me that he could be difficult to handle. True to form, Schmidt began to hammer at my case from the opening bell. He disputed every piece of evidence, argued long and hard with Judge Block about every legal issue, and harassed me at every opportunity, in a gruff, often brutally disrespectful tone. After the first few days I decided I hated Sam Schmidt. But I also could not help respecting him. Say what you wanted, he was not taking his client's case lying down. Instead, he was fighting with every ounce of his strength for an acquittal.

For a naive rookie trial lawyer, Sam's cross-examinations were shocking. He attacked every one of my witnesses relentlessly, bombarding them with questions in an angry, sarcastic, snide tone of voice. Sometimes he was effective, but at others, his style seemed counterproductive. He did not focus on a small range of coherent topics. Instead, he wove from one subject to another without warning and sometimes

without reason, an approach that clearly confused our jury. Sam also
had a bizarre nervous tic. On many occasions he would start to ask a
question, halt in the middle, and then withdraw the question before it
was completed. When Grogan was on the stand, for example, Sam asked,
"Based on your conversation with—withdrawn. It was you that first
suggested to—withdrawn. When you asked Mr. Saladino to make contact with Mr. Martinez, were you aware of Mr. Saladino's background?"
Or again: "But often—withdrawn. The inmate population, if there is a
person considered a leader, if they do—withdrawn." These halting, incoherent moments, punctuated by Sam's loud staccato shout of "WITH-
DRAWN," drove everyone in the courtroom crazy. At first, Judge Block
let Sam do whatever he wanted, and some of his crosses went on for
hours. Eventually, however, even the judge lost his patience. "Get to the
point," he would snap. "Mr. Schmidt, enough." "Mr. Schmidt, you have
to learn to discipline yourself like a professional lawyer."

Perhaps the most dramatic moment in the trial occurred when Sam
crossed Saladino. Block imposed no limits to questioning, just as in the
Artis trial, so Sam had an unlimited opportunity to attack my witness.
For four hours he assaulted Saladino, badgering, interrupting, making
sarcastic gibes, doing his best to dirty Saladino up. He asked Saladino
about pistol-whipping victims, destroying evidence, tying people naked
to trees, robbing senior citizens, threatening victims' families, and plotting to kill a schoolteacher. I had counseled Saladino to answer all these
questions in as matter-of-fact a manner as possible, and he did a great
job, responding in a deadpan tone, admitting to all of his horrible prior
crimes. He also told the jury that though his crimes were reprehensible,
he was now a new man, committed to honesty and a law-abiding life.

While Saladino dealt with Sam's questions, I put on an act of my
own. Throughout Sam's cross, I never objected to his questions. I assumed Block would overrule my objections anyway, and I didn't want to
look as if we had anything to hide. Instead, I slumped in my chair, looking bored and sleepy, trying to convey to the jury the notion that I
wasn't the least bit concerned with what was happening, that this was all
a charade, routine in these kinds of cases. The jury seemed to take its
cue from me. As far as I could tell, the jurors did not find Sam's revelations about Saladino's character interesting or relevant. Instead, they
appeared slightly disgusted by Sam's snide and bullying personality.

THE MARTINEZ TRIAL WAS DIFFERENT FROM ELCOCK'S in more than just intensity and tone, for unlike the teddy bear burglar, Martinez had a coherent defense. Midway through the trial, Martinez took the stand and proclaimed his innocence. Martinez told the jury that he was shocked and surprised when he received the first bribe, for he barely knew Saladino, and he was still half asleep from his nap, a claim that was corroborated, to some degree, by both the tape of the first bribe, in which Martinez was visibly groggy, and a doctor who testified that Martinez had a sleeping disorder. When he realized what had happened, Martinez said, he immediately went to the jail to confront Saladino, and when he did, the inmate, desperate to please his dim-witted law enforcement handlers, threatened him and his family. From that point forward, Martinez took the bribes not because he wanted to but because he was, in Sam Schmidt's words, "confused, frightened, and coerced." This last claim was critical, because coercion by a government agent—and Saladino, as a government informant, counted as a government agent—was a complete defense to the crime.

Though Schmidt's courtroom delivery was often rough and disorganized, the defense he offered was remarkably effective. To win a case as a defense lawyer, you cannot deny indisputable facts, like the fact that Martinez repeatedly took bribes on tape. Instead, you must explain to the jury why those facts are just as consistent with innocence as with guilt. If a defense attorney can do this, he will usually get an acquittal, for the government has the burden to prove guilt beyond a reasonable doubt. Schmidt had accomplished this, explaining to the jury how Martinez could be caught red-handed on tape taking bribes yet still be innocent of the crime.

Schmidt's defense strategy also accomplished the criminal trial lawyer's most important objective, shifting the jury's attention away from the opposing side's best evidence. My strongest proof in this case was the tapes, hard, solid evidence proving Martinez was crooked. In a perfect example of trial jujitsu, Schmidt told the jury that these tapes were irrelevant, since the crux of the case was not whether Martinez took bribes but whether he did so because he was threatened. The tapes, he suggested, shed no light on this issue. Instead, the jury would have to compare Martinez and Saladino and see which witness it trusted. With this tactic, Schmidt transformed a rock-solid tape case into a test of Saladino's credibility, the very thing I wanted to avoid.

Schmidt made it clear to the jury how it should resolve this credibility contest. In his opening statement, he said Saladino could not be trusted because he had been "feeding garbage to the government" and "what comes from his mouth is garbage." In case the jury missed his point, Sam went on to repeat, within a five-minute span, that Saladino's story was "garbage," "utter garbage," and "complete and utter garbage." Not very subtle but effective.

———

IN THE ELCOCK TRIAL, I did not face a great challenge in my closing argument. Every single piece of evidence favored a conviction, so all I had to do to win was summarize that evidence clearly, a closing tactic called marshaling the evidence. In Martinez's trial things were not so clear-cut. In order to win, I could not simply review the evidence, because after Schmidt's great effort, the evidence cut both ways. Instead, I needed to persuade the jury that my version of reality was correct: that Martinez had accepted bribes because he was crooked, not because of the alleged coercion. In short, I had to be a real trial lawyer.

How do you convince a jury to believe in your case? There is no single answer to this question. If you ask great trial lawyers the key to their success, however, they all tend to say roughly the same thing: "Stay true to yourself." Don't copy someone else's style in the courtroom. Figure out what is most natural to you, and stick with that.

As a rookie prosecutor I took this advice to heart. In court, my natural style is very simple and understated. "Jimmy Stewart," my colleague Kelly Moore once remarked, "not Tom Cruise." For that reason, I decided to avoid high-flying rhetoric, gimmicks, and emotional appeals and simply tell the jury instead, as clearly and sincerely as I could, the precise reasons why I did not believe Martinez's testimony. My approach might lack flash, but I hoped that if I truly believed every word I uttered, the jury would respond to my conviction.

I also made a strategic decision. I expected Sam to spend most of his closing argument calling Saladino a psychopathic liar, and I did not want to play into his hands, to give in to his trial jujitsu. For that reason,

I decided not to base any of my closing arguments on Saladino's testimony or trustworthiness. Instead, I would stick to my pretrial game plan and show how all the other evidence in the case—tapes, documents, and Martinez's own testimony—pointed to the defendant's guilt.

I delivered my closing argument on the afternoon of June 2, 1998. Standing before the jury in my favorite red tie, armed with one page of notes I knew I would not need, I wished the jury a good afternoon and then began with my planned introduction, one, I hoped, that would highlight my own strengths.

Closing arguments are a chance for the lawyers to get up and give you these big fancy speeches. I'm not going to do that today. Instead, I am going to do two simple things. First, I want to talk about the facts of the case, the events that took place. Criminal trials can be confusing. A lot of information was thrown at you very quickly. So what I would like to do is just run through the events as they happened. After we run through the events, I want to talk about the crimes that were charged and show you how the evidence in this case proves beyond a reasonable doubt that Anthony Martinez committed those crimes.

Following this introduction and my review of the facts, I talked to the jury about the evidence. My primary focus was on the tapes. If Martinez had been truly scared and coerced, I told the jury, you would see evidence of his fear on the tapes. But when you watched them, all you saw was corruption and greed. I also asked the jury to look closely at the prison records I had admitted into evidence, which showed that Martinez was granting a large volume of special visits and other privileges to ranking mafia members like Vic Orena, Frank Papagni, and Fabio Bartolotta before and after the first taped bribe. My theory here was simple: where there's smoke, there's fire. Finally, I dissected Martinez's trial testimony. Why, I asked, if Martinez had not arranged the first bribe, was he at his in-laws' house at the specific time and date Saladino told Grogan he would be? Why, if the first bribe was a total surprise, did he not simply report it to the warden? Why, if he was actually threatened by Saladino, did he not send Saladino to solitary confinement? Why, if the claimed threat from Saladino was real, did he fail to take any steps to protect his family? Martinez, I suggested, couldn't answer these questions because he was guilty. Then I sat down, and the Sam Schmidt show began.

During my closing argument, I used one prop, a simple black-and-white chart listing the four charged crimes. When I finished, I started to move the chart out of Schmidt's way, but Schmidt asked if he could use it as well, and I agreed. To my surprise, he gestured to my chart at the very beginning of this closing. "I left this here," Sam said, pointing to the chart on the easel, "because I think this basically gives you a nice cross-section of the government's case. It is a nice big piece of paper. Nice, beautifully done, black and white, and it means nothing. It says nothing here, nothing that you don't know. Because what the government has done here is put on a sideshow instead of proof. They put on a sideshow because they have a very, very heavy burden of proof in a criminal case—proof beyond a reasonable doubt." He then picked up my chart and tossed it contemptuously across the floor of the courtroom.

Sam's stupid trick surprised me, but I kept a straight face, looking out the corner of my eye to see how the jury was reacting. To my immense satisfaction, some of the jurors crossed their arms and scowled. This was, I thought, the "big fancy speech" I had warned the jury about in my introduction, the kind of cheap gimmick that I hoped would seem flat and meaningless after my own thoughtful discussion of the evidence.

In a criminal trial, my instinct, even as a rookie, was to look for opportunities to exploit my opponents' mistakes. I did so now. In any jury address it is critical that the lawyer attract and maintain the jury's full attention. Now, as Sam began to discuss why his client was innocent, I quietly got up, picked my abused chart off the floor, ostentatiously examined the corners that had been bent, dusted it off, and placed it carefully back on the government's table. All this was going on behind Sam's back, so he had no idea what was happening, but it broke the jury's attention. Most jurors kept their eyes on Sam, but others looked over to see what I was doing, and some even smiled.

Sam's closing argument was basically an attack on Saladino:

He put guns in people's faces and threatened to kill them, followed victims around so he knew their routine, beat up people, tied them to a tree, undressed them and threatened to kill them, had his girl-friend prepare to perjure herself for him, had his mother and girlfriend throw guns in the ocean, is looking to kill a school teacher—the list is forever . . . He's dangerous, deceptive, deceit-ful . . . I ask you to find Raymond Saladino a totally untrust-worthy despicable person . . . What I am saying to you is that Raymond Saladino's testimony is hogwash . . . complete garbage.

This went on for forty minutes, and though Sam was a little disor-ganized, his words sometimes unclear, his use of repetition was power-ful. By the time he finished, I thought the trial could go either way.

In every federal criminal case the government gets the last word, a few minutes for rebuttal after the defendant's closing argument. When asked to justify this practice, federal judges usually reply that since the government has the burden of proof, the government deserves the last shot at the jury. The truth is more complicated. In the federal criminal legal system, the procedural rules give the government numerous tacti-cal advantages, of which this is merely one example. Today this seems unfair to me. At the time, however, locked in the middle of a hard-fought trial, I wasn't too concerned about fairness. I simply wanted a chance to fire back at Schmidt.

Sam's closing had been effective, but his exclusive focus on Saladino and my "sideshow" created an opening. The evidence, I told the jury now, was not a "sideshow, but a TV show."

This case isn't about Raymond Saladino versus Anthony Mar-tinez. It is about the tapes, about lengthy conversations on tape. The tapes give you a window into the mind of Anthony Martinez and what he was up to. He was not a frightened man, he was not a scared man. He was a man who had bills and really wanted the money.

Then I reached down inside, and I closed my argument with as much drama as I could muster:

Now of all the things said on the tapes, one thing particularly leaped out at me: the third meeting, January 23, 1997. Mr. Mar-

tinez has just accepted a cigarette package full of what he thinks is dope, and he's talking with Lestrange and you know what he says? He says, "Whatever life you choose, you choose." True words. Every day, people got choices: good versus bad, right versus wrong, justice versus injustice, good citizen or criminal. And you choose. You choose.

Anthony Martinez chose. He chose in early December when he agreed to take the first bribe. He chose on December 15th when he took the first bribe. He chose on January 6th when he took the second bribe. He chose January 23rd, he chose again on January 24th, and you know this, you know how he chose, because [and here I held up one of the videotapes] it's on tape. That's why you should find Anthony Martinez guilty on all four counts.

The next day the jury retired to the jury room. After the Elcock trial, I had talked to Eric Corngold about jury deliberations, and he had given me a good piece of advice. "Never try to figure out what the jury is thinking," Corngold said. "If they send out notes, don't try to interpret them, to figure out if you are winning or losing. You will drive yourself crazy, and you will never be right. Juries are not rational, so don't pretend that they are. Just sit there and be patient. Read a novel. Try to think about something else."

I tried to follow Corngold's counsel. The first morning of deliberations I brought a book to read, *Macbeth*. Murder, witches, divine justice: the perfect courtroom reading. Unfortunately, I found it was impossible to focus on Shakespeare, for I was simply too tense.* I wound up sitting around with Grogan, talking about his children instead. As we chatted about his son's lacrosse season, I had a chance to observe Martinez and Schmidt. They seemed to have had a falling-out. They refused to sit next to each other and hardly ever spoke.

After an hour or so Martinez stood up and walked over to the government's side of the courtroom. He pulled up a seat next to me and started listening to my conversation with Grogan. This made both Steve and me feel awkward, and we paused. In the lull Martinez caught my

---

*Over the years I tried many different options: Jane Austen, Anthony Powell, even poetry. Regardless of what I chose, I never was able to read while the jury was out.

eye. Shyly, in his husky voice I knew so well from the bribery tapes, he addressed me: "Tough waiting, Mr. Kroger."

I raised my eyebrows a little bit. This is unusual, I thought. I didn't know what to say to Martinez. He looked very tired, and sweat had broken out on his forehead. As I looked him over, I did not feel like a hard-boiled prosecutor. Instead, I felt immense empathy for another human being who was clearly suffering. "I'm sure it must be, Mr. Martinez," was all I could think to say.

Martinez nodded, paused, and then asked, "How long do you think they will be out?"

Pretending to possess much more experience than I had, I repeated Corngold's words of wisdom: "I have no idea, Mr. Martinez. You can never tell. But if I were you, I wouldn't try to figure out what they are doing and thinking. It will just drive you crazy."

Martinez nodded again. A few minutes passed in awkward silence. He spoke again. "Where did you go to law school?"

"Harvard," I replied. And then, feeling that the conversation was heading in a very weird direction, I stood up. "Take care of yourself, Mr. Martinez," I said, and walked away. A few minutes later I heard Martinez say to his wife, "My prosecutor went to Harvard."

For the next two days I hung out anxiously in the courtroom, waiting for a verdict. Every few hours the jury would send out a note, requesting a piece of evidence. On one occasion the entire jury trooped out and sat in the jury box, just as it had during the trial, and Judge Block read, for a second time, the jury instruction on entrapment. At another point the jurors came out and listened as the judge read to them, in its entirety, Saladino's testimony about the first bribe. After two days of this, I was a nervous and exhausted wreck.

Finally, at the end of the second day, the jury informed us that it had reached a verdict. Mike Ianelli, the judge's courtroom deputy, rose and faced the foreperson and asked for the result. Martinez and Schmidt rose to receive the verdict. I slipped off my glasses and placed them on the table, reducing the world to a multicolored blur. After the longest thirty seconds on earth, we all knew the result: guilty on all four counts. I slumped in my chair, tired but content. Eyes down, I could hear Mrs. Martinez crying in the visitors' gallery.

I gathered my statute book and my trial notebook and walked out of the courtroom with Gordon Mehler, who had second-sat me throughout the trial. As we neared the elevator banks, he turned to me. "Well, John, I really don't know what to say. You tried a brilliant case, you got a conviction, and the defendant likes you more than his own lawyer." I smiled thinly. Then I went home and got into bed.

———

AFTER A FEDERAL PROSECUTOR WINS A TOUGH multiweek trial, he or she typically takes what the EDNY calls a victory lap. For a couple of weeks you try not to work very hard. You come into the office later in the morning, lazily dig through your e-mail, return some phone calls you ignored while in court, chat with your colleagues, take a long lunch, and then head home a few hours early. The victory lap is a time to relax, to recharge your emotional batteries, and to prepare, physically and psychologically, for your next big case. After *Martinez*, my victory lap got cut a little short. Two weeks after the jury returned its verdict, Jim Washington, the senior prosecutor who had helped me with my job interview hypotheticals the prior year, left me a voice mail message to call him "immediately." When I got Jim on the line, he had horrible news. "I did a proffer yesterday with Fabio Bartolotta, who's coming in to cooperate.* He says Ray Saladino was dealing heroin in the MDC during the Badfellas investigation." Jim paused. My mind reeled. Bartolotta's claim, if true, meant that Saladino had violated his cooperation agreement. It also raised a more disturbing specter. If Saladino could hoodwink us, committing serious crimes behind our backs, was it possible he had lied at trial as well? Could he have secretly threatened Martinez? As I listened to Jim, I grew worried. Had I been involved in a serious miscarriage of justice?

Saladino was my very first cooperator, and I had no idea what to do in these circumstances. Fortunately, Jim already had a game plan. "I am bringing Bartolotta in again tomorrow. You and Seth and the agent, Grogan, better come in and talk to him. I'll give you a couple of hours in the afternoon." I agreed and hung up, totally depressed.

The next day I walked over to our annex, a dingy office building on

---

*A proffer is a preliminary meeting between a criminal defendant and the government to see if the defendant possesses information that might be valuable to government investigators.

Montague Street, one block away from our main headquarters. The conference room on the seventh floor was packed: Seth Marvin, Grogan, Washington, four agents I did not know, a defense attorney, and Fabio Bartolotta, handcuffed to a chair, wearing a blue prison jumpsuit. Fabio was short and lightly built, with greasy, unwashed hair, a typical incarcerated prisoner. He had a very intense look on his face: wary, careful, uncertain. I knew little about him, but what I knew was horrible. An up-and-coming mobster and an experienced killer, he had, according to rumor, once aborted the pregnant girlfriend of a criminal associate by shooting the woman in the stomach. Now he wanted to cooperate, to avoid a life sentence. Jim introduced us to him, and then Seth and Grogan started asking questions. As the most junior person present I just sat and listened.

Fabio seemed smart and articulate, his demeanor calm, and he quickly told us what we came to hear: that Saladino ran a heroin business inside the MDC. The MDC's visiting room is an open bay, without glass partitions separating the prisoners from their visitors, and Saladino took advantage of this feature. Couriers would sneak drugs into the MDC and secretly pass them to him in the visiting room, right under the eyes of the guards. Saladino would then sell the drugs to addicted inmates. These customers would arrange for their friends or family to pay Ray's family for the drugs outside the prison. According to Fabio, this was not an isolated, one-time affair; Saladino was running a large-scale drug distribution ring. All I could do was hang my head.

Thankfully, Fabio did have some good news for us. After debriefing Fabio about Saladino, Grogan asked about Martinez. Fabio immediately told us that Martinez was crooked. Martinez, he said, had been taking bribes from mafia bosses in return for special visiting privileges and disclosure of confidential information about informants, information that could get people killed. Fabio himself had been paying Martinez for special favors, at a thousand dollars a pop.

After the interview, Grogan, Seth, and I huddled outside the conference room. We all agreed that Fabio seemed truthful: his demeanor was steady, his story plausible, and he had no clear incentive to lie. On the contrary, he and Saladino were close friends, and he knew he was screwing up Saladino's life. We had to take his claims seriously. Seth and Grogan agreed to go to Saladino's secret prison, confront him with Fabio's allegations, and see what he had to say for himself. If Saladino denied Fabio's story, then we would have to open a full investigation, to see if other inmates could corroborate Fabio's claims.

The next day Seth and Grogan drove to the prison to talk to Saladino. When Seth got back, he was furious. Saladino, he said, denied selling drugs at the MDC. He did, however, admit that he had "steered" forty or fifty drug transactions in jail, helping prisoners looking for drugs make a connection with someone who had drugs for sale. Ray, Seth told me, seemed to believe that admitting this conduct would not get him into trouble. His assessment was incorrect. Steering is a crime, aiding and abetting drug trafficking. Moreover, his failure to disclose his knowledge of these drug transactions when they were occurring was itself a serious violation of his cooperation agreement. For these reasons, Seth had decided to terminate Saladino's cooperation agreement. Termination would have two consequences. First, we would no longer be able to use Saladino as a witness, a foregone conclusion, for after Fabio's allegations, neither Seth nor I trusted Saladino any longer. Second, Saladino would serve his entire twenty-year prison sentence without any break.

The next week was a nightmare. Seth had two additional Badfellas trials scheduled, against prison guards Raymond Cotton and Derryl Strong. In both these cases, Saladino's testimony was essential, for unlike the Martinez case, there were no tapes. With Saladino out of the picture, Seth had to go to court and dismiss both these cases. Though we never discussed it, this must have been a painful moment for him.

Meanwhile, I had to deal with Martinez. The fact that Saladino had committed crimes while cooperating, in violation of his cooperation agreement, was what criminal lawyers call Giglio material (named for the defendant in a landmark Supreme Court case), information that could have been used, had it been known, to impeach Saladino's credibility at trial. Under the law, I was required to disclose all Giglio material to the defense. Accordingly, I sat down and wrote a brief letter to Sam Schmidt. Because Fabio's cooperation was secret at this time, and I was not yet certain if all his claims about Saladino were accurate, I did not discuss his information in my letter. I simply told Schmidt that Saladino had admitted to large-scale steering of narcotics transactions in violation of his cooperation agreement. I sent a more comprehensive letter to Judge Block, filed secretly under seal, asking the judge for time to investigate Saladino's conduct. I also asked the judge to delay Martinez's sentencing, as the allegations might result in a motion for a new trial from the defense. Block quickly granted these requests.

THE SALADINO DISASTER MADE ME SICK to my stomach. As a federal prosecutor I wanted to convict serious criminals, but I was equally committed to justice, and I wanted to earn these convictions fairly. I felt sure Martinez was guilty—Fabio's information only confirmed that—but I was ashamed that I had asked the jury to trust Saladino when in fact he was filled with deceit. I was also concerned about my professional reputation. When word leaked to the press, and the New York Daily News ran a story with a headline declaring PRISON GUARDS PROBE TAINTED, I worried people would think I was a thoughtless or careless prosecutor.

I tried to console myself. Seth and Grogan, I reflected, were very experienced law enforcement officers. If they had not been able to see through Saladino, after working with him for years, how would a rookie like me have spotted the problem after only three weeks? Alas, this excuse did not satisfy me. My goal was not just to be a competent prosecutor; I wanted to be a great prosecutor. And wouldn't a great prosecutor have some instinct, some sixth sense, to tell him when his witnesses were lying?

Over the next nine months I investigated Fabio's information. I contacted every AUSA in the district, asked if he or she had any cooperating witnesses who were living at the MDC during the relevant period in 1996 and 1997 when Saladino was there, and then interviewed as many of these witnesses as I could. Eventually Grogan and I found one reliable witness, a former addict who claimed that he had bought heroin directly from Saladino. This witness did not know Fabio and did not speak English, making it highly unlikely that the two men had fabricated their stories together. In January 1999 I sent another letter to Block and Schmidt. I told them that two credible witnesses had alleged that Saladino was dealing heroin in the prison and that the government accepted these allegations as true. Then I sat back and waited for Schmidt's next move.

If I felt bad when I learned about Saladino's treachery, I felt even worse after I received Sam Schmidt's motion. Schmidt claimed that I had intentionally suborned Saladino's perjury—that I had known, before the trial, that Saladino was engaged in crimes at the MDC but had covered up the fact in order to convict Martinez. Schmidt demanded that Martinez receive a new trial because of my reprehensible conduct. He also argued, in the alternative, that even if I had not known about Saladino's crimes—if I had just been too reckless or too stupid to discover the truth—the conviction should still be vacated.

Schmidt's motion was scathing, and when I finished reading it, I felt about six inches tall. Schmidt had no factual support for the claim that I had intentionally suborned perjury, and I did not think Judge Block would believe it, but this personal attack upset me greatly. I was very concerned about my reputation for justice and fairness, among both fellow prosecutors and the defense bar, and I believed that reputation had been sullied. My emotional reaction, one of true pain, showed my inexperience. Over the coming years I was to learn the hard way that in the world of big-time New York criminal law, it was a common practice for defense attorneys to allege that prosecutors were corrupt and dishonest. It happened so often, in fact, that I learned not to take it personally; it was simply part of the game. But I didn't know that at the time.

Once Sam filed his motion, I faced a basic choice: I could "confess error" and agree to a new trial, or I could fight to protect my conviction. There were arguments to be made on both sides. Had Martinez received a perfectly fair trial? No. Would the jury have been interested to know that Saladino could not be trusted? Definitely. Would that information have changed the result? Perhaps. These facts counseled granting a new trial. On the other hand, I now knew for certain that Martinez was corrupt, for we had discovered two new pieces of amazing evidence.

In one debriefing, Fabio Bartolotta told us that Martinez picked up Fabio's bribery money from Fabio's uncle, at a pizza parlor on Tenth Avenue in Manhattan. Fabio also said that he had served as an intermediary between Martinez and Nicky Corozzo, John Gotti's successor as the boss of the Gambino Family. In this role, Fabio had given Martinez the names of persons to be put on Corozzo's visitors' list. When Steve Grogan heard this information, a lightbulb went off in his head. Three and a half years earlier, when Martinez had been arrested on the MDC floor, Grogan had seized Martinez's wallet and personal possessions. Now, in a startling feat of memory, Grogan went back to his evidence storage locker and recovered two items. One was a handwritten note containing a list of names that Martinez had in his pocket at the time of his arrest. Written at the top, in Fabio's handwriting, was the heading "Nicky Corozzo List." The second piece of evidence, from Martinez's wallet, was even more damning: the business card for the pizza place on Tenth Avenue. This provided very strong corroboration for Fabio's claim that Martinez was on the take.

What is justice, the right result or a fair process? The philosopher in me wanted to think deeply about that question, but the prosecutor I had become had no time for reflection. My response to Schmidt's motion was due in two weeks, and I had one hundred other cases to handle in addition to Anthony Martinez's. In these circumstances, it was a relief (and probably wise as well) to defer to experience.

After I got the motion, I asked my boss, Eric Corngold, what I should do. He sent me to Jason Brown, the new chief of the public corruption unit, who was ultimately responsible for the Martinez case. Though I had doubts about the case, Jason had none. "You did nothing wrong, and we disclosed this stuff as soon as we learned about it. Saladino didn't lie about anything that mattered. He claimed he was reformed, but no rational jury would believe that. This was a tape case, not a witness case. So we fight to protect the conviction." Following this advice—or was it an order?—I filed my response with Judge Block. I told the judge that I had not been aware of Saladino's new criminal conduct when Martinez went to trial. I also described in detail Fabio's claims about Martinez's corruption. This information was not directly relevant to the motion, but I wanted Block to understand that if he granted Schmidt's request, he was taking a risk that a guilty man would go free.

I HOPED BLOCK WOULD RULE ON THE MOTION QUICKLY. Instead, I twisted in the wind for months. Every six weeks, it seemed, Schmidt would file new allegations of government misconduct or corruption, and though virtually all these were frivolous, Block (appropriately, under the circumstances) ordered me to investigate and report back on every single one, no matter how fanciful. Months passed, and I grew increasingly worried. Finally, more than a year after the trial, Block called us all into court to hear his decision. My heart was in my throat that day as I entered the courtroom. I was not just concerned about the conviction, though I knew that if we did the trial again, without Saladino I would probably lose. My terror was more personal. If Block was convinced that I had intentionally suborned perjury, I would lose my job as a federal prosecutor. I might even be disbarred.

Block told us that he was prepared to rule on the motion and that he would read his opinion from the bench. I could feel my heart racing; I had a lot riding on the decision. He began by analyzing whether I had known, or should have known, that Saladino was dealing heroin at the MDC prior to the Martinez trial. Block reviewed the facts and quickly concluded that there was no evidence to support Schmidt's claim. Instead, the judge commended me for my timely disclosure of Saladino's crimes and my honest handling of the case. At that instant I discovered that I had actually been holding my breath, and I quietly exhaled. My stress level declined by 90 percent. Even if Martinez got a new trial, I knew I was personally off the hook.

Block then turned to the substance of the motion. Even if, he said, the prosecution has done nothing wrong, posttrial discovery that a government witness committed perjury will still result in a new trial if the perjury was "material"—if it had a significant impact on a legal result. Thus the real question was: How important was Saladino's testimony? Schmidt argued that if the jurors had known that Saladino was not reformed but a lying, scheming drug trafficker, they would never have convicted his client. I took a different view. I pointed out that in my closing argument, I had never asked the jury to convict on the basis of Saladino's testimony. Instead, I had focused almost exclusively on the tapes, my "television show." For this reason I argued that no new trial was warranted.

Nonlawyers often think that in a legal case only one possible outcome is "right" or "just," but that isn't always true. Here both my position and Schmidt's were coherent, plausible, and defensible. Some judges would rule in the government's favor, and others in favor of Martinez. Block in the end gave me the nod. He ruled that Saladino had perjured himself by claiming to be an honest, reformed man but that the perjury was immaterial, of little consequence to the outcome of the trial. Saladino, Block noted, had been thoroughly impeached at trial; everyone knew he was a horrible person. More important, Block noted that at five or six different moments during my closing argument, I asked the jury to convict because of the tapes, not because of Saladino. As a result, he ruled, the key to the trial was the tapes, not Saladino's testimony.

I left court that day a happy man but also a sober one. I was glad the conviction was sustained. I was glad Martinez would not escape. But that did not change the facts. In my first case with a cooperating witness I had blown it.

ON NOVEMBER 20, 2000, more than two years after the trial, Block sentenced Anthony Martinez. Prior to this time, none of the Badfellas guards had received significant prison terms. The *Martinez* case, however, had educated Block on the evils of prison corruption. Before he rendered his sentence, Block sent a strong message to the court of appeals, which was likely to review his decision. "Just to make it clear," Block intoned, "I am absolutely at peace with myself that Mr. Martinez is an absolutely corrupt corrections officer." He then imposed a stiff seventy-eight-month prison sentence, the precise amount called for under the federal sentencing guidelines. That day Martinez was carted off to begin his prison sentence.

As I walked out of court, the case finally concluded after years of hard work, Mrs. Martinez, the defendant's wife, confronted me by the elevator bank. "Mr. Kroger!" she called out. I was tempted to walk on, but something made me stop and turn. Mrs. Martinez looked at me with piercing eyes. "Next time," she said, "be careful with your informants." I nodded and walked away.

For me, the *Martinez* case was a watershed. In federal law enforcement, reliance on informants is a necessary evil. The mission of the Justice Department is not to catch small-time crooks but to uncover and dismantle criminal organizations of national and international scope. These organizations are highly sophisticated; they cover their tracks well, leaving little evidence behind—and few witnesses alive. To discover their activities and bring them to justice, we have to rely on turncoats, members of the organizations themselves, who can be lured to work for our side in return for money or leniency. We are, in important respects, at the mercy of these informants, for we cannot do our jobs without them.

The Saladino disaster taught me, however, that reliance on informants, however necessary, is always fraught with peril. From this point on I scrutinized potential cooperators with extra care, putting their backgrounds and statements under a microscope, looking for signs of deception or dishonesty. If I had any doubts, I declined to sign people up; I wanted no more Saladinos. When I did agree to let defendants cooperate, I always told them the Ray Saladino story. Every time I concluded the story the exact same way. "If you ever lie to me or commit perjury, I personally guarantee you'll sit in prison for twenty years, just like Ray Saladino."

Did this extra care pay off? I like to think so. During the remainder of my career none of my cooperators was caught telling lies, by me or anyone else. The problem of course is that as a prosecutor you can never know for sure. I tried hard to keep my witnesses honest, and I hope and believe they were. But it is possible that some of my witnesses got away with deception despite my best efforts. Saladino got caught because of a fluke: one of his best friends cooperated. But for that fact he would have got away with his scam. That thought troubled me for the rest of my time as a prosecutor.

CHAPTER FIVE

The Human Factor

When I joined the U.S. Attorney's Office, I received very little formal training. At first, this did not bother me. I thought my job would be simple. People broke the law, and when they did, I would hold them accountable. If I had questions about the law, I could get my answers in the statute book and from case law.

This preconception turned out to be incredibly naive. Federal criminal law, I discovered, was immensely complicated. The problem was not the law itself; that was usually fairly clear. The real challenge was the human factor.

In every federal criminal case, you face dozens of potential traps. Witnesses may turn out to be dishonest or to have poor memories; important facts may never be discovered or may be discovered too late; the evidence you uncover may be ambiguous; judges may rule in unpredictable ways; defense attorneys may try to trick you. As a prosecutor you are responsible for cutting through the confusion and making a series of judgments. What actually happened in the case? Was a federal crime committed? Was the defendant responsible? Should you bring charges? Can you make your charges stick? Throughout this process you are always one small mistake away from disaster. If you fail to assess a situation correctly—fail to judge human nature correctly—a guilty criminal might go free. Worse, you might put an innocent person behind bars.

This job of the prosecutor is always challenging, but for the new recruit it is almost overwhelming. Making sure that justice is done requires excellent judgment, but that judgment comes only with experience. As a rookie AUSA you are flying blind. You can only learn from your mistakes.

————

DURING MY YEARS AS AN AUSA, federal agents in New York were required to seek and receive authorization from an AUSA to arrest a person and bring formal charges against him or her.* During the daytime this process was simple. Agents who had detained a suspect called Neil Ross, our veteran intake chief, and described the facts of the case. If Neil thought the case warranted federal prosecution, he authorized the arrest and told the agents to bring the defendant to the courthouse for arraignment. If Neil wanted to pass, however, he told the agents to cut their target loose or take the person to state prosecutors. The process was more complicated at night. There are two to four federal arrests every night in the Eastern District, and Neil would never get any sleep if he had to pass judgment on them all. To fix that problem, the most junior AUSAs in the office took turns standing "No. 1 arraignment duty," responsible for intake after closing hours.

At first I loved being on arraignment duty at night. It sounds a little pathetic today, but at the time the idea that I was "in charge" of the district for the night, responsible for making arrest determinations, gave me a slight thrill—and a decided feeling of power. Imagine you are out on a dinner date when all of a sudden your pager goes off. You suavely apologize for the interruption and return the call from your table. "Hey, it's John Kroger, the duty assistant . . . Yes . . . Yes . . . Any problems? . . . Two kilos? . . . Okay, sure, better bring him in." You hang up the phone and look over at your date. With any luck, she's thinking: How cool. What an interesting job. Alas, if she's a lawyer herself, she might know the truth: you have to be pretty low on the totem pole to get stuck on arraignment duty on Friday night.

Many arrest authorizations were simple. If an agent caught a defendant with a large quantity of heroin, we would certainly take the case.

---

*This was not a legal requirement but rather a function of the practical realities of federal law enforcement in New York. Because our caseloads were very heavy, we had to decline to prosecute a large number of potential federal cases. Because of this, it saved everyone time if the agents asked us for authorization to arrest right after they caught someone, instead of wasting time processing and transporting the defendant only to discover that the case was too trivial or flimsy to prosecute.

On other occasions, however, arrest determinations were hard to make, and arraignment duty was more challenging.

One night—Eeek! Eeek! Eeek!—my duty pager went off at 3:00 a.m. Groggy, eyes still closed, I made a grab for it on my bedside table, knocking my cheap plastic alarm clock to the floor in the process. "Fuck," I muttered quietly as I rubbed my eyes. I shut off the pager, put on my glasses, and turned on a light. In my limited experience, I had already discovered that you had to call agents back almost immediately, or they would get pissed off and call Neil, and that made him very angry. At the same time, you had to be totally awake before you called; no point in trying to make a decision when you are half asleep. So I got up, splashed some cold water on my face, poured a glass of orange juice, found a pen and legal pad, and then got back under the covers, ready for action.

When I called the number on the pager, the phone was answered by an angry cop at a Veterans Administration hospital out on Long Island. A drunken veteran had been caught at 2:00 a.m., trespassing. When the cops tried to escort him off the hospital property, he had become "verbally belligerent," and when the police got physical, the suspect pushed one cop and took a swing at another, landing a glancing blow. The cops wanted to charge him with assaulting a federal law enforcement officer, a serious felony offense. I wrote the facts down on my legal pad and then got out my EDNY declination guidelines, which I stored in a drawer of my bedside table just for these occasions.

The declination guidelines are an incredibly important document. Each federal prosecutor's office has limited resources, and it cannot possibly prosecute every federal crime within its boundaries. Instead, it has to exercise discretion, prosecuting the important cases and declining the trivial ones. To help individual prosecutors make these decisions, most large U.S. Attorney's Offices draft formal guidelines covering every kind of federal case. These guidelines set forth the offices' priorities. In the EDNY, for example, we would indict any case involving fifty grams or more of heroin but would decline anything below that amount, leaving it for state prosecutors to deal with.

The declination guidelines had a huge impact on the way we did our jobs. In the EDNY, for example, the front office believed marijuana was a minor problem, causing very minimal social costs compared with crack, heroin, and cocaine. As a result, it wrote guidelines requiring frontline prosecutors like me to decline any marijuana case involving less than two thousand pounds, anything short of a truckload. This was a wise call. We had more small pot cases in Brooklyn than we could possibly prosecute, and this high standard allowed us to focus on higher-priority heroin and cocaine cases. Still, the result always cracked me up. Almost every afternoon during the years I was a prosecutor, two old guys sat on a park bench in Cadman Plaza, right in front of the federal courthouse, and smoked joints. Every day hundreds of AUSAs, narcotics agents, and federal judges walked right past them, but no one did a thing. Sometimes I was tempted to go over to tell them to clear out, but they always looked so serene I didn't have the heart. Apparently, no one else did either. Busting these two guys was not our job, for our declination policies effectively rewrote the statute book. In Brooklyn, marijuana possession was no longer a federal crime.*

When I opened my copy of the guidelines that night, I hoped it would give me some clear guidance, for I had never handled an assault case before. Unfortunately, the guidelines simply provided general advice. "Assault cases," I read, "should be accepted or declined at the discretion of the AUSA, taking into consideration the nature of the assault, the degree of injury, the criminal background of the defendant, and any mitigating or aggravating factors." Hmm, I thought, that's vague enough. I asked the cop on the phone a series of follow-up questions, and I learned that the "defendant" was in his fifties, was a frequent patient at the facility, had no criminal history, and was very drunk. No one had been hurt, but the "defendant" had been really disrespectful. After looking back down at the guidelines once again, I realized this was not a black-and-white case. I did not want to make a decision on the fly, so I told the cop I would call him back in a few minutes.

Making a good arrest decision takes some imagination. Who is this drunk guy, I asked myself, running around a VA hospital at night? He was in his fifties. That made him a Vietnam-era vet, perhaps one who

---

*Declination guidelines ensure that cases within a district are treated uniformly, but no one has ever made any effort to ensure that the guidelines are uniform from district to district. Instead, each office sets its own priorities. This makes good sense; local U.S. Attorneys can better assess local needs than a bureaucrat in Washington, D.C. But it causes some serious discrepancies. In some districts, possession of even a small amount of marijuana will be prosecuted as a federal crime. In Brooklyn, it would never be charged.

had seen active duty. He appeared to have a substance abuse problem. If he was at the VA hospital, he might have medical issues stemming from an old wound. Perhaps, like many vets, he had serious, legitimate complaints about the quality of care he was receiving from the VA medical center. Was he causing trouble? Certainly. Did he need help? Yes. Did he need to be arrested and charged with a serious felony offense? On balance, no. No one had been hurt, no serious harm done. He was a veteran. We should cut him some slack. I called the cop back and told him to release the defendant.

I expected the VA cop to accept my decision calmly, for at this stage in my career no one had argued with my charging decisions. Instead, he went ballistic. "Look, I don't know who you think you are, but this is a serious crime. This guy attacked us. We got a tough job to do. You gotta support us. I never heard of a prosecutor who wouldn't stick up for us. I never heard of a prosecutor who didn't take it seriously when someone attacks a federal law enforcement officer. This guy is laughing at us. We need to hold him overnight and bring him down tomorrow and charge him!"

The cop's verbal assault really shook me up, and my confidence in my own decision immediately evaporated. Maybe the cop was right. Maybe we always charged these cases. How was I supposed to know? Attacking a cop was bad. Maybe I should do what they wanted. Pushed on the defensive, I told the cop I would call him back, and then I sat in my bed and fretted. What should I do? Paralyzed by uncertainty, the clock ticking, I chose to do the unthinkable: I called Neil Ross and woke him up.

I was a little afraid of Neil. He had been a prosecutor for years, first as a state prosecutor and then with the EDNY. Law enforcement agents loved him. He was gruff, a practical joker, not a stickler for rules. He was probably the only intake chief in the country who regularly broke the law himself, smoking giant smelly cigars in his office. Whenever I ran into him, Neil made fun of me, laughing at my inexperience and my self-importance. "How you doin' today, kid? Solve the crime problem yet?" Needless to say, my enthusiasm for waking him up at three in the morning was pretty limited. But I had a job to do, and I needed his help.

To my surprise, Neil was not mad that I called. He was extremely patient. I explained the facts of the case and my conflicting concerns: on the one hand, my desire to support the cops, and on the other, my feeling that arrest, overnight detention, and a felony assault charge were simply too severe. Finally, when I finished my anguished presentation, Neil sighed and said wearily, "Kroger, just write him a ticket."

A ticket? There are tickets in federal criminal law? Like parking tickets? Trying to hide my ignorance, I said, "Uh, right, but, uh, a ticket for what?"

Neil just sighed again. "Kroger, do you ever read the statute book? Eighteen USC Section 111. You can charge a misdemeanor assault. If it is a misdemeanor, the agents don't need to arrest him. They can just write the guy a summons and send him on his way. He'll probably get a fine. Okay?" I gulped, apologized to Neil for waking him up, and hung up. Ten minutes later, the VA cops had written the defendant a ticket and escorted him off the property—case closed. That night I learned an important lesson. Sometimes what appears to be a difficult ethical quandary is simply the product of ignorance about your options.

DURING THE CLINTON ADMINISTRATION, the Justice Department began to crack down on handgun violence by "federalizing," and thus punishing more heavily, select state firearms offenses, those in which the defendant had a prior criminal record or had committed a serious crime like armed robbery. These Triggerlock cases had a bad reputation in the office. Unlike most of our work, which was initiated by federal agents, these gun cases were typically brought to us by the New York Police Department. When I got my first gun case, a senior colleague gave me a chilling warning: "You have to scrutinize these cases closely. Most cops are honest, but their reports are not always accurate, and their cases have a much higher percentage of constitutional problems than those investigated by the FBI. And sometimes the officers will lie to hide their mistakes."

My first gun case looked open-and-shut. According to the police report, a man with a prior criminal record had tried to rob a convenience store owner at gunpoint. When the owner resisted, the suspect ran off. He was caught several blocks away. The robber was positively identified by the store owner, and the gun, unlicensed, with the serial number removed, was recovered as well. Because of the robber's prior record, the case was transferred to us for federal prosecution. I was supposed to indict the robber for a federal crime—use of a gun during a crime of violence—and for being a felon in possession of a weapon. If convicted, my defendant would spend ten years in federal prison.

Had this been a federal case from the get-go, I would not have examined the facts too closely; I would simply have put the agent in the grand jury and indicted the defendant on the basis of the facts set forth in his report. Since, however, I had been warned about the NYPD, I decided to analyze the police report more carefully, and when I did, some difficult questions came to my mind. If the suspect was armed, why did the store owner risk death by resisting? And how and why was the "resistance" successful? Did the owner have a gun as well? If not, why did the robber run off instead of simply shooting the owner or clubbing him over the head? I asked the arresting officer to come to my office to talk about the case. I assumed this meeting would clear everything up. Instead, it only made me more uncomfortable.

One morning the cop—let's call him Jackson—came to my office in uniform. He was a chubby guy, and with his utility belt, pistol, cuffs, and club, he barely fitted in my one spare office chair. I opened the meeting by asking Jackson to tell me what happened, and he repeated the story in his report. "I reported to a crime scene, chased down the bad guy, and got the bodega owner to ID him. It's an open-and-shut case. Let's get the guy locked up." The cop seemed self-confident. Almost self-satisfied. When, however, I started asking questions, he quickly lost his bluster.

"Where was the gun when you arrested the defendant?"

"Uh, he didn't have it on him. We recovered it from the bodega owner. The defendant threw it under an ice cream freezer before he fled."

"Was the bodega owner armed? How did he resist?"

"He wasn't armed. He physically resisted."

"Well, is the bodega owner a big guy?"

"Uh, no, he's Indian, uh, probably five feet two inches, one hundred twenty pounds."

"Then why didn't the robber just shoot him?"

"I don't know, he got nervous and ran."

"Did you see him run?"

"No, the owner called us to the scene a few minutes later."

"Did you fingerprint the gun?"

"No. You know, metal doesn't really show prints that well, so we don't print guns."

That's not exactly true, I thought. Fingerprints on nonporous surfaces like metal and glass can last for years. You rarely pick up prints off a gun's corrugated grips, but they can be recovered from smooth barrel surfaces and rounds left in the chamber. But I did not call Jackson on his claim. Instead, I simply asked, "Why don't we fingerprint it now?"

"Well, I mean, I handled the gun, the Indian guy handled it, so it won't be much help."

"Did the defendant admit he had a gun when you arrested him?"

"No, he says the Indian guy had one, but not him."

What was I supposed to make of this case? As I considered the facts, two possibilities came to mind. On the one hand, the suspect might indeed be an armed robber. Alternatively, he could have been framed. Sitting in my chair, listening to Jackson's answers, I quickly formulated a plausible alternative interpretation that fitted the facts of the case. The suspect, a black guy, was hassling the Indian store owner, scaring him, maybe threatening him, so the Indian store owner pulled an unlicensed gun and told him to take off. Scared the suspect might come back armed or with friends, the store owner called the NYPD and said the suspect had tried to rob him. Worried that the suspect would tell the police about the gun, which was unlicensed, he handed the gun to the cops and claimed it belonged to the suspect. The cops chose to believe the store owner because the suspect was a black guy with a record. In New York's tough neighborhoods this kind of stuff happens every day.

Did Jackson truly believe the defendant had tried to commit an armed robbery? Probably. Still, it seemed suspicious that he was reluctant to fingerprint the weapon, and his report was intentionally vague, leaving out many critical facts—for instance, that the gun was not found on the suspect but recovered from the owner. These facts suggested to me the cop knew the case was problematic but wanted to pursue it anyway. On a number of different occasions during my career, agents or cops have said to me, only half joking, "Don't worry if the defendant's innocent. If he didn't commit this crime, he undoubtedly committed others we don't know about." That kind of reasoning, and the desire to make an armed robbery bust, might have been in play here.

Ultimately, whether the cop was right about the case or not did not matter to me. My job was to prove cases beyond a reasonable doubt, and this one was so flimsy it would not hold up in court. For that reason, if nothing else, I decided to decline prosecution.

When I told Jackson I was not going to prosecute, he immediately got angry and defensive. "Whose side are you on, mine or the crook's? Are you calling me a liar?" I told the cop it didn't matter what I thought; the evidence was too weak to charge as a federal crime. Jackson complained to my supervisors, but the office backed me up. We already had so many cases, why charge one that was weak?

SHOULD I HAVE CONFRONTED THE COP and told him I thought the case might be a frame? Maybe. But before you reach that conclusion, let me tell you another story.

In the General Crimes unit, one of my closest friends was Eric Tirschwell, who started in the office two weeks before I did. One day Eric was assigned to an NYPD Triggerlock gun case. The defendant, Stanford Francis, had originally been charged by state prosecutors with attempted murder, but a jury acquitted him. Francis had a prior criminal record and had been carrying a gun at the time of his arrest. To keep Francis off the streets, Eric took a second bite at the apple, indicting him for a federal crime, felon in possession of a firearm.

A week before trial Eric met with James Sullivan, one of the two arresting officers, to prepare Sullivan's testimony. During the prep session Eric made an alarming discovery. At the prior state trial, Sullivan had testified under oath that the night Francis was arrested, he had picked up Francis's gun and locked it in his police cruiser's trunk, as required by police regulations. Now, however, Sullivan told Eric that his partner, not he, had picked up the gun, and that on the drive to the precinct the gun was not in the trunk but inside the passenger compartment. To Sullivan, these lies were no big deal; he had only changed the true story in minor ways because he didn't want to get busted for violating a petty police regulation. To a federal prosecutor like Eric, however, this was a major problem, prior perjury by a police officer under oath. Eric was the last guy to sweep something like this under the rug, so he confronted Sullivan with his inconsistent statements and advised him that he had committed perjury. That's when Sullivan made things worse. First he denied lying; he was just "confused." Then he said, "Tell me what you want me to say." This comment really bothered Eric, for it indicated that Sullivan was still willing to bend the truth.

The very next day Eric disclosed Sullivan's lies to the defense, just as I did in the *Martinez* case. Then he moved to dismiss his indictment, for he was unwilling to go to trial with a lead witness he could not trust. A few days later Sullivan was summoned to testify in federal court about his perjury and was told to bring a lawyer, since he might face criminal penalties. That day Sullivan never showed up.

Big city cops like James Sullivan are under immense pressure. They work long hours, make barely adequate livings, and constantly put their lives on the line. Every day when they wake up, they know they might get murdered by some stupid kid with a gun in his hand. Most feel wildly unappreciated by society.

For James Sullivan, a nine-year police veteran with more than a dozen commendations for excellent policing to his credit, with a wife and two small kids, the perjury allegation was simply one push too far. The night before his court appearance Sullivan drove his car off the side of the Sunken Meadow Parkway on eastern Long Island, took out his service pistol, and shot himself in the head. When Eric arrived at work the next morning, he got a voice mail message coldly informing him that his witness had committed suicide.

The Sullivan tragedy is an extreme example, but it illustrates a vital point. In federal prosecution lives are at stake every day. When a prosecutor decides to act, he or she will alter lives forever. You wield so much power, and can bring so much pressure to bear, that some people may crack. So when you make a decision, you'd better be right. Even if you are, your decision may have very high costs.

AS AN AUSA you work regularly with a dozen different federal law enforcement agencies, not just the FBI. Some are excellent. I usually enjoyed working with the Drug Enforcement Administration and Customs, for I found their agents were smart, dedicated, and careful. Other agencies, however, were problematic.

The United States Secret Service's primary responsibility is to protect the president, public officials, and visiting foreign leaders from assassination. This was not, however, its original function. It was created back in 1865 to fight counterfeiting, which had exploded during and after the Civil War, when the United States first printed its greenback dollars. Today the Secret Service continues to pursue these two very different missions. Unfortunately, the qualities that make Secret Service agents good at protection often render them hopeless in the field of counterfeiting. When your mission is to protect the president, results are all that count. Though Secret Service agents deny this when talking "on the record," they will admit (even brag) in private that they generally don't care too much about violating a potential assassin's civil rights and civil liberties if it means preventing the murder of someone they are assigned to protect. So they cut corners and break rules. Unfortunately, this cavalier attitude carries over to their less vital counterfeiting work. In sports, coaches tell you to "practice like you play" because the bad habits you learn in practice will come back to haunt you in a game. The same applies to criminal law. Secret Service agents who have developed bad investigative habits in the presidential protection area, failing, for example, to comply with constitutional rules regarding searches or interrogations, make the same errors when working on a simple criminal matter. That often means legal trouble: suppressed evidence or botched cases.*

In fall of 1997, after a few months on the job, I was asked to supervise a Secret Service investigation into a Colombian counterfeiting ring. The ring began when a drug cartel had a very good idea. The cartel was producing cocaine in Colombia and then smuggling it by suitcase into the United States, where it sold it for cash. Someone got the bright idea to cut out the first step entirely and just import money directly instead. The cartel manufactured hundreds of suitcases with false bottoms and sides. Behind these false structural walls, the cartel hid millions of dollars of counterfeit money, which it "printed" using high-tech photocopiers. Then it sent couriers with the suitcases to the United States on international flights through JFK, just as it did with its drugs. Once the counterfeit was safely inside our borders, it was traded at a discount for legitimate cash.

---

*I should stress that this judgment is based on my experiences in Brooklyn. My friend Matt, a prosecutor in California, totally disagrees. When he read a draft of this section, he told me that his Secret Service agents have been excellent, producing first-rate cases. This discrepancy may represent differences between the Secret Service's New York office and those in other parts of the country.

The Secret Service got wind of the scheme and brought the case to the EDNY for investigation. Our job was to uncover the ring and arrest any participants working in the United States. To be honest, this was a pretty serious case to assign to a rookie General Crimes assistant, and you might wonder why that happened. It was not, I can assure you, because I had shown any particular talent for investigating crime—or any other talent, for that matter. The truth is, the Secret Service had such a bad reputation in my office that no senior AUSAs would work with it, and so its cases had to be assigned to rookies, people like me who didn't know any better. If I had known this at the time, would it have changed the outcome of the case?

My cartel investigation began smoothly. The Secret Service agents came to my office, and together, using the leads they had compiled, we drafted a search warrant for a suspected cartel safe house, where we believed the conspirators disassembled the suitcases and stored the counterfeit. The night of the raid I gave the agents my home telephone number in case any legal questions came up. They called me about fifteen minutes after they had executed the search. The raid had gone perfectly, and the agents were excited. They had seized a large quantity of counterfeit bills, plus several of the smuggling suitcases. They had also arrested two men who were in the apartment, caught red-handed taking one of the suitcases apart. It looked like an open-and-shut case, and I gave them authorization to arrest the two men.

Because I had never run an investigation before, I had no idea what to do next, so I asked the agents to come to my office to plan our next steps. Unfortunately, our meeting was delayed—the agents were on protection detail for a presidential trip to New York—and before we could reschedule, something remarkable happened. One afternoon I got a call from a lawyer whom I will call Charles Mears. Mears told me he had been retained by one of the two arrested counterfeiters and asked for a meeting. When he arrived, I immediately sensed something unusual in the air. Mears was dressed in a somewhat gangsterish but clearly expensive black chalk-stripe suit, and when he gave me his business card, I saw that his office was located not on Brooklyn's lowly Court Street but at a prestigious address on Manhattan's Park Avenue. Now, the two guys we arrested in the apartment were what law enforcement calls mopes, low-level guys, illegal immigrants, hired to unpack suitcases for a tiny piece of the take. They were not the kind of men who could afford an expensive Park Avenue lawyer. So from the start I was thinking this guy was probably hired by the cartel itself.

Mears and I chatted for a few minutes, to no real purpose, and then he got up to go. I was wondering why he had bothered to drop by when almost as an afterthought, he handed me a document and said, "Oh, my client gave me this. I thought perhaps you would want it." I looked down, and as soon as I saw what he had given me, my face turned dark red. As I walked Mears to our office door—no one walks around a DOJ facility without an escort—I had a hard time focusing on him because my mind was tied up in knots.

The document was titled something like "United States Secret Service: Search Plan." It described the precise manner in which the apartment was to be searched, listing, for example, the names of the agents in charge of communications, security, hitting the door, and inventorying evidence. It also summarized the goals of our investigation. At the bottom, it read: "Assigned A.U.S.A.: John Kroger, EDNY." By my name I saw my home telephone number.

Like all great works of art, Mears's gambit was complex, operating on several different levels at once. I had no way of knowing how Mears had got his hands on the plan, which was, after all, a "secret" Secret Service document. Most likely, one of the agents had left it at the search location, and if that was true, it showed me that my agents were dangerously sloppy. It was also possible, however, that the document had been sold to the cartel by a corrupt Secret Service agent, a theory we could not afford to ignore. Finally, there was a personal angle. Mears had not threatened me, but he had let me know, in a very subtle manner, that the cartel knew who I was and how to find me. Perhaps he thought that would be enough to scare me off.

What was I supposed to do now? Clueless, I took the search plan into Corngold's office and told him what had happened. After I blew off some steam, ranting about the Secret Service, Corngold asked me what I thought we should do. I told him I was torn. I wanted to pursue the case, but that would be impossible if we had a corrupt agent on our hands. If, however, we opened an internal investigation to see if an agent was taking bribes, that would probably kill off the underlying counterfeiting case with the cartel still in business.

At that point Eric interrupted. Normally, he let me make my own decisions, part of the learning process at the heart of the EDNY's General Crimes unit.* Now, however, he simply gave me orders. "I'll call the Secret Service counsel's office and explain what happened. If they want to open an internal inquiry, and they probably will, that's their business. As for us, convict the defendants you've got and terminate the investigation. You don't want to work with these agents."

When Eric finished, I argued back. To me, the case seemed too important to abandon, and I hated the idea that Mears's strategy to derail my investigation was going to work. But Corngold cut me off. "Just trust me. For the rest of your career, work with agents you can rely on, and avoid the ones you can't trust. We have more criminals on our hands than we can manage as it is. If you don't do this case, you'll do a different one. Just drop it."

As I walked out, Corngold gave me one more piece of advice: "You'd better change your home phone number. Make sure it is unlisted. The office will pay for the charge. And never, ever, ever give it out to an agent again."

———

WHEN I FIRST JOINED THE EDNY, I was told that we did not plea-bargain. Under the federal sentencing guidelines, each defendant faces a specific, predetermined range of punishment for his conduct, which lawyers and judges calculate by assessing the seriousness of the defendant's crime and the extent of his or her criminal history. For a first-time credit card thief, that range might be ten to sixteen months; for a drug courier, sixty-three to seventy-eight months; for a drug kingpin, thirty years to life. When discussing pleas with defense attorneys, I was told to offer each defendant precisely what he was supposed to get under the guidelines, no more and no less. If the defendant didn't like our offer, he could go to trial.

The office's policy made sense: it was clear, ensured that defendants who committed similar crimes would receive the exact same sentences,

---

*My sense, talking to other AUSAs from other districts, is that my EDNY peers and I were given much more leeway to make our own decisions, and our own mistakes, than other rookie Justice Department prosecutors. This was one of the great advantages of working in Brooklyn, for it made us seasoned prosecutors early in our careers. But it came at the price of increased stress, for both us and our supervisors.

and prevented AUSAs from "underpleading" their cases just to clear them off their desks. I quickly learned, however, that our stated policy was totally untenable and that the gap between our stated policy and our actual conduct was immense.

In the mid-1990s customs officials caught roughly a thousand drug couriers at JFK Airport every year.* This barrage of drug importation cases threatened to swamp our office, so we had to find some way to get rid of them quickly and efficiently. The result was called the bump-down. In every simple courier case, we told the defendants that if they pleaded guilty rapidly, without making us do any further work, we would agree to a package of sentencing concessions that would reduce their sentences significantly—typically, to less than half of what they should have received. If, for example, they pleaded out before filing any motions or requesting discovery, we would dismiss any charges requiring a mandatory minimum sentence and agree to tell their sentencing judges that they were only "minimal" participants in the crime, entitled to a major "role reduction" at sentencing. This bump-down was so attractive drug couriers pleaded guilty in droves. Though I indicted more than one hundred courier cases during my time in Brooklyn, none of them ever went to trial. Everyone pleaded.

Of course the bump-down policy would not work unless judges agreed to respect our skimpy plea offers. The first time I told a judge that a drug courier deserved a minimal role reduction, I expected her to laugh in my face. After all, it is simply not true to say that the person actually carrying illegal drugs across the border is a minimal participant in drug smuggling. I quickly learned, however, that every single judge in the district had quietly agreed to support the policy. Some of the judges shut their eyes to this clear abuse of the sentencing laws because they recognized that this was the only way for the EDNY to manage its caseload efficiently. For many judges, however, a different issue was at stake. Many of the judges thought federal drug prison terms were way too

---

*Many of these couriers had narcotics hidden in their suitcases. Others were internal carriers, men and women who swallowed dozens of condoms or balloons filled with heroin or cocaine and then tried to bring the drugs into the country hidden in their digestive tracts. Customs inspectors were trained to look for signs that persons might be internal carriers: tickets bought in cash, no good explanations for why they were visiting the United States, nervousness, a lack of typical tourist luggage or possessions. They then ran persons fitting this profile through an X-ray machine, exposing any drugs in their body cavities.

long. Not surprisingly, they leaped at a chance to impose less drastic sentences.

From the outset of my time in the office, I was ambivalent about the bump-down. I recognized that the policy was probably necessary. I personally had more than sixty courier cases on my docket after six months in the office, and I would never have been able to deal with all these defendants without a way to get rid of their cases quickly and efficiently. In fact, I was grateful for the bump-down, because it freed up time so I could concentrate on the cases that really mattered to me, like *Elcock* and *Martinez*.

I also had no real objection to the results. Drug cartels tend to recruit the most vulnerable people to serve as their couriers: senior citizens, single mothers with small children, people in wheelchairs. These people are easy to recruit and to manipulate and they tend to receive less scrutiny at international borders. As a result, many of the drug couriers had horrendous stories to tell. In some of my cases the couriers agreed to smuggle drugs in order to buy medicine, pay for food for their children, or protect their families, whom the cartels had threatened to kill if they refused to carry drugs. Did it make a real difference, from a deterrence point of view, if these people went to jail for seven years rather than three? Probably not.

Still, I was not happy with the policy. Prosecutors and judges are supposed to execute faithfully the laws passed by Congress. In the EDNY, however, the judges and prosecutors were involved in what amounted to a conspiracy to circumvent the sentencing laws. This bothered me deeply. So though I used the bump-down all the time, I was looking for a chance to challenge it.

On December 24, 1997, two Russian women, Olga Zorina and Lyudmila Burmagina, arrived at JFK. They were gambling, I think, that Customs would let its guard down because it was Christmas Eve. They guessed wrong. Inspectors searched their suitcases and found large quantities of illegal Russian anabolic steroids—the kind used by weight lifters and sports stars to gain unnatural amounts of muscle. The women were placed under arrest and their case was assigned to me, a veteran, by now, of four months' prosecutorial experience.

In plea negotiations the two defense lawyers in the *Zorina-Burmagina* case—one was Abe Clott, soon to be my adversary in the Elcock trial—

demanded the bump-down on the ground that their clients were drug couriers, but I refused. This outraged my opponents, but there was little they could do. Since their clients had been caught red-handed, they would never win at trial. Lacking options, the two Russians pleaded guilty anyway to every single count in the indictment. That set up a showdown at sentencing.

The steroids case was assigned to Judge John Gleeson, a legend in the EDNY. As an AUSA Gleeson had brought mafia boss John Gotti to justice. Now on the bench, he was known for his calm demeanor, deep knowledge of criminal law, and sharp analytic mind. Here, I thought, was the perfect venue for my attack on the bump-down policy. Gleeson, I imagined, must be pretty tough on crime. Maybe I could impress him with my legal acumen.

One cold winter day the Russians appeared before Gleeson for sentencing. Veteran defense counsel Bobbi Sternheim spoke first. Sternheim noted that there was no plea agreement in the case because the government prosecutor had refused to offer the bump-down. She asked the court to sentence her client to probation and send her back to Russia, on the basis of her minimal role in the crime. Clott took the same position. After they had finished, Gleeson turned to me. I could see a quizzical look on his face, as if he were thinking: Hmm, what's this all about?

I was nervous—Gleeson's eyes did not look encouraging—but I did not back down. I told Gleeson that a bump-down reduction in sentence might be appropriate for a South American drug cartel courier, because a cartel courier is part of a giant organization and receives only a small percentage of the illegal profits from the crime. The case at bar, however, was totally different. There are no steroid smuggling cartels, and there was no evidence that the defendants were working for a giant organization rather than for themselves. Accordingly, there was no evidence to support the conclusion that they were minor participants in the crime and not the principals. For that reason, I asked the court to impose the guideline sentence and send the two women to prison without any reduction whatsoever.

Throughout my argument Gleeson stared steadily at me with his cold blue eyes. When I finished, he paused for a moment, and then he said, in his quiet, precise voice, "I couldn't be less interested in your argument." I blushed deeply, my face burning hot, and I felt incredibly

foolish. Two minutes later Gleeson sentenced the two women to probation. The judge, a great prosecutor in his day, was sending me a message:
If you want to be a hard-ass, save it for cases that matter.

———

DURING MY ROOKIE YEAR I faced many difficult choices. None of
them troubled me more than the case involving "Dora."

Every year foreign drug cartels make billions of dollars in the United
States. The cartels cannot simply deposit the money in banks in the
United States, for American bankers are required to report suspicious
deposits or wire transfers of ten thousand dollars or more to federal law
enforcement agencies. So, to enjoy their illicit profits, the drug lords have
to ship their money back to their home countries, where it can be more
easily spent, invested, or laundered. The cartels use many different
strategies to accomplish this. Some wire drug money overseas in small
batches of less than ten thousand dollars to escape the reporting requirements, a process known as smurfing. Some purchase expensive American products, which can then be sold or transported abroad more easily.
Some sell their dollars at a discount on the black peso market to persons
who are willing to buy dirty dollars and risk arrest. But most dealers prefer a more direct solution. They sneak their money out of the country
physically, in suitcases or shipping crates. They are, in essence, smuggling in both directions across the border: drugs in, money out.

To combat this flow of drug money, Congress has made it illegal for
any person in the United States to take more than ten thousand dollars
out of the country without declaring the money to Customs. Obviously,
drug cartels cannot comply with this rule, for if their money couriers declare they are traveling with large quantities of cash to Panama, Mexico,
or Colombia, the DEA and Customs will investigate. To avoid this, the
money couriers lie and hope they don't get caught.

Very early in my rookie year, a Colombian woman I shall call "Dora"
went through a routine outbound customs inspection at JFK prior to a
flight to Bogotá. The inspectors opened her suitcase, just as they do in
thousands of similar cases every day. Inside, they found something odd:
a bunch of automobile air filters. Most customs inspectors would let this
pass, but the inspector on duty was sharp. Air filters are readily available

in Latin America at a cheap price, so why, she wondered, would someone try to take them home from America? The inspector selected one box at random and opened it. The black plastic filter inside looked totally normal. When, however, she pried open the plastic filter casing, she didn't find a filter element; she found a tight roll of cash. The inspector and a team of agents tore all the filters apart, and when they were finished, they had roughly fifty thousand dollars in small bills piled on their inspection table. The agents called Neil Ross, and he authorized an arrest. The next day the case was assigned to me. My duty was to examine the facts and see whether Dora should be indicted or not.

In most federal districts, prosecutors would definitely charge Dora with a crime, for she was, without doubt, a drug money smuggler. In the EDNY, however, we had dozens of small money cases like this every month, so we had to be picky. I consulted the EDNY declination guidelines, but they did not provide a definitive answer. The guidelines stated that anyone caught smuggling less than twenty-five thousand dollars should be released after paying a fine, and everyone with more than a hundred thousand dollars should be prosecuted.* In cases like Dora's, where the dollar amount fell between these two benchmarks, the decision was "left to the AUSA's discretion." In short, the case was my call. Should I indict Dora and try to send her to prison or simply dismiss her case and deport her to Colombia?

As a brand-new rookie prosecutor I had no idea what I should do, so as always, I went to see my supervisor, Eric Corngold, for help. Corngold often reminded me of Yoda. Though capable, on occasion, of giving very specific advice, he usually refused to answer questions. Instead, he would reply with some abstract and cryptic remark, as impenetrable as a Zen koan. When I told him about the facts of Dora's case, he was no help at all. "The decision's up to you. Do what you think is right." Then he added, "Remember, every person is the hero of their own novel." I walked out of his office thinking: What's that supposed to mean?

The following week a legal aid lawyer named Mike Padden called me to talk about the case. "Just bring us in and listen to her story. I really don't think you should charge this one." A few days later I met with Dora

---

*Because the EDNY outbound currency guidelines have never been publicly disclosed, I have altered the actual numbers here.

and Mike in a small conference room at my office. This was my first face-to-face meeting with a criminal defendant outside court. Dora was short, about five feet one, and she looked very frail. She probably weighed less than one hundred pounds. Because she was not a U.S. citizen, she had been detained at the MDC after her arrest, and she was now wearing a blue prison jumpsuit. We took off her handcuffs, and she slumped in her chair, hands in her lap, eyes focused on the floor. She did not look nervous or wary. She looked like a person without hope.

I had no idea how to interview a defendant, let alone interrogate one, so I simply asked Dora to tell me what happened. She paused, and then she started to talk. Most defendants, I later discovered, need a lot of prompting before they talk about their crime. Dora was different. Her English was quite good, and she immediately confessed.

"Yes, I am guilty, I admit that. I was smuggling drug money for my husband, Carlito. He deals cocaine. It started several years ago. He told me that the government always suspects men, but they never check women, so I would be able to get the money to Colombia without getting caught. He told me he would do it himself, but he would be arrested. I was supposed to say I was visiting family back home. Once I was safely in Bogotá, I would deliver the filters to a man named Flaco, who always met me right at the airport gate. Carlito never told me how much money I was carrying. He kept me totally in the dark. He told me it wasn't much, not enough to get into trouble if I ever got caught. I was shocked when I learned it was fifty thousand dollars."

I asked Dora why she was willing to break the law. She replied, "If I refused, Carlito would beat me. He would leave me. I had to do it. I had no choice."

"Where is Carlito now?"

When I asked this question, Dora paused, and then tears leaked from the corners of her eyes. Padden gave her a Kleenex. She wiped her eyes, snuffled a little bit. Then she answered.

"He took off. I have not heard anything from him. My family tells me he is not at home, and he won't return my calls. I think he is in Miami. He has this whore he keeps."

At this point Dora broke down completely, her shoulders rising and falling as she gasped for breath between sobs. Padden did not say a word. I sat in my chair, watching her cry. I waited for a few moments, and then

I told Padden we should call it a day. Most defense lawyers would have made a pitch for their client on the way out the door. Padden, one of the best lawyers in the city, knew better. As we parted, he simply said, "Talk to you later." He wanted my last impression to be of Dora crying.

That afternoon I got out a yellow legal pad and began to list the pros and cons of indictment. On the one hand, Dora seemed honest and contrite. In my gut I felt she posed little risk of recidivism. If we deported her to Colombia, I thought she would probably not enter the United States again, for it looked as if she had learned her lesson about violating the drug laws. That suggested we pass on the case.

On the other hand, it was very possible Dora was trying to deceive me, that she was an experienced drug trafficker, perhaps in business for herself, and not the lowly mope she claimed to be. Padden might have prepped her to cry. None of her story might be true. Maybe Carlito did not exist. Maybe she was covering up for drug traffickers who were still alive and well in New York. Maybe my gut instincts were totally off base.

Experienced prosecutors like to believe—naively, perhaps—that we can distinguish between honest people and liars. We carefully probe a defendant's story, looking for contradictions or gaps in information, watching closely for the minute changes in body language that often signal dissimulation: a hunching of the shoulders, lip licking, fidgety fingers, sweating, repeated swallowing. Years later I would have employed this battery of interrogation skills to help make my decision. At the time, however, I had no such skills, and I had no idea whether she was telling the truth or not. Perhaps for that reason, I turned to philosophy for help.

As a prosecutor I was ethically required to seek a just outcome in the case. According to the utilitarians, those nineteenth-century British philosophers whom I had come to trust in college, justice is simply a fancy word for a result that maximizes social welfare. Thus a utilitarian considering Dora's case would ask: Would putting Dora in prison increase overall social welfare or not? When I considered this question, I quickly came to a clear answer: I had to indict. Cocaine trafficking is clearly a social evil. If we can stop drug traffickers from moving their money from the United States to Colombia, we can take away their profit motive, and this in turn will cut down on the drug supply. To do this, we have to seize as much of their money as possible and make it harder for them to recruit money couriers. Prosecuting Dora would help achieve these goals by sending a strong message to the drug trafficking community: people who work in the dirty money trade are going to pay a huge price when they get caught.

Rationally, I knew my analysis was sound. Yet I simply was not comfortable with it. If this is the right result, I asked myself, why does it feel so wrong? The more I thought about the case, the worse I felt about putting Dora in prison. Though I could not defend my instincts rationally, I simply did not think she would return to a life of crime, I did not think putting her in prison would make her a better person, and I felt sorry for her and her plight.

If you were Dora's prosecutor, what would you do? I pondered her case for several more days, and then, for better or worse, I decided to cut her loose. At the time I did not try to analyze the philosophical implications of my decision. I did not, for example, try to make sense of the obvious conflict that had emerged between my rational utilitarian beliefs and my intuitive sense of right and wrong. All I did was shrug. Maybe, I thought, philosophy just wasn't that useful to a prosecutor facing practical, real-world decisions.

To this day I have no idea whether or not I made the right decision in Dora's case. I will always be glad that I began my career by erring, if err I did, on the side of trust, compassion, and empathy. I am also sure, however, that if I had faced the same case years later, after hearing hundreds of defendants tell bullshit stories, I would almost certainly have indicted her.

PART II

Mafia Prosecutor

CHAPTER SIX

The Scarpa Crew and the FBI

I n June 1998, one week after the end of the Martinez trial, Eric Corngold called me into his office. Corngold was normally very jovial. Now he had a serious expression on his face. "I have surprising news for you. I just got off the phone with Valerie Caproni. She thought you did a great job on Martinez. She wants to know if you will join the trial team on the *Scarpa* case." Corngold paused, and for perhaps fifteen seconds the room was totally silent. He waited patiently.

Finally, I smiled weakly and managed to croak, "Are you serious?"

Mafia capo Gregory Scarpa, Jr., was one of the most dangerous mobsters in America. Scarpa and his mafia crew ran a big swath of the Brooklyn underworld, murdering at least twenty victims in the process. In 1995, after an investigation spanning more than ten years, the EDNY had charged Scarpa with racketeering and murder. Now the case was going to trial. As a General Crimes rookie, I had heard all about *United States v. Scarpa*, the highest-profile case then pending in the EDNY. To my surprise, I was now being asked to try it.

Corngold said that Valerie wanted an answer immediately. For me, the decision was easy. When I joined the EDNY, my secret hope was to join the office's fabled Organized Crime unit, the team that had brought down mafia boss John Gotti. Now that ambition was coming true. I tried to stay calm. I swallowed. And then I said, "Sure."

Corngold replied, "Trial's scheduled for September, but I think they've got motions due. You'd better give Valerie a call."

When I walked out of Eric's office, I was so excited every fiber in my body was tingling. I pumped my fist in the air, like a baseball pitcher who just got a critical strikeout. "Yes!" When I got back to my office, I was still so giddy it took me five minutes to regain my composure. When I finally calmed down, I called Valerie on the phone.

Valerie Caproni was the chief of the EDNY's entire Criminal Division, the supervisor of more than one hundred AUSAs. An experienced mafia prosecutor, Valerie had been battling the Colombo Organized Crime Family and its deadly Scarpa Crew since the mid-1980s. Valerie welcomed me to the case and told me, in her trademark Georgia twang, to "get up to speed" as quickly as possible. Trying to sound knowledgeable, I asked her if I could "pick up the file," as I had done when I took over the *Martinez* case. This just made Valerie laugh. "The Scarpa file"— she chuckled—"fills fifteen filing cabinets. For starters, I'll have the pros memo* and motion papers sent over." Valerie paused, and then she said, in a much quieter tone, "You better work hard. We can't afford to screw this up."

That afternoon a paralegal delivered a large box full of memorandums, reports, and grand jury transcripts to my office. Resting on top was a videotape. Curious, I slapped it into my office VCR and hit Play. The screen lit up, and there was Scarpa and two bodyguards, walking through the streets of Brooklyn, filmed covertly by undercover detectives. Scarpa appeared to be about five feet ten inches, with massive arms, a powerful chest, and a rich thatch of black hair that fell down in front over his mirrored sunglasses. He was wearing classic mafia garb: tight white double-knit slacks, white leather loafers with a golden fob, and a tight rose-colored sports shirt unbuttoned low enough to expose several gold chains lying across his hairy chest. Later I learned that Scarpa was bald; the "hair" I had seen was a cheap synthetic rug. Watching the tape, I could sense Scarpa's charisma. He didn't walk; he strutted, exuding an aura of confidence, power, and charm, like a well-fed alley cat. When he made a joke, he laughed deeply, from the belly, bent over at the waist, and the other men caught on the tape laughed with him.

---

*"Prosecution memo," laying out the facts of the case, relevant legal issues, and potential defenses. In the EDNY, all prosecutors submitted a prosecution memo to their supervisors in every case prior to indictment, in order to explain why a criminal charge was justified. This is clearly a good practice, but it is not followed in every district.

GREGORY SCARPA, JR., grew up in the mob. His father, Gregory Scarpa, Sr., was a notorious Colombo Family hitman. In mafia families, children who show an aptitude for what mobsters call the Life start in the business early. By age seventeen Scarpa was working for his father, and in time the two became partners. Together they built one of the most feared organized crime outfits in New York.

Mafia families, like secret espionage organizations, are divided into separate, independent cells, each with its own leadership. This structure ensures that if the government penetrates one cell, with an informant or a wiretap, that penetration will not compromise the rest of the organization. The mafia calls its cells crews. These crews serve as the basic tactical unit of the mafia. A small mafia family might have fifteen separate crews working the street; a large one, as many as forty.

In some respects, the Scarpa organization was a typical mafia crew. It was composed of approximately thirty men, all of full or partial Italian heritage. About a dozen were wiseguys or made men, fully initiated mafiosi, entitled to greater respect and a larger share of the spoils. The rest were associates, young mobsters in training who were not yet experienced enough—or trusted enough—to become full members of the Colombo Family. During the twentieth century most New York City mafia crews were based at storefront "social clubs" with colorful names. John Gotti was headquartered at the Bergin Hunt and Fish Club, Neil Dellacroce at the Ravenite, "Wild Bill" Cutolo at the Friendly Bocce Social Club. The Scarpas ran their crew from the Wimpy Boys Social Club, the name a rare instance of mafia irony, on Thirteenth Avenue in Bensonhurst, an old Italian neighborhood deep in the heart of Brooklyn. The club's decor was nondescript: cheap carpet, cheap wood paneling, card tables, a bar. Scarpa Senior had an office in the back. The crew met there every day, Monday through Saturday, to plot and execute crimes.

At the heart of the mafia lies a paradox. On the one hand, the mafia scorns hard work. Ordinary people who get up each day and go to steady jobs are suckers, weaklings, chumps, losers. In reality, however, most successful organized crime members are incredibly dedicated to their profession, just like ambitious doctors or lawyers. The Scarpa Crew was in the business of crime, and it expected its employees to be sober, serious, and disciplined. Members of the crew were required to report to work at the Wimpy Boys Club every morning ready to rob, steal, and kill. If an associate failed to show up regularly, drank too much, ran his mouth, or refused to carry out orders, he would be executed. The crew was also highly entrepreneurial. Though some mafia units specialize in one sort of crime only—pornography, labor racketeering, drug trafficking, gambling, or stock fraud—the members of the Scarpa Crew pursued many different scams at once. The Scarpas constantly encouraged their men to seek out new ways to "make a score." No good idea went untried.

The Scarpa Crew's core business was loansharking. For most of the twentieth century, working people in New York City had trouble getting legitimate loans. Their neighborhoods had very few banks, and discriminatory lending practices were common. For this reason, a person in Brooklyn who needed a loan to start a small business, buy an engagement ring, or pay a gambling debt would go to the only people in the neighborhood who had excess cash, the mobsters. In Bensonhurst, a loanshark customer could drop by the Wimpy Boys Club and borrow anything from one hundred to fifty thousand dollars that same day in cash, without posting collateral. The catch was, they had to pay unbelievably high interest. If, for example, a borrower took a thousand dollars at "five points"—5 percent interest per week, a common rate for new customers—he would have to pay fifty dollars per week. After just one year he would have handed over twenty-six hundred dollars in interest payments without making the slightest dent in his balance. If the debtor missed a payment, the crew would threaten to beat him up. I once asked Scarpa Crew loanshark Mario Parlagreco what happened if a beating did not work—if a person still refused to pay. Mario was nonchalant. "Oh, they always paid."

The Scarpas began to lend money in the 1970s, and by the mid-1980s they were running what amounted to a small bank, with several million dollars "out on the street." In time they became what Mario called "the loanshark's loanshark," lending money to other mobsters eager to start their own lending businesses. Parlagreco, then a young associate in the crew, was responsible for keeping the books. He recorded each loan in a notebook, with the addresses of customers and repayment information. Once a week he would sit down with the Scarpas at the club and "straighten out"—review outstanding loans, discuss collection problems, and hand over the Scarpas' profits. Though a tiny number of loans defaulted, the loansharking business was very dependable, easy to run, and extraordinarily lucrative. By the mid-1980s the two Scarpas, father and son, were clearing more than seven thousand dollars per week from loansharking interest alone.

They also ran the numbers, an illegal street lottery. Every day twenty or thirty numbers runners fanned out over the streets of Brooklyn and Staten Island to meet with a thousand working-class customers. These customers would give the runner a small bet, usually between one and ten dollars, and a three-digit number they picked between 000 and 999. These numbers, recorded on small slips of paper, were delivered to Scarpa at the Wimpy Boys Club every day by 4:00 p.m. Then, at 5:00, the Aqueduct horse racing track announced the daily handle, the total amount of bets placed at the track that day. The last three digits of the handle became the winning number. The next morning lucky customers who had picked the right number received their payoff, five hundred dollars for every dollar bet. Since the actual odds on each bet were a thousand to one, the crew made a huge profit. There was no need for the crew to cheat. Numbers, like loansharking, was a license to print money: steady, dependable, and low risk.

The Scarpas supplemented their loansharking and numbers income with armed robbery: gas stations, jewelry stores, car dealerships, liquor and cigarette delivery trucks. They even robbed a bowling alley once. The most lucrative of these heists were the fur jobs. Scarpa and his crew would locate a vulnerable fur store in Manhattan, Brooklyn, or Queens, preferably one with a door at street level. Early in the afternoon, before rush hour, the crew would drive a truck up to the curb, open up the back, and put down a ramp, as if they were conducting a routine delivery. As soon as the truck was in position, several crew members would charge into the store in ski masks, guns drawn, and roll dozens of clothes racks of furs out the door and up the ramp of the truck. As soon as the furs were loaded, typically a matter of seconds, the truck would take off, gunned through the streets to a nearby garage rented just for the heist. For the next few weeks all of the crew's associates would be out on the street, trying to sell fur coats at a steep discount.

The crew also committed more than a dozen bank burglaries. Joe Brewster, one of the crew's biggest earners, put an employee at a burglar alarm company on the Scarpa's payroll. Every few months the "alarm guy" would disable the alarms at a vulnerable branch bank in Brooklyn or Queens. Once the alarms were off, the crew would burrow into the bank from a nearby vacant house or break through the bank's weakest armored door using high-powered pneumatic drills. The vaults were usually too secure to penetrate, but in the 1980s the safety-deposit boxes in outer borough branches were rarely well protected. As soon as they got inside the bank, the crew pried and blasted its way into the boxes, using crowbars and dynamite, and took everything it could carry: cash, gold, jewelry, stocks. Senior members of the crew might make fifty thousand dollars for one night's work; the Scarpas, more than a hundred thousand. Parlagreco once got thirty thousand dollars just for purchasing some drills. The next day he bought a Cadillac.

Greg Senior, Scarpa's father, had a source who sold him credit card slugs, real but blank plastic cards, without names and numbers. The crew also possessed the tools needed to emboss information on the cards, making them look authentic. Using this equipment, the Scarpas manufactured fake cards by the dozen, handed them out to their young associates, and sent them on one-day buying sprees. The crew then sold the merchandise they bought to fences and pocketed the cash. This scam would not work today, of course, when most merchants use dial-up equipment or magnetic card readers to verify a card's authenticity, but in the 1970s and 1980s it was highly profitable.

In the mid-1980s Scarpa and two young associates, Larry Mazza and Jimmy DelMasto, decided to start a sports betting ring. Scarpa provided the working capital and took a huge cut of the profits; Larry and Jimmy did all the work. Seven days a week they took bets in person and over the phones at several different locations in Brooklyn and Staten Island. "The office," as their business was known, did not take small bets. Most of their customers were professional gamblers, risking five or ten thousand dollars a game. If the gambler won, he doubled his money. If, however, he lost, the crew took his bet plus a 10 percent fee. For Larry and Jimmy, the goal was constant balance. If the office was taking bets on a game between the Knicks and the Nets, they would adjust the odds every hour, altering the incentives, so that an equal number of bets would be placed on both teams. That way, no matter who won the game, the office would make a guaranteed profit equal to 5 percent of the total amount of bets placed without any risk. In time they became incredibly sophisticated at risk management, hedging exposure with other sports gambling operations to minimize losses and protect their stake. By the late 1980s the office was taking in more than one million dollars in bets a week, producing some fifty thousand dollars in weekly profit—two and a half million dollars a year.

Scarpa also entered a more dangerous business, drug trafficking. In 1985 a Staten Island marijuana dealer named Peter Crupi asked Scarpa for protection, and Scarpa agreed. Once, however, Scarpa figured out how much money Crupi was making at his drug "spot," at Staten Island College, he decided to conduct a hostile takeover. Crupi was gunned down. That same day Crupi's customers were greeted by their new suppliers, the Scarpa Crew. Within a few short weeks Scarpa and his men had transformed Crupi's small-time operation into a major drive-through drug mart replete with baggers, lookouts, runners, dealers, and supervisors all communicating by walkie-talkie. By 1986 the Staten Island College spot was serving more than a thousand customers a night, generating revenue of seventy thousand dollars a week. Charmed by the easy money, the crew diversified their product line, selling kilos of heroin and cocaine at wholesale prices to dealers all over the city.

Finally, the Scarpas collected what they called the drug tax. If someone like Crupi started dealing pot or cocaine in Brooklyn or Staten Island, the crew paid him a visit and offered him a deal. If he paid a hefty weekly kickback to the Scarpa Crew, he could stay in business. If, however, he refused, he'd go to the hospital. The tax collection business was run quite blatantly. Cosmo Catanzano, a young crew member involved in these drug dealer shakedowns, even hung personalized license plates on his Cadillac: 1289 TAX.*

Scarpa's criminal businesses made him and his father multimillion-aires. Scarpa drove a Mercedes convertible and lived in a beautiful house facing Staten Island's Wolfe's Pond, complete with stables. He also bought up and operated several legitimate businesses, including a Staten Island nightclub called On the Rocks and a Bensonhurst convenience store, Mike's Candy. Every year Scarpa filed false federal income tax returns, declaring thirty thousand dollars in income from work as a professional gambler.

---

*The prefix "1289" may have had some significance, but I never discovered what it was.

IN THE MAFIA some crews are famed for making money. In the 1990s, for example, the Colombo Family's Cutolo Crew made millions on Wall Street selling worthless stock to naive investors in boiler room pump-and-dump schemes.* Other crews ran multimillion-dollar business enterprises, using union control and extortion to eliminate their legitimate competitors. In New York in the early 1980s, for example, mafia crews controlled the Fulton Fish Market, the trash hauling industry, the garment district, window installation and replacement, and concrete, the latter through a multifamily extortion ring known as the Concrete Club. The Gambino Family, perhaps the most aggressive businessmen in the mob, ran grocery stores, packaged meat and poultry, and manufactured furniture and restaurant equipment. These sophisticated schemes netted mafia leaders hundreds of millions of dollars.

By comparison, the Scarpa Crew's illegal business was small, generating some five to ten million dollars in revenue per year. That did not mean, however, that the Scarpas were not powerful in the underworld. Every organized crime family needs muscle to protect its turf and maintain discipline. In the Colombo Family the Scarpa Crew was the premier muscle crew, always ready to kill, quickly, quietly, and professionally.

Starting in the early 1980s, Scarpa, his father, and their crew went on a murder spree, killing more than twenty people. Scarpa was intimately involved in most of these murders. Sometimes he planned the hit but left the dirty work to his men. On other occasions he did the shooting himself. Scarpa killed for many different reasons: to enforce mafia rules, kill off competitors, eliminate potential witnesses, or obtain revenge.

July 1981. Bucky DiLeonardi, a member of the crew, did something really stupid: he complained loudly about Scarpa's faulty lookout work on a bungled bank burglary. A few weeks later, after the controversy had died down, Scarpa asked DiLeonardi to give him and crew member Carmine Sessa a ride to a meeting. Sessa sat in the passenger seat of Bucky's baby blue Cadillac, while Scarpa got in back. They drove to a quiet tree-lined street on Staten Island, where they parked. There Scarpa

---

*In a typical pump-and-dump scheme, crooked brokers working out of temporary offices hype worthless stock to gullible investors. When the price starts to rise, the brokers sell their own holdings in the artificially inflated stock and then disappear. The brokers can make millions. The victims lose their shirts.

pulled a .38 and shot Bucky twice in the back of the head. From the crime scene photos, you could tell that Bucky knew, at the instant just before his death, that he had been betrayed, for his body was turned to one side, away from Scarpa's gun, and his dead hands were clutching the door handle.

July 1982. Limousine driver Alfred Longobardi got drunk and threatened Scarpa at Scarpa's own nightclub. At first Scarpa planned to kill Longobardi personally. One day Scarpa and his crew set up outside Longobardi's home. Scarpa used a knife to give the limousine a flat tire. Scarpa intended to shoot Longobardi when he stooped down to fix the flat, but when Longobardi came out of the house, he brought his infant son with him. Under mafia rules, you are not supposed to kill someone in front of his family, so the killing had to be postponed. Longobardi's reprieve was short-lived. At Scarpa's request, his father and Joe Brewster hired Longobardi's limousine one night and blasted the driver while he sat behind the wheel. To send a message about "respect," the two killers shot away Longobardi's face. When the family went to collect the body, they had to identify the victim by his tattoos.

January 1983. Scarpa suspected that Sal "The Hammerhead" Cardaci was ratting to the police about a series of car thefts committed by crew member Billy Meli. Scarpa lured Cardaci to Mike's Candy Store, ordered his murder, and watched while Sessa blew Cardaci's head off with a .357. Cardaci's body was stripped, covered with lime, and buried down in the candy store basement.

September 1984. Mary Bari was the girlfriend of Colombo Family consigliere Alphonse "Big Allie Boy" Persico, the brother of boss Carmine Persico. Big Allie Boy went on the lam to avoid arrest, but Bari knew where he was hiding. Afraid she was talking to the police, the Persicos ordered her murder, and the Scarpas took the contract. One night Bari was invited to a rendezvous. She arrived dressed to kill: tight designer jeans, pearl-studded belt, black halter top. As soon as she arrived, Scarpa grabbed her, threw her to the floor, and held her down while his father shot her dead. They wrapped the body in canvas and dumped it on the Brooklyn streets.

October 1985. Big Anthony Frezza, "Tony Muscles," was a Colombo Family associate. One night Frezza murdered an associate of the Gambino organized crime family without permission from the Commission, the organization that keeps the peace among New York's five mafia families. The Gambino Family demanded revenge, and Scarpa agreed to do "the work." Scarpa invited Frezza to his home on Staten Island, welcomed him, and then shot him in the heart at his own kitchen table. He showed the body to the Gambinos, to prove the killing had been done. The crew then buried the body on Staten Island's New Dorp Beach.

September 1987. Joe Brewster, the crew's bank burglary expert, conducted a series of heists on his own without sharing the loot with Scarpa, a violation of Colombo Family rules. Scarpa and his driver picked up Brewster one afternoon to take him to a meeting. Scarpa was sitting in the front passenger seat, Brewster in the back. A few minutes into the ride Scarpa spun around without warning and shot Brewster four times at point-blank range, twice in the head, twice in the chest. The police found Brewster's bloody corpse abandoned in a stolen car, the engine still running. Later that night Scarpa took the hit team to dinner at Romano's, a restaurant just down the street from the Wimpy Boys Club. As the table filled with antipasti and heaping plates of pasta and sauce, Scarpa congratulated his team effusively. "Nice piece of work! Nice piece of work!" he said, hugging them and pounding them on the back.

DURING THE 1980S the police solved none of Scarpa's murders. The reason for this was simple: mafia professionalism. Most homicides in the United States are crimes of passion committed by rank amateurs, and these crimes are very easy to solve. People kill their victims in front of witnesses, use weapons that can be traced, or leave forensic evidence at the scene of the crime that links them to the murder: fingerprints on a doorknob, skin cells under the victim's fingernails, a hair or fiber from clothing lying near the body. In the Code of Silence Murders case, you may recall, we identified one killer using DNA collected from dried saliva found on the lip of a beer bottle abandoned at a murder scene. Scarpa, in contrast, murdered like a pro. Weapons were thrown into the sewer or Wolfe's Pond, fingerprints wiped clean, bloody clothes burned. Bodies were dumped far from the murder scene, often in stolen cars, or buried underground or at sea, never to be found. When Scarpa killed Frezza in his kitchen, he immediately brought in contractors to remodel the room from floor to ceiling, just to make sure that no microscopic

DNA samples from blood remained to be found. These tactics made detection well-nigh impossible.

———

WHILE THE SCARPA CREW WAS ROBBING, extorting, and killing, where was the government? Why was the Scarpa Crew, and more than eighty similar crews spread all across New York City, allowed to operate with impunity? Where was the law? Here are two preliminary answers. First, for most of the twentieth century the government did nothing to combat mafia crime. Second, far from being a target of government heat, the mafia was largely the government's creation.

Back in 1900 the American mafia did not exist. Many large cities were plagued by ethnic gangs—German, Irish, Italian, Jewish—but these groups had little impact on American society. Their weakness stemmed from one simple but profound factor, lack of a reliable source of income. Gangs like New York City's Daybreak Boys and the Dead Rabbits were involved in prostitution, robbery, burglary, extortion, and strikebreaking, but these crimes were not very lucrative. As a result, the gangs could not afford to bribe local politicians and police for protection, a fatal disability. After the turn of the century, urban progressives forced police to crack down on the gangs. By the end of World War I they were in clear decline. Unfortunately, that positive trend came to an abrupt halt in 1920. To understand why, you need a little background information.

For the past one hundred years, American public policy has been shaped primarily by a utilitarian calculus. Faced with a policy proposal, experts estimate whether in aggregate, the proposal increases social welfare or not. Unfortunately, this policy assessment process does not always provide reliable answers. Human society is so complex it is often impossible to predict precisely what will happen when you tinker with government policies. Sometimes a law will achieve its designed objectives but will also have unintended side effects, some of them harmful. This happens so often policy experts speak of a law of unintended consequences: for every predicted consequence of a change in economic or social policy, you will get several effects you did not foresee and do not want. That happened with the urban gangs.

On January 16, 1920, the Eighteenth Amendment to the U.S. Constitution went into effect, prohibiting the manufacture, sale, and transportation of alcohol. Prohibition took an enormous sector of the legitimate economy and criminalized it overnight. This may have reduced alcohol consumption, but it also had another, less savory consequence: it increased crime. Honest brewers, distillers, and tavern owners abandoned the liquor business, and criminals took control. Bootleggers smuggled alcohol into the country from the Caribbean and over the long, largely unmonitored Canada–United States border, and then they funneled their alcohol to the urban gangs, which sold and delivered booze and "protection" to thousands of illegal speakeasies. This system instantly gave the gangs access to hundreds of millions of dollars in illicit profits, which they used to bribe police, politicians, and the courts. Not surprisingly, the moribund urban gangs revived overnight.

Prohibition radically altered the structure of the American criminal underworld. With immense bootlegging profits at stake, violent competitive turf wars broke out in every major city. Throughout the urban North, the outcome was the same: ruthless and ambitious "families" composed of Sicilian and Italian immigrants pushed out, sometimes wiped out the older Irish and German gangs, who were not as violent or well organized. In Chicago, for example, the Capone organization fought for years against the Irish North Side Gang to control liquor distribution in the city. The battle ended in 1929, when Capone gunmen dressed like cops blasted six North Siders with machine guns in the notorious St. Valentine's Day Massacre, an event that led the Irish gang to capitulate. The same thing happened in New York. Over the course of the 1920s five well-organized Italian families eliminated all their competitors. These Five Families then consolidated their power through a cooperative cartel system, dividing up geographical turf and rackets among them in order to reduce friction and keep the peace. The Five Families entered into similar treaties with the Italian gangs controlling other major cities like Cleveland, Chicago, and Detroit, and the American mafia was born.

———

IN 1933 CONGRESS repealed Prohibition. Repeal gave local and federal law enforcement agencies a golden opportunity to attack and eliminate the newly emerging mafia. They let this chance pass. For fifty years, from 1930 to 1980, law enforcement took very little action to combat the mafia.* This lengthy reprieve gave the mob the breathing room it needed to revamp its business model, which shifted from almost exclusive reliance on bootlegging to a more diversified approach, with mafia families drawing income from a multiplicity of criminal schemes, not just from one potentially vulnerable source.

Letting the mafia dig in and diversify was, in retrospect, one of the biggest failures of American law enforcement in the twentieth century. It forces us to ask: Why did we make this blunder? The answer reveals a great deal about how we fight crime in America.

Under our federal system, state and local governments do the bulk of America's law enforcement work, handling more than 95 percent of the criminal cases in the country. Thus fighting the mafia was, in the first instance, the responsibility of police forces and district attorneys. Unfortunately, these local institutions had real trouble coming to grips with the mob. One problem was bribery; in New York City a huge number of cops and judges were on the take by the 1950s. But the real problem was resources. In the United States virtually every urban police force has less money than it needs to do its job. As a result, the police tend to allocate their manpower to two kinds of cases, those that are cheap and easy to investigate and those initiated by citizen victims who file criminal complaints. Complex mafia cases slip easily through this net. In most mafia crimes there are no real victims (like numbers or sports betting), dead victims (murders), or victims who are too scared to talk to the police (loansharking and extortion). Since no one is demanding that the police get involved in a case, they don't.

Mafia investigations are also prohibitively expensive. The mafia works largely in secret, covering its tracks and hiding its activities. Mafia

*There was one great exception, the Manhattan District Attorney's Office in the 1930s, under District Attorney Tom Dewey. Dewey possessed political ambitions, and he recognized that taking on and beating the mafia would be a huge public relations coup. In 1936 Dewey convicted Lucky Luciano, the top mobster in New York, for running a large-scale prostitution ring. In 1937 his investigation of a mafia murder forced top Luciano deputy Vito Genovese to flee to Italy. And in 1941 he gained convictions against a notorious mafia hit squad, dubbed Murder, Inc. by the press. Dewey's success proved that an aggressive prosecutor could put the mob on the run, but his progress was very short-lived. In the 1940s the mysterious deaths of several critical government witnesses and the outbreak of World War II took the heat off Genovese and other leading mobsters. Then, in 1943, Dewey was elected governor of New York, a political promotion that shifted his attention from the mafia to the presidency, an office he was fated never to win. Following the war, no one stepped up to fill Dewey's shoes, and the promising prewar antimafia effort fizzled.

killers like Scarpa never leave forensic evidence behind for investigators
to find, and if mafia members do get caught, they will do anything to
avoid conviction, including murdering government witnesses and bribing juries. As a result of these barriers, you cannot bring the mob to justice unless you are willing to devote a significant amount of time and
money to sophisticated, long-term, proactive investigations that may, in
the end, fail to reach any conclusive results. Throughout most of the
twentieth century no one in state and local law enforcement thought
this effort was worth the trouble. Instead, local cops and prosecutors
chose to focus on the low-hanging fruit, amateur street crime.

When local cops and prosecutors fail to address a criminal threat,
because of bribery, lack of resources, lack of expertise, or incompetence,
the federal government is supposed to step in and help. From 1930 to
1980 the IRS and the Immigration Service brought a small number of
useful mafia cases, as did the Bureau of Narcotics, the precursor to today's Drug Enforcement Administration. But the FBI, the largest federal
law enforcement agency, chose to leave the mafia alone. Responsibility
for this decision lies squarely with the notorious J. Edgar Hoover, the director of the FBI from 1924 to 1972. Initially Hoover refused to admit the
mob existed. Later, by the 1960s, when so much mafia evidence had piled
up that denial was impossible, he conceded the mafia existed but still refused to take any action. Though Congress and some attorneys general
occasionally prodded the FBI to attack, Hoover stubbornly insisted that
battling mobsters was a state and local responsibility.

Law enforcement experts still debate the motive for Hoover's inaction. Professor James Jacobs of New York University, the dean of organized crime scholars, has ably summarized the competing theories:

> Some believe that he was being blackmailed by mobsters who knew
> about his (supposed) homosexuality. Other scholars believe that
> Hoover did not regard organized crime as a national problem; did
> not believe that the FBI had jurisdiction to investigate local gang-
> sters; feared that FBI agents would be corrupted if they became in-
> volved in investigating the vice crimes that the mafia was engaged
> in (gambling, drugs, and so on); or perhaps, prior to the exposure
> of the organized crime conclave in Apalachin, New York, in 1957,
> he did not believe there was any connection or coordination

*among local organized crime families. Still other scholars empha-
size that Hoover did not want to divert resources away from investigating communists and political subversives. Although we will
probably never be able to choose definitely among these explanations, the facts are indisputable: until after Hoover's death in May
1972, the FBI did not devote resources to investigating organized
crime while assigning top priority to exposing and prosecuting
communists (broadly defined).*

My own assessment is slightly different. When Hoover took over the
FBI in 1924, it was a small, disreputable organization with virtually no
clout in Washington. Hoover changed that dramatically. He initiated
some significant reforms at the FBI, including better agent recruiting
and training and development of the first truly scientific forensics lab,
but his true talent was for public relations. During the Depression
Hoover crafted a new image for his G-men: tough, smart, all-American,
and impossible to beat. When the media picked up on Hoover's story,
agents like Eliot Ness became national heroes. In response, Congress
gave the popular Hoover ever larger appropriations to fuel his growing
law enforcement empire. Hoover could have used these resources to
tackle the mob, but he understood that if he did, the FBI's carefully
crafted image might collapse. When law enforcement pressured the
mafia, the mobsters always responded with bribery. Hoover knew that if
some of his agents succumbed to this temptation, it would tarnish the
FBI's squeaky-clean image. Hoover also recognized that if the FBI went
toe-to-toe with the mafia, it might easily lose, destroying the myth of
FBI invincibility. And so, to protect the FBI's reputation and power,
Hoover decided to keep it on the sidelines. While the mafia grew in
strength and power, Hoover focused the FBI's attention on unsophisticated, low-level thugs who were easy to catch, people like John Dillinger
and Pretty Boy Floyd. For fifty years the FBI did not win a single major
mafia case.

The FBI's biggest institutional problem is its reluctance to change
and adapt. When Hoover died in 1972, FBI Headquarters did not rethink
its mafia policy. Instead, it blindly continued down Hoover's path, leaving the mafia free to operate with impunity. The FBI's weakness received
national attention in 1978, when members of the Lucchese Family

walked off with $5.8 million in a single night, in the Lufthansa airfreight robbery at JFK Airport. Since the robbery interfered with international commerce, it clearly fell within the FBI's jurisdiction, but the Bureau lacked the mafia intelligence, the informants, and the expertise needed to solve the crime. No one was arrested for the heist for years.

In sum, neither federal authorities nor local law enforcement made a significant, sustained effort to tackle the mafia for more than fifty years. This neglect led, inevitably, to massive mafia growth. By 1980 there were major mafia crews operating all across New York City, running illegal loansharking, gambling, extortion, drug trafficking, and robbery schemes. Through their union and extortion power, the Five Families of New York controlled huge slices of New York's economic life. Business leaders casually spoke of a mob tax, the inevitable financial kickback required just to keep their companies operating. Not surprisingly, the leaders of the mafia became very rich. Joseph Bonanno, leader of the Bonanno Family, acquired a mansion on Long Island, a vacation home in Arizona, and a 280-acre estate near Middletown, New York. Thomas Gambino amassed a fortune of at least seventy million dollars. Worst of all, bodies were dropping left and right.

Enforcement decisions made in Washington have huge ramifications on the street. When I watched my video surveillance tape of the Scarpa Crew in Brooklyn, I quickly realized that the crew thought it was invulnerable. It made no effort to hide the fact that the Wimpy Boys Club was its criminal headquarters. Since the weather was nice on the day the tape was made, fifteen mafiosi had pulled their chairs onto the sidewalk in front of the club, and I could see the crew members basking in the sunshine, collecting loansharking payments and numbers from their runners right out in the open. Carmine Sessa showed up carrying a paper bag full of cash. Dozens of gaudy Cadillacs and Mercedes sedans were double-parked on Thirteenth Avenue. When a police cruiser drove by, the mobsters all waved—and the cops waved back.

IN THE EARLY 1980S the federal government reversed course and decided to take on the mob. The primary catalyst was the election of President Ronald Reagan in 1981. Reagan and his team believed that

Washington was a corrupt and inefficient cesspool. Though an oversimplification, this view came with one clear benefit, a willingness to reexamine existing government policies and to question the status quo. The Reagan Justice Department took one look at the government's mafia policy and decided enough was enough. Virtually overnight, the new administration declared war on the mafia, with Reagan publicly promising, in a televised speech in 1982, that the government would go on the offensive and root out mafia crime.

At the same time the DOJ was reviewing its mafia policy, a group of senior FBI agents in New York, many of them military veterans in search of a meaningful mission in life, independently decided to make the mafia their top priority. These agents, now FBI legends—men like Jim Kallstrom, Jim Kossler, and Bruce Mouw—proposed the creation of new FBI squads devoted exclusively to organized crime work and a dramatic expansion of bugging and electronic surveillance. In the FBI, new ideas that bubble up from the bottom are often quashed by cautious bureaucrats at FBI Headquarters. In this case, however, the agents got support from their bosses, perhaps because they could sense that the Reagan administration wanted real progress. By 1982 the FBI assault on the Five Families was in full swing, with, by one estimate, some 350 agents assigned to organized crime investigations.

The FBI received essential support from the new United States Attorney for the Southern District of New York, a former AUSA in his late thirties named Rudy Giuliani. An Italian American from Brooklyn, Giuliani was personally dedicated to bringing the mafia to justice. He assigned many of his top prosecutors to work on organized crime; they included Louis Freeh, later the director of the FBI, and Michael Chertoff, President George W. Bush's Secretary of Homeland Security. Together with the FBI, these AUSAs adopted an audacious goal: to prosecute the Commission, the board of mafia bosses who collectively governed the New York underworld. A daring FBI agent posing as a television repairman installed a number of bugs in the house of Paul Castellano, the boss of the Gambino Family. These bugs revealed the existence of an illegal billion-dollar multifamily cartel that controlled construction in Manhattan. Armed with these devastating audiotapes, the prosecutors indicted four of New York's five mafia bosses in 1984. When the dust cleared, three of the bosses had been sent to prison for life. The fourth, Castellano himself, never made it to trial, for he was gunned down in the streets of Manhattan by one of his own ambitious capos, John Gotti of Queens, who wanted to run the Gambino Family himself.

The success of Giuliani's Commission case permanently changed the relationship between the federal government and the mafia. The case demonstrated that after decades of law enforcement neglect, the mafia had become sloppy and vulnerable. By the mid-1980s both the SDNY and the EDNY had opened up dozens of major new mafia investigations.

THE FBI should have targeted the Scarpa Crew early in its assault on the mafia, for it was one of the most powerful and dangerous crews in New York. The Bureau, however, decided to ignore the Scarpa Crew, for reasons that were at the time totally unclear to outsiders. Fortunately, the Drug Enforcement Administration filled the vacuum. When the DEA saw increased funding flowing to the FBI for mafia cases, it decided to horn in on the act. In New York, the DEA and New York law enforcement officials created a Drug Enforcement Task Force to investigate mafia drug trafficking. In 1985 these agents stumbled onto Scarpa's marijuana mart at Staten Island College. The investigation and trial, later dubbed *Scarpa I*, was a bumpy ride. Before the DEA could make any arrests, Scarpa disappeared, almost as if he had been tipped off. He was eventually tracked down and forced to trial, but he and his underlings walked on the DEA's two murder charges; without an informant inside the crew, the government simply could not produce sufficient firsthand evidence to win. Scarpa and his men were convicted, however, of racketeering and drug dealing. Scarpa got a stiff sentence, and the young lead prosecutor, Valerie Caproni, began her rise in the EDNY.

Scarpa I was a clear but limited victory. Prison did not put Scarpa out of commission. He secretly ordered a homicide from the pen, and he and his family continued to get his regular financial cut from the loansharking, numbers, and gambling businesses. His father, who was not arrested, immediately began to rebuild the crew, recruiting a new batch of tough young associates to replace those who had been busted. From jail Scarpa planned for the future. Early in his sentence he sent a message to his team: "Stay tough. We will all be together again soon."

MAFIA FAMILIES have one profound organizational weakness: no clear rules for succession. In the early 1990s the Colombo Family was torn apart by a violent struggle to see who would replace boss Carmine "The Snake" Persico, who had been imprisoned for life in the Commission case. Two-thirds of the family backed the powerful Long Island capo Vic Orena (who later bribed Anthony Martinez in the Badfellas mafia prison bribery scheme). The remainder, including the Scarpa Crew, backed Alphonse "Allie Boy" Persico, Carmine's son.* From 1991 to 1993 the two sides shot it out in what became known as the Colombo Family War, the last great mob war in history. By the time it was over, ten men had been shot dead.

The Colombo Family War proved a huge boon to the FBI. Armed with recordings from strategically placed bugs and secret information from a top informant hidden inside the family itself, the FBI began to arrest Colombo Family hit teams and their superiors, like top mobster Vic Orena. Then, in 1992, Colombo mobster "Joey Brains" Ambrosino, who faced a massive prison term, flipped. His decision had a domino effect. The next year Carmine Sessa, the respected consigliere of the family and an alumnus of the Scarpa Crew, decided to enter the Witness Security Program as well. Sessa was a huge catch, one of the highest-ranking mafia members ever to cooperate. He knew where all of the Scarpa Crew's bodies were buried. When he flipped, four other crew members realized the jig was up. Over the next two years they all cooperated as well. Together these five witnesses gave the government, for the very first time, an accurate picture of the Scarpas' violent killing spree in the 1980s and 1990s.

Armed with these new witnesses, the government decided to take a second stab at bringing the Scarpa Crew to bay. Scarpa's father, Greg Scarpa, Sr., was the first to go. In 1992, Senior was indicted for several homicides committed during the war. Suffering from AIDS, which he had acquired from a tainted blood transfusion, Scarpa Senior quietly pleaded guilty and died in prison in 1994. Then, in June 1995, AUSA Ellen Corcella indicted Scarpa and twelve other members of the crew for com-

---

*Often called Little Allie Boy, to distinguish him from his uncle, Big Allie Boy Persico, who had ordered the murder of his girlfriend Mary Bari in 1984.

mitting a dozen murders. The case, *United States v. Gregory Scarpa Jr.*, or *Scarpa II*, landed in my lap three years later.

———

IN A TYPICAL MURDER CASE, the government makes a very tough plea offer, one that will keep the defendant in prison for the rest of his life. In *Scarpa II*, in contrast, Ellen Corcella offered the Scarpa Crew deals ranging from seventeen to twenty years. These were really light sentences, given the number of murders involved. Ultimately, every single defendant accepted the government offer except one, Gregory Scarpa, Jr., himself.

Why, one might ask, would Corcella, a skilled and experienced mob prosecutor, offer sweetheart deals to such hardened killers? The answer was simple: she thought she might lose the trial. Her fear was not irrational, for the crew possessed what was widely viewed as an unbeatable "atom bomb defense." It even had a name, the Scarpa Defense, in honor of Scarpa's dead father, Gregory Scarpa, Sr. Though the defense was complicated, it rested on one simple and incontrovertible fact: during the Scarpa Crew's long reign of terror, Scarpa Senior had been secretly on the government payroll.

When the FBI decided to attack the mob in the early 1980s, it was desperately short of one critical asset, inside intelligence. To shore up this problem, agents were encouraged to contact and try to "sign up" mafia members as informants. Special Agent Lindley "Lin" DeVecchio, the supervisor of the Colombo Squad, was one of the most successful. In 1980 he managed to recruit Gregory Scarpa, Sr., who had been an FBI informant long before, in the 1960s, but inactive ever since. Senior agreed to provide detailed information about the Colombo Family's organization and ongoing crimes. DeVecchio in return provided Scarpa Senior with two very attractive gifts, legal protection and cash. DeVecchio never authorized Senior to commit crimes, but he knew Senior was engaged in many different criminal schemes. DeVecchio agreed to ignore this as long as Senior produced the goods.

At first the Scarpa Senior–DeVecchio agreement worked well for both men. When Senior got arrested on a credit card fraud case, DeVecchio intervened to ensure that he stayed out of jail. In return, DeVecchio got good scoop. In a profession in which your reputation is based, at least in part, on your ability to flip key informants, DeVecchio became a major player.

Unfortunately, Scarpa Senior quickly started to take advantage of the relationship. Under his informant agreement, Senior was not supposed to commit any violent crimes. Instead of honoring this commitment, he and his son went on a murder spree behind DeVecchio's back. Had the FBI investigated the Scarpa Crew closely, it might have discovered these killings. Unfortunately, DeVecchio's Colombo Squad did not do so. Scarpa Senior was viewed as a highly valuable informant. If the FBI put his men under surveillance, Scarpa Senior might stop providing information. DeVecchio did not want to kill the goose that laid the golden eggs. For this reason, the Colombo Squad left the Scarpa Crew alone.

Lin DeVecchio's motives, at least initially, were sound. In the 1980s mafia informants were hard to come by, so having Senior on the payroll was a huge break. Over time, however, DeVecchio seems to have lost his moral bearings. In all agent-informant relationships, the government is supposed to ensure that information flows in only one direction, from the informant to the "controlling agent." According to several witnesses from the mafia and the FBI, DeVecchio ignored this basic rule. In the mid-1980s, according to these witnesses, he began to disclose confidential law enforcement information to Gregory Scarpa, Sr. He told Senior, for example, that the Wimpy Boys Club had been bugged, foiling a New York State investigation in the process. He also gave Senior advance warning about *Scarpa I*, Valerie Caproni's DEA marijuana case, allowing his son to escape arrest temporarily. Senior may even have used DeVecchio to locate deadbeat loanshark customers. According to one FBI agent, Senior provided the names, and DeVecchio told him where to look. The FBI should have put a stop to this, but at the time no one understood what was happening. Normally, an informant is controlled by two FBI agents, who ensure together that all the relevant rules are followed. DeVecchio, however, told the FBI that Senior would deal only with him, so there was no way for a second agent to monitor DeVecchio's behavior.

To this day it is not exactly clear to me what happened to DeVecchio.

He may have been so excited to have a TE informant on his payroll* that keeping Senior happy became more important to him than preventing violations of the law. I suspect, however, that something more complex was afoot. In law enforcement, a small but appreciable number of men run the risk of "moral capture."† They spend so much time living in the underworld, with crooks and crooked informants, they come to adopt its perspective. Almost imperceptibly at first, they begin to envy their targets' apparent moral independence, the criminal's freedom to do whatever he wants, free of conventional societal constraints: to take risks, break taboos, kill, and rob anyone they choose. For someone stuck in a government bureaucracy, hemmed in by rules, crime can start to look attractive. That happened to the prison manager Anthony Martinez in the Badfellas case. It is possible it happened to DeVecchio as well. But only he knows for sure, and he is not talking.

The Scarpa-DeVecchio mess grew worse during the Colombo Family War. In early 1992 the FBI received information that Senior was involved in violence. These reports were accurate. By this time Scarpa had already committed two murders in the Colombo Family War, as well as some seven or eight earlier killings. In March a senior FBI supervisor stepped in, terminating Scarpa Senior's informant status. DeVecchio, however, insisted these reports were wrong, and he used his bureaucratic clout to have Senior reinstated. This move was shocking but not surprising. By the spring of 1992 DeVecchio appeared to have lost all perspective.

Throughout the Colombo Family War, FBI Special Agent Chris Favo provided DeVecchio with daily morning briefings about events on the street the night before. One morning Favo reported that Larry Lampesi, a member of the Orena faction, had been gunned down by Scarpa Senior's Persico group. According to Favo, DeVecchio became extremely excited at the news. Slapping his desk with his hand, DeVecchio crowed,

---

*When the FBI signs up a rare top echelon, or TE, informant, only a small number of persons with the "need to know" are informed of that fact. DeVecchio told one EDNY mafia prosecutor that he had recruited Scarpa Senior, but no one else at my office knew. When that prosecutor left government service, he failed to pass on this critical information to his replacement. As a result, the government was working at cross-purposes during the 1980s. Valerie Caproni and other EDNY prosecutors were trying to investigate the Scarpa Crew, with the help of the DEA, the New York Police Department, and the New York State Police. Meanwhile, the Colombo Squad was trying to give the Scarpas cover, to protect Senior's work as an informant.

†This problem appears to affect men more than women. I am not sure why this is true, but it may be that the outlaw life simply holds more attraction for men than for women.

"We're going to win this thing!" According to Favo, it was clear from De-Vecchio's reaction that he had forgotten he worked for the FBI. His position was now "blurred," as one federal judge later reported, for he was clearly, in Favo's words, a "cheerleader" for the Persico faction.

By the late summer of 1992 the government could no longer ignore the obvious truth: its own informant was committing serial murder. Several prosecutors and agents wanted to arrest Senior. They worried, however, that DeVecchio might leak word to Scarpa of any impending arrest. So prosecutors arranged for the bust to be handled by the NYPD, not the FBI. Even then DeVecchio intervened. Scarpa Senior should have been locked up until his trial, for he was charged with murder. DeVecchio, however, helped arrange for him to be put out on bail. Back on the street, Scarpa committed one more shooting, the last straw. In December 1992 he was arrested a second time and put behind bars for good.

The FBI and the Justice Department opened up a major internal investigation into DeVecchio's conduct.* Unfortunately, it was too late; the damage had been done. When, in 1994, the government publicly disclosed the truth about Scarpa Senior and DeVecchio, the story hit Brooklyn like a bomb.

THE SCARPA SENIOR–DEVECCHIO SCANDAL derailed the government's assault on the Colombo Family. In 1993, the year before the facts were revealed, the EDNY obtained eighteen Colombo convictions. We were on track to dismantle the entire family. When, however, the truth about Senior and his ties to the FBI became known, defense attorneys concocted what became known as the Scarpa Defense. Within a year it had radically altered the legal playing field.

The Colombo Family first employed the Scarpa Defense in the summer of 1994, when Allie Boy Persico went on trial. The government claimed that Persico, the son of incarcerated boss Carmine Persico, had encouraged and financed the violence within the Colombo Family in an effort to succeed his father as boss. Persico in turn raised the Scarpa De-

---

*Main Justice opened an investigation into DeVecchio's case in 1994. Ultimately, the Public Integrity Section concluded that DeVecchio should not be prosecuted, and he was allowed to retire. More recently, the Brooklyn district attorney indicted DeVecchio for aiding and abetting several Scarpa Senior homicides. This case was a fiasco, based on totally flimsy evidence, and was ultimately dismissed.

fense. According to Persico, the so-called Colombo Family War was really the Scarpa-DeVecchio War, a wave of violence instigated by Scarpa Senior and his crooked FBI boss in order to kill everyone who suspected Senior was an informant. This claim was, in the words of one federal judge, "bizarre, but not entirely implausible." After all, Senior had been an informant, Senior was one of the deadliest shooters in the war, and DeVecchio had apparently provided him with confidential law enforcement information. Ultimately, however, the power of the defense had little to do with plausibility. Persico and his lawyers were shooting instead for nullification. They hoped that if the jurors learned that a de facto government employee had been out on a killing spree, they would refuse to convict out of anger, frustration, and disgust. This instinct proved right on target. In the *Persico* case the jury specifically found, on its special verdict form,* that Allie Persico was a murderer. Nevertheless, it acquitted him on all charges, an unprecedented result. Persico walked out of court a free man.

The government's loss in *Persico* was only the beginning. In December 1994 Colombo Family captain "Wild Bill" Cutolo and six hitmen from his Orena faction crew went on trial before Judge Eugene Nickerson. The government's case was strong. Wild Bill's crew had been arrested while driving around Brooklyn in armed caravans, looking to kill its opponents. In the end, however, this evidence did not matter, for Cutolo raised the Scarpa Defense. The defendants conceded that they had been armed but claimed they were acting in self-defense, trying to protect themselves from the murderous Scarpa Senior and his bloodthirsty federal handler, who were trying to murder everyone who suspected Senior was a rat. When the smoke cleared, every single defendant was acquitted. A few months later, the capo Victor Orena, Jr., Vic Orena's son, went on trial with his crew, and they were acquitted as well. The EDNY's Colombo Family cases, once so promising, had become a complete fiasco. As long as the defendants put the Scarpa Defense into play, an acquittal was all but guaranteed.

The Scarpa Defense changed the balance of power in plea negotiations. Previously, Colombo defendants had had to beg for deals. Now defense attorneys told prosecutors that unless the government's offer

---

*In racketeering cases, the court typically uses a special verdict form, which requires the jury to make specific findings of fact as well as return a verdict.

was really sweet, they would be happy to go to trial and raise the Scarpa issue. To the gun-shy AUSAs who tried and lost the *Persico*, *Cutolo*, and *Orena*, *Jr.*, cases, this was a very powerful threat.

In *Scarpa II*, Corcella hoped that Scarpa would plead out, but Scarpa refused all offers, even one for seventeen years. Scarpa was a gambler. He knew how well the Scarpa Defense worked, and he believed he could use it even more effectively than Persico or Cutolo. He was the informant's son, so he could plausibly claim inside information about Lin DeVecchio's misdeeds. He was also, as I learned to my disgust when I joined the Scarpa trial team in 1998, an FBI informant himself.

SCARPA SHOULD HAVE GONE TO TRIAL in 1996, before I even became a federal prosecutor, but the case was delayed for two years, while he filed and lost a double jeopardy appeal. In criminal cases, trial delays are a wild card; lots of things can happen in the interim, from death of a key witness to the discovery of new evidence. In *Scarpa II*, one bizarre thing happened after another.

In 1995, Scarpa was imprisoned with Vic Amuso, the boss of the Lucchese Family. One day Amuso called Scarpa Senior a rat. When Scarpa tried to defend his father, Amuso replied, "The apple doesn't fall far from the tree." His honor insulted, Scarpa attacked. He banged Amuso's head repeatedly against a metal bed frame, then brained him with a heavy porcelain bowl. Amuso, beaten almost senseless, was carted off to the prison hospital.

Assaults are pretty common in prison, but Scarpa's crime had unusual real-world consequences, for his victim was a mafia boss. Amuso put out a contract on Scarpa's life, promising generous compensation to any inmate who put Scarpa into a grave. Word of the contract soon leaked to the FBI and the Federal Bureau of Prisons.

When an inmate's life is in danger, the Bureau of Prisons moves him into protective custody. For Scarpa, that meant Floor Nine South of Manhattan's Metropolitan Correctional Center, the MCC. Nine South is one of the federal government's most secure prison units. It houses two types of inmate. A small number, like Scarpa, are in mortal danger from their peers. The remainder, also like Scarpa, are homicidal sociopaths. When Scarpa was moved to Nine South in 1995, he wound up in a cell next to just such a man. Ramzi Yousef was one of the most dangerous terrorists in the world. In February 1993 he masterminded the bomb attack on the World Trade Center that killed six Americans, wounded a thousand others, mostly from smoke inhalation, and caused more than five hundred million dollars in damage. Two years later he bombed a Philippines airliner, part of a practice run for larger-scale attacks on U.S. aircraft. In 1995, after an international manhunt, he was arrested in the Philippines. When Scarpa was moved to the MCC, Yousef was already there, awaiting trial on terrorism charges.

A few weeks after Scarpa got to Nine South, he sent word through his attorney that he wanted to meet with the FBI. At this meeting Scarpa shared electrifying news. According to Scarpa, Yousef admired the mafia, which he viewed as being at war with the United States. This admiration created a bond of trust between the two men, which led to frequent discussions about their criminal careers. Scarpa now proposed to exploit that friendship. Yousef, Scarpa claimed, had begun to describe his ideas for future terrorist attacks. Scarpa offered to cooperate against Yousef by providing the FBI with detailed information about Yousef's plans.

Under normal circumstances, the government would have refused to allow Scarpa to cooperate. The problem was not that he had killed a dozen people; the government recruits murderers as witnesses all the time, as long as they have testimony to give against even more culpable criminals. The real barrier was trust. After stalking Scarpa for years, EDNY prosecutors felt they knew him very well, and everyone thought he was dishonest and treacherous. The fact that his father took our money and killed behind our backs made matters worse. As Valerie Caproni later told me, "it would have been a cold day in hell before I would have signed him up." Terrorism, however, is a special case. When someone comes forward with intelligence about potential terror strikes, the federal government always listens. Yousef was an extraordinarily dangerous man, with ties to terror cells all over the world. If there was even a small chance that Scarpa's information was accurate, the government had to take it seriously. The EDNY passed Scarpa's proposal to AUSA Pat Fitzgerald of the Southern District, then involved in a major investigation of ongoing radical Islamic terror.* Fitzgerald wanted

---

*The same Fitzgerald who later earned nationwide acclaim for his prosecution of vice presidential aide I. Lewis "Scooter" Libby for perjury and obstruction of justice.

Scarpa's information, and the EDNY agreed. The FBI gave Scarpa a miniature spy camera and told him to get to work.

For the next several months Scarpa regaled the FBI with tantalizing intelligence. Yousef, Scarpa claimed, was planning to blow up a federal judge, murder several prosecutors, bomb the upcoming Atlanta Olympics, and bust Scarpa out of jail. To corroborate his stories, Scarpa provided the FBI with photographs of "kites," informal prison letters from one inmate to another, in Yousef's handwriting, apparently describing these plots. Scarpa even claimed to be able to intercept Yousef's messages to terror cells on the street. Unfortunately, it turned out that Vic Amuso was right: like father, like son. When FBI agents and terrorism prosecutors from the Southern District of New York tried to follow up on Scarpa's leads, they quickly determined that Scarpa's cooperation was a ruse, the product of collusion between Scarpa and Yousef. Yousef apparently agreed to provide Scarpa with false information about upcoming attacks in order to waste government resources and throw terror investigators off the track. Scarpa in turn received a chance to bargain with the government, exchanging the fake terror intelligence for a shot at a lighter sentence.

The FBI terminated Scarpa's cooperation, but not before serious damage had been done to the EDNY's case. After Scarpa's scam with Yousef, the Scarpa Defense looked even more powerful than before, from a nullification perspective. Scarpa would now be able to tell the jury that he too worked for the FBI, just like his father. Corcella doubled her efforts to get Scarpa to plead, but Scarpa hung tough. He understood that his fake stint as a terrorism spy had strengthened his position.

THE NEXT UNUSUAL DEVELOPMENT in the *Scarpa* case was caused by the prosecutors. In early 1998, on the eve of trial, the FBI learned that Scarpa was threatening several important government witnesses. In a typical federal case, the government would bring this information to the attention of the judge, who would warn the defendant not to obstruct justice. Usually, this is enough to bring any witness tampering to an end. In the *Scarpa* case, the government took a different route. By 1998 Scarpa had killed more than a dozen people, escaped conviction in a prior murder case, gone on the lam, lied to the FBI about terrorism, and violently assaulted another inmate. This conduct made him, in the eyes of the EDNY brass, public enemy number one, our highest prosecution target. Instead of simply disclosing the tampering to Judge Raggi, Ellen Corcella and her trial partner, AUSA Sung-Hee Suh, did something extraordinary: they stuck a bug, an electronic listening device, in Scarpa's Nine South prison cell, in the hope of gaining evidence of witness tampering from Scarpa's own mouth.

For thirty days the FBI monitored Scarpa's conversations with other inmates. The result was pretty comical. Scarpa was a very savvy guy, and he could sense that someone might be bugging his cell, so he was generally very guarded in his statements. Much of the time he ranted about Valerie Caproni, his former prosecutor, now the chief of the EDNY Criminal Division, who he thought (correctly) was out to get him (and every other murderer she could identify). Every once in a while he would shout out things like "If anyone is listening, the next few statements are covered by attorney-client privilege!" In the end the bug did not reveal a single conversation about witness tampering.

The Scarpa prison bug was perfectly legal, but it was controversial nevertheless. Prison bugs are used very infrequently, and they are almost never used right before trial, when a defendant is likely to be talking to other inmates about his upcoming ordeal. When the government disclosed the existence of the bug, Scarpa's defense attorney, Larry Silverman, reacted violently. At an emergency status conference before Judge Raggi, Silverman claimed that the bug was a desperate attempt by the government to discover Scarpa's secret trial strategy. Silverman moved to dismiss the entire case for outrageous government misconduct. He also asked for an adjournment of the trial date, so that he could listen to the tapes and move, if he wished, to suppress the bug evidence. Larry's motion to dismiss the indictment was frivolous, but he certainly had the right to challenge the bug. Regretfully, Judge Raggi delayed the case once again, to the fall of 1998. This second delay changed my career.

By this point it seemed clear that Scarpa was not going to plead, and that a trial was inevitable. Hoping to gain an important advantage, Ellen Corcella filed a pretrial motion seeking to preclude him from using the Scarpa Defense. That motion triggered a major courtroom drama. Judge Raggi is brilliant, but she is also quite stern; you have to watch what you say in her courtroom. If you fail to show respect, you are asking for trouble. During argument on the motion, Corcella stepped over that line. Corcella had already seen dozens of dangerous mobsters get acquitted using the Scarpa Defense. For her, the issue was very serious, both personally—she did not want to lose another big trial—and as a matter of public safety. When it looked as if her motion might be denied, she started to lecture Judge Raggi in a hectoring tone. Shocked, the judge lashed out in response, demanding that Corcella show proper deference to the bench. That should have ended the dispute, but Corcella did not back down, and the argument escalated. A friend who was present told me later that both Judge Raggi and Corcella were yelling at each other, something that never happens in federal court. It was a very ugly moment.

After the court appearance, Valerie Caproni recognized that Ellen could no longer serve as lead prosecutor, for her relations with Judge Raggi were permanently damaged, and that might jeopardize our chances to win. Caproni did not want to try the case herself. Later she told me, "I had already tried Greg Scarpa once. I had moved on." There was, however, no other senior mafia prosecutor quite like Valerie, a proven winner in big cases in the courtroom. Zach Carter, the U.S. Attorney, asked Valerie to replace Corcella as lead, and reluctantly she agreed. Corcella in turn resigned from the office, taking a job as a senior prosecutor in another jurisdiction.*

Corcella's decision to leave the EDNY had huge implications for me. Normally, the EDNY would staff a big trial like Scarpa with two senior AUSAs. Valerie was worried, however, that two prosecutors were inadequate, for her supervisory responsibilities as the chief of the Criminal Division made it impossible for her to give Scarpa her undivided attention. For that reason, she and Sung-Hee Suh decided to add a third prosecutor to the case. Though they discussed several options, I was their first choice. The Badfellas case proved I could handle a complex, hard-fought trial, and my reputation was already strong, "the best of the new Assistants," Sung-Hee later told me. A few days after Ellen resigned, Corngold called me into his office and told me that Valerie wanted me. Ellen's fight with Judge Raggi had changed my career.

---

*Ellen did not resign out of pique. She had recently adopted a baby girl, and she wanted a job offering more family time, something in short supply for an EDNY mafia prosecutor. She had been planning to leave after the Scarpa trial. Now she was able to accelerate her plans. I should note for the record that she was and is a fantastic prosecutor.

CHAPTER SEVEN

Hitmen

When I joined Valerie and Sung-Hee on the Scarpa trial team in late spring of 1998, I expected to play a very limited role: draft legal papers, examine three or four uncontroversial witnesses, perhaps do the opening statement. My work on the case began that way. When we had our first status conference, which lasted for more than an hour, I did not say a single word. My height made the situation even more comical. At six feet one inch, I am a foot taller than both Valerie and Sung-Hee. Every time they put their heads together to discuss a legal point, I had to bend over almost in half, like a jackknife, in order to hear what they were saying. Even then I had nothing to add to their discussions. I felt completely useless, hovering way above them, not really part of the case. After that status conference, a fellow prosecutor walked up to me and mockingly remarked, "Nice job." I blushed.

A few weeks later all that changed. One morning Valerie announced that she was resigning from the EDNY to take a top job at the Securities and Exchange Commission, America's Wall Street cop. This was a good career move for Valerie, but it left Sung-Hee holding the bag, with only a General Crimes rookie for help. I did not envy her.

Right after Valerie made her announcement, Sung-Hee asked me to come to her office to discuss the staffing of the case. We had two options: we could try the case on our own, or we could add another experienced prosecutor to take Valerie's place. I assumed that Sung-Hee would want to add another AUSA, and so, as I walked over to her office, I didn't give the question too much thought.

Sung-Hee Suh was one of the best prosecutors in the EDNY, a brainy, chain-smoking workaholic with a number of important organized crime cases under her belt. She exuded total confidence. This aura was reinforced when she was sitting in her own office, the walls covered with law enforcement awards, the bookshelves crowded with thick black binders, the transcripts of her previous trials. As soon as I arrived, Sung-Hee got down to business. "Well," she asked, "do you think we should add another AUSA to the case?"

To be honest, I was stunned by Sung-Hee's question. Since I was a very junior AUSA, I expected her to tell me what she had decided, not to ask me for advice. With only seconds to respond, I had no time to think. I simply blurted out, "I think we should try it together, just the two of us."

Sung-Hee just smiled. "Great," she said simply, "that's what I think too. But you are going to have a lot of work on your hands."

Years later Sung-Hee told me that in truth she had serious doubts about trying the case alone with me. The Scarpa trial was her first opportunity to be lead prosecutor on a major case, and she was worried that I did not have enough experience. If, however, we added a third prosecutor, she believed it might change the atmospherics in the courtroom. At this point in the case Scarpa was represented by a single attorney. If we, in contrast, had three lawyers at our table, it might look to the jury as if we were ganging up on an underdog, something Sung-Hee wanted to avoid.

WHEN I TELL PEOPLE I was a mafia prosecutor, the first question they always ask is: "Did you ever fear for your life?" As an AUSA I always gave a stock answer: "Most criminal groups know that killing a federal prosecutor is not in their best interest. If they killed a prosecutor, three more would take her place, and DOJ would really turn up the heat. If they want to kill someone, they take out a witness." This is true, but only to a degree. Sometimes one persistent AUSA will be responsible for convicting an entire gang or mafia family, bringing dozens of cases year after year until the whole group is brought to its knees. In these rare cases some crooks decide to strike back.

Cathy Palmer was one of the most dogged investigators in the EDNY, personally responsible for dismantling a host of Asian tongs and heroin smuggling rings. Finally, her targets got fed up. One day she received an odd-looking package in her office. Suspicious, Palmer asked a detective to open the parcel. The detective did so with extreme care and found inside a sawed-off .22-caliber rifle, triggered to fire when the package was opened. This was not an isolated example. My friend Greg Andres personally convicted dozens of members of the Bonanno Family, and they in turn put a contract on his head. For months Greg lived with an armed guard of U.S. Marshals.

Fortunately, Greg and Cathy are still with us. Other cases have ended more tragically. On October 11, 2001, a great AUSA named Tom Wales was gunned down in his home office in Seattle, shot by a sniper while he worked at his computer. According to media reports, the FBI suspects that Wales was killed by one of his former defendants, but the murder has never been solved, and no one has ever been charged. In another case closer to home, the Colombo Family put out a contract on Southern District AUSA William Aronwald, who had worked on several major mafia prosecutions. Tragically, the Colombos bungled the hit and gunned down Aronwald's elderly father instead.*

Was I nervous about a potential hit? Hemingway once wrote that courage is the ability to repress one's imagination. For me, that's never been easy to do. For twenty-three hours and fifty-six minutes of every day, I didn't give the danger a thought. But every day, if only for a few fleeting seconds, something reminded me that there was always the potential for an "accident." Gregory Scarpa was a rogue mafioso, a killer, and a psychopath. New as I was to the mafia world, these facts made me a little bit paranoid. When I walked home from work through the streets of Brooklyn, I looked for the classic sign of a Colombo Family hit, idling "crash cars" waiting up and down the block. When I turned the key in my door, I always expected an explosion. Fear never affected my work. I always knew that statistically I was much more likely to die in a car wreck than be shot by an angry defendant. But I won't deny that I felt it now and then.

---

*The Aronwald case remained unsolved until 2001, when AUSA Patricia Notopoulos and I flipped a key witness, gunman Frankie Smith, who had helped commit the hit. With Smith as a witness, Notopoulos charged Colombo capo Joel Cacace with ordering the murder. In 2004, Cacace, age sixty-three, pleaded guilty to the crime. I hope and expect he will die in jail.

WHEN SUNG-HEE AND I began to prepare for the Scarpa trial, our first priority was to identify and mark all the pieces of physical evidence that could be used to prove Scarpa's guilt. For more than a decade the DEA, NYPD, and, more recently, the FBI had been investigating the Scarpa Crew, using every law enforcement tool imaginable: wiretaps, bugs, video surveillance, tailing, subpoenas, searches, garbage pulls, raids. All the resulting evidence had been collected in the "Scarpa war room," a locked, windowless tomb on the EDNY's fifteenth floor. One night shortly after Valerie had dropped from the case, Sung-Hee and I met outside the war room in order to survey our new empire. I assumed that everything would be shipshape. When, however, Sung-Hee and I unlocked the door, we discovered that we could open it only a few inches wide; too many boxes were stacked in the way. I forced the door open with my shoulder, causing a minor avalanche of boxes inside, and quickly learned that we had inherited a total mess. File cabinets and boxes had been packed so deeply against the walls I could not even locate a light switch. They rose in perilous piles all the way to the ceiling. The room smelled pervasively of old cardboard and ancient, calcified masking tape, the scent of despair. Sung-Hee and I looked at each other and our hearts sank. We quickly retreated to Starbucks for coffee.

The next morning Sung-Hee and I met at the office early, Sung-Hee in jeans, I in an old pair of khakis, and we began to clean up the war room. We moved forty or fifty boxes out into the hallway to free up some space inside, brought in two lamps to give us more light, and began to unpack the boxes. My hands were soon covered in dust, my allergies flaring, but I did not really mind, for I was totally mesmerized. The Scarpa war room was like a mafia museum. Every time I tore open a box, I had no idea what I would find. In the first half hour, I uncovered hundreds of wiretap tapes, several pairs of scales for weighing cocaine and heroin, and stacks of old NYPD crime scene photos, pictures of Scarpa's victims. In one giant carton, I found half a dozen antiquated telephones and answering machines, seized almost a decade before during a raid on the Scarpa sports gambling business. In another corner of the room, I uncovered several bulletproof vests, two hunting rifle cases, holsters, several boxes of ammunition, and a scope—evidence from the Colombo

Family War. One small box was labeled "biohazard." Inside I found a number of human bones, the last remains of Sal "The Hammerhead" Cardaci.

Sung-Hee and I spent one whole week digging through the war room, working from morning until late at night. Every time I found something I could not identify, Sung-Hee would come over, read the evidence labels, tell me what I had found, and explain why it was or was not useful to our case. In this way, cleaning up the war room served two distinct purposes: we put our evidence in order, and I got a thorough education about the case. Generally, I deferred to Sung-Hee's judgment about the value of the evidence, but sometimes we disagreed. "John," she would yell, "the Gambuzza phones are worthless!"

"No, you don't get it," I would shout back. "This will make the gambling business come alive, seem more real."

Usually, we compromised. In this way, cleaning up the war room was a bonding experience. By the time we finished, we were not just colleagues but friends.

SUNG-HEE AND I decided to use almost a thousand pieces of evidence from the war room: wiretap recordings, crime scene photos, surveillance videotapes, loansharking and gambling records, several hundred photographs, and about two dozen bullets, most of them pried from the bodies of Scarpa's victims. This sounds like an impressive haul, but in truth the case was really weak.

Prosecutors tend to classify criminal cases on a spectrum, based on the predominant type of evidence. The strongest cases—slam dunks like *Elcock*—are based on solid physical evidence. These cases are easy to win because the jury can rest its judgment on tangible exhibits, without having to rely on testimony from fallible human beings, who may have poor memories or an incentive to lie. At the other end of the spectrum, the weak end, are cases based exclusively on witness testimony. The worst of these are called straight cooperator cases. In a straight cooperator case the prosecution has no evidence except the stories of cooperating witnesses, criminals who have flipped and are testifying in the hopes of receiving a lighter sentence. Juries tend to hate these witnesses and the "sweetheart" deals that brought them to the government side. So winning a straight cooperator case can be tough.

After digging through the Scarpa war room, Sung-Hee and I realized that our case was close to the weak side of the spectrum: almost, though not quite, a straight cooperator case. We had lots of fascinating exhibits, including loansharking records, bullets, bones, and so on. These exhibits could be used to prove that loans had been made, bets taken, and people killed. Alas, none of this evidence directly incriminated Scarpa; he had been too cagey, too careful to leave any traces of his own involvement behind. His name never appeared on any gambling or loansharking records; he was never caught with any incriminating evidence on his person; we never found any solid evidence in his house or in his car. This meant that in the final analysis, our hopes of conviction would rest almost entirely on the testimony of our cooperating mafia witnesses, former members of Scarpa's own crew.

The strength of a straight cooperator case depends on the number of cooperating witnesses the government has in its stable. A case with ten cooperators is going to be hard to lose. If, however, your case is based on only two or three witnesses, then the burden of proof is harder to meet. That was our situation. When Scarpa was indicted in June 1995, the case was built primarily on the testimony of five former Scarpa Crew members, all of them killers: Carmine Sessa, Larry Mazza, Jimmy Del-Masto, Billy Meli, and Mario Parlagreco. For a mafia murder case this was pretty strong, giving us a reasonable chance to win. By the time we went to trial, however, much of this strength had dissipated.

The first cooperator we lost was Carmine Sessa, the Colombo Family consigliere. Sessa and Scarpa had committed many murders together, so he was a very valuable witness. Sessa, however, had known for years that Scarpa Senior had a secret source of information inside the FBI, who tipped him off to the existence of wiretaps and arrests. Sung-Hee believed that if we used Sessa at trial, he would do more harm than good, for Larry Silverman, Scarpa's attorney, would be able to elicit incredibly damning information from him about the Scarpa Senior–DeVecchio relationship. "Our primary strategic goal is to minimize, to the extent we can, the impact of the Scarpa Defense," Sung-Hee told me one day early in trial prep. So we decided not to call Sessa.

The other loss was Larry Mazza, comanager of the Scarpa sports betting business. Mazza was still in prison, where telephone conversations to the outside world are routinely monitored and recorded. One day Mazza was caught on a recorded prison telephone making a bunch of outrageous statements: that Valerie Caproni was more powerful than President Clinton; that jurors were stupid; that he expected a very light sentence for his crimes. After this blunder, the government called Mazza twice to testify in mafia trials. On both occasions, defense attorneys used Mazza's taped remarks to crush him on cross-examination, resulting in two acquittals. This should have come as no surprise. Juries, after all, will not react well when they learn a mafia cooperator thinks they are dumb. Given this record, Sung-Hee decided that Mazza too was more trouble than he was worth.

As a rookie mafia prosecutor I had no reason to second-guess these judgments, but they still made me nervous. Prosecutors frequently have to make tough judgments about the value of witnesses, cutting their losses if a witness's "baggage" outweighs his potential contribution. Still, going from a five-witness case to a three-witness case really upped the pressure. Our margin of error, always tight, had grown even more narrow.

———

THE DAY AFTER Valerie resigned from the case, Sung-Hee and I sat down to map out a game plan for the summer. Our highest priority was to prep our cooperators for trial. In multiple prosecutor cases, the trial team splits up responsibility for the witnesses. Sung-Hee had much more experience than I did, so she agreed to take two of our cooperators, Jimmy DelMasto and Billy Meli. I got the third, Mario Parlagreco. To get them ready for trial, we had to go on the road. First up was Jimmy DelMasto.

One sultry July morning I went into the office early to meet Sung-Hee and Maggie Carmichael, the lead FBI agent on the Scarpa case. Together the three of us drove south to a Bureau of Prisons PCU, or protective custody unit, where Jimmy DelMasto was jailed. During the drive Sung-Hee told me Jimmy's life story. Jimmy, I learned, had been a star baseball player in high school, scouted by the New York Yankees. As he got older, sports proved his undoing. In the mid-1980s Larry Mazza, a childhood friend, asked Jimmy to help him set up a sports gambling business with Scarpa's protection and support. Jimmy leaped at the chance. The operation they established was the single most professional criminal scam run by the Scarpa Crew, grossing more than a million dollars a week. Within a few years it had made Jimmy rich.

Though Jimmy had joined the mob to run a gambling business, he found himself committing murder. Jimmy was not involved in the Scarpa Crew's murder spree during the 1980s. He kept his head down and focused on gambling instead. When, however, the Colombo Family War broke out, it was impossible for him to stay neutral. During the war Jimmy rode shotgun with Scarpa Senior, helping him kill several Orena faction enemies. The FBI caught up with Jimmy in 1994, after Carmine Sessa cooperated, and he was placed under arrest. Jimmy's profession was risk assessment. He knew that if he ever wanted to get out of prison, the smart call was to play ball with the government. So he flipped.

For most of the drive south, I thought about Jimmy DelMasto. I had never met a murderer before, and I wondered what he would be like. It may sound incredibly naive, but I thought I might like the guy. This was in part because I have great faith in baseball. Anyone who loves the game, I thought, cannot be all that bad.

Jimmy's prison was modern, cold, and antiseptic. The warden had turned the air conditioning on high, trying to beat the summer heat. A few minutes after we arrived, two guards brought Jimmy to us in the visitors' lounge. I took a close look: medium height; prisoner's tan jumpsuit; short brown hair; pale skin; the slightly pigeon-toed walk of an athlete. As soon as I saw him, I realized how clueless I had been. Jimmy seemed as cold as the room, with a vacant look in his dull blue eyes. Sung-Hee and Maggie said hello as warmly as they could, and then they introduced me. I shook Jimmy's hand. His grip was limp, clammy, and noncommittal. Over the next several hours Jimmy never looked me in the eye.

Sung-Hee had met with Jimmy several times before, and she had all her questions for trial scripted out, line by line, in her black trial binder. For the next hour or two, she ran through these questions in a highly formal manner, just as if Jimmy were on the stand. I quickly realized that Jimmy was not going to be our star witness. He sat up dead straight in his chair, staring blankly at Sung-Hee, his feet planted firmly on the ground, his hand resting on a cold can of Coke. When Sung-Hee asked a question, he would pause, think about it for a moment, and then answer in a laconic, abrupt, almost insolent manner. Often his "answers" to questions were single one-syllable words.

SUNG-HEE: What happened to Joe Brewster?
JIMMY: Killed.
SUNG-HEE: Who killed him?
JIMMY: The crew.
SUNG-HEE: What crew?
JIMMY: Mine.
SUNG-HEE: How was he killed?
JIMMY: Shot.

After this had gone on for five or ten minutes, Sung-Hee got mad. "Jimmy, you have to try to answer these questions fully! It's important!" Jimmy just nodded. For a question or two he would try to provide a litle more detail. Within two minutes, however, he was back to monosyllables, his right hand gripped tightly around his soft-drink can. To me, the whole exchange seemed a little inhuman. I was glad when we wrapped up the prep session and got back out in the sunshine.

Driving that night to dinner—a pancake house, Sung-Hee's favorite—I commented on Jimmy's personality: "He's like a shell of a human being. He's not really there. The jury's gonna hate him. I thought he would be more outgoing."

Sung-Hee looked at me contemptuously. "What do you expect? He's a stone-cold killer."

That night I thought about what Sung-Hee had said, and I concluded she must be right. Maybe, I thought, only cold and emotionless people like Jimmy can kill other human beings. Later, however, I met many other killers during my prosecutorial career, and I concluded Sung-Hee was wrong. Murderers, I learned, come in all stripes, as diverse in character as humankind itself. Some killers are quiet, and some are loquacious. Some cold, some friendly. A few seem utterly changed by their experiences, and others totally untouched. You cannot generalize.

In Jimmy's case, I do not think you could attribute his burned-out personality to some basic character flaw. Instead, I suspect he was suffering from deep clinical depression.

THE NEXT WITNESS WE VISITED was Billy Meli. Billy grew up on the streets of Brooklyn, and he was in and out of prison throughout his teens and twenties: assault, burglary, drugs. Big, strong, and tough, Billy was used in the Scarpa Crew as muscle, to beat up recalcitrant loan-shark customers and extortion victims. Once he bit off the ear of a cop. Billy was also an experienced killer. During the relatively brief periods he was out of jail, he had killed, or helped kill, nine different men.

In 1987 Billy was busted for marijuana dealing and sent to prison in the *Scarpa I* case. At first he hung tough, but in 1993 he decided to coop-erate with the FBI. Most men cooperate out of simple self-interest; they face massive prison sentences and believe working for the feds is their only chance of freedom. Billy's decision to cooperate was more idiosyn-cratic. Billy had spent his entire life in and out of prison, and the prospect of rotting in jail until he died did not really scare him. By 1993, however, Billy was really angry and disappointed with the mob.

In the mafia, incarcerated members and associates expect their crews to look out for their spouses while they are locked up. If someone starts a sexual relationship with the wife of an incarcerated mafioso, that person's life is forfeit. When Billy's wife, Christine, began to cheat on him in the early 1990s with another Colombo Family member, Billy sent a message to the crew that he wanted the interloper murdered. Billy be-lieved deeply in the Colombo Family rules, and he was confident that the family would give him his due. When, however, he submitted his re-quest, the family blew him off, for they valued a man "on the street" more than a man in prison. For Billy, this was more than treachery; it was a violation of a sacred contract. As he told me years later, "If they aren't going to follow the rules, then I don't have to follow the rules." In September 1993, Billy began to cooperate against his former colleagues. By 1998 he was out on bail, living in the Witness Security Program.

Meeting with incarcerated mafia witnesses like Jimmy was easy. We made a call to OEO, the Office of Enforcement Operations at Main Justice in Washington, and the trip was quickly arranged. Meeting a WITSEC witness who has been released into the community is much more difficult. First, the U.S. Marshals, who manage the WITSEC pro-gram, picked Billy up in his current home, a location kept secret from me and Sung-Hee, and hopscotched him and an armed escort all around the country, a serpentine process designed to make it hard for him to be tracked or followed. Once he was plunked down in a geographical location where the threat from the mafia was very low, we were flown out to meet him. I can't tell you where we met. The Marshals like to keep their meeting locations secret.

Our neutral site (as we call meetings with WITSEC witnesses out on bail, since the locations are supposed to be neutral, free of mafia influence) with Billy lasted for only two days. The first morning the Marshals brought Billy to us at our hotel. He was friendly and gruff, with a host of tattoos peeking out from underneath his muscle shirt. For the first half hour, Sung-Hee, Maggie, and Billy talked about Billy's new life, hiding out in Middle America. This conversation was intended to make Billy feel relaxed and comfortable, so he would be more cooperative during trial prep, but it also had a more significant purpose. Every person in WITSEC has an AUSA sponsor and an FBI handler who are together responsible for the witness's conduct. As I learned firsthand later in my career, this is a serious burden, for you are always worried that a former murderer released into the real world will crack up and kill again. When Valerie Caproni and Ellen Corcella left the U.S. Attorney's Office, Sung-Hee became Billy's sponsor. She wanted to talk to him about his life to ensure that if there was any potential trouble on the horizon, it could be spotted and corrected before it blew up.

Billy told us he had few complaints; he liked his new community, he was gainfully employed, and he had a new girlfriend to replace the treacherous Christine. For a hitman in the Witness Security Program, he seemed pretty well adjusted. He had only one gripe. When he entered the program, he had been given a forged high school diploma and a transcript that matched his new identity. Unfortunately, the Marshals had given the "new Billy" the same grades he had received in school in Brooklyn, mostly Ds and Fs. Billy thought this was outrageous. "Come on now, Sung-Hee. If they are gonna forge me a diploma, can't they give me some better grades?" Sung-Hee told him he was out of luck.

In that first half hour I discovered that I liked Billy Meli—liked him a lot. To an ordinary citizen, that may sound bizarre. Billy was, after all, a mafia hitman, a guy who killed people for a living. But that is the truth. Most cooperating defendants are like Saladino: obsequious, a little oily, trying to keep "their prosecutor" happy. Not Billy. He was blunt and honest, radiating strength and common sense. Early in the meeting, Sung-Hee told him that Scarpa was going to trial, and Billy would have to testify. Billy did not whine or look scared, as many witnesses do. He just shook his head and said, "That guy is a defiant bastard." Later I asked him if he regretted killing so many men. I expected Billy to repeat some pious cant about rehabilitation, like the Morgan Freeman character Red in the parole board scene in *The Shawshank Redemption*: "Yes, sir. Absolutely. I've learned my lesson. I can honestly say I'm a changed man. I'm no longer a danger to society. That's the God's honest truth. No doubt about it." Instead, Billy was totally unremorseful. "All those guys, they broke the rules. They chose the life they chose. They knew the rules. They had it coming, most of them." I was astounded by this remark, but I liked it nonetheless. After my Saladino disaster, I was nervous about slick, lying cooperators. With Billy, there was no pretense, no bullshit, no effort to please. He said what he thought, and that was that.

Billy was also funny. He had a thick Brooklyn accent, and I imagined that if I'd encountered him as my new neighbor in Middle America, I would immediately think: mafia hitman in the Witness Security Program. During a break in our morning session, I questioned Billy about this. Did he think his neighbors had any questions about his past? What, I asked, did they make of his New York accent? Billy's reply cracked me up. "They always ask, but I got a good answer. When they say, 'You have a funny accent; where are you from?' I just say, 'France.'"

As a witness Billy had some definite pluses. He had committed a bunch of murders for and with Scarpa, and his testimony about these killings was generally clear and convincing. He was also good at cross. When, during a practice session, Sung-Hee commented that Scarpa's defense lawyers would try to rough him up, Billy replied, "I've been through worse." Unfortunately, the rest of his testimony was weak. Because he had been in and out of prison constantly in the 1980s, Billy's grip on the Scarpa Crew's criminal business operations was hazy, his memory for dates was bad, and his understanding of mafia organization and structure was poor. Worst of all, he kept forgetting how many men he had killed. Every time Sung-Hee asked, "How many men did you murder?" Billy would reply, "Eight . . . No, no! Nine, I killed nine."

Each time he did this, Sung-Hee would yell at him, "Billy, you have to remember how many people you killed, or the jury will think you don't take it seriously!"

Billy just grumbled. "I know," he said sheepishly, "but there's that one I don't really count. I keep forgetting it."

The sight of Sung-Hee, who probably weighs less than a hundred pounds, shouting at a strapping mafia killer always made me laugh.

On the second day of the neutral site, the Marshals gave us permission to take Billy out for lunch. Sung-Hee has an endless appetite for junk food, so we wound up at a food court in a suburban shopping mall. As shoppers swirled around us, Sung-Hee, Billy, Maggie, and I got our food, and we met back at our cheap metal table. A careful observer might have noticed that we appeared to be an odd group of friends. Sung-Hee is petite, well dressed, stylish, and sophisticated, while Billy sports a lot of tattoos and looks, well, like a member of the mafia. But no one gave us a second look. As I ate my chicken sandwich, I glanced around at the other folks at the mall, wolfing down their burgers and Chinese food, and I was filled with a sense of the surreal. Here I am, I thought, eating at the food court with a mafia hitman. To this day, whenever I am at a shopping mall, I always look around at the other shoppers, wondering: Anyone here in WITSEC?

The last night of the neutral site, after Sung-Hee had finished preparing her direct, she gave me an hour or two to ask my own questions. My selection of questions was driven by trial strategy. Juries judge a witness's credibility by two primary factors, his demeanor on the witness stand and corroboration, the extent to which his testimony is backed up by, or interlocks with, other witnesses and other pieces of evidence. One of my main goals with my own cooperator, Mario Parlagreco, was to use his testimony to bolster the credibility of Billy and Jimmy by getting him to repeat and confirm as many facts from their testimony as I could. To do this effectively, I had to identify areas of common knowledge. This entailed asking Billy lots of detailed questions about random matters: the kinds of cars the crew members drove, what a particular hardware store looked like, the weight of canvas used to wrap a body, or the interior decoration of Scarpa's house. Unfortunately, Billy was tired, and his answers to my questions were increasingly abrupt. Every once in a while he would shake his head and grunt, "Why do you want to know that? Why would I remember that? Who cares?" Finally, as I headed into my last set of questions, I made an offhand comment, trying to cajole him into one more effort.

"All right, Billy," I said, looking down at my notes, "don't kill me, I've got just a few more things to ask." As soon as this remark slipped out, I froze and then slowly looked up. Billy was staring at me strangely, a puzzled expression on his face. For a moment he looked like a small, hurt child. For me, "don't kill me" was a common colloquial phrase, a figure of speech meaning "don't get mad." But to Billy, "don't kill me" was not a figure of speech at all; it was something he had heard from his victims in their last moments of life, before execution. Several tense seconds passed, the room totally silent, and then we both broke up laughing. I slapped him on the shoulder, and we ended the neutral site.

OUR FINAL COOPERATOR, Mario Parlagreco, was my responsibility. Mario was incarcerated at the same WITSEC prison facility as Ray Saladino, a few hours' drive from New York. One morning in late July, I drove up to the prison to introduce myself. When I first went to this prison to meet with Saladino, just three months before, I had been a self-conscious rookie. Now, on my second WITSEC case, I felt like a hardened pro. As I signed into the green WITSEC logbook, the guard on duty remarked, "Back again, Mr. Kroger?" It will sound pathetic to you, I imagine, but I swelled with pride at that moment. I thought: I'm really in the big leagues now.

When I met Mario, I was struck by his immaculate appearance. His tan prison uniform was ironed into sharp creases; his black shoes were carefully polished; his hair was oiled and combed back neatly over his sleek skull. Special Agent Dayna Better, his FBI handler, told me later that Mario got up early on mornings when he was meeting with the government to get his clothes and shoes ready, in order to show respect.

That day I talked with Mario about his childhood and his decision to join the mob. I quickly concluded that Mario had the makings of a star witness. He was a natural storyteller, with a great memory for details, and when he recalled his past experiences, he often acted them out, gesturing with his torso and his arms as he relived his past. More important, and to my great surprise, Mario was a mafia rarity, a killer in touch with his feelings.

Most mobsters have stunted emotional lives. Though many mafia members have powerful passions bottled up inside them, the mafia trains them not to think about, let alone express, their fears, anxieties, hopes, and sorrows. Most mafiosi never develop the habit of self-reflection or the vocabulary needed to analyze their feelings. When you talk with them, you discover that they are incapable of discussing the moral consequences of their actions. They cannot describe, in more than trivial terms, how their decisions in the past have affected themselves or other people. For men like Jimmy, this leads to profound and deeply rooted depression they cannot even identify, let alone address. It also makes them horrible witnesses, like cold, checked-out robots.

Mario was different. Somehow, the mafia never killed off his ordinary emotional responses to horror and pain. On the street this was a detriment. Despite his powerful build, his colleagues in the crew called Mario "Marianne" because of his "womanly" emotions. During murders, Mario was never asked to be the triggerman. Instead, he always played a supporting role, luring the victim to the murder location or disposing of the body afterward. Had he stayed in the mob, Mario's rich emotional life would probably have led to his death; "weak" mafia members are often whacked because they are viewed as a risk. Now, however, his ability to talk about his feelings was a godsend.

I discovered Mario's emotional depth early in the prep process. One day he and I were talking about the murder of a car thief, Sal "The Hammerhead" Cardaci. This was the first murder Mario helped commit. After Mario described, in graphic detail, how he cleaned up Cardaci's blood and brains in the bathroom of Mike's Candy Store, I asked him if participating in the homicide had changed his status in the crew. Mario's eyes narrowed, and he looked away from me, as if he were gazing off into the distance. "When I was first in the crew, I was the coffee boy. Anybody wanted coffee, I had to run to the diner and get it. After the killing, I didn't have to be the coffee boy no more." Mario's face wrinkled up, and he began to cry quietly, not sobbing, just a few tears. He was, I think, reflecting on his loss of innocence. All I could think of, as I waited for him to finish, was how to use his sorrow to my advantage. Please, I thought, let me tap into this same emotion in front of the jury.

My meetings with Mario had their comical moments. On that first day I discovered that because of our prep session, Mario would miss his prison lunch. I asked Sung-Hee what I could do to remedy this, and she told me that I could bring him food, so we could work a full day without having to break. At our next session I asked Mario what he wanted to eat, and his eyes lit up. "I want a sub, a sub with prosciutto, pepperoni, provolone, mozzarella, and roasted peppers. Don't have 'em put on the oil and vinegar, have 'em put it on the side. That way the bread won't get soggy." The morning before my next visit, I went over to Cranberry's, the fancy Brooklyn deli by my office, to order our lunch. I got a turkey on rye with mayo. Then I scanned the menu board for a sandwich that fit Mario's description. I quickly found it, and I had to laugh when I ordered. "I'll also have a Godfather, oil and vinegar on the side."

Over time I got to know Mario well, and though I still found his prison incredibly depressing, I looked forward to our sessions just to hear what he would say. One day he and I prepared his testimony about Scarpa's loansharking business. When Mario talked about this line of work, he sometimes called it loansharking, but more commonly shylocking. He would refer to shylocks, the shy-business, shy-money. This terminology fascinated me. How, I wondered, did Shakespeare wind up in the mafia lexicon?* But it also concerned me. After a while I told Mario that I would prefer him to use the term "loansharking," not "shylocking." Mario asked me why.

"Well," I said, "the term 'shylocking' may be offensive to Jews, and I expect we will have some Jewish people on the jury, since the trial is taking place in Brooklyn."

Mario was puzzled by this response. "Why," he asked me, "would Jews get mad about calling it shylocking?"

I paused for a moment and thought: This is going to get interesting. "Do you know where the term 'shylocking' comes from?" I asked. Mario shook his head and said no. "Have you ever heard of Shakespeare, the playwright?" Mario nodded, though from the fuzzy look on his face, I gathered that reading the Bard was not part of his regular routine. "Well, Shakespeare wrote a play called *The Merchant of Venice*, about a loan-

---

*This is not the only example. Mafia killers often refer to murder as a piece of work. Compare *Macbeth*, act II, scene III. When the king's murder is discovered, Banquo comments:

And when we have our naked frailties hid,
That suffer in exposure, let us meet,
And question this most bloody piece of work,
To know it further.

shark named Shylock." Mario nodded again, taking it all in. "In the play, Shylock is pretty horrible. One guy can't pay him back, and Shylock tries to carve a pound of flesh from his body with a knife. The play is basically anti-Semitic, portraying Jews very negatively, tapping into a racial stereotype about Jews being greedy. So the name Shylock, for many Jews, carries negative connotations."

Mario thought about this silently for a moment, his face scrunched up in concentration. "You mean," he said very tentatively, as if he were slowly thinking this through for himself, step by step, "that it would hurt a Jew's feelings if I called loansharking shylocking?"

I nodded and thought: Well, he seems to have got that much. Then I couldn't resist. "You really should read *The Merchant of Venice* sometime, Mario. It is one of the few great literary portrayals of the loansharking business in Western culture."

Mario looked blankly at me. I might just as well have told him to become an astronaut. We quickly moved on to a new topic.

As the Scarpa trial date grew closer, Sung-Hee decided to come to one of our sessions, to make sure everything was going well. To honor this visit, Mario told me that he had received permission to use his prison unit kitchen to make us lunch. I tried to put Mario off. The idea of eating lunch made in the prison, probably not the most sanitary of places, really grossed me out. But Mario was insistent, and I realized that if we refused, it would hurt his pride. I didn't want to eat his cooking, but I did want him feeling happy and confident in the stressful month before trial. So I agreed. Anything for the case.

The next week Sung-Hee came along with Dayna Better and me, and she listened to part of his direct, the section focusing on the murders. Once we finished work, Mario brought out a giant plastic bucket of soggy pasta and chicken cacciatore. The ensuing meal was hilarious. Mario was very proud of his cooking and nervous about its reception, so Sung-Hee and I were effusive, just to get him to calm down. "Mario," we said, "this is amazing." At the same time, both of us were visibly concerned about the food. Sung-Hee kept asking questions about the recipe, fishing around for any indication that she was about to get salmonella. "So, Mario, how long did you cook this chicken for?" Meanwhile I was picking at my lunch, trying to calculate precisely how much I had to eat in order to satisfy Mario's honor. Eventually I sucked it up and munched away. As I did so, I was overcome by a sense of the absurdity of my life. Here I am, I thought, eating a really disgusting lunch so as not to hurt the feelings of an overly sensitive cook who happens to kill people for a living. Later, on the drive home, Sung-Hee told me that she had wondered if Mario might try to poison us.

EVERY DAY PROSECUTORS are faced with stunning evidence of human brutality. To deal with it, many prosecutors turn violent crimes into a joke. As we packed up our briefcases to go on the day that Mario cooked us lunch, I turned to Sung-Hee and asked, "Of all the murders, which is your favorite?"

I did not specify the grounds by which Sung-Hee was to judge, but she needed no clarification. Somehow, she knew exactly what I meant: most gruesome, most shocking, most inhuman. She immediately replied, "I like the Longobardi homicide best: gunned down in his own limousine, his face shot away beyond recognition."

I nodded but disagreed. "For me, it's the Cardaci murder: childhood friend of Billy Meli, murdered and buried in a candy store basement, only the knucklebones for evidence. Pretty much sums up the human condition." Sung-Hee just laughed and continued packing her bag.

Suddenly Sung-Hee and I became aware that Mario was staring at us, his dark eyes like day-old bruises, a hurt, disappointed look on his face. Mario did not say a word, but his stern expression conveyed an unmistakable message. I helped kill these people, he seemed to be thinking, and it is no laughing matter. Sung-Hee and I grew quiet, packed up the rest of our stuff, and left the prison in a somber mood. Hmm, I thought, a lesson in values from a mafia hitman.

To this day I am a bit ashamed that I could laugh about something so horrible as murder. My conduct may seem insensitive to you, perhaps even disgusting. All I can say, in my own defense, is that in violent crimes prosecution, a sense of morbid humor is a common coping device and that for prosecutors, a lack of moral perspective is a common occupational hazard.

CHAPTER EIGHT

A Mafia Murder Trial

The trial of Gregory Scarpa, Jr., began on September 23, 1998. That morning, before the jury arrived, I took a good look at our opponent. Scarpa was stocky and strong, just like his 1980s video footage, but he looked much older than his forty-seven years, as if prison had worn him out. Like many defendants, Scarpa had undergone an "extreme trial makeover." He had abandoned his toupee. His bald head was now framed with close-cropped gray hair. He wore a blue cardigan sweater, gray wool slacks, and gold-rimmed glasses. He was trying, I thought, to look like someone's grandfather. When he talked to Larry Silverman, his lawyer, he tended to cover his mouth with his cupped hand, apparently so we could not read his lips, maybe an old mafia habit.

For the first three weeks of the trial Sung-Hee and I slowly presented our case to the jury, witness by witness, exhibit by exhibit. Looking back, I remember this as a period of great stress. In addition to Mario Parlagreco, I had twenty-five witnesses to juggle. Every morning I would get up early and go to the courthouse. Short of sleep, drugged on coffee, I would meet with my morning witnesses and finalize my directs for the day. We were in court from nine to five, with only a short break at noon to wolf down some lunch—sometimes, for me, just one more cup of coffee. In the evening I prepped more witnesses, and then I spent several hours at my computer, looking for helpful cases online or drafting motion papers. Sung-Hee, I learned, was a master of the paper war. During the trial we filed a blizzard of legal motions, often several per day. These motions always had a legitimate purpose: to limit cross-examination, to block lines of argument, or to seek evidentiary rulings in advance. At the same time, we were trying to keep Silverman so busy replying to our motions that he could not focus on his own work. By the time Sung-Hee and I went home, it was often well past midnight.

Not surprisingly, Sung-Hee and I quickly grew tired and irritable. One afternoon, as we were walking out of the courtroom, my friend Kelly Moore, a fellow AUSA, stopped me and asked me how the trial was going. As I was describing the day's events, Sung-Hee interrupted. "You don't have time to talk," she snarled. "You have witnesses to prep!"

Larry Silverman increased our stress levels. Larry was a former AUSA in the Eastern District who had "joined the dark side." He had a good reputation and was always outwardly affable, but he drove me crazy. From the very start of the trial he went on the offensive, trying to raise the Scarpa Defense. In his opening statement, he told the jury that the entire trial was a cover-up designed to hide the FBI's crimes by framing an innocent man. Scarpa's father was the real culprit, our cooperators were liars, the FBI was corrupt, and Sung-Hee and I were hiding evidence of Senior's guilt. The constant refrain of government incompetence, misconduct, and criminality got on my nerves. So did Larry's endless supply of petty but annoying tricks.

To make the trial go faster, Judge Raggi ordered us to sit down with Larry and try to reach an agreement about which government exhibits were admissible, so that we did not waste the jury's time with evidentiary objections. For me, this process was a nightmare. One day, for example, Larry and I were reviewing a series of exhibits from a 1992 search. After a cursory glance at my evidence, Larry casually told me that he would seek to preclude only one item, an envelope with the name Gregory Scarpa, Sr., on it. I was trying to be reasonable, and the envelope in question was of marginal importance, so I told Larry we would not offer it.

A couple of days later the detective who conducted that search was on the stand, authenticating several pieces of evidence, those to which Larry had not objected. When I finished my questions, Larry got up for cross. He asked, with a sneering tone, "Do you recall recovering an envelope that was addressed not to Gregory Scarpa Jr., but to Gregory Scarpa Sr.?" The detective said he could not remember. Larry then walked to the

government's table, picked up the Scarpa Senior envelope he had asked
me not to use, ostentatiously stuck a defense exhibit sticker on it, and
produced it with a flourish. "I would like to show you what has been
marked for identification Defendant's Exhibit K. I ask you first, sir, do
you recall retrieving this envelope?" The detective paused, referred to his
records, and then authenticated the document. Larry rolled his eyes at
the jury and shook his head with mock regret—another effort by the
government, he seemed to imply, to hide all the evidence relating to the
real criminal, Gregory Scarpa, Sr. Then he said, with deep satisfaction,
"No further questions."

Later that day I objected to Judge Raggi. "What we observed with
Government Exhibit 533 was a classic sandbag. This was an exhibit that
I intended to offer, it was given to Mr. Silverman on Friday, it was one
that he objected to and I removed it from the Government Exhibits because he objected to it. We wind up with a staged event as if the government is hiding material involving Gregory Scarpa Sr."

Judge Raggi cut me off. "What is the application to me?"

I paused. Should I ask that Larry be sanctioned? Admonished? Disbarred? Fined? I paused, made a quick calculation, and realized that
the correct answer was: do nothing. My reasoning was simple. In any
criminal trial, a motion for sanctions against a defense attorney will
backfire against the government. If I claimed that Larry had acted un-
ethically and Scarpa was later convicted, Scarpa could use my allegation
to get a new trial on the basis of "ineffective assistance of counsel."
My job was to protect the government's shot at a guilty verdict that
would stick. That required me to pretend Larry had done nothing
wrong, to avoid a potential issue on appeal. Defense lawyers like Larry
understand this calculus, and it emboldens some of them to play dirty
tricks. Judge Raggi knew all of this too, of course; that was why
she cut me off short. Faced with her question—do you want to put
up or shut up?—I had no real choice. I humbly muttered, "There is no
application."

This was not Larry's only stunt. One day he was cross-examining
a detective about a wiretap. The detective testified that according to a
transcript, one intercepted telephone call started at "01:18 p.m." Larry interrupted. "Sir, when I was in the army, sir, I thought if it was written that
way it would be 13:18."

The detective responded, "I didn't put the times on these so they're not all in military time."

Was Larry really trying to clarify the time of the call? Not in the least. Our jury contained four Vietnam-era veterans. When Larry alluded gratuitously to his prior army service, he was trying, improperly, to forge a link with the jury that might redound to the benefit of his client. This little trick really burned me up, and I decided to fight fire with fire. That afternoon I borrowed a Marine Corps Eagle, Globe, and Anchor tie clasp, which I was entitled to wear as a Marine veteran, from one of the court security officers. Our jury panel included two Marines, and I knew they would recognize it. For the rest of the trial I wore it every day. My new accessory did not go unobserved by my colleagues. One day Andrew Weissmann, the deputy chief of our Criminal Division, stopped me in the hallway of the courthouse. Andrew was something of a fashion plate: Armani suits, Italian suede shoes. He asked with concern, "What is that hideous tie clasp thingy?" I told Andrew the story about Silverman, and he sighed. "Well, as long as it's for an advantage at trial."

Interestingly, it was Scarpa himself who tried to decrease the tension in the courtroom. Once, early in the trial, I glanced over at him and discovered, to my discomfort, that he was staring at me with an open, somewhat curious look on his face. When our eyes made contact, Scarpa winked. A few days later, during a break, Scarpa spoke to me directly. "Mr. Kroger, you a Giants fan?"

I looked at him, a bit startled, and then replied, "Uh, yes, yes, I am."

"Did you see the game on Sunday?"

I knitted my brows and frowned at him. "Uh, actually, Mr. Scarpa, I've been pretty busy lately." Scarpa chortled and turned away.

For the rest of the trial Scarpa looked for opportunities to make some personal contact with me. Sometimes he was downright funny. One afternoon, after extensive testimony about the Scarpa sports gambling business, he accosted me on my way out of the courtroom. "Mr. Kroger, you got the line for the Jets game?" I couldn't help chuckling. On another day Silverman and Sung-Hee were going at it hammer and tongs, furiously debating an abstruse legal point in front of Judge Raggi. Scarpa caught my eye and gave an exaggerated shrug. "Lawyers," he said, shaking his head in disgust.

THE CORE OF OUR CASE against Scarpa was the testimony of our three cooperating witnesses. In cooperator trials, the government typically uses a bookends strategy, like a relay team in track. You start the case with your second-best witness, bury your mediocre ones in the middle, and finish the trial with your strongest. For us, that meant our order was Billy, Jimmy, then Mario.

Billy Meli was compelling on the stand, blunt and clear. The FBI agents had helped him pick out a dark navy suit, and he looked great. When he answered questions, he looked straight at Scarpa, as if to say, "I am not afraid of you." Altogether, his was a remarkable performance. His testimony was damaged, unfortunately, by its rapidity. Sung-Hee and I possessed very different theories about direct examination. I was interested in vivid storytelling, which I thought made the witnesses more convincing. Sung-Hee disagreed. "You win these cases in your closing argument," she told me. "All you need to do is elicit the basic facts you need to close." Sung-Hee used her terse approach with Billy, and though it was certainly a competent direct, it went way too quickly. Billy's descriptions of the murders, for example, took less than a minute or two apiece, a pace that failed to convey the moral gravity of the crime. Sometimes the subjects being discussed changed so rapidly I thought the jury got lost.

Billy was at his best on cross. Sung-Hee had carefully prepped him to pause and think about questions before he answered, to answer, "I don't know," if he was uncertain about the facts, and to decline to answer any questions he did not understand. Billy used these tactics as weapons to tie Larry Silverman up in knots. At one point, for example, Larry tried to get Billy to describe a notorious 1991 newspaper article that reported a rumor that Scarpa Senior was a government informant.

SILVERMAN: Do you recall, sir, that there came a time that there was an article in the newspaper about Mr. Scarpa Sr.? [Pause, without an answer.] Do you recall that?
MELI: Could you be a little more specific? What article are we talking about?

SILVERMAN: Well, was it often, sir, that there were articles written about Greg Scarpa?

MELI: There was a few articles, yes.

SILVERMAN: What is the first article you recall reading about anybody named Scarpa? [Pause, without an answer.] Let me make it easier for you. When is the first article, newspaper article, that was called to your attention, either that you read yourself, or someone showed it to you or told you about, that had the name Scarpa in it?

MELI: When I was indicted in 1988.

SILVERMAN: And was that an article about the people who were arrested?

MELI: Yes.

SILVERMAN: Other than that article, sir, when was the next article that you read or heard about that had the name Scarpa in it?

MELI: I can't recall that, counselor.

SILVERMAN: Well, how many articles do you recall either reading yourself or being brought to your attention that referred to someone named Scarpa?

MELI: I can't recall how many, counselor.

SILVERMAN: Well, could you give us some idea, a number?

MELI: There was a few: five, ten, maybe a dozen. A dozen would be fair enough.

SILVERMAN: Okay. When was the first one, other than the one that took place in '87? When was the next one?

MELI: Oh, I don't know. I don't recall, counselor.

SILVERMAN: Was it in 1988?

MELI [incorrectly]: You just said besides the one in '88 . . .

SILVERMAN: Besides the one in '88? Was there another one in '88?

MELI: Well, there was two months of trial in '88. We were in the paper every day.

SILVERMAN: Let me make it easier. I am not referring to any article that referred to the ongoing trial that was taking place in '88.

MELI: Okay.

SILVERMAN: Let's take this beyond the trial itself.

MELI: Okay.

SILVERMAN: 1989. Do you recall any articles in 1989?

MELI: I—I can't recall, counselor. I . . . I am sure there was articles about . . . [long pause].

SILVERMAN: What is the subject matter of the next article after the trial that concerned someone by the name of Scarpa?

MELI: The next article besides the trial?

SILVERMAN: Yes, sir.

MELI: Excluding the trial?

SILVERMAN: Excluding the trial.

MELI: I can't recall, counselor.

SILVERMAN [visibly frustrated]: Well, was there one article that came out, sir, that caught your attention because of the subject matter?

MELI: And what article was that?

SILVERMAN: Concerning someone by the name of Scarpa.

MELI: Okay. I'm . . . I don't understand what article you are speaking of, counselor.

SILVERMAN [yelling]: ANY ARTICLE, SIR, ANY ARTICLE!

JUDGE RAGGI [interrupting]: All right, Mr. Silverman, this is not productive. If you want to lead, you can do that. Go ahead.

SILVERMAN [slowly and carefully]: Mr. Meli, was there an article that occurred sometime in the year 1991 . . .

MELI [interrupting]: Okay . . .

SILVERMAN: . . . that mentioned the name Gregory Scarpa . . .

MELI: Right . . .

SILVERMAN: . . . in the context of being an informant?

MELI: Okay. Now I know what you are talking about, counselor. [With a smile]. Nice and easy, nice and easy.

JURY: Laughter.

In contrast with Billy, Jimmy DelMasto was a borderline disaster. Sung-Hee had carefully scripted his direct, and she knew that he was capable of answering every one of her questions because he had done so in trial prep. On the stand, however, he had a suspicious attack of amnesia. When Sung-Hee asked him simple questions, he answered: "I can't be sure"; "I don't remember"; "I don't know"; "That's all I know"; "I don't remember exactly"; "I'm not one hundred percent sure"; "I guess"; "I'm guessing"; and "I would be guessing." To make matters worse, he alternated between mumbling and whispering. When Sung-Hee pressed him for more detailed answers, she drew repeated objections for leading. Soon she started editing her direct on the spot, cutting down the number of questions to the bare minimum. When he finally got off the stand, she was furious. Jimmy had been a very weak witness, and because of his "poor memory," Sung-Hee had not been able to elicit all the evidence from him that we needed. When it came time for Jimmy to be sentenced, Sung-Hee would be a very lukewarm advocate.

Finally, Mario Parlagreco got up to testify. Mario's direct was a work of art, featuring lavish, detailed, dramatic accounts of the murders. Later, after the trial, Judge Raggi said he was clearly our best witness. On cross, however, he crumbled. This was my fault, not his.

Prior to trial, a basic responsibility of an AUSA is to review his witnesses' 3500 material—all the law enforcement reports and grand jury testimony transcripts containing the witnesses' prior statements about the case.* In my two previous trials, I was diligent about this. Before Scarpa, however, I never closely examined Mario's prior statements, a major, major blunder. My negligence was due in part to the fact that Mario's FBI debriefings had never been typed up. The 3500 material consisted of hundreds of pages of handwritten notes I could barely read. When I tried to review them, I got easily frustrated and quit. I was also overwhelmed with work, and this was the area where I decided to cut corners. But the most important contributing factor was my own naiveté. During trial prep, I found Mario such a convincing storyteller, with such a vivid memory, it never even occurred to me that parts of his story had changed over time.

During trial prep Mario described a trip he took to the Scarpa farm in New Jersey to pick up fifty thousand dollars in cash for a loanshark loan. Mario's memory of this loan seemed crystal clear, and so I asked him about it during the trial, and he repeated what he had told me to the

---

*These documents are collectively called 3500 material because a statute—Title 18, *United States Code*, Section 3500—defines what items must be disclosed to the defense.

jury. Years before, however, Mario had told the FBI that the money was not for loansharking but for a numbers payoff. Had I reviewed the 3500 material, I would have seen this contradiction and left the entire incident out of my direct, but because I failed to do my job, Mario was left a sitting duck.

In contrast with me, Larry Silverman had studied Mario's prior statements carefully, and he pounced on this relatively minor issue like a hungry tiger, using it to show that Mario was unreliable. Caught in a clear contradiction, Mario panicked and lost all self-confidence, something Silverman could clearly see. For several hours Silverman hammered away at my witness. Were his statements really true? Didn't he say something different years ago? Was he sure? Wasn't he making things up? Mario melted under this barrage, mumbling over and over, "I don't know, I may have said something different, I don't know, maybe." Meanwhile, Sung-Hee was ready to kill me. Shooting daggers with her eyes, she kept hissing, sotto voce, "Didn't you even bother to look at the 3500 material?"

By the time I got up for redirect, I was furious: mad at myself, mad at Mario, mad at Larry for turning the trial into a game of gotcha. Barely in control of my emotions, my voice quivering with anger, I elicited from Mario, for a second time, the basic facts of the case: that Scarpa was a mob captain, that he ran the Scarpa Crew, and that he had ordered Mario to murder five different men. After five minutes Mario burst into tears, and that was the end of the government's case.

WHEN SUNG-HEE AND I RESTED, after three weeks of testimony, our mood was guardedly optimistic. Obviously, we had hit some bumps. We felt sure, however, that we had convinced the jury that Scarpa was a murderous mobster. And that put Larry Silverman in a bind.

In every criminal case the most important strategic decision for the defense is whether the defendant should testify or not. Some lawyers think that if the defendant does not testify, the jury will conclude he has something to hide. Other lawyers believe that it is better to take potshots at the government's evidence than to put forward evidence of their own, particularly when, as is common in criminal cases, the defendant is stupid, likely to make blunders on the stand.

In *Scarpa*, this decision was particularly complex. On the one hand, there was a strong argument that Scarpa *had* to testify. Scarpa's best strategy was to raise the Scarpa-DeVecchio scandal and hope for jury nullification. After all, that approach had worked 100 percent of the time in prior Colombo Family trials. Silverman's effort to broach the issue had been derailed, however, by one of Sung-Hee's best ideas. When we put together the government's witness list, way back at the start of the summer, Sung-Hee had insisted that we leave off every witness, no matter how useful to our case, who possessed any firsthand information about the Scarpa Senior–DeVecchio relationship, not just cooperator Carmine Sessa but every FBI agent from the tainted Colombo Squad as well. Because of this tactic, Silverman made almost no progress raising the issue. When he asked our witnesses about DeVecchio, the only answer he ever got was: "I don't know anything about that." Because our tactic worked, there was only one way for Silverman to get his gold-plated nullification defense into evidence: Scarpa would have to testify and raise the issue himself.

On the other hand, conventional trial lawyer wisdom suggested that Scarpa should remain silent—indeed, *had* to remain silent. On two separate occasions in the 1990s—once before his indictment in 1994 and once during his fake cooperation against Ramzi Yousef in 1996—Scarpa had discussed his life with FBI agents investigating Lin DeVecchio. At the second proffer, Scarpa bizarrely confessed to being involved in several murder conspiracies. He told the agents that he had supervised the digging of graves for murder victims and that on the day limousine driver Alfred Longobardi was killed, he had been part of the hit team, riding in a crash car, responsible for crashing into the police if they tried to chase and arrest the fleeing shooters. Scarpa even admitted that he had attempted to kill Longobardi himself, months before the successful slaying, but had abandoned his plan when Longobardi's son appeared at the murder scene. The agents were flabbergasted that Scarpa would incriminate himself, but they quietly wrote down everything he said.

To this day it is unclear to me why Scarpa made such a foolish mistake. Maybe he was trying to boost his credibility. Or he may have thought that since his "cooperation" was going so well, he would never be held accountable for his crimes anyway, so his confession would not matter. Regardless, his blunder had a huge impact on the trial.

According to the proffer agreements that Scarpa had signed before the two interviews, the government was not allowed to use these devastating statements in its case-in-chief. This gave Scarpa some protection and an incentive to talk. The agreements authorized us, however, to use his statements in cross-examination if Scarpa ever testified at trial. Thus, if Scarpa took the stand, we could blast him out of the water with his own words.

In short, Silverman was caught in a terrible bind. If Scarpa took the Fifth, he might very well lose the trial. But if he testified, his prior proffer statements about participating in murders would be thrown back in his face. As the trial went on, Sung-Hee and I increasingly wondered: How would Silverman resolve this dilemma?

ON OCTOBER 13, 1998, Gregory Scarpa, Jr., took the stand to testify in his own defense. His testimony was a clever mix of truth and perjury. He claimed that when he was a teenager, his father took him aside and told him he worked for the FBI, and that his mobster identity was just a cover (false). Whenever the local police got interested in the Scarpa Crew, DeVecchio and the FBI repeatedly intervened, tipping it off to wiretaps, raids, and arrests in order to keep Scarpa Senior in business (true to a degree). Scarpa told the jury that his own mafia career had been FBI cover as well, designed to hide his father's work as an informant (false). Though he joined the Colombo Family (true), he did so on the orders of Lin DeVecchio (false). Scarpa bolstered his claims by describing, in fascinating detail, his antiterrorism work for the FBI. He had cooperated against Ramzi Yousef (sort of true), he told our jurors, preventing an attack on the 1996 Atlanta Olympics and saving the lives of several prosecutors and judges (false).

Scarpa was a good storyteller. When he wanted to emphasize a point, he would pause, turn toward the jurors, look them in the eye, and gesture with his hands. While he spoke, I watched the jury closely. Sometimes, when a defendant testifies, the jurors' body language is very revealing: they scowl, roll their eyes, cross their arms, or snicker. The Scarpa jurors showed no such signs of skepticism. They did not seem hostile, just puzzled. I could tell they did not know what to make of Scarpa's story.

At this moment Silverman could have concluded Scarpa's testimony, relying on what lawyers call an authorization defense; though his client may have committed crimes, he had done so with the express approval of the government. Indeed, I personally thought Larry should have stopped here because the jury looked, if not convinced, at least interested. That gave him just enough leverage to try to win the case in his closing argument. Silverman, however, had other ideas. As soon as he finished the DeVecchio and Yousef stories, Scarpa shifted gears and deployed an entirely new defense, the "I'm totally innocent, Daddy did it" defense. For half an hour Scarpa repeatedly denied he had ever committed any serious crimes in his life. He blamed everything on his father. Here's one exchange:

SILVERMAN: Numbers business?
SCARPA: Senior.
SILVERMAN: Gambling?
SCARPA: Mazza and DelMasto and Senior.
SILVERMAN: The marijuana business?
SCARPA: Nicky DiCarlo and Senior.

He took the same tack on murder. Did he kill Bucky DiLenoardi? "No, sir." Alfred Longobardi? "No, sir." Sal Cardaci? "No, sir." Asked whether he had killed Joe Brewster, Scarpa replied: "That's sick, sir . . . I was devastated." Scarpa claimed that he tried to save lives, not take them. In one situation, he intervened with his father. "I says, 'Dad,'—because I know where his mind is—I said[,] 'Dad, don't even—this kid is a beautiful kid, alright?'"

Scarpa finished with a description of his father: "He was—he was a real feared person. Everybody feared him. He was like a—he was like a Caesar. You know what I'm saying? With guys all around him, muscle guys around him. And whatever he said, this [gesturing], this [gesturing], people would jump. He controlled everybody and everything."

By the time Scarpa finished, the mood in the courtroom had changed. The jurors were clearly shocked by Scarpa's blanket denials. On several occasions they looked over at Sung-Hee and me, incredulous, almost as if they expected us to leap out of our chairs and denounce him as a liar. To me, it seemed obvious that Scarpa had overplayed his hand.

By denying any criminal wrongdoing whatsoever, he had gone too far and damaged his credibility.

At this point, you might wonder: If Silverman was such an experienced attorney, why did he let Scarpa put on this totally lame defense? Consider the following story:

On July 11, 1987, at 4:15 p.m., mafia defense lawyer Barry Slotnick was getting into his chauffeured car on Broadway. All of a sudden, a man wearing a motorcycle helmet, a black visor covering his face, jumped out at him, swinging a baseball bat spiked with nails. The bat smashed into Slotnick's left wrist, breaking bones and puncturing his skin. The bloodied Slotnick tried to run. When a bystander came to his aid, the assailant jumped onto a motorcycle and raced away into traffic. Later the FBI learned that the assault had been ordered by Colombo boss Carmine Persico. Slotnick had been representing some Colombo Family defendants, and their trials had ended in convictions. Persico was angered by Slotnick's courtroom tactics, so he decided to send a message: try harder!

The Slotnick assault was an extraordinary, but not unprecedented, event. Other mob lawyers have faced similar pressure. In 1989, for example, John Gotti threatened to throw his attorney Gerry Shargel down an elevator shaft. Needless to say, incidents like these turn the normal attorney-client relationship upside down. Mob lawyers often let their clients call all the shots. If Scarpa wanted to tell the jury that he was pure as driven snow, Silverman was unlikely to object.

As for Scarpa himself, I'll bet the pressure of the trial interfered with his judgment. For three weeks, he had been forced to sit quietly in his chair while government witnesses called him a killer. He was probably feeling desperate. Getting up in front of the jury to deny everything probably felt great, though I think it damaged his case.

WHEN JUDGE RAGGI told the jury it was time for cross-examination, the jurors sat up in their chairs, eyes flashing with interest, eager to see the confrontation. By Justice Department tradition, the senior prosecutor always questions the defendant, for it is typically the decisive moment at trial. In *Scarpa*, that meant cross fell to Sung-Hee. When, however, Judge Raggi asked us to proceed, I stood up instead.

To this day I am not really certain why Sung-Hee asked me to do the cross. She is a very rational lawyer, so she must have figured it was best for the case. As lead attorney she was weighed down with a load of responsibilities, so getting one off her plate must have been a relief. She may also have figured that Scarpa was unlikely to testify, given his incriminating proffer statements. Still, she was taking an enormous risk. I was a total rookie, with only two trials under my belt. If I screwed up the cross and we lost the trial, her decision would be heavily criticized.

When I stood up to cross Scarpa that afternoon, I had two immediate goals. The first was easy to accomplish. Under the Federal Rules of Evidence, I could not call an FBI rebuttal witness to recount Scarpa's incriminating confession unless Scarpa denied making those statements. So right off the bat, I asked Scarpa whether he had ever told the FBI about his involvement in murders: planning attacks; digging graves; driving crash cars; attempting to kill Longobardi. Scarpa replied that he had never been involved in any violence whatsoever during his years in the Colombo Family. He had never even punched anyone, he said, except once, when ordered to by Lin DeVecchio. Scarpa's claim left me totally exasperated. How can you be in the mob for more than two decades and never even slap someone? "What?" I blurted out. "Is the Colombo Family kind of like the Boy Scouts?" The jury laughed out loud. Judge Raggi kept a poker face and told Scarpa he didn't have to answer.

My second goal was more complicated and requires a little context. When a man joins the mafia, he takes a vow of *omertà*, or silence, never to talk to outsiders about life in the mob. Because of this vow, mafia members never testify in court. When Scarpa got up on the stand, he was breaking new ground, the first "made" or fully initiated mafia member in history, I was told, to testify at his own criminal trial. I was breaking new ground too, for I was the first AUSA to take a crack at a sworn mafioso on the stand. Because my situation was novel, there were no clear models to follow. No one knew what would work, or not work, when you tried to cross-examine a mafia capo.

Prior to trial, Sung-Hee and I met with Andrew Weissmann to talk about cross. In the meeting Andrew, the most experienced mafia prosecutor in the office, came up with a clever proposal. "When you get up there, ask Scarpa detailed questions about the personnel and operations of the Colombo Family. Ask him to name the current boss of the family, to disclose the identity of persons involved in loansharking, and to describe his initiation ceremony." Andrew believed these questions would put Scarpa in a bind. "He can't answer any of them, because it will violate his vow of *omertà*. And when he refuses to answer, it will prove that he took that vow, prove that he is in fact in the mob." I nodded. That seemed to make sense.

"And if he does answer, we win too," Andrew said with a laugh. "If he identifies Allie Persico as boss of the family, Allie will have him whacked!" Andrew was joking—sort of.

We decided to follow Andrew's game plan, and the result was a total fiasco. Scarpa, it turned out, did not give a damn about *omertà*, and he appeared to recognize belatedly that his blanket denial of guilt in his direct testimony had not been convincing. So he adopted a new approach, one that proved risky but fruitful. He denied any involvement in homicides, the core of our case against him and which carried the risk of life in prison. But to my amazement, he freely admitted in response to my questions that he had long been a member of the mob. He identified Persico as the boss of the Colombo Family, described his initiation ceremony, and conceded that when he became a mafia member, he promised to kill on demand. He ratted out his own fellow crew members, provided the names of several other Colombo Family capos, and admitted to committing bank burglaries, a crime not charged in the indictment. In short, he appeared honest and candid, willing to admit some guilt, and this greatly boosted his credibility. I thought he seemed very convincing, as if he were trying to be helpful. As for me, I was dying up there at the podium, and I was deeply grateful when Judge Raggi decided to halt the trial for the night. It was close to five o'clock when we paused, so time may have driven her decision, but I also sensed some pity. She could tell I was getting slaughtered.

As we walked out of the courtroom, Sung-Hee lashed out. "You have to do better than that," she snapped, with a hard edge in her voice.

I nodded numbly; I knew she was right. When I got back to my office, I didn't tarry. I packed up my briefcase, walked out the door, and headed for home. I needed some quiet time to gather my thoughts and rally my spirits. Later someone remarked, "Andrew's idea was pretty clever, but you know, he would never have done that cross in one of his own cases. Too reckless."

Back at the MCC, Scarpa was exultant. The next morning a jailhouse informant at the MCC called his prosecutor, my friend Dwight Holton. The informant told Dwight, "That guy Scarpa, he was bragging about how good he was doing. He was saying, 'I kicked Kroger's ass!'" And it was true. He did.

———

THAT NIGHT, soaking in the bathtub, I reflected on the day's events. There was no point in beating myself up. I had to focus on the task at hand. To that end I tried to analyze what had gone wrong. The answer was simple: I had ignored the basic rules of trial lawyering.

When I first joined the EDNY, the office sent me and a few other rookies down to Washington, D.C., to attend the Justice Department's weeklong trial advocacy training program. The course was, for the most part, a total waste of time. Very few topflight AUSAs are interested in leaving the courtroom to join the DOJ's corps of instructors. Most of the classes were dull, and some were downright unhelpful. There was one great exception, however, a lecture delivered by a prosecutor from Virginia I will call "Thompson" on the art of cross-examination. For one brief hour Thompson told us everything we needed to know to conduct a simple, competent cross. Today, years later, I can still repeat much of what he told us verbatim.

"Most young prosecutors," Thompson intoned at the start of the lecture, "think cross-examination is about having a Perry Mason moment, when the defendant breaks down under relentless questioning and admits his guilt to the world. Look, that's never gonna happen. Well, maybe it will happen once in your career, but that's not your goal. You don't win a trial on cross, you win it in your case-in-chief, with your own witnesses and your own evidence. When you cross a defendant, all you want to do is not lose, and that means play it safe. Select one basic theme, force the defendant to admit some facts that help establish that theme, and then get out quick."

Thompson also gave us some basic rules about technique. The most important, he stressed, was always to use leading questions, questions that can be answered only with a yes or a no. If you ignore that rule, he told us, the defendant will make you pay. Imagine, for example, that you want to prove that the defendant was at home on a particular night. Never ask, "Where were you on the night of January twenty-fourth?" That kind of open-ended query gives the defendant a chance to deliver a self-serving answer. "Well, after a tough day at work, earning money to put food on the table for my family, I went home to play with my kids." Instead, you should ask, "On the night of January twenth-fourth, you were at home, correct?" This keeps a defendant's testimony headed in the precise direction you want, so the jury can follow what you are trying to prove without getting distracted. It also shows the jury that you are in control.

Thompson also stressed style. "Sound confident, like you know what you are doing. You are an Assistant United States Attorney. You represent the United States in that courtroom. The jury will trust you—they want to trust you—and they will take their signals from you. If you seem panicked by the defendant's testimony, they will panic too. But if you seem totally unsurprised and act as if the defendant's claims are a bunch of lies, then the jury will believe your case is still in good shape."

That night, immersed in my bubble bath, I realized that my cross of Scarpa had broken every one of Thompson's cardinal rules. My rambling questions about the Colombo Family were open-ended, not leading, and conveyed no clear theme or point. The next day, I needed to go back to basics. I went to bed early that night, got up at 4:00 a.m., and started to work while it was still dark outside, writing a new cross. By 9:00 I was in the courtroom, ready to go.

———

THAT MORNING, as our starting time drew near, I felt a slight buzz, a change in the courtroom atmosphere. I looked up and saw that the gallery was packed to capacity: reporters, lawyers, clerks, judges. The whole courthouse community had heard that a capo was on cross and wanted to watch the fireworks. As I looked out at the crowd, I saw Judge John Gleeson, who before his appointment to the bench had convicted John Gotti, and his presence gave me a boost.

As the jury filed in, I laid out on the podium several pieces of paper, my new set of cross-examination questions. This was just for insurance.

I had spent the last hour memorizing them, and I knew I would not need my notes. I looked up at the witness stand. Scarpa looked relaxed and happy, as if he were home free. As soon as Judge Raggi told me to go ahead, I went after Scarpa, hard. My theme? That Scarpa was a violent thug.

KROGER: Mr. Scarpa, do you recall that in June of 1991, you were incarcerated at Lewisburg?

SCARPA: Yes.

KROGER: Do you remember someone with the name "Cottone"?

SCARPA: Cottone, no[,] sir, but if it is Sal, maybe.

KROGER: Did you assault Mr. Cottone at Lewisburg?

SCARPA: Mr. Cottone attacked me, sir.

When Scarpa gave this answer, I played an unethical trick. I ostentatiously looked down at the podium, picked up a piece of paper, read it silently to myself in front of the jury, and then walked toward Scarpa, the paper in my hand, trying to look as menacing as I could. I paused a few feet away from him and barked, "Is it your testimony that you didn't"— and here I looked down at the paper again—"approach inmate Cottone and push him backwards to the ground?" My goal here was threefold: to show the jury that I was not afraid of Scarpa and was prepared to confront him physically with the report if he kept up his lies; to make Scarpa realize that yesterday's free lunch was over; and, most important of all, to let the jury see that I was not making this allegation up but was reading from an official report. Judge Raggi understood exactly what I was doing. She immediately interrupted. "Mr. Kroger, I am going to ask you to question from the podium. I am also going to remind you not to read in front of the jury from documents that are not in evidence. Go ahead."

I returned to the podium, turned, and confronted Scarpa again.

KROGER: When he was on the ground, did you kick him in the groin?

SCARPA: Excuse me, sir?

KROGER: When he was on the ground, did you kick him in the groin?

SCARPA: No[,] sir.

KROGER: Once he was on the ground, did you hit him in the face?

SCARPA: No, sir.

For the next fifteen minutes I battered Scarpa with leading questions. Didn't you savagely beat up Vic Amuso? Didn't you get caught with an eight-inch knife while in prison? Didn't you dig graves to hide bodies? Didn't you plan to kill Cosmo Catanzano? These questions accomplished my primary goal, to set a new tone for the day. In response, Scarpa repeatedly denied any involvement with violence. I could tell, however, that he wasn't having any fun, that my questions were hitting their target. His face grew pale, and he stopped looking me in the eye, staring down at his own hands instead. Sometimes he paused and glanced over at silent, stone-faced Judge Raggi, as if he were looking for help. Soon he started to weave and dodge. He refused to respond to my leading questions directly. Instead, he would interrupt, start a rambling story, or offer to provide "context." Each time he tried to wiggle away, I cut him off. "Just answer my question, Mr. Scarpa." "Mr. Scarpa, just answer my question, please, yes or no." Eventually, Scarpa started to wilt, and the tone of his answers changed. When I accused him of involvement in attacks, he did not deny participation outright, in his original self-righteous tone. Instead, he replied quite weakly, "I don't remember that."

Finally, when I felt he was on the ropes, I sprang my last trap. In his direct testimony Scarpa had claimed to have known since he was a teenager that his father was an FBI informant. In his 1994 proffer with the FBI, however, Scarpa had said nothing about this, even when asked directly. So I closed my cross by stressing this point.

KROGER: Mr. Scarpa, you stated you had known your father was an informant since 1970?

SCARPA: Probably before, sir.

KROGER: Do you recall a proffer session in 1994 with FBI agents?

SCARPA: Oh, yes, yes.

KROGER: It was an interview, correct?

SCARPA: Yes.

KROGER: You and the FBI?

SCARPA: Yes.

KROGER: And you were asked to tell them what you knew about your father, correct?

SCARPA: Sir, at that point I thought I was being set up to be killed, they came to the penitentiary . . .

KROGER [interrupting]: Mr. Scarpa . . .

JUDGE RAGGI: Mr. Scarpa, try to answer the questions that you are asked.

SCARPA: Yes, sorry.

KROGER: FBI agents came, is that correct?

SCARPA: Yes.

KROGER: They asked you whether you knew he was an informant, correct?

SCARPA [With panic in his voice]: I don't know what they asked me. I didn't hear them. I didn't acknowledge nothin', that's how set up I was to be killed, sir.

KROGER: Is it your testimony, Mr. Scarpa, that you didn't tell them at that time, that you really didn't know anything about your father and his relationship with the FBI?

SCARPA [whining]: I don't remember that. I may have, I don't know . . .

Throughout my cross, Sung-Hee had been watching the jury closely, trying to assess their mood. Now she passed me a note: "Wrap it up." I asked my last few questions, sat down, and we all took a break. Sung-Hee never said much about my cross that morning, but in my heart I knew I had taken care of business. I did not have a Perry Mason moment. Scarpa did not break down and confess. But I beat him up a bit, landed a few good blows, made him look deceptive, and changed the momentum of the trial. Years later the office circulated my cross of Scarpa as a model for young attorneys to follow.

———

WHEN SCARPA SAT DOWN, Silverman faced a choice: up the ante or fold. Silverman chose the former option and called retired FBI agent Lin DeVecchio to the stand. I had never seen DeVecchio before, and I was curious to see what such a controversial man looked like. I have to say his appearance was impressive. Now in his fifties, he was tall and held himself ramrod straight, with a full head of curly hair, military-style mustache, long nose, and sharp-eyed, almost arrogant look on his face. When he walked to the witness stand, he seemed very calm, in full command of his emotions. He did not look like a criminal. He did not look as if he had anything to hide. I remember thinking: This is going to be interesting.

Before the jury entered the courtroom, DeVecchio took the Fifth in a loud, self-confident voice, refusing to answer any questions on the ground that he might incriminate himself. Once, however, he had been immunized, he had no choice but to testify.* The result was one of the most bizarre hours I ever observed in court. Silverman thought he could show that DeVecchio was corrupt, that he had been helping, not stopping, the Scarpa Crew commit crimes. Instead, his tactic totally backfired. DeVecchio denied any misconduct whatsoever and did so in an incredibly convincing manner. Stern, precise, and indignant, he asserted again and again that he had never violated government laws and regulations, that Scarpa Senior had been kept under close control and that as soon as evidence existed that Scarpa Senior was up to no good, he had been arrested, convicted, and jailed until his death. DeVecchio came off as a good agent, perhaps even a good man. Watching the jurors, I became convinced they believed that the FBI had done nothing wrong. Indeed, he almost convinced me.

DeVecchio's testimony was great for the government, undercutting Scarpa's defense, but it made me very uncomfortable. Normally, you win cases when the jury learns the truth. Here, however, the jury was not learning the true story of the Scarpa Senior–DeVecchio relationship. In this situation Sung-Hee and I faced a dilemma. Should we try to steer the jury straight and harm our own case? Or let DeVecchio's testimony stand and allow the jury to remain in the dark? Without discussion, we took the latter course. We were under an ethical obligation to prevent

---

*Only the government can immunize a witness from criminal prosecution. Normally, we would not have immunized one of Scarpa's witnesses; if the witness took the Fifth, that was Scarpa's problem. There is, however, a rule that states that if the government has immunized a witness in a prior proceeding, for its own benefit, then it has to immunize the witness again if the defense wants to call him. Years before, the government had granted DeVecchio immunity when it first began to investigate his conduct during the Colombo Family War. Now we had to do the same for Scarpa.

our own witnesses from committing perjury, but we had not called DeVecchio to the stand; Silverman had. Silverman was privy to all the same negative information about DeVecchio that we had. If he could not prove DeVecchio was lying, that was his problem. To this day I am not sure what else we could have done. Still, it felt wrong. The paths of truth and justice are not supposed to part ways. But in this case they did.

———

WHEN SILVERMAN CONCLUDED the defense case, Sung-Hee and I felt great. My second day of cross had battered Scarpa's credibility, and DeVecchio's convincing claim that the FBI had done nothing illegal or improper helped sink the Scarpa Defense. More to the point, we expected our rebuttal case—two FBI agents testifying about Scarpa's prior confessions—to be devastating. Unfortunately, our optimism was misplaced. Before we could call our rebuttal witnesses, we got hit with a bombshell.

During my cross of Scarpa, I was shocked when he denied making any statements to the FBI about his past involvement in murders. I was not surprised he was lying—I expected that—but it seemed such a stupid tactical blunder. How, I wondered, does Scarpa think he can get away with deceiving the jury when he knows I have FBI agents waiting in the wings, ready to contradict him? What's the trick? Now we got our answer.

On October 14, the day after DeVecchio testified, Silverman tried to block our whole rebuttal case. Silverman told Judge Raggi that he had been present at both interviews with the FBI and that he had taken extensive and detailed notes. He had now reviewed those notes. Scarpa, he told the court, had never confessed that he had ordered graves to be dug, driven a crash car, or tried to kill Alfred Longobardi. Moreover, such a confession would have been impossible, for "if he did start talking about anything that I felt would be incriminating, I would have stopped him in his tracks." In short, the government's claim that Scarpa had confessed to murder was made up, a corrupt effort to frame his client. To emphasize the seriousness of his contentions, Silverman told the court he would put his objections in an affidavit under oath and submit his notes to the court.

Silverman concluded with a clever gambit. He told Judge Raggi that if the government's agents testified about Scarpa's alleged statements, Silverman himself would have to take the stand to defend his client. And since, under the code of professional ethics, a lawyer cannot testify at the same trial in which he serves as an advocate, the result would be a mistrial. To avoid the hardship of a second trial—a pretty dire prospect for all of us, after years of delay and a month of hard work in court— Silverman asked Judge Raggi to preclude the government witnesses from testifying at all.

When Silverman finished his presentation, I sat stunned in my chair. If Silverman's motion was granted, the FBI would be silenced, and Scarpa would get away with his lies, perhaps get away with murder. Judge Raggi's discussion of the legal issue was, as always, succinct and precise:

> *The government has a witness who is prepared to testify under oath that Mr. Scarpa made certain admissions about his involvement in the Longobardi murder during this meeting. Mr. Silverman, who was present, tells me that he is prepared to testify under oath that his client made no such statement. If we were before trial, there would be an easy resolution to this. I would have to relieve Mr. Silverman and appoint other counsel so that he would be available to Mr. Scarpa to call on this point. But we are not before trial, we are four weeks into trial on the defense case. And I am not interested in declaring a mistrial. I gather the defense is saying that since Mr. Silverman can't testify, the government's witness should not be allowed to testify.*

Judge Raggi's analysis suggested that she was leaning toward precluding our witnesses, since it was the only way to avoid a mistrial. She did not, however, rule on the subject. Instead, she sent the jury home and let us go back to our offices. When Sung-Hee and I got there, we convened a meeting of the top lawyers in the EDNY to analyze and assess our options.

That night was one of the most depressing I ever spent as a prosecutor. For hours we sat around Andrew Weissmann's office, trying to find a way out, but Silverman had trapped us, and none of our alternatives looked good. We did not want a mistrial; after all, we thought we were going to win. At the same time, preclusion of our rebuttal case would be a disaster, for Scarpa's horrible lies would go unchallenged. In my cross, I had claimed that Scarpa had made incriminating statements to the

FBI. If we could not call witnesses to back me up, the jury might conclude that Scarpa was telling the truth, that my assertions were just empty posturing. Indeed, Silverman would be legally entitled to tell the jury that there was not one shred of evidence that his client had confessed. That argument alone might put our verdict in jeopardy.

For the rest of the evening, Sung-Hee and I debated the issue back and forth with our supervisors, trying to discover a good solution. Finally, around 11:00 p.m., we reached a sobering conclusion. Scarpa, we believed, had to be convicted; that was an overwhelming public priority. He had gambled when he testified, hoping that he could get away with blatant lies because our rebuttal case would be blocked. We could not let his strategy succeed. Around midnight we faxed a letter to Judge Raggi's chambers, asking, with regret, for a mistrial. We told the court that we thought our rebuttal testimony was essential to our case, given Scarpa's lies on the stand. We were not prepared to go forward unless we could call our rebuttal witnesses. We would rather do the entire trial all over again.

The next morning the courtroom felt like a morgue. Judge Raggi sent the jury to its deliberation room. Then she turned to our motion for a mistrial. She asked Silverman if he was willing to present his testimony to the jury on paper, anonymously, but Larry refused. He insisted on his right to be a witness. Judge Raggi then told us she wanted time to assess the situation. She sent the jury home early for the second day in a row and called a recess until the afternoon. As the jurors filed out of the courtroom, I thought, with a sinking feeling: Well, that's it. Train wreck. Case over.

———

LATER THAT AFTERNOON Judge Raggi, Scarpa, and the lawyers gathered in the courtroom to discuss the future of the case. From the moment the judge swept in, I felt that the atmosphere had changed, though how I could not articulate. Raggi's courtroom deputy called us to order: "Case on trial, United States versus Gregory Scarpa, Jr." Then Judge Raggi did something remarkable: she asked all the spectators and reporters in the courtoom to leave and had the Marshals shut and lock the doors. To me, this was shocking, since open and public trials are guaranteed in the Constitution. But Raggi had her reasons. Once the doors were sealed, Raggi spoke.

When matters come up relatively quickly, as this one has, the parties and the court are left to try and deal with alternatives rather rapidly. I proposed one this morning. I have this afternoon also taken Mr. Silverman up on his suggestion, made early when matters arose, to look at his notes, myself. Having done that, having given the matter some thought and recognizing the public interest in the case being brought to a conclusion, the government interest in putting in relevant evidence, I think that for me to decide to preclude evidence would not be appropriate without a full hearing as to exactly what evidence Mr. Silverman could provide his client if he is available as a witness.

Judge Raggi's proposal mystified me. A hearing? Outside the presence of the jury? What for? The facts were not in question. We already knew what Silverman would say, from his repeated representations to the court and the affidavit he had filed under oath: that Scarpa had never made any incriminating statements and that if he had, Silverman would have stopped him. So what would a hearing accomplish? Wouldn't it just waste time?

With some judges, I might have asked for an explanation. Judge Raggi, however, was not to be trifled with. Besides, she was brilliant. If she wanted to hold a hearing, there must be a good reason for it.

To prepare for the hearing, Sung-Hee requested a copy of all of Silverman's notes from the interviews. Judge Raggi smiled, something she rarely did in court. Then she told us that she thought only a couple of pages would be needed. She asked her clerks to copy just those pages and then to pass them out to us. "I think," she said, in a coy voice, "we will all be able to speak more intelligently when the government has that much."

For the next five minutes, while we waited for the notes to be copied, Sung-Hee and I quietly discussed our strategy for the hearing. Suddenly Silverman piped up.

SILVERMAN: Your Honor, do you have a copy of my notes in front of you?

RAGGI: I just sent them to be copied.

SILVERMAN: I noticed for the first time—I don't know what
   relevance it has—but if I could hand up to the Court my
   copy. I didn't notice this before. On the right side of page
   two . . .

RAGGI [interrupting abruptly]: I saw that. I know what you are
   referring to . . .

SILVERMAN: I don't know what . . . it has no reference point.

I looked up. Silverman's face was bright red, and something was
wrong with his voice. He looked surprised, perhaps mortified, but something about his appearance struck me oddly. I remember thinking: It's
almost like he is acting, like he is trying to look surprised.

At that moment a clerk bustled in with several copies of the notes. He
handed one copy to the judge and one to Silverman and Scarpa. Then he
walked over to the government table and put a copy into my hands.

I have a bad back, and in trial, it often goes haywire, the result of
stress and hours of sitting. So I put the notes on the table in front of
Sung-Hee, where she could read them easily, and then stood behind her
chair, trying to read over her shoulder. Before I could make any progress,
Judge Raggi interrupted me with an arch look.

RAGGI: Are you reading the notes, Mr. Kroger? Have you been
   given a redacted copy?

KROGER: Yes, Your Honor.

RAGGI: I would suggest you sit down.

Judge Raggi's request was bizarre. Why did I need to sit? Was standing disrespectful? But I figured, what the hell, she's a federal judge. I
should do what she says. I pulled up a chair, sat down, and refocused on
Silverman's notes. After a few seconds, I got the judge's joke. I turned to
Sung-Hee and quietly muttered, "Holy shit, I don't believe this." There,
in the notes, as plain as day, were references to driving crash cars, digging
graves, and, a little more cryptically, but still quite clearly, the foiled early
attempt to kill Alfred Longobardi. Sung-Hee and I just looked at each
other, stunned. There was nothing to say. Silverman, it appeared, had
been trying to get away with a massive fraud.

While we were absorbing the truth about the notes, Raggi spoke once more from the bench. A few moments before, she had been making sly jokes. Now her air of amusement had disappeared, clearly replaced by anger.

> *I think the easiest thing I can say is that the notes . . . I find the notes . . . perplexing . . . in light of the affirmation that was submitted and the representations that were made to the Court, but I am prepared to have my confusion cleared up at a hearing. I mean, when a statement is in a note like "Longobardi—Junior tried to act (son)," given the representation the government has made about Mr. Scarpa Jr. trying to kill Longobardi but stopping when the son was on the scene, I am not sure I do understand how Mr. Silverman would give testimony at odds with what the government has proposed to put in in rebuttal. As I said, I am prepared to hold a hearing, tomorrow morning, 10:00.*

With that she dismissed us for the day. As I walked out, I realized why she had emptied the courtroom. Larry was an old friend of hers, and furious as she was, she did not want to embarrass him.

That night, for the first time since the trial began, Sung-Hee and I quit work early and went to get a drink with a bunch of our colleagues. For several hours we ate fried calamari and talked about Silverman's scam, trying to understand what had happened. One explanation was outright fraud: that Silverman had intentionally lied to Judge Raggi in an effort to derail our case. A second theory was sloppiness: that Silverman had denied that Scarpa had confessed before carefully reviewing his notes, and that once he had started down that road, he had found it difficult to back off his inaccurate position. A third possibility was fear: that Scarpa had threatened Silverman into making his false representations.

That night we did not reach a conclusion. Andrew Weissmann thought Silverman was simply lying. That seemed incredible to me, but as Andrew noted, strange things happen in mafia trials. Eric Corngold, in contrast, thought it was all a big mistake: that Larry was guilty, perhaps, of carelessness but not fraud. I was confused and did not know what to think. I leaned toward Andrew's explanation. Today, however, I tend to believe Corngold got it right.

Sometimes, when a lawyer makes a bad mistake, he deals with it by simply forgetting what he did. A good lawyer would never have let Scarpa incriminate himself in those FBI interviews; it was a dreadful, dreadful error. Silverman thought, with good reason, that he was an excellent lawyer. To escape from the inevitable cognitive dissonance arising from this tension, he blocked out all recollection of his mistake. When the government claimed that Scarpa had confessed to involvement in murders, Silverman objected strenuously, before bothering to check his notes, because to him, the government's position seemed obviously untrue. He knew in his heart that if Scarpa had started to confess, a good lawyer like him would have stopped the session immediately!

As a trial lawyer I have come to recognize that witnesses are incredibly unreliable. Humans often remember not what happened but what they wish had happened. What we label "a memory" is often self-deception. Perhaps that is what happened with Silverman.

———

THE NEXT DAY PASSED IN A FLASH. In the morning Judge Raggi asked Silverman to take the stand. Sung-Hee was licking her chops, looking forward to cross. Silverman, however, refused to testify, for he wanted to avoid Sung-Hee. Instead, he proposed that Judge Raggi ask him any questions she thought were pertinent. This "interview" ended in farce. Every time Judge Raggi asked about his notes, Silverman replied, "My client has directed me not to explain that," or, "My client prohibits me from commenting on that." This charade gave Raggi the leverage she needed. Quick as lightning, she denied Silverman's motion to preclude our rebuttal witnesses. Then, just as swiftly, she told us to conclude the trial.

Our rebuttal case took only a few hours. I had thought our evidence was dynamite, but in the end it fizzled. The two FBI agents testified about Scarpa's confession, and their testimony should have been devastating, but the jurors just looked bored and confused. After a month in the courtroom and two days off they clearly wanted to go home.

I think our rebuttal fell flat because the jurors found the idea that Scarpa had confessed to murder too bizarre to contemplate. If he had confessed, after all, there wouldn't be a trial, right? I understood how they felt. Unfortunately, I had no way to explain to them that when Scarpa decided to go to trial, he was gambling that he and Silverman would be able to keep his confession secret.

WHEN I FIRST became an AUSA, I was terrified by the prospect of closing a tough case. There are a million potential arguments one could make to a jury. How could I, a rookie, select the one perfect thing to say that would convince the jury to convict my defendants?

By the time I got to *Scarpa*, one year into the job, I realized that this view was naive. In most cases, your strategic options at closing are severely limited by the evidence in the case.

For Silverman, for example, the die had been cast when Scarpa testified. Scarpa had denied committing any serious crimes, blaming everything on his father. Now, at closing, Silverman had no choice but to repeat that argument. He told the jury that Scarpa Senior was the real killer all along, that Billy Meli and Mario Parlagreco had conspired to frame Senior's son because they needed a target to cooperate against after Senior had died, that DeVecchio was corrupt, and that his client was an innocent counterterrorism spy.

My own options were limited as well. When you stripped our case of all the bells and whistles—autopsy reports, crime scene photos, surveillance videos—*Scarpa* remained a straight cooperator case. We were asking the jury to convict the defendant for five murders and six murder conspiracies almost exclusively on the basis of the testimony of his former accomplices. If the jury did not believe our three cooperating witnesses—all admitted killers, all of whom had committed perjury at some point in their criminal careers—they would have to acquit.

Silverman understood that the credibility of our cooperators was the key to the case. As an AUSA Larry had used informants and cooperators all the time. Now, in his own closing, he tried to convince the jury that this practice was corrupt.

> *Right now, Mr. Meli is out on bail. I asked him: "Mr. Meli, didn't you want to start serving your time for the murders?" He has not spent, and I suggest to you, doesn't believe he will spend one day in jail for the multiple murders that he admits, the ones he admits he was involved with. Accomplice testimony—Meli, Parlagreco, Del-Masto—that is typical purchase and sale. The witnesses want to know: [H]ow much money am I going to get? How can I help re-*

duce my criminal exposure? And what kind of sentence? Can I
benefit by saying what would help them most? Now, it sounds repugnant. The reason it does is, it is repugnant. The judicial process
is tainted when someone's factual testimony is bartered like
that . . . What you should look at, ladies and gentlemen, when you
go to deliberate, is: Did the government put on people—Meli, Parlagreco, and DelMasto—that you, in a very important decision in
your life, could rely on, that you could trust?

Larry's arguments made my challenge clear: I had to convince the
jury that Billy, Mario, and Jimmy were honest and could be trusted. If I
failed, we would lose—simple as that.

When you deliver a jury address, it is hard to fake conviction. Juries
can sense insincerity. For that reason, a lawyer should always focus most
of his attention on arguments he personally believes are powerful and
compelling. In *Scarpa*, I asked myself: Why do I trust Billy, Jimmy, and
Mario? The answer, which became the core of my closing argument, was
corroboration.

In federal cases, the prosecutors and agents are never supposed to
show, or tell their witnesses about, the physical evidence in the case. That
way it can be used to prove, independently, that our witnesses are telling
the truth. In my closing, I explained this fact to the jury, and then I spent
an entire hour showing how the testimony of Billy, Mario, and Jimmy
was backed up by specific physical exhibits. Some of the corroboration
was incredibly weak. I spent less than fifteen seconds discussing the 1985
Frezza murder, because there was simply no good evidence to prove the
cooperators were telling the truth about it. In contrast, I spent a solid ten
minutes on the 1987 murder of Joe Brewster because it was by far the
strongest homicide in the case. As you read my argument, ask yourself
this: If you were a juror, would you find my arguments convincing?

Both Billy Meli and Mario Parlagreco told you that the murder of
Joe Brewster was done in a white car. Here's the car from the crime
scene [holding up a photo so the jury could see and pointing].
There's the white car. Mario Parlagreco even said it was parked on
the right side of the road. The car is there [pointing with my index
finger], parked on the right side of the road . . .

Billy Meli told you that the murder was set up through beeper communication. Greg Scarpa Jr. told him that he had been paged by Joe Brewster, and that Meli was supposed to call Brewster back and set up a time at which they should meet. This [holding up a piece of evidence with my left hand] is a piece of paper. As you heard, it was found on the body of Joe Brewster at the time he was murdered, when he was discovered. It's got a number on it. Lo and behold, that number matches [holding up an exhibit with my right hand] the number of a beeper contract, a pager contract made out to Gregory Scarpa, 436 Holton Avenue, Staten Island. They tell you this is how the murder got set up. They are telling you the truth. How do you know it? From this corroboration . . .

Both Mario Parlagreco and Billy Meli told you that Greg Scarpa Jr. was the shooter. That he had been sitting in the front seat. That Joe Saponaro was driving. Greg Scarpa Jr. was on the passenger side. Frank Gargano, who was the investigating officer who investigated the crime scene, told you that in his opinion, the shots would have to have come from the front seat, because rounds were found in the back of the seat, and one was found in the trunk. So they passed through from the front to the back. He also told you that from the placement of the rounds, he was able to draw the conclusion that they were most likely fired from the passenger seat. That's how you know that these two people are telling you the truth about the murder, because when they describe what happened, it's backed up by independent facts.

Billy Meli told you that he supplied the gun that Joe Brewster was killed with. He told you that he took a .38 and slid it underneath the white mat of the car, when he handed it over to Joe Saponaro to be driven. These [I held up a small yellow envelope filled with used bullets] are the bullets that came out of Joe Brewster's body. They are .38's. It's the kind of gun Billy Meli said he left in the car. Again, independent corroboration . . .

Final point about corroboration. Billy Meli testified that not only was the Brewster murder done with a .38 revolver, but the Frezza murder was done with a .38 revolver. Mario Parlagreco said that when he was taught how to kill people by Greg Scarpa Jr., Greg Scarpa Jr. said to always use revolvers because they tend to jam less. How do you know they are telling the truth about who committed these murders? You know because in these cases here [I held up envelopes holding bullets recovered from the DiLeonardi, Brewster, and Longobardi murders] we recovered the spent rounds either in the body of a person who was murdered, or in the car where they were murdered. In each case, the rounds are .38's.

At the end of her closing, the government prosecutor typically asks the jury to return a verdict of guilty. I did that with a twist. After I had made my last argument, I paused for a moment and looked each juror in the eye. Then I said, as earnestly as I could, "Throughout his entire life, Greg Scarpa Jr. has spoken with treachery and acted with violence. When you go back to the jury room, speak truth to his treachery . . . and answer his violence with justice."

Of all three jury arguments, the most interesting by far was Sung-Hee's rebuttal. Normally, the government uses the rebuttal to attack the defendant's case head-on. In *Scarpa*, we did not have that luxury. We could not claim that DeVecchio was completely honest; we did not think he was. We could not argue that Scarpa Senior was not a government informant; he was. And we could not really undercut the terrorism spy story. Though Scarpa was distorting the facts, the core of his story—that he was used as an FBI informant against Ramzi Yousef—was true. This put Sung-Hee in something of a box. To get out of it, she engaged in a first-class piece of trial jujitsu. Instead of discussing Scarpa's story directly, she spent most of her rebuttal attacking Silverman. While Silverman was giving his summation, Sung-Hee sat alertly at our counsel's table, frantically writing notes as he talked and looking up facts in the transcript of prior days' proceedings. Then, in her rebuttal, she pointed out six specific examples of moments when Silverman had misrepresented the facts of the case. This was devastating, for it suggested that Larry was so unreliable his entire closing should be disregarded. Then, to finish, she went after Scarpa himself.

What this defendant did on the stand, both a week ago when he first testified, and then again today, was to make a mockery of the criminal justice system, to make it seem like he can just fabricate things and convince a jury of average citizens such as yourselves *that there was this government cover-up, that he was authorized to commit all these crimes, that he had a career in the Colombo Family for over twenty years in which all he ever did was slap one person, and that at the direction of the FBI. He made a mockery of the criminal justice system. Ladies and gentlemen, don't let him get the last laugh.* *

WHEN THE SCARPA JURY disappeared to deliberate, we expected it to be out for several days at least, for it faced a tough decision. Neither the government nor Scarpa had presented an overwhelming case. Scarpa's claim of complete innocence was, I thought, almost impossible for a jury to swallow. At the same time, our case was vulnerable to criticism as well. If the jury agreed with Larry Silverman that deals with informants were improper, we were sunk. Even if we cleared that hurdle, we still faced a big challenge, for we were asking the jurors to convict a man for murder on the basis of the word of three admitted killers with track records of perjury and a potential incentive to lie. I had tried to make our cooperators look as reliable as I could, but there are limits to what you can do. If the jurors looked closely at the "independent proof" I highlighted in my closing, they would discern a potentially fatal weakness. Most of our corroboration proved only that Billy and Mario were killers. It was much less convincing on the core issue, whether Scarpa had been involved in these homicides as well.

For the next several days Scarpa, Silverman, Sung-Hee, and I gathered in the courtroom to wait. We were not a happy group. Scarpa seemed to have lost his ebullience; he no longer tried to catch my eye or crack a joke. Gray-faced and weary, he sat quietly in his chair. I think the enormity of the situation had finally hit him. Sung-Hee was equally out of sorts. She was so furious at Silverman for the "proffer notes" fiasco she

----

*Actually, Scarpa did get the last laugh. As soon as Sung-Hee sat down, Larry Silverman objected to her final comment, which he claimed was prejudicial. Judge Raggi agreed. She told the jury: "These remarks could be interpreted as appealing to your emotions, rather than your reason, and it's improper to do so . . . And so, I now strike the last remarks made by the prosecutor in rebuttal summation. I order you to disregard them in your deliberations and I instruct you to focus your attention on the evidence before you." In some offices, Sung-Hee's tactic might be viewed as an error. In the EDNY, however, she generally received praise. There is an old saying in the office, attributed, whether correctly or not I don't know, to John Gleeson: if you are not drawing objections, you are not trying hard enough.

could barely speak to him. When she had to ask him a question about deliberations, she dispatched me as her ambassador, so she did not have to talk to him face-to-face. As for me, I was totally exhausted, a burned-out shell. Every couple of hours I slipped out of the courtroom on a coffee run.

While we waited, I was struck, for the first time in my career, by the essential artificiality of criminal trials. In criminal law, the real story is often going on behind the jurors' backs. The rules of evidence, the whims of judges, and the two parties' own tactical judgments whittle away at the evidence. Key exhibits get suppressed, a critical witness takes the Fifth, or a party drops some witnesses from its list, and this, not the evidence heard by the jury, proves decisive.

In our trial, the jury was presented not with the truth but with a carefully tailored, strangely manipulated slice of reality. It never heard the full truth about Lin DeVecchio, never got the real story about Scarpa's fake terror cooperation, did not hear a shred of information about Scarpa's desperate effort to block our rebuttal case, never heard the testimony of Carmine Sessa or Larry Mazza. Whether suppression of all this evidence made it a good or a bad trial is very hard for me to tell. But it certainly kept the jury from knowing the whole story.

———

FRIDAY, OCTOBER 23, 1998. When the trial began, exactly one month before, we were enjoying an Indian summer. Now it was fall, a cold gray morning in Brooklyn. In Courtroom Two, the Scarpa jury sent out a note. We all expected this was a verdict. Juries hate to come back to court after the weekend, so many juries reach decisions on Fridays. We gathered in front of the bench, and Judge Raggi read us the note. It said: "Can we have brunch instead of lunch?" For the first time in days the courtroom broke into laughter. Judge Raggi sent the jurors a note in return, telling them that brunch was fine. Later we heard they'd ordered steaks and eggs from our local diner.

Though the note cracked everyone up at first, the tension in the courtroom immediately returned as we tried to follow their reasoning. Why would a jury order brunch? Only one reason came to mind. It was going to render a verdict this morning, before lunchtime, but still wanted one more free meal.

At 11:40 a.m. Jimmy, the court security officer, scuttled into the courtroom and handed a note to Eileen Levine, Judge Raggi's courtroom deputy. While Eileen read the note, Jimmy looked over at me. Silently, he mouthed the word "verdict." It took ten long minutes for us to gather all the relevant parties in the courtroom. As soon as we all were present, Judge Raggi brought in the jury. As the jurors filed in, I glanced over my shoulder at Scarpa. He looked tired and defeated.

When a case goes to verdict, what does a prosecutor think about? In that moment I was not reflecting on Scarpa's crimes or the critical role of the jury in civil society or even about my own career. Indeed, I was not thinking at all. My mind was like a badly scratched CD that endlessly replays the same loop: "please, please, please, please, please . . ." My desire to win was intense. Scarpa's must have been unbearable.

When both the government and the defense have flawed cases, what does a jury do? In theory, the defense should win; the government, after all, has the burden of proof beyond a reasonable doubt. Often, however, the jury decides to "split the baby"—to give each side a partial victory. That happened in *Scarpa*. The jury was clearly uncomfortable convicting a man for murder solely on the basis of cooperator testimony. At the same time, it was convinced that Scarpa was a dangerous mobster who had lied through his teeth. On all five murders, it gave the nod to Scarpa: not proved. But it convicted on almost everything else, finding him guilty of racketeering conspiracy, four murder conspiracies, loansharking, gambling, and tax evasion. Later that afternoon Judge Raggi told Sung-Hee and me not to feel bad; we had tried a very good case. I almost laughed. Feel bad? I was ecstatic! Scarpa was going to jail. "A win," Andrew Weissmann commented, "is a win."

A WEEK AFTER THE TRIAL Sung-Hee and I took Maggie Carmichael and Dayna Better, the two lead FBI agents, out to lunch to celebrate. We could have gone to a fancy place in Manhattan or a clubby law enforcement hangout in Brooklyn Heights. Instead, we drove down to Bensonhurst and went to Russo's, Scarpa's favorite restaurant on Thirteenth Avenue, just down the street from the shuttered Wimpy Boys Club. When we walked in, everyone stared. Russo's is a neighborhood place, and outsiders are rare. The agents sat with their backs to the wall, and I remember thinking: I'm glad Maggie's packing heat. We ordered drinks, and then Sung-Hee offered a toast: "Nice piece of work, everyone, nice piece of work."

Six months after the trial, Scarpa came up for sentencing. If we had convicted him of murder, he would have received a life sentence. As it was, Raggi gave him more than forty years, enough to keep him locked up in prison until his late eighties. Last time I looked, Scarpa was being held in "Supermax," the "Alcatraz of the Rockies," in Florence, Colorado. He spends twenty-three hours of every day in solitary confinement.

CHAPTER NINE

How We Beat the Mob

The *Scarpa* case was unique, filled with endless treachery and intrigue, but in one important respect, it was a typical DOJ mafia prosecution; it ended successfully, with the defendant in prison. During the last twenty years the Justice Department has given the mafia a very thorough beating in the courtroom. Outside the New York metro area, from Boston to Los Angeles, the mafia has been almost totally eliminated. In New York City, the mob limps on, but its power is negligible. We have jailed all five bosses of the Five Families and every one of their replacements. We have forced the mafia out of garbage carting, labor unions, the Garment District, airfreight, construction, the Fulton Fish Market, and Wall Street. Today's mafiosi are no more than ordinary street thugs. They steal, and they deal drugs, but they no longer control whole industries or vast criminal empires. They possess, in my estimation, less than 5 percent of the influence they wielded at their peak in the late 1970s. If you made a list of serious crime issues in the United States back in 1975, the mafia would have headed the list. Today it would barely crack the top twenty. In contemporary America the most influential mafia family is not the Colombos or the Gambinos; it is the Sopranos. The mafia is no longer a public threat. It has become a cultural artifact.

The government's victory against the mafia is incredibly significant from a public policy perspective. In the United States today we are faced with numerous organized criminal threats: domestic and international terrorist groups, drug cartels, crooked corporate management teams, and sophisticated computer fraud and identity theft rings. Most of these criminals are extraordinarily dangerous; we have no option but to try to eliminate them. Sometimes, however, these battles look impossible to win. Some people believe that these problems are here to stay for good, permanent and immutable aspects of contemporary life. I acknowledge that these criminal threats are hard to control, let alone defeat, but I am optimistic about our ability to prevail, for one very good reason. Back in the 1970s we felt the exact same way about Italian American organized crime: hopeless. Now, less than thirty years later, we have that problem beat. This historic achievement suggests that under the right circumstances we can succeed against even the most sophisticated criminal groups and the most intractable kinds of crime.

Mob prosecutors and agents rarely talk publicly about the strategies we have successfully employed against the mafia; no one wants to give away the family jewels. If, however, we are going to replicate our mafia victory in new, even more challenging criminal contexts, we need to understand precisely what our strategies were and why they worked. So before we go any further, I want to explain how we beat the mob.

IN THE JUSTICE DEPARTMENT and the FBI, there is broad agreement that our success against the mob can be attributed to smart law enforcement policies and tactics. According to this conventional wisdom, Congress created excellent antimafia tools like RICO, the Title III electronic surveillance statute, and WITSEC. Federal agents and prosecutors then used these tools aggressively, even brilliantly, to dismantle our opponents. Back in the old days, when I worked as a mafia prosecutor, I agreed with this assessment. I could see its truth with my own eyes, in my own cases. Today I still agree with it . . . to a degree.

THE CORNERSTONE of our antimafia program is RICO, the Racketeer Influenced and Corrupt Organizations Act. Passed in 1970, RICO is a complex criminal statute designed to give federal prosecutors the legal power they need to take on and beat the mob. The statute has a very interesting history. When Congress wrote RICO, it assumed that federal prosecutors would employ it immediately to bring organized crime to bay. Instead, prosecutors ignored it. During the statute's first ten years the United States did not file a single significant RICO case. This failure was, in part, a by-product of larger government inaction; as I note in Chapter Six, the FBI and DOJ failed to attack the mafia aggressively until the early 1980s. It was also a matter of statutory novelty. RICO is a bizarre and untraditional law, with so many moving parts that initially prosecutors simply did not understand its value. Strange but true, it took federal prosecutors more than a decade just to figure out how RICO actually worked.

RICO's primary provision—Title 18, *United States Code*, Section 1962(a)—makes it a crime for mobsters to invest in or take over businesses engaged in interstate commerce. This tool was designed to block the most lucrative aspect of the mafia's business model, its use of extortion and union control to compete and make money in the legitimate marketplace. At the time RICO was passed, almost all congressional attention was focused on this provision, which was viewed as having great promise. Unfortunately, it flopped. AUSAs and the FBI quickly discovered that it was virtually impossible to trace mafia money to its source or determine where it went. We might suspect that loansharking profits had been invested in a legitimate business, but since almost all mafia transactions are conducted in cash, without the generation of any traditional business records, proving such suspicions was tough. To this day Section 1962(a)'s investment provision remains a dead letter. I never used it during my career.

Thankfully, RICO contained several additional weapons, ones that attracted virtually no congressional comment in 1970. The most significant of these was Section 1962(c). This provision makes it a federal crime, punishable by up to twenty years in jail (or, in cases involving murder, life), for a person to commit two or more specified state or federal crimes as part of an "enterprise"—an organized group—that affects interstate commerce.

At first blush, prosecutors concluded that 1962(c) was worthless, and perhaps you can see why. In 1970, when the law was passed, prosecutors were finding it almost impossible to convict mafia members of even one single federal crime. Section 1962(c) appeared to make matters worse because it increased the government's burden of proof. To get a conviction under this section, you had to prove the defendant had committed at least two crimes, not just one. You also had to prove the defendant had committed these crimes as a member of an organized enterprise like a mafia family that was big enough to affect interstate commerce, a difficult task at a time when many people denied that the mafia even existed. Not surprisingly, prosecutors thought this newfangled statute was more trouble than it was worth.

In the early 1980s, however, prosecutors in New York took a second look at RICO, and they quickly discovered that Section 1962(c) possessed immense untapped potential. This is not because, as some "experts" commonly assert, RICO lets you target mafia bosses, not just underlings; federal prosecutors have always had that power.* It is, rather, because Section 1962(c) radically extended federal criminal jurisdiction.

Under the United States Constitution, Congress's power to make new federal criminal laws is not unlimited. Congress can criminalize conduct only if it affects interstate commerce or some other clear federal interest. Everything else—crimes without an impact on the national economy or the operation of federal programs—must be left to the fifty states. Thus Congress can make it a federal crime to kidnap someone and take him or her across state lines or to steal money from Medicare, but it cannot criminalize a simple local burglary.

Because of this traditional limit, many of the most important crimes committed by the mafia were not violations of federal law prior to 1970. For instance, federal prosecutors could not charge a mafia member with murder unless the killer traveled across state lines to commit the crime.† This fact had serious implications for law enforcement. In the mafia, most hits are committed by locals against locals; no interstate travel is involved. As a result, virtually all mafia murders fell outside federal control. The importance of this fact cannot be overstated. The Scarpa Crew, to give one example, committed roughly twenty murders, but none of them involved interstate travel. Under traditional law prior to RICO, these kinds of murders were not federal crimes, and they could not be investigated or charged by federal prosecutors.

RICO changed all that. As you may recall from my brief summary, Section 1962(c) makes it a federal crime to commit two or more speci-

---

*For example, Title 18, Section 2, the 1948 aiding and abetting law, provides that any person who "counsels, commands, induces or procures" the commission of a federal crime—anyone who gives orders—is just as guilty as the actual perpetrator.

†Or used the U.S. postal system to commit the crime, a fact pattern that rarely occurred.

fied state or federal crimes as part of a criminal enterprise that affects interstate commerce. Among the eligible crimes listed in the statute is what federal prosecutors call state murder, a murder in violation of state law.* Though it took prosecutors more than a decade to figure it out, this provision gave them the stick they needed to bring the mafia to justice because it brought mafia murder within federal criminal jurisdiction. As a result of Section 1962(c), federal prosecutors could, for the first time in history, bring multiple mafia homicide cases like *Scarpa*.

RICO's expansion of federal jurisdiction totally altered the legal playing field. In the past federal prosecutors had indicted a small number of mafia members for crimes like tax evasion and loansharking. The government won some of these cases, but the victories were hollow, for the sentences imposed for such crimes were low: two years, three years, maybe even probation. With RICO, however, we could indict defendants for multiple homicides and send them to prison for life.

Federalization of murder also changed the balance of power in plea negotiations. In virtually all mafia investigations, the government cannot uncover the truth unless it flips a cooperating witness or two. John Gleeson, the AUSA who convicted John Gotti, once commented:

> *One characteristic of organized crime is that the most culpable and dangerous individuals rarely do the dirty work. Although the organization's leaders are ultimately responsible for its crimes, they typically deal through intermediaries and limit their own participation to behind-the-scenes control and guidance. Consequently, their guilt usually cannot be proved by the testimony of victims or eyewitnesses or by forensic evidence. And they never confess. Generally speaking, successful prosecution of organized crime leaders requires the use of accomplice testimony.*

Given this fact, finding a way to convince major organized crime targets to plead guilty and cooperate is critical. Sometimes a desire for

---

*Federalizing state murder in this manner does not violate the traditional restriction on federal criminal jurisdiction, because the government still has to prove that the overall criminal group has an impact on interstate commerce, even if the individual RICO predicate crimes like murder do not. This is usually not too difficult. In the *Scarpa* case, for example, we proved that the Scarpa Crew took loansharking and gambling customers from many states and traveled from New York to New Jersey to conduct mob business.

revenge will do the trick. In one of my later cases a mafia prince named Billy Cutolo, Jr., bravely volunteered to wear a wire in meetings with members of the Colombo Family in the hope of gathering evidence against the men who killed his father, capo William "Wild Bill" Cutolo. But normally, the only way to flip a mafioso is to "jam him up"—to convince him that his only chance to avoid rotting in prison for decades is to testify against his criminal associates.

That's where 1962(c) comes in. Prior to 1970, it was almost impossible to flip a mafia defendant. If you told a mafia member you were going to indict him for illegal gambling, he would laugh, because the sentences were so short. After passage of RICO, in contrast, you could threaten him with murder charges and a life in prison. In *Scarpa*, all three cooperators who testified for the government at trial were brought to cooperate this way: by the threat of federal RICO murder charges.

RICO also included a second revolutionary tool, Title 18, *United States Code*, Section 1964. Section 1964 gave government lawyers the right to seek all sorts of civil legal remedies to prevent ongoing RICO violations, including the dissolution or reorganization of any mobbed-up organization. No one saw the potential of this provision until 1982, when AUSAs in New Jersey used Section 1964 in a big teamsters case. The AUSAs proved at trial that powerful Teamsters Local 560, with more than thirty-five thousand members, was run by Tony Provenzano, a capo in the Genovese Family. After the government victory, Judge Harold Ackerman invoked Section 1964 to throw out the mafia leadership, impose his own trustee, and free the union from mob control. Since that time the Justice Department has used Section 1964 to clean up dozens of unions.

Finally, RICO gave federal prosecutors a host of technical procedural advantages that made it easier to bring the mafia to justice. Most of these advantages were not created intentionally by Congress but flowed inevitably from the statute's complex structure. Many took years to discover and exploit. Let me give you just one example.

In a traditional criminal case, two defendants cannot be joined together in the same indictment and tried in the same trial unless they committed crimes together. If, for example, you busted two members of a mafia family for separate crimes—one for gambling, one for loansharking—you would have to try them in two separate cases in front of two different juries. RICO altered these traditional joinder rules, for it authorizes the government to include in a single indictment all defendants who belong to the same "enterprise," even if they were involved in separate criminal schemes and had very little personal contact. In a case filed in 2000 against Colombo boss Alphonse Persico and his underlings, for example, AUSAs Amy Walsh, Noah Perlman, and I combined in one indictment eleven defendants and a dozen different crimes: loan-sharking, money laundering, three separate extortion schemes, illegal gambling, securities fraud, telecommunications fraud, and marijuana and Ecstasy dealing. This permissive joinder gave us a huge advantage in the case, for it allowed us to exploit what lawyers call prejudicial spillover. Here's how it works.

In any criminal investigation against multiple targets, your proof is inevitably going to be strong against some defendants and weak against others. If you have to try each defendant separately, you win the strong cases and lose the weak ones. If, however, you can put together all the defendants in one trial, the jury will have a tough time keeping the defendants and evidence clear and separate in their minds. Over the length of the trial, the strong proof against some defendants will "spill over" and "infect" the defendants against whom your evidence is weak, and this gives you a very good chance of running the table—of convicting the whole bunch.

Prejudicial spillover is critical in mafia cases. In the mob, most of the shooting, stealing, and dealing is done by young thugs. The capos and bosses, as John Gleeson noted, tend to stay out of the fray, insulated from contact with all but a few trusted subordinates. As a result, it is very hard to gather incriminating evidence against them. Without RICO's permissive joinder rule, mob bosses would go to trial alone, against weak government cases. Under RICO, in contrast, they go on trial surrounded by their underlings, and the jury hears extensive evidence about all the crimes these henchmen have committed. An unfair advantage for prosecutors? Perhaps, which is one reason defense attorneys loathe RICO. But I have to admit, it never troubled me greatly. When you are fighting the mob, you need every advantage you can get.

RECRUITMENT OF COOPERATING WITNESSES is an essential part of our antimafia campaign, for only they can provide the trial testimony needed to put their fellow mobsters behind bars. Prior to 1970, law enforcement flipped only two significant mafia informants, New York gunman Abe "Kid Twist" Reles and the low-level Genovese Family thug Joseph Valachi, the first in 1940, the second in 1962. Today that trickle has become a flood, with several major mafia members changing sides every year. This radical shift has been brought about in part because RICO gives us the leverage we need to flip more accomplices. But we also learned from our mistakes.

In 1940, Reles, the first great mafia informant, disclosed the existence and operations of a bloody mafia murder and enforcement squad dubbed Murder Inc. by the press. His fate did little to encourage other mafia members to cooperate. In 1941, while under close police protection, Reles fell from the sixth-floor window of a Brooklyn hotel and died on impact. It is possible that Reles jumped, distraught, perhaps, over his own treachery to the mob, but no one really believes that. In the mafia world there are no coincidences, no bad luck. Though it will never be proved, everyone thinks he was thrown to his death by mafia killers who paid the cops to look the other way or perhaps by the crooked cops themselves.

Valachi's story is equally revealing. The first major mafia informant since Reles, he flipped in 1962. He spent the next half dozen years being debriefed by FBI experts and testifying before Congress. His reward, however, was meager. As the only living mafia cooperator, the only walking, talking proof that the mafia even existed, Valachi was a priceless asset. To keep him alive, he had to be kept under very close guard, for it was generally agreed that if he were freed, even under a new name, he would quickly wind up dead. To prevent that, he was kept under lock and key, living more or less in solitary confinement in a series of bleak federal facilities until his death in 1971.

The government's experiences with Reles and Valachi suggested that if we wanted to encourage more mafia members to flip, we needed to devise a more attractive way to protect mafia turncoats, one that would give them a true second chance at life. The solution was the Witness Security Program, created by Congress in 1970. Witnesses and their families entering WITSEC are moved to new homes in areas with little mob activity, given new identities, and provided with temporary financial assistance to get them started. They go on to lead lives of relative normality, blending in with the ordinary families around them. Though originally designed to counter the mafia, the program is now used to protect informants from all walks of crime: drug traffickers, terrorists, gang members. Over the course of the program's existence, not one WITSEC witness has been harmed.

As a prosecutor I found WITSEC invaluable. When potential mafia witnesses asked about their safety, I could say with confidence, "If you enter the program and follow the rules, I guarantee that you and your family will be safe." Some people refused—they figured they could disappear quite successfully on their own. Many others, however, accepted our offer. For these men and women, safety comes with a price. WITSEC is attractive to mafia cooperators because it offers a real opportunity to start life over again, but entering and living in the program can be a harrowing experience. On the day of entry the witness and his or her immediate family are scooped up off the street by FBI or DEA agents and taken to a temporary safe house under twenty-four-hour protective surveillance. The family is allowed to bring only two suitcases, so virtually all their personal possessions are left behind. They must also abandon any items that could disclose their true identities—all photographs, letters, scrapbooks, memorabilia. From that moment on, their old selves simply do not exist. They are provided with new, permanent identities, given medical treatment, and trained in program safety procedures. When everything is ready, they are moved by the U.S. Marshals to another part of the country, typically in a small or medium-size town with no history of mafia infiltration.

For most witnesses, this process is totally disorienting. The move from Brooklyn to a place like Minnesota (to choose at random one location where mafia witnesses might be placed) is very strange for your average mafia member. People talk differently, eat different foods, and live in different types of houses. The witness's sense of alienation is increased by the total destruction of his or her existing social and family network. When you enter the program, all your links with life back home are severed. You leave behind your friends, your parents, and your siblings. At best, the Marshals might arrange one or two monitored phone calls with family members per year. If you are divorced or separated from your spouse, and you have children who do not enter the program, your contact with them, for the rest of your life, will be limited to rare phone calls and short visits in neutral sites. If the witness contacts friends or relatives from his past life or makes an unauthorized trip to his old community, he and his family are immediately uprooted and moved to a second new life, under a second new name, and they have to adjust all over again. Not surprisingly, many witnesses react to this experience by developing severe cases of depression. One of my witnesses became a drunk. Several needed psychological counseling. Sometimes a witness in the program would call me just to chat, just to hear someone call him by his real name.

WITSEC can be equally nerve-racking for prosecutors. As a WITSEC sponsor you are responsible for placing trained and experienced killers, some of them borderline sociopaths, in small, unsuspecting communities. So far no mafioso has lost his cool and committed murder while in the program, but it could happen any day.

Consider the case of Carmine Sessa. From the early 1970s to 1993 Sessa was a leading member of the Colombo Family. As an associate in the Scarpa Crew and then as the family's consigliere and underboss, he was responsible for thirteen brutal murders. In 1993, Sessa flipped, the highest-ranking member of the family ever to cooperate and one of the most important mafia witnesses ever. Initially, we kept Sessa safe in one of WITSEC's secret prison units, but eventually he was released on bail. He and his family were given new identities, moved to a small town, and began new lives as law-abiding citizens.

Sessa was a star witness, helping the government convict more than forty other mobsters. Unfortunately, his adjustment to the real world did not go smoothly. Back in Brooklyn, Sessa had run a billion-dollar criminal empire and held power over life and death. He was feared for his ruthlessness, admired for his prowess as a killer, respected for his business sense and cool, deliberate judgment. In his new life, however, he had no skills to market and no significant employment record. As a result, the only work he could find was manual labor, on the very bottom of the totem pole. This dramatic fall from mob boss to minimum-wage earner ate away at his self-esteem. So did a new fact of life: if someone at work yelled at him or failed to show "respect," he could not simply have the culprit whacked; he had to keep quiet and take it.

Inevitably, the stress mounted. After a few months Sessa began to abuse his wife. Later things got worse. Many mafia members are slightly paranoid, constantly imagining they are about to be murdered. Now Sessa's mind started to spin, and he began to wonder if his own son was trying to have him killed. Though Sessa was prohibited from carrying weapons, he got his hands on a couple of guns just to feel safe. Had things continued down this path, Sessa might have easily lost control and killed someone. Fortunately, his wife contacted the U.S. Marshals, who supervise the WITSEC program, and they called in prosecutors and the FBI. Within forty-eight hours Sessa was back in jail.

After we revoked his bail, Sung-Hee and I met with Sessa back at a WITSEC prison facility to talk to him about his behavior. Sessa admitted that obtaining the guns was wrong. He even agreed, after a lot of prodding from Sung-Hee, that he did not have the right to hit his wife, though that idea struck him as totally counterintuitive, for he assumed all husbands were allowed to hit their spouses. Still, I was worried about him and his prospects on the street. Sessa told me how hard it was for him to be a nobody, an aging minimum-wage worker without power or prestige. "These people," he said, "they don't know who I am, what I can do." Then he said in his calm, deliberate manner, "I tell you, John, I feel like a ticking time bomb." Today Sessa is back on bail, buried in middle America, deep in the heart of WITSEC. Let's hope all goes well.

COOPERATORS ARE ESSENTIAL in any mafia case, but they have two significant limitations. First, most mafiosi will not flip until they are indicted. By the time they see the light and cooperate, they are already in jail. As a result, they cannot provide real-time intelligence about crimes being committed out on the street. Second, their credibility is always subject to attack at trial, for most have committed perjury at some point in their careers, and they have an undeniable interest in keeping their prosecutors happy. For these reasons, electronic surveillance is often crucial in mafia investigations. Wiretaps and bugs allow us to detect crimes as they occur and then fling a defendant's own words back at him on tape.

In 1968, Congress passed Title III, a law authorizing the FBI and other federal law enforcement agencies to engage in the bugging and wiretapping of criminal suspects. In 1981, when the FBI began to hunt the mafia in earnest, it finally took advantage of this law, creating a special electronic surveillance unit in New York City to intercept and record mafia conversations. From the outset this special operations team recognized that conventional wiretaps were unlikely to be effective—most mafia bosses are simply too smart to talk business over the telephone—so the unit relied mostly on bugging. The results have been stunning. In 1989, for example, the FBI broke into a tiny apartment over the Ravenite Club in Little Italy and installed hidden microphones. Soon monitors picked up John Gotti, the boss of the Gambino Family, explaining why certain people had to be killed. These tapes led directly to Gotti's conviction.

Title III also helped us in our case against Gregory Scarpa, Jr. We had no bombshell tapes; our prison cell bug was largely ineffective. Still, electronic surveillance conducted during our investigation, before the case was charged, played a very useful corroborative role at trial. We played for the jury intercepted telephone calls placed by crew members in prison to their colleagues on the street to show the crew's organization and membership and wiretap tapes of gamblers placing bets to prove the existence of Scarpa's gambling business. More fundamentally, electronic surveillance helped us get the case going in the first place.

In 1992, five years before I became an AUSA, the FBI bugged a car driven by a Colombo mobster named Joey Ambrosino. The Ambrosino car bug was an evidentiary gold mine, for during the Colombo Family War, Ambrosino and his colleagues used the car as a mobile hit squad command post, driving around Brooklyn, hunting for members of the Orena faction, looking for people to shoot. These crimes were caught on tape. When the devastating evidence was revealed, Ambrosino flipped. The fall of this first Colombo domino set off a chain reaction: Ambrosino incriminated Sessa, and when Sessa flipped, he implicated Billy Meli, Mario Parlagreco, and Jimmy DelMasto, among others. They too decided to cooperate and became government witnesses at trial. It is not an exaggeration to say that bugging was the key to our case. Without it, we would never have been able to indict Greg Scarpa.

OUR SUCCESSFUL ANTIMAFIA STRATEGY involved one additional tactical innovation, proper organization. In my experience, law enforcement personnel work most effectively when they have a clear, discrete, and specific mission. If you tell agents to go out and arrest all drug traffickers, they will feel overwhelmed. But if you tell them to bust every drug trafficker working in a particular five-block radius, they will view the task as a challenge. Recognizing this fact, the FBI in New York has, for most of the last twenty-five years, assigned a separate FBI squad of ten to fifteen agents to investigate each of the Five Families. This simple organizational structure has paid immense dividends. Each squad knows precisely what its mission is and where to focus its energy. It also creates productive competition, with each squad trying to destroy its target more thoroughly and more quickly than the other squads. Finally, it has provided transparency of results, generating obvious metrics to track success or failure. If you want to know how the Lucchese Squad has been doing, for example, you can simply count up the number of Luccheses who have been busted in the last twelve months and how many are left on the street.

SO HOW did we beat the mob? The explanation I summarized above, one widely accepted in law enforcement circles, places emphasis on the federal government's wise law enforcement policies and tactics. This assessment is accurate, but only to a degree. Smart, aggressive law enforcement was certainly a key factor in our victory over the mob. But this explanation is also misleading because it is incomplete.

Why do some criminal organizations prosper while others ultimately die out? To understand this phenomenon, we might think about it in terms borrowed from the theory of natural selection.

In the natural world, a species flourishes not because it is, in some abstract manner, more "fit" than other animals but because it occupies a specific environmental niche to which it is well adapted. The tree sloth, for example, is incredibly slow and inactive, too slow to run from predators. A bad bet to win the battle for survival, right? No! In the South American rain forest, the sloth thrives precisely because of its slow speed and limited movement. If you look closely at a wild sloth—not something, admittedly, most of us have time to do—you will see that algae grow in its fur. When rainy season comes, the algae turn bright green, providing camouflage. When the rainy season is over, the algae fade to a duller shade, once again turning just the right color to conceal their host. The lesson is simple. Survival is not the product of abstract qualities but the way in which those qualities interact with the environmental context. The sloth will do well as long as the rain forest flourishes. But if environmental conditions change, a species like the sloth that is well adapted to prior conditions must change as well or die out. A sloth would not last long in the desert.

Criminal groups, in my experience, rise and fall in the same way. To survive, a criminal organization must be more than "good at crime" in some abstract sense. It must also exist in an economic and social environment that favors the particular organizational structure, type, and style of crime it practices. A criminal group that comes to power in one era, when conditions favor its existence, may die out when conditions change.

This evolutionary model helps explain the history of the American mafia. In the first half of the twentieth century, the mafia rose to power because our society provided a particular evolutionary niche, a set of legal, social, and economic conditions, that made it easy for the mob to prosper. In the second half of the twentieth century, however, those conditions changed drastically. Like species that face rapid extinction when the temperature or rainfall is altered, the mafia had to adjust or die. Fixed in its ways, the mafia perished. If my thesis is correct—you can judge for yourself as you read my analysis below—then law enforcement strategies do not really explain the fall of the mob. Instead, our explanation needs to focus on ways in which the economic and social playing field, so favorable to the mob in its first fifty years, ultimately doomed it to decline.

SINCE 1933, when Prohibition was repealed, the mafia has made the bulk of its profits through four criminal businesses: loansharking, illegal gambling, drug trafficking, and labor racketeering. Criminal enforcement has helped suppress these schemes, but changes in economic and regulatory conditions have had a much more powerful impact.

Consider loansharking. In the old days mafia loansharks like the Scarpas made millions of dollars in profits (billions for the mafia as a whole), financing all kinds of basic needs. Mafia loansharks helped their customers pay rent, buy used cars or washing machines, open small businesses, and eliminate gambling debts. Their lending business prospered for one reason: millions of residents in the ethnic urban enclaves where the mafia operated did not have easy access to credit from any other source.

In the last several decades, however, we have seen a revolution in consumer credit. In 1950 credit cards did not exist. Today 73 percent of Americans have at least one. Not surprisingly, total revolving credit, the kind you get with credit cards that allow you to run a balance, has exploded, from $2 billion in 1968 to $626 billion in 2000. This trend has not been

limited to the middle class. Today over one-quarter of the bottom 20 percent of households in America have a credit card. For the remainder,
short-term credit can be obtained easily from tens of thousands of money
stores and payday loan companies, which have proliferated in working-
class neighborhoods to supplement more traditional pawnshops.

A similar revolution has occurred in small business lending. In 1953,
Congress created the Small Business Administration, which subsidizes
loans to small and new businesses. Since then the SBA has put more than
thirty billion dollars in loans into the hands of over twenty million businesses. Even the poorest of the poor have gained access to some business
credit, from microlenders who make business loans to indigent entre-
preneurs. Accion USA, for example, is a microlending institution that
started on the Colombo Family's home turf in Brooklyn. During the last
two decades it has lent more than ninety million dollars to more than
ten thousand low-income American residents.

As a result of these developments, consumers have much greater access to credit today than they had in the 1950s or 1960s, and this has totally destroyed the loansharking business. In contemporary America, no
one goes to a loanshark like the Scarpas anymore to finance his or her
credit needs. Instead, he or she simply goes to a legitimate lender. The
only people who still find loanshark loans attractive are outcasts who,
for unique reasons, cannot access credit in any other way: low-level drug
dealers looking for short-term loans to finance narcotics purchases, or
hard-luck gamblers who can't pay off their debts. Needless to say, these
two lending pools are small and risky. Gamblers have a very high default
rate and often disappear before repayment. Drug dealers are an even
worse customer base. Most reliable dealers can get better credit terms
from their suppliers, a very common practice in the drug trade. Thus
only the rankest amateurs or dealers who have proved to be incompetent
look to the mob for help. And when dealers do borrow money from
loansharks, they may ultimately prefer to shoot their lenders rather than
repay them. After all, dealers are typically comfortable employing violence as a business practice.

In sum, mafia loansharking exists as part of a larger credit market. In
the early and mid-twentieth century, loansharks faced no real competition
in their market niche. Today that is no longer true. Legal lenders offer consumers interest rates and lending terms that are comparable to or better

than those offered by most loansharks, free from the prospect of broken kneecaps. Loansharks can't compete, so their industry has collapsed.

The mafia numbers racket has also imploded, for the same reason: competition. In the 1950s and 1960s New Yorkers spent billions of dollars a year on the mafia's numbers game. In 1967, however, the government of New York decided to enter the same market by introducing a state lottery, with tickets on sale in every neighborhood convenience store. At first the mafia tried to fight back. According to several mafia cooperators I debriefed on this subject, the Colombo Family increased the size of its numbers payouts after 1967 in order to make its game more competitive, and numbers runners were instructed to remind their customers that if they played the mafia numbers game, they could keep all their earnings, but if they won from the state, they had to pay taxes. Today, however, the mafia has given up trying to compete with legal lotteries. The government offers multimillion-dollar lotto prizes in games that can be played openly, easily, safely, and legally. A small, illegal lottery game run by a bunch of crooks simply does not have sufficient market appeal to survive.

The mafia's grip on drug trafficking has been similarly eroded. From 1950 to 1980 the mafia controlled heroin distribution in the United States because it had a significant comparative advantage over other potential rivals. Most of the world's heroin supply was refined by Corsican and Sicilian mobsters in Sicily and the south of France. When these European criminal groups hunted for an American distributor, they naturally chose to deal with their New York mafia cousins, who were discreet and well organized and spoke Italian. The fact that mafia unions controlled every major port on the eastern seaboard did not hurt either. As a result, the mafia made billions from the drug trade.

In the late 1970s, however, Latin America replaced Europe as the major source of international drug production, and the mafia lost its niche. No one in the mafia spoke Spanish, had significant family ties to Colombia or Peru, or had established reliable transportation routes from Latin America to the United States. As a result, mafia drug traffickers lost control of the wholesale trade to Colombians, Mexicans, and Dominicans. Today many mafia members sell drugs, but only in relatively small amounts. Compared with that of the Latin American cartels, the volume they distribute is trivial.

Finally, labor racketeering profits have dried up almost entirely. In the 1950s and 1960s the mafia used its control over dozens of powerful national labor unions to generate massive amounts of revenue. Mafia unions extorted billions of dollars from businesspeople in exchange for "strike insurance." They also treated giant union pension funds like private piggy banks, to be raided at will. The most sophisticated mafia families went one step further, using union control to gain market share for their own businesses. A mafia manufacturing operation was guaranteed cheap labor contracts, union peace, and reliable product distribution services from mobbed-up teamsters and longshoremen. If a legitimate business tried to compete, it faced union strikes, transportation foulups, and mysterious warehouse fires. Labor control, in short, gave mafia business enterprises a major competitive advantage.

Since the 1980s, however, mafia union power has been almost totally destroyed. The sharp decline in labor racketeering has been the result in part of the Justice Department's RICO-based civil enforcement efforts. But in reality, the most significant factor in the collapse of labor racketeering has not been enforcement but the decline of the American labor union movement itself. For most of the twentieth century the mafia was powerful because unions were powerful, exerting massive influence on the American economy. In 1953, to give one basic indicator, more than 32 percent of American workers belonged to unions. Today, in contrast, only 7 percent of private-sector workers are unionized, largely because of pressures from the new, more competitive global economy. This sharp decline has been accompanied by the evisceration of union negotiating leverage. Strikes, once a feared labor tactic, are increasingly viewed by management as a paper tiger. If workers want to go on strike, fine; companies simply hire permanent replacement workers or move their plants overseas.

The decline of organized labor has led inevitably to a commensurate decline in the profitability of mafia labor racketeering. Though some old-school union locals are still mobbed up, these operations are no longer central to the mafia's business model, producing only limited revenue. One revealing fact: in recent years the mafia has made little effort to expand its labor base by infiltrating and taking over other legitimate union locals. That is not because it fears getting caught, but because it thinks that labor racketeering is not worth the effort.

Collectively, these four structural changes in the American and international economy—the radical expansion of consumer credit, the legalization of many games of chance, the shift of drug production to Latin America, and the decline of unions—have done more to ensure the mafia's fall than any of our intentional law enforcement actions. Aggressive enforcement since 1980 has certainly accelerated the mafia's decline. By forcing the mafia underground, we have raised its administrative and transaction costs. But enforcement would probably have failed or produced much more modest results were it not for the immense boost we received from these changes in the economic playing field. The mafia's power has always been a function of its economic strength. Since 1970 all four of its core product and service lines have collapsed in the face of competition. This loss of market power has made the mafia's extinction all but inevitable.

The mafia has tried to adapt to changing market conditions, branching out over the last ten years into new lines of work, including securities and telecommunications fraud, excise tax scams, and 9/11 and Hurricane Katrina charity rip-offs. Some of these efforts have paid large short-term dividends, but none has resulted in significant, stable revenue flows, which the mafia desperately needs. In part, this failure reflects the maturity of the new criminal sectors the mafia is trying to enter. Stock fraud, for example, is already a crowded field, filled with many talented practictioners, white-collar criminals with M.B.A.'s. But another force is also at work. In these new areas the mafia has no particular comparative advantage over its competitors. For this reason, it is not likely to gain any permanent traction.

THE MAFIA'S POWER has also been undercut by significant changes in its social environment. Between 1910 and 1920, more than two million Italians immigrated to the United States. America was slow to welcome these new immigrants. Most did not speak English, they typically possessed little education, and 75 percent were from small agricultural communities, with no job skills transferable to an industrial society. When they tried to find work, they faced massive discrimination in the workplace. Given these facts, it is not surprising that a very small number of smart, ambitious, and ruthless men would turn to crime to satisfy their cravings for power, money, and status.

When you read about early mafia leaders, it is hard not to be impressed. They were violent killers, but they were not mindless thugs. Charles "Lucky" Luciano imposed an organizational structure on the New York underworld that has lasted for more than seventy years. Carlo Gambino, the model for *The Godfather*'s Don Corleone, supervised a criminal empire with revenues roughly the same size as General Motors. Joseph Profaci became America's olive oil king. These men had brains, discretion, self-discipline, and the ability to think strategically. They probably would have succeeded in any line of work they chose.

Today things have changed. Italian Americans no longer face language barriers or significant job discrimination. If a young American of Italian descent has a lot of brains and ambition, he has no need to enter the mob; he can become a Supreme Court justice, a CEO, a mayor, or a mafia prosecutor. This transformation in the economic and social opportunities available to Italian Americans has had a huge impact on the mafia. To put it bluntly, only an idiot would choose to be in the mafia today, so idiots are the only persons the mafia can recruit. Today there are no Carlo Gambinos in the mob. The new recruits are rock stupid, incapable of planning or carrying out sophisticated criminal schemes. If an organization is only as good as its people, the mafia is in trouble because its new recruits are pathetic.

The mafia could have avoided this problem, of course, if it had been willing to alter its recruiting policies. Historically, the mafia has been open only to men of at least partial Italian descent. If a corporation adopted that approach, it would be out of business in six weeks, strangled by a dearth of talent. The mafia, however, has never been willing to change its rules, to recruit talented women and non-Italians. This lack of flexibility in the face of changing social conditions has made its survival extremely unlikely.

Another social trend has had an equally devastating effect on the mob: the decline of traditional urban Italian American neighborhoods. In the 1920s and 1930s, almost 450,000 Italian immigrants lived in New York City, packed into tenement slums like Manhattan's Little Italy and Brooklyn's Bensonhurst. These homogeneous neighborhoods provided a perfect breeding ground for the mafia. They were hard for police to penetrate, for law enforcement personnel stuck out like sore thumbs, and residents tended to have more loyalty to mobsters of their own ethnic heritage than they did to Irish American cops or an abstract notion of the rule of law. These neighborhoods produced a steady stream of mafia customers, persons to play the numbers and borrow money from loansharks. They were also great recruiting grounds.

These enclaves no longer exist. The huge Italian American community in East Harlem has totally disappeared, and Little Italy is a shrinking tourist trap, losing more blocks to Chinatown with each passing year. Today its population is only 8 percent Italian American, about the city average.

Asked to explain why communism was hard to defeat, Mao reputedly answered that "the people are the ocean and the Communists are fish." Today's mafia members are like fish out of water. With the decline of the great Italian American neighborhoods, they have lost their natural habitat. That makes it even more difficult for them to make money, to recruit new members, and to hide.

THE MAFIA has also been hampered by a significant change in the legal landscape. For much of the twentieth century a primary purpose of the criminal justice system was rehabilitation, to turn criminals into law-abiding citizens. To achieve this goal, our prison sentencing systems employed two basic strategies. First, judges had broad discretion to tailor prison sentences to the individual defendant, depending on each judge's assessment of the defendant's past history and the likelihood of rehabilitation. Confronted with two thieves who committed identical crimes, a judge could sentence one to six months and the other to ten years on the basis of his sense of their character and future prospects. The judges did not, however, have the last word. The sentences they imposed were actually indeterminate in length because they were subject to administrative review by parole and probation officers. These officers—often trained psychologists, sociologists, or social workers—had the power to terminate prison sentences as soon as they believed it was safe to release a defendant. Thus the thief who received a ten-year sentence might actually be out in two if he appeared to have learned his lesson.

Indeterminate, discretionary sentencing has a lot of surface attraction, for it is based on an appealing idea, that criminals can reform. By the late 1970s, however, a growing number of criminal justice experts had concluded that our sentencing system was broken. Scholars were split, and remain split today, on the potential for and value of rehabilitation. They generally agreed, however, on a more central and damning conclusion: that it was virtually impossible to predict, with any reliability, which individual prisoners were rehabilitated and which remained risks. When the parole system was created, psychology was on the rise. People believed it was (or would soon become) a hard physical science, as reliable as chemistry or physics. Alas, forty years of data from parole and probation boards indicated that our predictions about rehabilitation and recidivism were horrifically inaccurate. Armed with the latest social science methods, our parole boards had released millions of supposedly reformed defendants back on the streets, only to see a huge percentage return to committing crimes. The idea that we could tell who was good and who was bad was, in short, a wrongheaded fantasy. We might as well have been throwing darts.

By the 1980s dissatisfaction with the traditional sentencing approach had grown to a fever pitch. On the political left, liberals were convinced that judicial discretion allowed judges to discriminate against poor defendants and racial minorities. On the right, conservatives believed the whole idea that criminals could be rehabilitated was weak-kneed left-wing rubbish. United, for once, in contempt for the status quo, both political parties voted for a radical overhaul of federal sentencing. The Sentencing Reform Act of 1984 brought some of the most sweeping changes to American criminal law ever passed by Congress. The act rejected the goal of rehabilitation entirely, constrained judicial discretion, and eliminated parole. Federal judges could no longer pick a prison sentence out of thin air; they had to follow strict, formal sentencing rules. And once a defendant was sentenced, he had to serve his entire term, without any chance for probation or parole.*

The Sentencing Reform Act altered federal criminal practice in numerous ways, most of which were unintended. For example, it boosted the ability of federal prosecutors to recruit cooperating witnesses. Under the traditional sentencing system, a defendant convicted of RICO might be sentenced anywhere from zero years in prison to life, depending on the whim of the judge. To make things even more random, a parole officer might eventually curtail whatever sentence the judge imposed. In these circumstances, the government's "stick" was pretty weak: "Cooper-

---

*Our sentencing scheme provides a slight sentencing discount that can be earned in prison for good behavior, to provide an incentive for inmates to follow the rules.

ate now, or maybe, your sentence will be stiff." Many defendants replied: "I prefer to take my chances with the judge and the parole board."

The sentencing guidelines changed these sensitive negotiations by injecting a greater amount of certainty into the process. To calculate how much time a defendant faces for his crimes under the sentencing guidelines, you simply look at a chart. For murder, the minimum is life in prison. Since parole has been eliminated, you know that sentence will stick. As a result, prosecutors now have immense leverage when dealing with potential cooperators. In these meetings, they can say, with total conviction, "If you don't flip, you will die in jail." Even more important, the defendant will hear the same analysis from his own lawyer because it is based not on a hunch but on a chart. As John Gleeson has commented, "if federal prosecutors had been asked to create a sentencing regime that would place the maximum permissible pressure on criminal defendants to cooperate with the government, they could hardly have done better."

The Sentencing Reform Act was not passed as an antimafia tool. In the debate on the bill, no one in Congress suggested that determinate sentencing would help us dismantle organized crime. It has, however, had that effect. The mafia profited greatly from the prior sentencing regime. Because the incentives for cooperating were fuzzy and weak, the traditional sentencing system helped it maintain discipline, loyalty, and unity. Today, however, under determinate sentencing, the trickle of co-operators in the 1980s has turned into a flood.*

DURING THE LAST TWENTY-FIVE YEARS the mafia has been almost entirely destroyed, but many organized criminal threats remain. Some of

---

*In 2005, in *United States v. Booker*, 543 U.S. 220 (2005), the Supreme Court altered federal sentencing in ways that may affect this trend. Freddie Booker was convicted by a jury of possessing with intent to distribute 92.5 grams of crack cocaine found in his duffel bag. At sentencing, the judge, applying the federal sentencing guidelines, determined that Booker had sold an additional 566 grams of crack, on the basis of evidence that was never presented to the jury. The judge then sentenced Booker to thirty years in prison, nine years longer than the twenty-one years he would have received on the basis of the facts proved to the jury. The Supreme Court reviewed Booker's case and declared that mandatory sentencing guidelines were unconstitutional because they undercut the traditional power of juries to decide the facts relevant to sentencing. As a result, the guidelines are now "advisory," not binding, in the federal courts. This decision may ultimately undercut the DOJ's efforts to recruit cooperating witnesses by undercutting sentencing determinacy. So far, however, I have heard no such complaints. That may be because most federal courts have continued to follow the guidelines in the vast majority of cases. We shall have to monitor this situation closely to see how it plays out.

these are relatively powerless. The media-hyped "Russian mob," for example, has never really taken root here, for good reason: given the incredibly lucrative market for crime and corruption in post-Communist Russia, where law enforcement is close to nonexistent, only a fool would decide to set up as a gangster here instead. But other groups, like Mexican and Colombian drug cartels, urban gangs, white supremacy groups, and terror organizations, pose major threats. As we confront these groups, it would be tragic if we ignored the lessons we ought to have learned from our fight against the mafia.

First, to destroy an organized criminal group, you have to try. One reason the mafia flourished from 1930 to 1980 was that the federal government left it in peace. Had the government moved aggressively to eliminate the mafia in its early days, it might never have taken root. When a new organized criminal threat emerges, the government must strike hard and fast.

Second, to destroy an organized criminal group, you need the right legal tools. In the case of the mafia, our enforcement efforts have been greatly boosted by RICO, Title III, WITSEC, and the sentencing guidelines. When faced with new enforcement challenges, we need to consider if we possess the right mix of legal tools to win, and if we do not, we need to create them.

Finally, to beat an organized criminal group, the prospects for success depend, to a great degree, on the character of the economic, social, and legal environment in which that group operates. In our battle against the mafia, the FBI and DOJ did a great enforcement job, but we never would have won as quickly and decisively as we did were it not for the enormous boost we received from social and economic trends that made it difficult for the mafia to compete and survive. In short, smart law enforcement tools and tactics are essential, but may not be sufficient, to destroy a sophisticated criminal threat.

With the mafia, some of the trends that helped us out, such as the rise of Latin American drug trafficking, were clearly beyond government control, the result of powerful changes in technology, tastes, and international markets. Other positive developments, however, were the direct product of public policies. To give two examples, the creation of state lotteries and the intentional expansion of consumer and business credit after World War II clearly helped us get the mafia under control. Of course these policies were not designed to destroy the mafia. No one knew that when we created the New York State lotto, it would dismantle the numbers racket. To that extent, we simply got lucky. If we are wise, however, we can learn from our luck.

In the future, when faced with similar organized criminal threats, be they drug cartels or terror groups, we should try to replicate this result intentionally instead of leaving it to chance. Tough enforcement measures will not succeed if social and economic conditions greatly favor the criminals. To get them under control, we also need to poison their environment, manipulating economic and social conditions so as to eliminate their "evolutionary niche." This sounds like a tall order. Later in the book I'll give an example of how it might work in the field of narcotics enforcement.

———

WILL THE MAFIA ever make a comeback? Since 9/11, the FBI has cut the number of agents working organized crime cases dramatically in order to beef up its counterterrorism squads. At the same time *The Sopranos* has made the mafia lifestyle attractive again to young Italian American hoods. Some observers have suggested that if we decrease our pressure, the mob will regain its power. Though I think we have to continue to hammer the mob until it dies for good, I do not predict a mafia resurgence. Today's mafia is an eight-track tape trapped in a digital world, a group of aging mediocrities employing an antiquated business model that was designed for a world that no longer exists. When conditions change, criminal groups must adapt or die. The mafia shows no sign of evolution. As long as that is the case, it is headed rapidly toward extinction.

PART III

The War on Drugs

CHAPTER TEN

Wiretaps

carpa was my third trial, so I was eligible, once the case was finished, to be reassigned from General Crimes to a senior unit. For me, the choice was simple. Traditionally, the office's best prosecutors worked on mafia cases, and that was where I wanted to be. One month after the trial I formally requested a transfer to Organized Crime. To seal the deal, I asked to meet with Mark Feldman, the OC chief. Mark was a very good manager, and his unit got great results, but he always cracked me up. After years of prosecuting mobsters, he had started to adopt some of their mannerisms, including a deep love of secrecy. He never liked to talk about cases in his own office, which he appeared to believe might be bugged. If he wanted to pass on some piece of information, he would stop you in the hallway or on the sidewalk outside the office instead. And he never spoke out loud. He would whisper in your ear, in veiled or coded terms. "About that thing, the thing we talked about the other day. I spoke to that guy, and he says okay." Mark pulled me into a vacant office and told me he had endorsed my request. "You did an excellent job in the Scarpa trial. We'd be happy to have you on board."

A few days later Alan Vinegrad, Valerie's replacement as the chief of the Criminal Division, asked to see me. I expected him to tell me I was headed to OC. Instead, I got a shock. Alan congratulated me on the *Scarpa* result, and then he declared, with a weird look on his face, "John, we are sending you to Narcotics." I almost threw up.

Viewed objectively, Alan's decision to send me to the Narcotics Unit was eminently reasonable. In narcotics cases, prosecutors rely heavily on wiretapping. Some supervisors in the office, Alan among them, thought young AUSAs would be more proficient prosecutors later in their careers if they spent an apprenticeship doing drug cases so that they could master this important investigative tool. Alan was also probably worried about his budget. In the late 1990s narcotics enforcement was a growth industry. Congress and Main Justice were throwing lots of funding at the "war on drugs." Indeed, it was the only part of the EDNY's budget that was increasing. To tap into this money, Alan had to show that our office could bring big drug cases, and that meant sending skilled AUSAs to Narcotics. My situation was not unique. At the same time I got my marching orders, my friends Eric Tirschwell and Linda Lacewell, both excellent rookie prosecutors, got the same news.

I knew all this at the time, but I was still depressed by my fate. In the EDNY, Narcotics was a traditional dumping ground, the place where the worst AUSAs were sent. To give just one indicator of status, Organized Crime was located way up on the fifteenth floor of our main building, which had a marble lobby and views of Manhattan. Narcotics was located in an old, run-down building across the street, with threadbare carpets and dirty, scuffed linoleum. Most of the Narcotics offices had a view of the giant leaky air conditioning unit bolted to the roof of the building next door.

My concern was not just with status. I was also unenthusiastic about my new unit's mission. I was under no illusions about the evils of the drug trade. One of my best friends from college had overdosed on heroin and died on the streets of New Jersey just a few short years after we graduated. But as a General Crimes assistant I heard Narcotics was a mess. Jim Washington, the guy who had helped me cheat on my EDNY entrance interview, was a supervisor. Jim, I heard, cherry-picked all the good cases as they came in and then dumped all the junk onto his assistants. I also heard that DEA agents liked to "cut corners," violating their targets' civil rights. And wasn't the whole thing futile? Weren't we losing the war on drugs?

The next day I met with my new boss, and I was instantly reassured. Jodi Avergun was one of the top drug prosecutors in the country, and she was used to dealing with reluctant new recruits. I expected her to give me a pep talk: go, Narcotics! Instead, she totally disarmed me with her candor. "I know you would prefer to be in Organized Crime, and if you want to go there when your two years here are up, I will help you do that. In the meantime, I want you to have fun. Despite what you may have heard, we do great cases here. You'll learn a lot, and you'll make a difference. Do you have any ideas about the kinds of cases that would interest you most?"

I paused for a second to gather my thoughts. I was tempted to tell Jodi about my worries, but I thought I might get off on the wrong foot. So I decided to put a positive spin on things. "I would rather be in OC," I said, "but I'm a team player, and I want to make a strong contribution to the unit. If there are cases with violence, I'd like to focus on those. I guess a second priority would be cartel cases. Something that might have an impact. I'm not that interested in pot or Ecstasy." I did not explain why I thought pot prosecution was a waste of time, but I did not need to. Jodi just nodded.

"We have some good Ecstasy cases against organized trafficking groups, mainly Israelis and Europeans," she said, "but I can spare you those. We have some big Colombian cartel wire investigations. I'll send one your way. Welcome."

A few days after my meeting with Jodi, I moved into my new office. Its provenance was not auspicious. The prior occupant—we'll call him Roberts—had been asked to resign for unspecified (but much rumored) misconduct. As I started to unpack my pens and pencils, I opened a desk drawer and discovered that no one had bothered to clean it out. I found a used toothbrush, some hair gel, a comb encrusted with dandruff, and a pack of condoms. I shut the drawer with a shudder. I asked my new secretary if someone could clean out my office, but all I got was a shrug. For the next two years I never used the desk drawers; Roberts's junk sat right where he had left it. Ultimately, I bequeathed the contents to my own successor.

———

FROM 1998 TO 2000 I worked eighty hours a week in the Narcotics Unit, battling drug traffickers. From the outset I realized that the odds were stacked against us. Today sixteen million Americans buy drugs from roughly five hundred thousand dealers. To catch this army of traffickers, our nation employs four thousand DEA agents and eighty-seven hundred "federalized" cops and sheriffs, who work with the DEA on combined local and federal task forces. Given the odds, trying to catch every street distributor is impossible. On the federal level, we chase after the biggest fish we can identify and hope local police forces will deal with the rest.

To bust drug traffickers, federal agents and prosecutors use three main techniques. The most basic is the buy-bust. An undercover agent or police officer wearing a wire approaches a suspected drug dealer, offers to make an illegal drug purchase, and then arrests the dealer on delivery. Buy-busts are an effective but crude tool. They work best against low-level dealers, the kind you can catch out in the open. This is useful if you want to clear retail dealers out of a narcotics point source, like a drugged-up housing project or an intersection near a school. To make a real dent in drug trafficking, however, you have to attack the problem at the wholesale level, by arresting the drug importers and distributors, the men and women who sell multikilo quantities to the retail dealers who work the street. These professional drug dealers cannot be apprehended by using buy-busts, for they will not do business with strangers but only with street dealers they trust or who have been vouched for. To get these bigger targets, DOJ uses two main alternative strategies, the wiretap investigation and the flip-bust-flip. As a Narcotics prosecutor, I became an expert in both.

ONE DAY IN JANUARY OF 2000, two FBI agents from Group C-39 in Manhattan showed up in my office. Mike was a former state prosecutor who decided life would be more fun carrying a gun than a briefcase; he was smart, experienced, and a little cocky. Greg was a former deputy sheriff from South Florida, ground zero in the war on drugs. Greg was a weight lifter, with a pumped-up chest and a boyish smile. One day I ran into him in the basement of 26 Federal, the FBI's main headquarters in Manhattan. He was heading out on a raid, wearing full black body armor, with a sawed-off shotgun over one shoulder. Whistling.

In our first meeting, Mike did most of the talking. "Last fall one of our top informants, a guy who has got us a dozen convictions and hundreds of kilos, tipped us off to a major Colombian trafficker. He goes by the names Kitochet and Salabar, but his real name is Nicolas Garcia. So far the investigation's been a dry hole. The CI* has given us a couple of different phone numbers, but every time we are about to go up on a wire, Garcia drops the phone. We've been through this drill a couple of times, and we're not getting anywhere. Jodi told us to come see you."

I asked Mike who was handling the case now, and he frowned. "Anne, and she's okay, but she's so damn slow. Kitochet changes phones every three weeks or a month, and that's killing us. From the moment we get a new number from the CI, it's taking us almost a month to get authorization from Washington to tap it. By the time we are ready to go, the phone is dead."

As I listened, I thought: the problem here might not be Anne but sexism. Mike and Greg were pretty macho, and they might be having trouble working with a woman prosecutor. I made some inquiries, however, and I found that their complaints were well founded. In the EDNY, like most districts around the country, it typically takes prosecutors at least a month to "go up" on a phone: a week or two to gather sufficient evidence to establish probable cause to intercept calls; a couple of weeks to draft the application and get it approved internally; another week for review by Main Justice in Washington; and a final day or two to get the warrant signed by a federal judge in New York. Drug traffickers are aware of this delay, and they take advantage of it. Most professional traffickers change their phone service every couple of weeks, to cut down on the risk of interception.

The simplest solution to this problem is the so-called roving wiretap, which allows agents to listen to any phone a target uses, no matter how often he switches. In the EDNY, however, we were discouraged from seeking roving taps, for reasons that were never clear to me. Perhaps they were harder to administer, or maybe someone in Washington thought they raised civil liberties concerns. With that option off the table, there was only one way to solve Mike's problem: faster wiretap approval. I asked around and got the name of the most helpful wiretap reviewer

*In fed-speak, there are two kinds of informant. A CI, or confidential informant, provides information in exchange for cash. These informants work secretly and never testify at trial, so we can protect their covert status. A CW, or cooperating witness, is different. A CW provides intelligence and may wear a wire or work undercover, but his cooperation agreement requires him to testify publicly at trial if necessary. Generally, a law enforcement agency like the FBI or DEA recruits, pays, and supervises CIs, while CWs answer to prosecutors.

down at OEO, the Office of Enforcement Operations in Washington. I told this guy about our problem and made a rare request: expedited review of my next wire application. The reviewer was surprisingly helpful. Though he made no promises, he told me he would do everything he could. Then I called the agents back. My message was simple: "The next time the CI gives you a new number for Kitochet, get it to me ASAP. We're gonna set a new world speed record for wiretaps."

For the next couple of weeks we sat on our hands, waiting to hear from the CI. Then, in mid-February, our informant called: Garcia was using a new phone. Armed with the new telephone number, we leaped into action.

To get legal approval for a wiretap, you need to establish, to the satisfaction of a federal judge, that there is probable cause to believe that the phone is being used to commit a federal crime. Our CI had a good track record of reliability, and he told us Garcia's new phone was dirty, but in most cases, information from one informant alone is not enough for PC; you need corroboration. The same day we got Garcia's new number, I went to a judge and got approval for a pen register, a device that allows agents to record every number the target telephone calls. For the next few days the agents carefully examined Garcia's phone tolls, looking for evidence that he was using the phone for narcotics deals. After several days we got what we needed, four calls to a telephone number in Colombia belonging to a known cocaine trafficker named Lora. Once I got this confirmation, I raced our wiretap application through the screening process: first Jodi; then Washington; then a judge over in the courthouse. Finally, on February 18, after only one week's delay, we got approval to go up. This celerity proved critical, for sixteen days later Garcia dropped the phone. If we had taken three weeks to get wiretap authorization, we would not have heard a call. But because we moved quickly, we intercepted more than two weeks' worth. In wiretap investigations, speed kills.*

On February 18, the day the wiretap was signed, I went down to 26 Federal to brief the monitoring team on the legal rules it had to follow to ensure that our evidence would be admissible in court. Then, starting

---

*Getting approval in one week was pretty good, but my friend Eric Tirschwell was even faster. Eric put up more wires than anyone in our unit, and he did so with incredible speed, often in as little as forty-eight hours.

that afternoon, a relay team of Spanish-speaking investigators manned our wire around the clock. Their task was both difficult and dull. Most traffickers talk in coded language and slang, just in case someone is listening. To make matters worse, Title III, the federal wiretap statute, requires monitors to "minimize." Whenever a call involves personal matters, not crime, the monitor has to turn the wiretap off, wait a few minutes, and then listen in again, to see if the subject of the call is still personal or not. Under these conditions, it is often hard for monitors to figure out what is going on. When I reviewed the translations of the daily call summaries, I found most of the conversations were incomprehensible. Others, however, were priceless. Let me give you one example.

On March 2, 2000, at 10:45 a.m., Garcia called Lora, his boss in Colombia. He told him he was at a hotel in Miami, one of the most expensive in the country. Lora cut him off: "You seem to be living well."

Garcia just laughed. "No, working for you, boss."

The two men then got down to business. Lora reported that he had done the count, and it was "311 plus," a reference, I thought, to the size of Garcia's last money shipment, which probably totaled more than $311,000. Garcia replied that by the end of the week he would have more money and would send it right away. The Colombian then asked for an update: "I don't know what's going on."

Garcia told him, "They already started with the first half; they will arrive at the border tomorrow. We are just waiting for it to arrive." This was clearly a reference to a pending drug shipment that was currently in Mexico, headed for the United States, split into two loads.

BEFORE I DID MY FIRST WIRETAP CASE, I thought the government role would be passive: we would listen to calls, wait for the targets to incriminate themselves, and then make a bunch of arrests. In truth, wire cases are not so simple. Because serious traffickers use coded language, most intercepted calls are ambiguous. "Did you get the two sweaters?" "Yes, and then I sent you a basket." Even when defendants talk more clearly, they still rarely incriminate themselves completely. If, for example, I indicted Garcia on the basis of the March 2 call, he could claim at trial that he was importing fruit or handbags. And because the government has to prove its case beyond a reasonable doubt, he might actually get away with it. For this reason, I needed something more than suggestive phone calls; I needed a drug seizure. To get one, we could not just sit on our butts, recording conversations. The agents had to get out on the street and "work the wire." Fortunately, Group C-39 needed no prodding. Its members were, I discovered, masters of the wire investigation.

On March 1, 2000, Garcia called an unidentified male and asked him to wire some money to Texas, probably for expenses related to Garcia's drug shipment from Mexico. The two men then agreed to meet at "the cinema." Many agents would have simply recorded the call. C-39, in contrast, immediately put Garcia under surveillance. The agents followed him from his apartment to the College Point Multiplex in Queens, where he met with a guy driving a black Nissan Sentra. The agents ran the Nissan's plates, determined that the car was registered to a man named Erick Lopez, and then confirmed, by examining DMV photos, that it was in fact Lopez who had been behind the wheel. As a result of this operation, we had a name and face to go with that voice on the phone. Then we traced Lopez back to his home. When, a few days later, Garcia called the same guy and told him to "start checking out the streets"—lining up customers—because he had some of the "same stuff" coming and he wanted to "make some money," we were not flying blind. We knew on the basis of our prior surveillance work that Garcia was giving instructions to his subordinate, Erick Lopez. When it came time to pull down the case, Lopez would be on our arrest list.

ON MARCH 6, 2000, we picked up a bizarre call. It did not involve Garcia but two unidentified men talking about a payment to be arranged with one "Oscar De Leon." A few hours later Garcia's phone went completely dead, a development we had been expecting. That evening I met with Greg and Mike at our local Brooklyn Heights bar to discuss strategy. Though we had intercepted many good calls, we all agreed it was too early to make arrests. The wiretap had done its job, helping us identify several of Garcia's workers, three suspected customers, and two possible stash houses. With the wire down, we had more manpower to work the street. Greg and Mike thought we should put all our suspects under surveillance and see if we could pick up a seizure.

The next morning we put the plan into effect. The agents woke up early and tracked Garcia and one of his workers to a street corner in Queens, where they met with a guy we had never seen before, a man we later identified as Oscar De Leon. When the meeting broke up, after about five minutes, Greg and Mike decided to tail De Leon. They followed him discreetly to a car wash in Flushing, where intriguingly, he picked up a suitcase. The agents could have "hit the bag" at that moment, but they did not want to tip off Garcia and his men to our investigation. So they kept their heads down and followed De Leon and his bag to De Leon's house, on Sixty-second Road in Flushing. That night, when De Leon went to bed, agents were parked down the street. As soon as the house's lights went off, they called me and gave me a heads-up: possible seizure tomorrow.

In the morning De Leon exited the front door of his house carrying two suitcases. He put both bags in the trunk of his black Maxima, and then he drove to a street corner in Jackson Heights, a predominantly Latino neighborhood filled with cheap Colombian restaurants and bodegas. He got out of the car and walked around, looking at his watch. A few minutes later a young woman named Fernanda Cruz came walking down the street. The two never exchanged a word. De Leon handed Cruz the keys to the Maxima. Cruz took them, walked straight to the Maxima, and drove off, the agents once again tailing her at a cautious distance. A couple of minutes later she pulled over next to a black Jeep Cherokee and began to shift the bags to that vehicle. The agents called me quickly on their cell phone. Did they have probable cause to search the bags? I gave them the okay, and they swept in.

The luggage Cruz had picked up from De Leon contained $300,000 in small bills. The agents read Cruz her *Miranda* rights, and surprisingly, she agreed to talk, probably because she was scared out of her wits. She worked, she said, for people who collected and stored drug money. She had received the money from a man named De Leon. The agents wrote down everything she said on an FBI confession form, read it back to her, and had her sign it. When they were done, Greg called me. He was elated, as agents always are after a successful seizure. "We got a couple of bags, three hundred thousand dollars, plus one target in custody. She confessed, so she's done. Do you want us to bring her in?"

I paused, sitting in my office chair, thinking about our options. Sometimes, in investigations, you want to stir the pot. At other times you want to lull the opposition into a false sense of security. I thought about how the case might play out, and then I told the agents to let Cruz go. "If we arrest Cruz, we need to grab De Leon as well, or he'll flee. And if we nail De Leon, Garcia might disappear, so we'd have to grab him too. But arrests would be premature. If we hold off for a couple of weeks, we'll get more bodies and a stronger case. So cut her loose."

I was taking a big risk. If De Leon or Garcia learned what happened, they might flee to avoid arrest, and it would be my fault. But I had a hunch it would work out fine, and Mike and Greg, two very experienced agents, agreed. Cruz, we figured, would never tell her associates that she had ratted them out, for they would shoot her if she did. Instead, she would downplay what took place. "Oh, they grabbed the bags, but they had no idea what was going on. I told them it was money to open a restaurant, and they bought the story and let me go." Perhaps the traffickers would not believe her, but I thought they would, for most humans would rather deceive themselves than face bad news. The agents gave Cruz an FBI receipt for the money, so she could prove to her bosses that she had not stolen it, a nice touch that probably saved her life. Then they took off their cuffs and released her.

———

DURING THE TIME THE WIRE WAS ACTIVE, we tailed one of Garcia's associates, Christian Orejuella, to a third-floor apartment at 110-51 Sixty-third Avenue, in Queens. Once Garcia's phone died, we put the house under constant surveillance. For a couple of weeks after the money seizure, things were pretty quiet. On March 22, however, agents saw something promising, a short male nicknamed Chin Che leaving the house carrying a white bag. Chin Che got in a blue Nissan Sentra—this crew sure liked its Nissans!—and drove off down the street, tailed as always by FBI agents. The agents were in something of a bind. They could not arrest Chin Che or search the bag. Though they had their suspicions, they did not have sufficient proof—probable cause—to believe the bag carried drugs. But it looked as if Chin Che were driving to the other suspected stash house, and once he was inside, their chance of a seizure would disappear. So they decided to stir the pot.

The agents called in backup, two cops in a marked NYPD patrol car. The cops started to tail Chin Che's Sentra very openly, to see if they could make him panic. Not surprisingly, this tactic worked. For a couple of minutes Chin Che glanced repeatedly into his rearview mirror, a look of horror in his eyes, and then he suddenly pulled over, threw the white bag out of the car, and made a dash for it down the street, into an alley, and over a fence. Chin Che must have felt good, getting away from the cops. When he got back to his friends, he would no doubt tell them he had skillfully eluded arrest. He would have felt less thrilled if he'd known we let him get away intentionally; it was still too early to make arrests. The cops recovered the bag and handed it over to the FBI. Inside, the agents found more than a pound of cocaine and a separate smaller bag of crack.

When the agents called me about the seizure, I told them to come down to the EDNY immediately, for their discovery that the white bag definitely contained drugs gave us enough evidence for a warrant to search the third-floor apartment on Sixty-third Avenue. Mike, Greg, and I spent several hours crafting a search warrant application, and then we took it to a judge for review. By 5:00 p.m. it had been signed.

That night, around nine, a large force of FBI agents and NYPD detectives arrived at the apartment building and split into two teams. The security team established a perimeter around the building, to ensure that no one could enter and attack the searching agents from behind. Once that was accomplished, the search team propped open the front door and sneaked quietly up the stairs to the third floor. When the whole team was in place, they hit the door, guns drawn, yelling in Spanish and English. "*Abajo! Abajo!* Get down on the floor!" Inside they found a woman named Monica and her two small kids, whom they must have terrified. Two agents sat Monica and her kids in a chair and kept them covered, while the rest of the team dug through every drawer, closet, and bag in the place. They quickly discovered 688 grams of white powder, which they assumed was cocaine or heroin. When, however, they placed a small sample of the powder on a testing strip, it came up negative. Later we determined it was a cutting agent, a laxative powder that dealers use to stretch and bulk up their product to make it go farther, a sort of "heroin helper."

Once the search was over, the agents asked Monica where her husband was. She replied, "In the basement with Miguel, doing *trabajo de droga* [drug work]." The search team immediately peeled off and raced down the stairs. They discovered, however, that the security team had got to the basement first.

While the search had been under way on the third floor, the security squad had remained downstairs, watching the building. At nine-forty, they saw a man we later identified as Miguel Gomez appear in the well-lit first-floor foyer, peer out the open front door with a quizzical look on his face, and then close and lock it. The security team did not want a locked door between them and the search team, so two agents got up, knocked on the door, and flashed their badges. "We're FBI. What are you doing here?"

Visibly nervous, licking his lips, Gomez looked at them and said, "I am visiting friends, I just got here," a lie, for the agents had all the entrances and exits covered, and no one had come or gone for at least forty minutes.

As the agents talked with Gomez, they noticed an open door leading down to a basement, the place, perhaps, where Gomez had just come from. Two agents took Gomez outside. They would detain him until the search was finished, for safety. Another agent and an NYPD detective drew their guns and crept down the stairs, which led to a narrow basement corridor. They padded silently down the hall for a few yards and then came to an open doorway. Loud voices, talking in Spanish, were coming from just around the corner, inside the room. The detective peered quickly around the doorway and then yanked his head back. He saw two men sitting at a table, wearing latex plastic gloves, handling big mounds of white powder. Gun still raised, the detective rotated his torso to face his partner. He silently held up two fingers and then pointed them toward the open doorway, signaling "two men inside." Then he pointed upstairs with his index finger, which he rotated: "Get backup." Within thirty seconds two more agents arrived silently in the hallway. When the team was ready, they spun through the doorway, guns drawn, yelling in Spanish, "*Abajo! Abajo!*" They grabbed the two men and threw them roughly to the floor, then pointed their guns at their heads. Once the men were immobile, arms cuffed behind their backs, facedown on the concrete floor, the agents took stock. On the table they saw a big white chalky cube, straight from a Latin American processing lab, and three clear plastic bags of white powder. The agents did a quick field test: heroin. That night the agents weighed the drugs before putting them in the evidence vault: 665 grams. Sold retail, at the going rate of $1,000 per gram, it was worth $665,000.

The agents paged me from the search site, and I returned their call from home. I authorized the arrest of the two men in the basement, Henry Valencia and Orlando Rincon. The case of the third man, Miguel Gomez, was more complex. We did not catch him with drugs, and the only evidence tying him to the heroin in the basement was Monica's statement, and she would almost certainly disappear that night, moving to escape the FBI.* Still, I told the agents to bring Gomez in. I figured that eventually someone would flip and implicate him.

WHEN WE ARRESTED RINCON, Valencia, and Gomez, we took a risk that Garcia would disappear. Still, we did not take the case down. Having picked off one of his distribution cells, we thought we might get lucky and nail another. For the next five weeks the agents worked surveillance aggressively, but we had no further breaks. I suspected that our arrests had frightened our targets, and they were lying low, hoping to stay off our radar screen. After a while we decided we should not be greedy. On May 3, 2000, C-39 fanned out over Queens and arrested Garcia, Orejuella, and Oscar De Leon. Erick Lopez managed to slip through our net, but he eventually surfaced in June, and we picked him up then. We even busted Chin Che, who was very unhappy to learn that we had had him under surveillance the whole time he thought he was free. Cruz, however, escaped. After we stopped her in March, she had wisely disappeared. In the end we arrested eight men.

THE GARCIA CASE had all the makings of a dramatic trial: a large cast of thuggish defendants, three dramatic drug and money seizures, smart law enforcement tactics, and a group of intriguing wiretap interceptions. I looked forward to presenting this story to a jury. We would let the jurors hold bags of crack, heroin, and cocaine in their hands, see

---

*We could not arrest Monica. Though she was obviously aware that her husband was a drug trafficker, we did not possess any evidence that she was affirmatively aiding the drug business, and thus she was not liable as an accomplice. I could have arrested her as a material witness but decided not to do so, for if I had, her children would have wound up in foster care.

what $300,000 in cash looks like, and let them listen in as a drug lord in Colombia talked to his contact in New York about a drug shipment crossing the United States–Mexico border. If we presented our evidence creatively, we could make the drug trafficking world come to life in the courtroom. I was confident we would win.

Unfortunately, we never got our chance. Though it took a year of negotiations, conducted by both my colleague Nicky Kowalski and me, we ultimately convinced all eight defendants to plead guilty, and the whole crew was sent off to prison. From the office's perspective, this was a big win. It guaranteed convictions without the risk of trial, and it conserved our most precious resource, prosecutorial time. Instead of devoting three months exclusively to this one case, for trial prep and trial itself, I was able to spend that time supervising new investigations and making new arrests.

From a professional perspective, I was glad we got everyone to plead guilty. I was even commended by Jodi Avergun in my annual fitness review for resolving the case efficiently. But personally I was disappointed. A trial would have been fun.

The anticlimactic outcome of the *Garcia* case was not unusual. During my time in the Narcotics Unit, almost all my investigations ended in guilty pleas. At first, I gave myself a lot of credit for this. I've run skillful investigations and made wise charging decisions, I told myself, so I have the proof on my side. And the defense attorneys know I am good in the courtroom, so they're afraid to face me. In time, however, I realized that this egotistical explanation was off target. I was not the only prosecutor who got most of his drug defendants to plead. The same was true for almost everyone else in Narcotics. This forced me to look for a deeper explanation. Ultimately I found two.

IN FEDERAL NARCOTICS CASES the defendants often face massive prison sentences if they are convicted after trial. In these circumstances, some defendants plead in return for a lighter sentence. Others decide to cooperate with the government. In my drug cases, for example, I could usually count on 20 to 30 percent of my defendants to flip and testify against their former friends and colleagues. As a result, my proof always got stronger after indictment. In *Garcia*, for example, several of the defendants quickly signed up as cooperators. This left their peers in a hopeless position, facing strong accomplice testimony in addition to the wiretap and surveillance evidence that had led me to arrest them in the first place. Faced with this evidence, all of them wisely decided to cave rather than risk trial. The fact that I was the prosecutor was probably irrelevant. The same would likely have happened even if the case had been in less skilled hands.

A second dynamic was also at work. If you watch a lot of federal drug trials, you quickly see that juries will convict narcotics defendants even when the government's case is relatively weak. The reason for this is really depressing. When juries consider the evidence, their deliberations are inevitably tainted by bias. Most of the defendants fit our society's stereotype of the typical drug dealer: young, male, a person of color, poorly educated, living in a marginal, troubled neighborhood. Because the narcotics defendants look just like the drug dealers on television, jurors find it easy, cognitively, to accept the government's assertion that they are in fact involved in the drug trade. Defense attorneys know this. They know that even if the evidence is weak, they run a serious risk of conviction in these cases. As a result, they are often quick to recommend a plea or to suggest that their clients cooperate. For a prosecutor, in short, winning a federal drug case is like running with the wind behind you. You may be breaking speed records, but that is not because you are so fast; it is because you have an unfair advantage.

CHAPTER ELEVEN

Bushwick

Some narcotics prosecutors and agents love the wiretap, but I was never a huge fan. It is an essential tool if you are hunting down drug traffickers overseas, where visual surveillance and seizures are impossible, but for purely domestic cases, it has a lot of drawbacks. Getting a wiretap requires a lot of time-consuming and mind-numbing paperwork. Wiretaps are also expensive because you have to pay dozens of employees to monitor the wire and even more to translate the results if, as is common in drug cases, the targets speak a language other than English. In one of my cases, we burned more than one million dollars this way, trying, unsuccessfully, to catch a suspected cop killer in the Russian mob.

More important, I discovered that wiretaps are not always needed to investigate a narcotics case successfully. To get approval for a wiretap, you need to have probable cause to believe you will uncover evidence of a crime. In most drug cases, the only way to establish PC is to use an informant to infiltrate your target group. But if you have that kind of solid intelligence to begin with, an informant on the ground who can identify at least one key player and a telephone number, you can usually make a good case without a wiretap, through careful surveillance alone. My favorite DEA agent, Jeff Higgins, never asked for a wiretap during all the years I worked with him. "They're just a hassle," he told me once. "I'd rather be out working the street."

If you cannot or will not wiretap your narcotics targets, how do you round them up? The answer is the flip-bust-flip. You "jam up" a defendant by catching him selling drugs, get him to cooperate, and then put him back out on the street. He helps you set up more dealers, and when you arrest the second set, you convince some of them to flip too. If you do this properly and have a bit of luck, the case never ends; you just keep arresting and flipping targets, one wave after another.

My favorite case of my entire career was a flip-bust-flip. The case began in 1997, when I was a rookie, and it is still going on today, in 2008. When cases last a decade, prosecutors and agents tend to name them, for convenience. This case was called Bushwick, for the grim neighborhood in which it unfolded.

———

ONE NIGHT IN LATE 1997, when I was a brand-new federal prosecutor, DEA Special Agent Jeff Higgins conducted a classic buy-bust in the rough Bushwick neighborhood of Brooklyn. The target, a Dominican immigrant named Manuel, was a pharmacist back in Santo Domingo, but unable to find work in America, he turned to selling drugs. Jeff caught him red-handed, on tape, trying to sell fifty grams of heroin he had in his pocket. Because the case was small, involving a single defendant and a negligible quantity of heroin, Neil Ross, the EDNY's cigar-smoking intake chief, sent the case to General Crimes, not Narcotics. The case folder wound up in my mailbox.

To be honest, I was totally uninterested in Manuel's case, and when his attorney offered to cooperate, I wanted to decline. I already had dozens of small drug cases, more than I could handle comfortably. My only goal was to terminate Manuel's case as quickly as possible, with an effortless guilty plea. Signing up Manuel as a cooperator, with all the supervisory responsibilities that entailed, seemed like more work than it was worth. Jeff Higgins, however, pressured me. "We've got to put this guy out on the street. I can make good cases with him." Ultimately, I agreed. Jeff seemed very smart, and I thought his aggressive drive should be encouraged. I was also worried that if I said no, Jeff might complain to my boss that I was dragging my feet. Manuel pleaded guilty in the spring of 1998 and was then released on bail, so he could work for Jeff. At the time I gave Jeff a warning: "I don't have time to work this case. Manuel's all yours. Do what you want. Let me know if something good happens."

For nine months I paid no attention to Jeff's investigation; I was too busy with the Badfellas and Scarpa trials. When, however, I arrived in the Narcotics unit in late 1998, my attitude changed. A great AUSA "makes her own cases," flipping her defendants and using their testimony to take other criminals off the street. At that point Manuel was my only active cooperator. If I were going to make some cases, I would have to start with him.

I also had a broader purpose in mind. During our year in General Crimes, my friend Dwight Holton and I often discussed the EDNY's severe crime problem, and we concluded that our office's crime-fighting strategy was too diffuse. Instead of waiting for agents to bring cases to us, we should be more focused and proactive. Eventually Dwight and I developed an idea for community prosecution. We would identify the worst high-crime neighborhoods in Brooklyn and Queens, and then small teams of AUSAs would take responsibility for those neighborhoods, working with federal agents and the NYPD to arrest the area's worst criminals and put them permanently behind bars. Dwight and I floated the idea to our supervisors, but we had so little seniority in the office no one took us seriously. We decided to implement our plan quietly on our own.

Dwight and I surveyed our options, and our eyes quickly landed on Bushwick, a small but dense neighborhood with roughly 110,000 African American and Dominican residents in northern Brooklyn. Bushwick was very poor. More than one-third of the residents were on public assistance; the streets were lined with burned-out buildings; kids played in empty lots strewn with garbage and broken glass. It was also a total war zone. In 1990 there were 77 reported murders, 2,242 robberies, and 1,173 violent assaults in Bushwick's tiny Eighty-third Precinct alone.* Bushwick's main drag, Knickerbocker Avenue, was known on the street as the Well, because its supply of heroin was so reliable. If you wanted to try to clean up one bad neighborhood, Bushwick seemed like a logical place to start. More to the point, both Dwight and I had assets there. I had the cooperator Manuel; he had a cooperator named Orlando, a dealer who had been involved in a bunch of murders. Together we decided we would use these two informants to build as many Bushwick cases as we could.

*By comparison, there were 18 murders that year in downtown Brooklyn's Eighty-fourth Precinct, 8 in Manhattan's Midtown South Precinct, and 6 in Chelsea's Tenth Precinct.

Jeff Higgins and I had our first serious meeting on the Bushwick case in my office in early November 1998. Jeff was in his late twenties, thin, wiry, and tough. He had lost most of his hair prematurely, and his shaved head and alert gaze gave him a slightly satanic look. Later, I learned that our defendants in the Bushwick case called him *el diablo calvo*, the bald devil. I asked Jeff what was happening with Manuel, and he grinned. "I knew you were busy with that big mafia trial, so I tried to keep out of your way. But we are ready to roll. Manuel has been out on the street for five months, telling everyone in Bushwick that his case was dismissed. At first no one really believed him, but I think they do now. He's been talking with a couple of dealers, and they are prepared to sell to him. So if you are game, I want to make some cases."

I asked Jeff who the targets were. He looked down at his notes. "There's a guy named Ricochet, and he has two partners, Cabeza—that's Spanish for 'big head'—and David Jimenez. There's also an assistant, a worker, who they call Number Seventeen. According to Manuel, Ricochet's crew is moving about one kilo of heroin a week. They sell it in fifty- and one-hundred-gram amounts to street dealers, who peddle it up and down Knickerbocker Avenue and in the projects. I checked in with Mike Zeller at the Eight-Three.* He says he doesn't have much hard proof, but Ricochet's a top suspect in a homicide."

I smiled and interrupted. "His name is certainly promising."

Jeff smiled too, and then he continued. "On October 29 we wired up Manuel, and he got a heroin sample from Ricochet, so we know he is prepared to deal." I asked Jeff what his plan was. He shrugged, as if the answer were obvious. "Make some recorded calls and set up some buys."

———

FROM NOVEMBER 1998 TO MAY 1999, Jeff and Mike Zeller of the NYPD set up a series of meetings among Manuel, Ricochet, and Ricochet's men. These meetings took place at a number of different drug safe houses and Latino restaurants in Bushwick. At each meeting, Manuel wore a tiny recording device and transmitter, so Jeff and his team could intervene if things got dangerous. Manuel would give our targets large stacks of cash, courtesy of the DEA, and our targets gave us small sacks

*The NYPD's Eighty-third Precinct.

of heroin. We also pulled a harsh trick. Under federal law, the punishment for selling crack is one hundred times more severe than that for selling cocaine powder.* To make sure Ricochet got hammered at sentencing, we asked him for crack and bought some of that too. By mid-May we had gathered enough evidence on Ricochet, Cabeza, Jimenez, and Number Seventeen to guarantee convictions. Jeff swooped in and arrested all the targets.

Had the case stopped there, it would have been a success. Jeff and I, however, had larger ambitions. In a debriefing session, Manuel told us that Ricochet got his drugs from "Oscar," one of the biggest drug suppliers in the neighborhood, who ran a Bushwick telephone and pager store called Tele Global Communications. Manuel made Oscar look like a very attractive target. "He's big, very big, moves lots of drugs, knows everybody. He's got Ricochet on tap for muscle. No one fucks with him. Very dangerous. Very cold." Manuel was a low-level dealer, and he could not safely approach Oscar without raising suspicions. Fortunately, Jeff came up with a solution.

According to Manuel, a dealer nicknamed Gordo, the Fat Guy, was a major player in Bushwick. In the fall of 1998 I had wanted to make him a target, but Jeff waved me off. Now Jeff told me that Gordo was a secret DEA informant who provided information in exchange for cash. Though Manuel could not approach Oscar, Gordo could. There was some risk in making a blind approach, but Jeff told me Gordo would do it gladly. "To be honest, I don't think he does this for the money anymore. He likes a little bit of danger." There was only one catch. Since Gordo was a highly valued informant, Jeff made me promise that no matter what happened, I would never "burn him"—force him to testify in court, where his status as an informant would be disclosed. To fix this problem, we developed a simple ruse. During the spring of 1999 Gordo met repeatedly with Oscar and his assistants to buy heroin. At each meeting Gordo was accompanied by his "bodyguard," a Latino DEA agent working undercover. This protected Gordo's covert status, for if

---

*Providing more severe punishment for crack than for powder cocaine has been a highly contentious criminal justice issue for years. Some justify the disparity because crack is more addictive and associated with more intense street crime and violence. Critics allege, however, that the difference is rooted in racism, for crack is more widely consumed by African Americans, while powder is favored by whites. Experts on the U.S. Sentencing Commission have recommended that the disparity be reduced, but Congress has refused, for there is no political gain to be had by reducing criminal penalties for any crimes, let alone crack dealing.

we had a trial, the agent could testify about the meetings instead of him, and the dealers would blame the "bodyguard," not Gordo himself. Eventually, Oscar trusted our undercover agent so much he sold him heroin directly. By June 1999 we had three buys with Oscar on tape, enough to guarantee guilty pleas from Oscar and his assistants.

On June 23, 1999, at 3:00 p.m., Jeff and his DEA team put on combat gear and assaulted Tele Global, putting Oscar and his two workers under arrest. A few minutes later Jeff called me at my office. I asked him how things had gone. "Everybody safe?"

Jeff just laughed, still jacked up on adrenaline. "Everything's fine. We've got Oscar and his two helpers, Red and Primo, all under arrest. I'll have them down for arraignment as soon as I can."

"Did you have to use any force?"

"Nah. I like to announce our presence with authority. We practically drove through the storefront. They were scared shitless and hit the floor. They were easy to round up."

"Great."

"I've got a favor to ask. When we hit the door, there were two other men with Oscar in his back office, behind bulletproof Plexiglas. I'm holding them now. My gut tells me these guys are big, probably Oscar's suppliers. I want to pick them up too."

I did not reply immediately. I was tempted to tell Jeff to forget it. I did not want to authorize additional arrests off the cuff. But by this point in the investigation I knew that Jeff was a brilliant agent. His instincts were so good they deserved respect. So after a few moments I said, "Okay, tell me what you've got."

Jeff laughed again, nervously, perhaps because of the adrenaline, or maybe because he knew his evidence was too weak. "Not much. One of them is named Granados. Yesterday, when we were doing the last buy from Oscar, we picked him up on surveillance. When Oscar drove up, Granados was in the passenger seat of his car. While Oscar was inside, meeting with the informant, Granados was out on the sidewalk, looking up and down the street, like a lookout."

"Anything else?"

"No, that's all we got on Granados."

"Okay, what about the other one?"

"Uh, his name is Alberto Longas, recently arrived from Colombia. I got almost nothing on him. Before we hit the door, I wanted to make sure Oscar was here, so I asked Gordo to check it out. He told us Oscar was in his office with two Colombian associates from the drug business. These guys are Colombian. So it's probably them."

Agents always want you to arrest every suspect, even if there is no evidence. As a prosecutor you cannot afford to play that game since you have to defend your arrest decisions in court, before a judge. I cut in. "Come on, Jeff! I can't write a complaint on that! You really don't have anything else?"

"Well, he's Colombian, and Manuel says Oscar's supplier is a Colombian, but he's never met him . . ." Jeff's voice trailed off.

I paused, thinking. After a few minutes Jeff got impatient. "Trust me, this could be huge. If you let me arrest them, I promise you, I will dig up enough evidence. Give me two weeks, and you'll have a good case."

"Shut up for a minute. Let me think," I said. The phone went silent. Jeff was waiting; I was thinking through our options. It took me a minute, but eventually I worked out a plan I was comfortable with.

"Jeff, what are you guys doing now?"

"We're searching Tele Global."

"Do you have a camera with your search gear?"

"Yeah, a Polaroid."

"Okay, here's what you do. You can hold Granados and Longas for a few minutes, for security reasons, while you finish up the search. Take a quick Polaroid of them and run the photos over to Gordo. Ask him if he can identify them and if he knows anything else about them. Then call me back."

Jeff said, "Roger that," and hung up. Ten minutes later he was back on the phone. "Gordo IDed them both. He said that Granados came with Oscar to a meeting one time, when they discussed a big heroin deal. And last week, when he bought seven hundred grams from Oscar, both Granados and Longas came with Oscar to deliver. He says they probably were there for protection."

"Okay, here's the deal. You can take them into custody for now. Come on down as soon as you can, and we'll write the best complaint we can. If the judge signs it, fine. But I am not indicting them as it is. You've got a couple of weeks to dig up some more evidence. If you don't, we cut them loose."

"No problem," Jeff replied. "I guarantee you we will find it." He sounded confident and elated.

That afternoon I wrote the weakest criminal complaint of my career. It stated that according to Manuel, Oscar's suppliers were Colombian, and both Longas and Granados were of that nationality; that Gordo, an informant, said both men were present at a big heroin deal; that Granados had been seen by DEA agents on another occasion acting like a lookout; and that when we raided Tele Global, both men were with Oscar, behind the Plexiglas partition. I believed this was sufficient evidence to arrest, but it was pretty thin, as we say in the business, and I was worried that some reviewing magistrates might disagree. Fortunately, Judge Cheryl Pollak was on duty that day. Before she became a judge, Pollak was one of the best narcotics prosecutors in EDNY history. At arraignment she read my complaint and signed it without comment. At the end of the day we had five new arrests to our credit.

FROM THE MOMENT OSCAR entered my consciousness, I knew he would make a great cooperator. Oscar occupied a strategic middle position in the Brooklyn drug world, obtaining large amounts of drugs from Colombian importers and then passing them on to various distribution organizations, like Ricochet's. If he flipped, we could work him both up and down the distribution chain, busting both smugglers and distributors. At his arraignment, I tried to plant the seed. I took his lawyer out into the marble hallway and said, "Look, there is no way Oscar is going to escape conviction. I've got him on tape doing deals directly with an undercover. If he wants to fight the case, he's going to get hammered. His only way out is to cooperate, but if he wants to get on that boat, he has to move quick. I'd like to get him in to proffer immediately, if we could."

The next morning the lawyer called. "Oscar is interested. When can we come in?"

I replied: "How about tomorrow?"

On June 25, Jeff picked up Oscar at the MDC and brought him down to my office, where we handcuffed him to a chair in the main Narcotics conference room. Oscar was about five feet eight inches tall and weighed some two hundred pounds, a little fat but strong. He was wearing prison garb: dark blue pants; a voluminous light blue cotton shirt;

dark blue slippers with white rubber soles. His head was massive and square, his hair greasy, and he seemed very nervous, licking his lips, glancing from one corner of the room to the next, as if he expected an attack. I explained our standard proffer agreement to him, and I discovered to my delight that he spoke English. Then I started my pitch.

In most first proffers, I move very slowly, progressing step by step through the defendant's criminal career, testing his honesty and judging his credibility. With Oscar, I did not have that luxury. Normally, defendants decide to cooperate weeks or months into their case, and though they may have important information to provide us, their knowledge about crimes occurring at that moment out on the street is limited because they have been sitting in jail. Oscar, in contrast, had been arrested only two days before our meeting, and some of his intelligence might be actionable. So, as soon as he signed the proffer agreement, I cut to the chase.

"Oscar, I don't know if we are going to let you cooperate or not. But I do know one thing: the chance of you getting a light sentence down the road is going to depend on what you say and do in the next five minutes. This is a very serious moment for you, a fateful moment. If you fuck it up, you are going to rot in jail for years. At least ten, probably fifteen, maybe more. I'm not making that up. Ask your lawyer; he'll tell you the same thing. So, here's my question. I want to know where I can seize some drugs right now. I want to know the places where your suppliers and your customers store their stash. Don't hold back on me. If you do, you are only fucking yourself. Tell me everything you know."

Oscar stared at me blankly, looked over at his attorney, swallowed, and then said, "Can I have a few minutes to talk to my lawyer?" Jeff and I walked out of the room, though Jeff kept the door slightly ajar so he could keep an eye on things from the hallway. Five minutes later the attorney called us back in. Some defendants are tough to flip; Oscar was butter.

"I get my drugs from a cartel in Colombia. At first my contact was Felix, but a few months ago Felix left, and they sent me Longas. Longas meets the couriers, gets their heroin, and then I pick it up from him at his house. I don't know the address, but I can describe where he lives."

"What about Granados? Is he a supplier too?"

Oscar shook his head wearily, a look of disgust on his face. "He's a nobody, practically homeless. I let him work at my store. He sweeps it out, runs errands, gets coffee. Sometimes I use him to deliver drugs. He is useless for protection, but he looks sort of tough, so I bring him along sometimes just for show."

I interrupted. To have probable cause for a warrant, your information must be "fresh," not out-of-date. So I asked, "When was the last time you picked up drugs at Longas's house?"

"Oh, a week ago, maybe two."

That was good enough for me. "Oscar, this is really important. If you help us here, it may do you a lot of good. Tell me everything you know about the house."

For the next few minutes Oscar described Longas's house. He did not know the address, but he knew it was on Junction Boulevard in Queens, around Fifty-third Street, and he told us about the house's shape and color. Longas, he said, did not live in the main part of the house but in a separate basement apartment, which had a door around back. We pumped Oscar for every extra bit of information, and then Jeff dispatched a recon team to Queens to see if the agents could find the house. Twenty minutes later, they called in: there was a house at 5308 Junction Boulevard that fitted the description perfectly. I told the agents to secure the perimeter, so no one could enter or leave, and then to knock on the front door and see if they could confirm that Longas lived there. Two minutes later they called back. Affirmative, he lived in the basement apartment.

At that point I terminated Oscar's first proffer. One team of agents bustled him downstairs and back to the MDC. Another headed to Queens, to join the recon team. Meanwhile, I called the duty magistrate and told her I would be bringing over an emergency warrant in twenty minutes. Jeff and I retired to my office, and I batted out in fifteen minutes a search warrant application for Longas's apartment. Then we sprinted over to the courthouse. Normally, that walk took five minutes. Jeff and I did it in two. The judge took the warrant, read it in our presence, and signed. A few minutes later Jeff called his recon team from the front steps of the courthouse and told the agents they were authorized to hit the apartment. Then we walked back to my office to wait for the results. Unfortunately, the search team called back quickly. The search result was negative. No drugs. Jeff was dejected. I was not surprised.

When we wrote the search warrant for Longas's apartment, Jeff and I had slightly different motives. In the DEA an agent is judged, to a significant degree, by the number and size of his drug seizures, because the DEA places great emphasis on getting narcotics off the street. So Jeff wanted a seizure badly. I would have loved to seize some drugs, but that was not my main goal. Colombian cartels are very professional, so I assumed that when Longas was arrested, another worker had probably gone to his apartment and cleared out any drugs. There was, however, a chance that he had still left good evidence behind. When the searching agents told me they had not found drugs, I immediately asked, "What else did you find?"

"Well, we've got some paperwork, it looks like they might be drug records, listing dates and dollar amounts, and we got a scale."

"Test the scale. See if it has any drug residue on it."

"I don't need to test it, it's got white powder in one of the cups."

"Look around, see if you can find anything with Longas's name on it. I want to be able to prove he lived there."

"Roger, give me a minute." I waited. "Okay, we've got some mail addressed to him and a bank statement."

"Great. Seize all that stuff. Try not to handle the envelopes. We may be able to get prints."

"Right. Sorry we didn't find any drugs."

"No problem. This was a great search. That scale guarantees that if Longas goes to trial, he loses. Good work."

AFTER THE LONGAS SEARCH, I brought Oscar back in for a comprehensive debriefing. When I was satisfied that he was being completely honest and had admitted all his past criminal conduct, or what I believed to be all his past crimes, he pleaded guilty and signed a cooperation agreement. I did not publicly disclose that Oscar was cooperating, but in the courthouse, the defense lawyers can always tell who has cut a deal, because a cooperator's guilty plea is done not in open court but behind closed doors, under seal. Rumor apparently spread that Oscar had come in, for his guilty plea set off an avalanche. Oscar's own assistants pleaded guilty first. Red got four years in prison; Primo and Granados, two. Ricochet's crew was next. Ricochet and Cabeza got ten years each; David and Number Seventeen, four. Longas was last. Though I knew in my heart he was a major heroin importer, he got only six years, because I could never prove how much heroin he had brought into the country.

Once these cases were out of the way, Jeff and I prepared another wave of arrests. In his debriefing, Oscar gave us the names and physical descriptions of several other major Bushwick dealers. Jeff tried to identify these men, using criminal background checks, immigration records, surveillance, and the database of the Department of Motor Vehicles. Eventually, he located two: Nelson Aguirre and Jose Correa, who was also called El Viejo, "the old man." According to Oscar, Aguirre and Correa sold large quantities of heroin to dealers in the neighborhood. For almost a year Jeff and I worked to corroborate this information. First we found, arrested, and flipped another Bushwick dealer. When we handed him a book of fifty mug shots, some of Bushwick suspects, some chosen at random, he identified both Aguirre and Correa as major-league dealers, whom he knew from prior narcotics deals. This gave us a second witness. Jeff also brought to my office numerous boxes of records he had taken from Tele Global, Oscar's store, and together we dug through them, looking for useful evidence. After several days of hunting, we found wire transfer receipts showing Aguirre and Correa had shipped hundreds of thousands of dollars to Panama and Colombia using their own names. This was very useful. Who besides drug dealers ships huge amounts of cash overseas?

Unfortunately, Jeff and I were unable to uncover any additional evidence, leaving us with two very weak cases. I thought if we indicted Aguirre and Correa, a jury might acquit them. Still, we had nothing to lose. Our cases were never going to get better. In 2001, Jeff arrested them both. El Viejo, as his name implied, was an old man who looked and acted like a grandfather. He had a lot of potential jury appeal, and I was happy when he agreed to take a four-year plea.

Resolution of the Aguirre case was more complicated. Left to his own devices, Aguirre would have gone to trial. His chief assistant in the drug business, however, was his young wife, Marysol. I was never very interested in busting the wives of drug traffickers. In many cases, they are coerced into helping their husbands in the drug trade. In this case, however, I thought Marysol was guilty as sin, and I knew I needed leverage. When we arrested Aguirre, we took Marysol into custody as well. Then we made an offer. If Aguirre pleaded guilty, we would cut Marysol loose. Aguirre loved his wife, or maybe he just wanted her released so she could restart the drug business. Regardless, he accepted our offer and went to prison for nine years. This brought our conviction count in the case up to twelve.

IN THE EDNY we never signed up a defendant to cooperate unless we were confident he had divulged all of his past crimes. We adopted this position for two reasons. First, we believed that if a cooperator started his work for the government by getting away with deception about his own past, he might be tempted to lie again, about other people's crimes. That could result in the conviction of an innocent man. Second, we wanted to make sure that we were not inadvertently giving sweetheart deals to mass murderers or drug kingpins who were hiding their past crimes. The only way to avoid this was to get them to confess to every crime they had ever committed.

Unfortunately, getting most defendants to confess is hard work. Virtually all new witnesses tend to "minimize," to hide or downplay their criminal histories. They will admit to selling drugs but lie about the amounts or "forget" to tell you about murders or assaults. Most witnesses do this because they think that hiding the full extent of their crimes will work to their advantage, resulting in a lighter sentence than if they are totally honest. For some others, however, it is a matter of shame. When you take criminals off the street and put them in a controlled environment, where being a killer is no longer valued and respected, a few of them recognize that their past conduct has been abhorrent. They want to earn the respect of their prosecutors and handling agents, so they lie about their past or downplay their roles. When this happened in my own cases, I was always disgusted. Nothing is more offensive than listening to a man insist that he is not really such a bad guy, because he was only the lookout in a shooting, not the triggerman. But from an ethical point of view, these evasions are important, for the defendant's lack of comfort about his own past often represents a necessary first step toward greater moral self-reflection.

To get a reluctant cooperator to "come to Jesus," prosecutors engage in a process called, somewhat inelegantly, beating up the witness. Whenever we suspect that a witness is lying about his past—and our suspicions are often correct, for virtually every dealer or shooter lies at first—we pressure him. Some prosecutors shout: "Look, this is such bullshit! If you want to play games, you can go to trial!" I did that on occasion. At other times you get better results using a more solemn, quiet, regretful approach: "Well, I have to say, I don't feel like you are being totally honest here, so maybe we should wrap this up. I don't really need your cooperation anyway. I'd just as soon send you to prison." Then you shake your head in mock sorrow at the infirmity of human nature.

The challenge of course is to distinguish between truth and lies, to be able to sense when your witnesses are covering up. Consider Oscar. When Oscar began to cooperate, he was incredibly forthcoming about his drug business, and he even admitted to threatening some of his customers with violence when they were late in paying him off. But when I asked him about murder, he denied any involvement. If I pressed him, he begged and whined, "Why do you keep doubting me? I am telling you everything I know. Believe me. Please. Pleeeeease. Be-leeeve me."

I had no evidence that Oscar had committed a murder, but I did not trust his denials, and neither did Jeff. It is hard to articulate why: something about the way his voice changed and his eyes flashed when I asked him if he was lying. Finally, I threw down the gauntlet. I told Oscar he had one last chance to be completely honest. If he kept lying, the deal was off. This was a dangerous tactic, for in truth I wanted his cooperation badly, but I believed I had no other choice. I left Oscar alone with his lawyer for half an hour, and when I came back, I asked him if he was ready to talk. He nodded and spoke.

"I told you about those Dominican guys from Boston, Ramon, Jesus, Francisco. They would come down to New York every few months, to buy heroin. Sometimes they would come to Tele Global. Sometimes Red and I would take drugs to them in the Bronx. Then they would drive it up to Boston and sell it at their spot. I was giving them stuff on credit, but then Ramon fell behind in their payments. I pressured him to come up with the money, but he had no way to pay. Finally, he came up with an idea. One of his men had left the crew and was selling heroin he bought from other dealers . . ."

Oscar paused. I could tell this was difficult for him. I waited for a few seconds, and then I prodded him. "What happened next?"

"I told Ramon, 'You can't put up with that shit; you have to send a message,' and he agreed. He told me he would kill this guy, steal his heroin, sell it, and then use the money to pay me back. He asked me for help in finding a hitman, and I put him in touch with one, but they could not work out a deal. I think it was too expensive. After that I forgot all about the whole thing. Then, one day back in the spring, Ramon shows up at Tele Global. He tells me that he needs money, he has to flee the country. I asked him why, and he told me he had killed that guy who used to be in his crew. He had lured him to a quiet place to talk and then cut his throat. Now he had to go. So I lent him money, and he went to the Dominican Republic."

Oscar's confession had two immediate consequences. First, I told him that if he wanted to cooperate, he had to plead guilty to murder conspiracy, which exposed him, potentially, to life in prison. Oscar hated this and tried to push back, but I made it a condition of his cooperation, and ultimately he swallowed it. He knew that if he went to trial on his drug charges, he would definitely lose and receive something like a ten- or fifteen-year sentence. Worse, he might eventually find himself charged with murder too and face life in jail. Given these facts, he was better off cooperating with me than fighting against me, even if that required him to plead to a murder charge.

Second, Jeff went to work, investigating Ramon's group, which we dubbed, for convenience, the Boston Crew. He debriefed Oscar in detail, getting him to reveal every scrap of information he knew about Ramon, his men, and the date and method of the murder. Then he went to Boston and started digging around. With the help of the Boston police, he found the victim, Jose Antonio Fabian, whose body was found in a Boston alley on April 12, 1999, covered in blood, with multiple stab wounds and a slashed throat. Jeff also identified four of the crew members: the leader, Ramon Medina; his brother Jesus; and two of their dealers, Francisco Matos and Jose Bautista.

Once these basics were nailed down, Jeff began to build a case. He found phone records that proved that the men knew one another and Oscar. He discovered that several cars registered to members of the crew possessed covert "traps," secret storage places dealers use to hide drugs when they are transporting them. He located several key witnesses. One told us that Ramon Medina had been looking for Fabian just before Fabian was killed. The other said Ramon was skilled with knives. Jeff uncovered evidence that Ramon and Matos had been involved in two earlier stabbings. Most important of all, he learned that on two occasions Matos and Bautista had been caught by the Boston police selling heroin. These prior arrests, which had resulted in very short jail terms, were of priceless evidentiary value, for they would prove to a jury that this Boston heroin ring did in fact exist, just as Oscar claimed. By early 2000 we were ready to make arrests.

Jose Bautista and Francisco Matos went down easily: located quickly, arrested, indicted, convicted. Bautista got fourteen years; Matos, eleven. The Medina brothers were more trouble. After the Fabian murder they both had disappeared, and when we tried to find them, we came up short. In this situation, most agents would have been passive; they would have posted the arrest warrants on the National Crime Information Center, or NCIC, database and left the arrests to chance. Jeff, in contrast, went on a protracted manhunt. He gathered the telephone numbers of every one of the Medinas' friends and family members, and then he analyzed all their phone traffic, looking for clues. Eventually he learned that one family member kept calling Alaska. This seemed bizarre—there are not too many Dominicans in Alaska—so we traced the calls. On August 14, 2000, DEA agents found Jesus Medina in Anchorage. Soon he was under arrest and on his way to Brooklyn.

Before Jesus arrived at the Brooklyn MDC, Jeff Higgins prepared a little surprise. He called the prison and arranged for Jesus to be sent to the same floor as Oscar. Legally, this maneuver was a bit dicey. As a cooperating witness Oscar was a de facto government agent. In the landmark case of *Brewer v. Williams*, decided in 1977, the Supreme Court held that government agents cannot "deliberately elicit" incriminating statements from criminal defendants who are represented by counsel unless the defendant's lawyer is present, because such questioning violates the defendant's right to have counsel present at all interrogation sessions. If we placed Oscar and Jesus together at the MDC, and Oscar questioned Jesus about his past crimes, that would violate *Brewer*—and the U.S. Constitution.

There are, however, a couple of important loopholes in the Brewer doctrine. In a later case, *Kuhlmann v. Wilson*, the Supreme Court held that it does not violate the right to counsel for the government to place an informant in a cell with a defendant and instruct the informant simply to listen to, rather than question, the defendant. Another case, *McNeil v. Wisconsin*, held that the right to counsel is "offense specific," applying only to charged crimes. Though an informant cannot legally question a defendant about charged crimes, he can make inquiries about new or uncharged criminal conduct. In Jesus's case, I planned to exploit both these exceptions.

One afternoon, while Jesus Medina was still in transit from Alaska, Jeff got Oscar out of prison and brought him to my office, where I gave him a special briefing. "You may," I told him, "run into someone you know at the MDC in the near future. I am not going to tell you who he is. I am, however, going to give you some instructions for how to deal with this person should you recognize him. I want you to follow these instructions very carefully. If you violate them, that will be a breach of your cooperation agreement."

I then gave Oscar his rules of engagement. "You must not initiate any contact with this person: don't say hello; don't walk up and talk to him. If, however, the person recognizes you and wants to talk, you can respond. Whatever you do, do not ask him any questions about his past crimes. It sounds bizarre, but if you do, you are breaking the law. If, however, he wants to talk about the past, you can listen, and I want you to listen carefully, so you can repeat accurately what he says to Jeff. If he proposes committing any new crimes, like a prison break, or attacking a guard, or selling drugs in the prison, you can discuss those crimes with him. Then report back to Jeff immediately."

Oscar waited for me to finish, and then he asked, "Who is it?" I declined to answer, for I had learned my lesson from the Scarpa-DeVecchio disaster: information should flow only one way, from the informant to the government, never the other way around.

Our decision to put Oscar and Jesus on the same floor at the MDC paid immediate dividends. When Jesus ran into his former drug supplier, he greeted him effusively and pulled him aside to talk. Jesus told Oscar that his brother Ramon had escaped to the Dominican Republic. Ramon had a good drug distribution network in the United States, which he could run from the Dominican Republic, but he needed a new source. Could Oscar hook them up again? Oscar told Jesus he would check, and then he reported this information back to Jeff. Jeff gave Oscar the phone number of a "drug importer," an undercover NYPD detective. Soon Ramon, Jesus, and the detective were in contact by phone. Ramon and Jesus offered to buy thirty kilos of cocaine, worth $600,000 wholesale, and this offer was captured on tape. Needless to say, this tape finished Jesus off. Though he might have been tempted to fight my original case, which was based primarily on testimony from only one witness, he had no stomach to contest a tape case. He pleaded guilty and got six and a half years.

The monitored cocaine telephone calls also helped us track Ramon Medina to an address in the Dominican Republic. Unfortunately, we had no power to arrest him there. Under the principle of comity—do you remember that basic rule of international law, from the *Elcock* Teddy Bear Case?—we were prohibited from conducting any law enforcement actions inside Dominican borders. Instead, Jeff and I had to ask the Dominican police to arrest Ramon for us. We gave the Dominican police a detailed description of Ramon and the address we believed he was at, and then made a formal arrest and extradition request. A few weeks later the Dominican police called Jeff and told him they had the house surrounded. I was very excited, since you don't bust a murderer overseas every day, but my elation was premature. Several hours later Jeff called me, his voice filled with disappointment, and told me the arrest was canceled. According to the Dominicans, Ramon had escaped, perhaps, they told us, to Spain. I slammed the phone down in its cradle. It is possible that Ramon was a master of escape. It is more likely, however, that he had bribed his way to freedom.

For years Ramon remained a fugitive. When I resigned from the DOJ in 2003, he was still loose. But in 2005 I got an unexpected e-mail from Kelly Currie, the EDNY's highly respected gang chief. Ramon had been tracked to the Netherlands and placed under arrest, and he was on his way to Brooklyn for trial. Justice may be delayed, but in this case it was not to be denied. In September 2007, just as I was finishing this book, Currie sent me an e-mail: "Thought you'd want to know that Ramon Medina finally pled guilty to the Fabian murder this week. Without your persistence, he likely would have gotten away with it."

———

JEFF HIGGINS AND I began the Bushwick investigation with a single small-time defendant. The case was so intrinsically unimportant I was tempted to ignore it, and I would have had Jeff not been so aggressive. Because of his great investigative work and my decent lawyering, we turned that one arrest into a major case, with sixteen narcotics and murder convictions to our credit. Twelve of the defendants were from Bushwick proper, working within a six-block radius of one another.

During the exact same time period, AUSA Dwight Holton, my partner on the Bushwick initiative, and NYPD detective Gene Torriente, his lead agent, had even greater success, convicting seventeen Bushwick drug dealers on narcotics and murder charges. Together, within three short years, we had collectively pulled almost thirty wholesale drug dealers off the Bushwick streets.

When Dwight and I first floated our proposal for community prosecution, no one was interested in the idea, and we had to launch our initiative on the sly. Thankfully, the EDNY respects results. In 2001 the office formally adopted our program, and today it still continues, run with the help of the NYPD, the FBI, and the DEA. This development has proved critical. Though Dwight and I made solid progress in Bushwick, that progress was not permanent. When we pulled Oscar and our other defendants off the Bushwick streets, new drug groups like the Woodbine Crew and the Four Horsemen swept into the neighborhood, to meet the market demand for heroin. If our office had let the program die, Bushwick would have slid back into mayhem. Instead, the office increased its commitment. Between 2001 and 2006 the EDNY's gang unit, led by AUSAs Kelly Moore and Kelly Currie, busted sixty-five more dealers in the neighborhood.

The impact of the EDNY's Bushwick initiative can be seen on the Bushwick streets. When we started the case, the neighborhood was dying. In June 2006, in contrast, *The New York Times* wrote a gushing article about Bushwick, praising its "peaceful tree-shaded blocks," the abundance of good housing, the recent influx of artists and young professionals, and its "much safer environment." The *Times* noted that serious crime was down 67 percent. "Knickerbocker Avenue, once known as 'the well' for its unending supply of narcotics, is now a bustling outdoor mall with modestly priced shoe and clothing outlets." One recent arrival, a woman who worked in the fashion industry in Manhattan, enthused, "We'd like to stay here . . . It seems really obvious to us that the neighborhood is going to get better and better."

Obviously, Dwight Holton, Jeff Higgins, and I did not single-handledly cure Bushwick's crime problem. If you look at the crime statistics, you can see that things were already improving by 1995, two years before we launched our initiative, primarily because of radically improved economic conditions in Brooklyn. The NYPD too deserves immense credit. The cops in the Eighty-third Precinct, like our partner Mike Zeller, have done an amazing job stamping out street crime. But I like to think that our Bushwick initiative made a very important contribution. Street cops are reactive. They are great at busting low-level retail dealers, but they lack the time and resources to launch the kinds of skillful investigations needed to catch major drug suppliers. In the Bushwick case, our federal team did just that. By eliminating most of the big dealers from the neighborhood, we choked off the flow of drugs. More important, we showed that community prosecution can produce steady, measurable results, ones you can see.

IN MAY 2004, after five years of cooperation, Oscar came before Judge Allyne Ross for sentencing. Because he pleaded guilty to large-scale drug trafficking and conspiracy to commit murder, Oscar faced roughly thirty years in prison under the federal sentencing guidelines. Judge Ross, however, was allowed to "depart" from this guideline sentence to reward his cooperation. The question was: How much did she think that effort was worth? What sentence would you give him?

Kelly Currie told the court that Oscar had been a major cooperator, responsible for a dozen drug and violence convictions. Then Paul Nalven, Oscar's lawyer, made an impassioned plea for his client.

Being a defense attorney in this courthouse, and having many clients at the MDC, I got wind that this was a very significant anticrime initiative in the Bushwick area, which was an area of the city crying out for help. Large quantities of drugs were being meted out and packaged in smaller quantities, coming directly from wholesalers in Queens. It really was, I think, a significant government effort. I know that there were federal agents from different agencies, there were homicide detectives, there were state and local narcotics detectives, but the defendant can fairly be said to be the main, initial, seminal witness in the whole investigation. I think law enforcement learned a lot about that neighborhood and made a big dent and got a lot of intelligence that was very, very helpful.

When Nalven was finished, Judge Ross sentenced Oscar to "time served," and he was released from jail that very day. You might think that sentence was too light. As a prosecutor, however, I was very happy with it, for Oscar's release will help us recruit new witnesses. When a major cooperator with a bad criminal record receives a light sentence, word travels quickly through the criminal underworld, both in and out of prison. When future narcotics defendants are arrested in Brooklyn, they will look at Oscar's example and say to themselves: Oscar served only five years in jail, so maybe I should cooperate too. Oscar is now living somewhere in the Northeast. I hope he stays on the right side of the law from now on.

Normally, the lead agent in a case appears at a cooperator's sentencing. In Oscar's case, however, Jeff Higgins was absent. After the 9/11 terror attack, Higgins volunteered to go to Afghanistan, to fight that country's booming opium industry. Last time I checked, he was still there.

CHAPTER TWELVE

Hunting "The Puma"

D uring my tenure in the Narcotics Unit, every single defendant I arrested pleaded guilty. Fortunately, I still got to go to
trial. The case involved a drug kingpin. His name was "The
Puma."

DARRYL ALBONICO was a veteran detective with the New Jersey State
Police. He ran a wide network of informants up and down the Meadow-
lands, a polluted industrial wasteland of petrochemical plants, shipping
warehouses, and freight yards in northeastern Jersey. On January 19,
1999, one of his sources, a motel clerk at a Newark Ramada, called in
with a tip. A Hispanic male named Noe Gutierrez with a Texas driver's
license had checked in that afternoon. Gutierrez was acting odd: walking
in circles through the motel lobby and parking lot; looking around;
making periodic calls from the pay phones. Albonico took the name and
driver's license number and ran it in NCIC, the National Crime Information Center database. The search quickly returned a match: Noe
Gutierrez was wanted for aggravated assault—a hit-and-run—in Brownsville, Texas.

   Albonico was a very good detective, and he quickly concluded that
Gutierrez was probably a drug trafficker. Why else would a guy from the
Texas-Mexico border be walking around a Ramada in New Jersey? But
even if he wasn't, the case was worth a little investigative effort. If Gutierrez turned out to be clean, Albonico could always arrest him on the hit-

and-run and ship him to Texas, a cheap and easy way to bolster his arrest statistics.

The next day, at 7:00 a.m., a five-man covert surveillance team in unmarked cars with tinted windows set up quietly around the perimeter of the motel. At 9:00 a.m. Gutierrez popped out of his room in his underwear. He was in his early thirties and very good-looking: piercing brown eyes; aquiline nose; high cheekbones; long black hair down to his shoulders. He scanned the parking lot from his balcony and then disappeared back inside. At 11:00 he appeared again, this time fully clothed. He took a quick walk around the parking lot, made an outgoing call at the pay phones, and then walked back to his room. The detectives sat and watched for several more dull hours.

Finally, at 1:30 in the afternoon, things picked up. A green Ford Crown Victoria sedan pulled up into the hotel parking lot with two Latino men inside. One stayed behind the wheel. The other, dressed in a white tracksuit, went straight to Gutierrez's motel room. Tracksuit knocked, the door opened, and he disappeared inside. More than an hour later Gutierrez and Tracksuit reappeared. The two men jumped into the Crown Victoria, the driver fired up the engine, and the car pulled quickly out of the motel lot and onto Frelinghuysen Avenue.

Tailing a car in the New York metro area is generally tricky work because of the traffic congestion, but it is much more difficult when the targets are experienced criminals, skilled at countersurveillance. When Gutierrez and his friends pulled out of the Ramada parking lot, they did not drive straight to their destination. Instead, they drove north on the avenue, U-turned quickly and headed back south, and then flipped around once again toward the north. They were not lost. Each time they turned, they were scanning their rearview mirrors, trying to see if anyone was following them. Normally, this tactic would have worked, revealing the law enforcement tail making the same U-turns, trying to keep up. Fortunately, the Jersey cops were pros. They were using two cars in radio contact and tailing very loosely, one running ahead of the target, one running behind, and they managed to keep in contact without blowing their cover.

That day the surveillance was anticlimactic. Gutierrez and Tracksuit drove to a Jersey check cashing store, used a pay phone, and then returned to the Ramada. But for the New Jersey State Police, the day was a huge success. Gutierrez and his colleagues thought they were smart, conducting countersurveillance. Instead, all they had done was heighten the cops' interest. If someone "boxes the blocks," a standard countertailing measure, he is almost certainly a crook. That night Albonico placed some calls down to law enforcement officials on the Texas-Mexico border looking for more intelligence. What he learned was no real shock. Two paid narcotics informants, one working for the Harlingen, Texas, Police Department, the other for the Texas Department of Public Safety, believed Gutierrez was a major drug trafficker, involved in shipping cocaine.

The next morning Albonico set up surveillance once again. This time he brought a nine-man team, later expanded to twelve. For the next three days this enormous surveillance unit quietly tracked Gutierrez and the man in the white tracksuit all over New Jersey and New York. They tailed the men to a motel by the Lincoln Tunnel, where the targets drove slowly past a parking lot, scrutinizing a parked eighteen-wheeler truck; to a truck stop on the New Jersey Turnpike; to a check cashing facility in Kearny, New Jersey; to a warehouse in Queens; to the Hunts Point produce market in the Bronx; and to a Manhattan copy shop. At the end of the odyssey, the cops tracked the targets to a Holiday Inn on Manhattan's West Side, on West Fifty-seventh Street between Ninth and Tenth Avenues, where both men got rooms.

Albonico approached the hotel security staff, flashed his badge, and demanded some registration information. Tracksuit had registered as Mr. Pugr, 1002 Elton Street, Houston, Texas, using a Texas driver's license. Albonico sent a query to the Texas Department of Public Safety. There was, the DPS replied, no Pugr in Texas, and the license number was fake. It did, however, have a listing for Rigoberto Puga on Elton Street. Could that be your man? DPS wired up a photo, and it matched: Tracksuit was Rigoberto Puga. Albonico ran a criminal background check: 1981: arrested trying to smuggle 150 pounds of marijuana across the Texas-Mexico border; 1991: arrested in the middle of a 200-pound marijuana deal. Puga too was a major drug trafficker.

On Saturday, January 23, Albonico requested assistance from Drug Enforcement Administration Group T-21, based in Manhattan. T-21 was a veteran narcotics enforcement crew specializing in truck cases: large-scale drug shipments coming from the Mexican and Canadian borders in eighteen-wheelers. Months later I asked Albonico: "Why did you call in the feds?" After all, his own operation was very professional. Albonico told me that after several days of tight, pressure-packed surveillance, his team was starting to wear out. I asked the DEA agents the same question and got a slightly different response: "Those guys just hate to work weekends." Regardless of the reason, the Gutierrez-Puga investigation was now a joint state and federal case.

SPECIAL AGENT Brian Conneely was a DEA veteran, with eleven years of service and hundreds of drug cases under his belt: quiet, stolid, thorough, patient. "I hate being on surveillance with that guy," one agent told me later, his voice filled with equal parts respect and good-natured bemusement. "He'll sit on a truck for days, practically living in his car, waiting for something to happen. Drives me crazy." His partner, Jimmy Duffy, was new to the DEA. Young and good-looking, with slicked-back hair, Jimmy had pierced his ears with two gold loop earrings, a rarity in law enforcement. His colleagues on T-21 called him Rings. On January 23, Brian, Jimmy, and a team from T-21 picked up surveillance from Albonico.

During the next day and a half nothing happened. The DEA agents watched Puga feed a parking meter with coins, and later they tracked the men to a sushi restaurant on Houston Street. Then, at 4:30 a.m. on January 25, Gutierrez and Puga exited the hotel, got into a white Ford cargo truck parked on a nearby street, and headed toward New Jersey. Two other Latino men followed in the Crown Victoria. The DEA called Albonico and then tailed the truck to New Jersey. After a short ride, the truck and the sedan pulled into CS Integrated, a freight warehouse in Secaucus. A few minutes later backup arrived: almost a dozen members of the New Jersey State Police. Together the DEA agents and the New Jersey cops sat and watched the truck.

At 9:00 a.m., after several hours of delay, the white Ford truck pulled into a loading dock. Puga appeared, driving a small forklift, and quickly loaded six wooden pallets of boxes into the truck's cargo hold. Some of the boxes were marked with a large A on the side; others, with a large B. The B pallets were pristine, the boxes perfectly stacked, sealed with clear tape, apparently handled with great care. The A pallets, in contrast, were stacked too high, and some of them were crushed. They looked as if they had been handled a lot. Some of the *A* boxes were sealed with clear tape; others, with brown tape.

At 10:15 the Ford truck pulled out of the loading dock at CSI and began to drive toward New York, following the Crown Victoria. The surveillance team tried to tail them surreptitiously, but it was tough. The truck kept pulling on and off the freeway, to check if it was being followed, and the surveillance teams had to stick close; they could not afford to lose the truck. About ten minutes into the drive, the two men riding in the Crown Victoria both turned around in their seats, craning their necks, and looked straight at the lead surveillance vehicle. After a quick conference on the radio, the surveillance team concluded their cover was blown. The detectives sped up, popped red lights on the tops of their cars, and pulled over the two vehicles. Both quickly stopped.

Albonico approached the cab of the truck and asked Puga, the driver, for his license. When Puga handed it over, Albonico noticed his hands were shaking. Like all good detectives, Albonico had come prepared with consent-to-search forms written in both English and Spanish. Albonico read him the English version. Then Detective Serrano, a Spanish speaker, read Puga the Spanish one. Serrano gave the form to Puga to review. Puga read the form for a few moments—his brain was probably spinning, trying to figure the odds, the angles, the best strategy to adopt—and then he took a pen and signed. The New Jersey State Police was now legally entitled to search the truck. I have always wondered why Puga agreed to let them search. Did he think a search was inevitable? Did he think the cops might not find his load? We shall never know.*

Albonico climbed into the back of the Ford truck. He took a knife and sliced open one of the *A* boxes sealed with clear tape. All he found inside was frozen cauliflower. Next, Albonico grabbed a box sealed with brown tape. As he lifted it clear of the pallet, he immediately noticed that it weighed much more than the first box. He cut open the top. Inside, he found several dozen heat-sealed plastic packages filled with white

---

*If Puga had not signed the consent form, the agents would have searched anyway. They almost certainly had probable cause to do so, and because warrants are not required to search cars and trucks, that search would probably have been upheld by later courts. Still, getting consent was a very smart move, for it made it all but impossible for anyone to challenge the search later.

powder. Albonico punctured one of the packages with his knife, dipped the blade into the powder, smelled it, tasted it. Cocaine.

Albonico and his team grabbed the men, emptied their pockets, cuffed them, and read them their rights. As they did so, they made a startling discovery: Noe Gutierrez had disappeared. Apparently, he had slipped out from under the surveillance net at CSI while the detectives were focused on the Ford truck. The detectives quickly questioned the men they had arrested, and one of them blurted out that Gutierrez had left to catch a flight at Newark Airport. Albonico split up his team. Half stayed with Puga and the drugs. The rest raced off to the airport. They got there just in time. Gutierrez was already on his plane back to Texas, American Airlines Flight 1723, sitting at the gate, a few minutes away from takeoff. The detectives boarded the aircraft. They quietly approached Gutierrez, identified themselves, and asked him to step off the plane. Gutierrez looked stunned, but he did not resist. He stood up, collected his carry-on bag, and walked off the plane with the police. When they got back to the boarding area, the detectives put him in handcuffs, read him his rights, and placed him under arrest.

That afternoon the New Jersey State Police drove the Ford truck to a police station in Totowa and conducted a detailed search. For several hours the detectives unloaded boxes, sliced them open, and pulled out plastic packages of cocaine. Eventually, the pile of cocaine stretched all the way across the garage. Once they were finished, Albonico counted up the score. Fifty of the boxes contained cocaine. In each of those boxes, the detectives found twenty-four separate shrink-wrapped packages weighing one kilo—2.2 pounds. The total take was 1,200 kilos, or 2,600 pounds, well over one ton of cocaine. Sold wholesale by the kilo, the cocaine was worth roughly $24 million; sold on the street gram by gram, between $180 and $200 million. That evening the New Jersey State Police handed Noe Gutierrez over to the DEA for questioning. From this point forward, the DEA would run the case.

SOME DRUG TRAFFICKERS are easy to flip; others, almost impossible. Noe Gutierrez was on the easy side. He had been transporting drugs since 1990, and he was a professional. From the moment of his arrest, he knew how his case would play out. He had been caught with his hands on twelve hundred kilos of cocaine and handed over to the feds. That meant at least twenty years in prison. Brian Conneely told him that the only way to save himself was to talk, and Noe knew it was the truth. That night he agreed to cooperate with the DEA.

When DEA agents make a big seizure, they have a very short window of opportunity to work the case before word of the seizure leaks out into the drug trafficking community. When Noe agreed to cooperate, Brian and Jimmy moved fast. Their goal was to investigate the case both up and down the distribution chain, to catch, if they could, both the shipper and intended recipient of the drugs.

First, they moved against the recipients. Noe told the agents that the cocaine was destined for three major customers and that Puga, who was responsible for delivery, had the contact information for them in his wallet. The agents looked through Puga's personal belongings, which they had seized at the time of his arrest, and found a small sheet of paper with three names and pager numbers. Under Brian's supervision, Noe used his cell phone to page all three numbers. Two of the customers never responded; word had apparently already spread that the shipment had been intercepted. One guy, "Julio," did call back. Noe told Julio tersely that the shipment had been delayed but that he would call the next morning to arrange delivery. This bought Brian and Jimmy some time. That night they planned a controlled delivery.

The next morning Guillermo Dudley, a Spanish-speaking New York cop detailed to T-21, paged Julio's number. Dudley introduced himself as Tio, Puga's code name for the operation, and told the customer that he was ready to deliver the drugs, more than four hundred kilos. The cop and the trafficker agreed to meet at 3:00 p.m. at an Exxon gas station on the corner of Tenth Avenue and Twenty-third Street, on the west side of Manhattan.

At 2:30 p.m. Brian and a team of eight agents set up surveillance, with unmarked cars on every street, plus a plainclothes NYPD detective, Diane Spence, inside the Exxon station minimart. A few minutes before 3:00, Spence saw two Hispanic men walk into the minimart and take up position inside the store, looking out the front window toward the street. A few minutes later Detective Dudley came into view, walking slowly to the corner, a folded newspaper under his arm, an identifying signal he had arranged with Julio that morning. As soon as Dudley came into sight, one of the men walked out of the store, while the other remained on the lookout. The man—we later learned his real name was Rojas—approached Dudley and identified himself as Julio. Rojas asked, "Are you Tio?" Dudley said he was. Rojas handed Dudley the silver key to a Ford van, into which the cocaine was to be loaded. Dudley told Rojas he would have the van loaded and returned in half an hour. Rojas looked around nervously and told Dudley that he did not feel safe. It was his last statement in freedom. Dudley removed his knit cap, the arrest signal. The DEA team swooped in immediately and put both Rojas and his lookout, Rigoberto Justi, under arrest.

THE NIGHT OF THE SEIZURE Brian and Jimmy were also focused on moving up the distribution chain. Their goal: to catch Noe's boss, the shipper of the cocaine. To start, they interviewed Noe and listened to his story.

Noe Gutierrez was born in 1965 and grew up in the Valley, the fertile South Texas agricultural region just north of the Mexico border. Noe's early years were unimpressive: one year of community college; work for a slaughterhouse loading and unloading trucks; drug and alcohol abuse. In 1989, when Noe was twenty-four, his worried father got him a steady job at H&H, the meatpacker where he was transportation manager. Noe started as a driver's helper, riding shotgun on meat deliveries, helping with directions and unloading the truck, but he was soon promoted to full driver, with better pay and benefits. Noe started on local deliveries: Harlingen, McAllen, Brownsville. Then, in 1991, he was assigned to work the three-hundred-mile Houston route. Typically, H&H drivers heading to Houston were paired with another driver, so they could split time behind the wheel. That was how Noe met Juan Jose Rodriguez.

Juan was short and wiry, with a thin mustache and a nice smile. He was also very smart: ambitious, entrepreneurial, creative. Had he been born into a richer, more privileged family, he might have grown up to be a CEO, maybe even worked for Enron. As it was, he got work driving meat, a job that failed to provide the challenges and rewards he desired. Juan's friends called him the Puma.

One morning, as Juan and Noe left the H&H plant bound for Houston, Juan announced an unscheduled stop. He pulled off Highway 77 onto a back road and drove into the countryside for two miles, to a solitary turnout. Juan's cousin Carlos was waiting there in a pickup truck. Juan got out of the H&H truck and talked to Carlos for a moment. Then Juan and Carlos grabbed two big boxes out of Carlos's pickup, walked over to the H&H truck, opened the cab's passenger-side door, where Noe was sitting, and threw the boxes inside, behind the seat. Each box weighed about fifty pounds. Noe later told me, "I could immediately tell they were filled with marijuana. The smell was really strong." When he got back in the truck, Juan asked, "Is this okay?" Noe nodded; his career in drug trafficking had begun.

The two men began to drive to Houston. Because the marijuana smelled so powerful, they had to pull over and shift it to the rear of the truck. In the back the marijuana boxes blended in perfectly with the truck's load of boxed beef. A couple of hours later, the men hit the Sarita immigration checkpoint on Highway 77.

The Sarita checkpoint occupies a key choke point in South Texas. It is easy to get across the border from Mexico to the Texas Valley, but to get from the Valley to Houston, you have only two options: cross over one hundred miles of inhospitable desert on foot, or take Highway 77. Most illegal immigrants—and every truck driver with a load of Mexican drugs—take Highway 77. To stop them, the Immigration Service operates a checkpoint on a dusty stretch of the highway, just like a border crossing, with drug dogs and immigration inspectors. When Juan and Noe arrived there with their truck of meat and marijuana, Noe was trembling. Two Latino men with a cargo truck: What could be more suspicious? The guards just smiled and waved them through. Juan was a familiar face, for he drove the Houston route once a week.

That same morning Noe and Juan reached Houston and made their meat deliveries to butcher shops and grocery stores. At one supermarket Juan made a phone call. A guy showed up, unloaded the marijuana boxes, gave some money to Juan, and drove off. Later that day Juan handed Noe a thousand dollars in cash.

Soon after that first Houston run, Juan resigned from H&H to work full-time as a drug trafficker. Whenever he had a shipment to transport to Houston, he contacted Noe and asked him to come to the turnoff on his next H&H delivery trip. There Juan and a team of helpers loaded hefty fifty-pound boxes, marked "beef" on the side, into the trailer of the truck. Noe drove the drugs past the Sarita checkpoint to Houston and then met Juan at a designated supermarket parking lot, where Juan picked up the load. When he got back home, Noe went to Juan's house in Elsa, another small Valley town, and Juan paid him in cash, between five thousand and fifteen thousand dollars a trip, depending on the value of the drugs.

Juan bought a comfortable suburban home and started two new businesses: a trucking company based in Texas that was designed in part to explain to the IRS how he was making so much money and a pager and cellular telephone business down in Mexico. He moved most of his assets down south. He figured if the cops ever got wind of his involvement in drugs, he could simply hop across the border and live the good life in Mexico. Noe spent a lot of his earnings on cocaine, which he abused regularly, but he also bought an eighteen-wheeler and went into business as an independent trucker. Sometimes he carried legitimate loads. Other times he carried drugs for Juan.

During the 1990s Juan's operation grew in size and sophistication. NAFTA, the North American Free Trade Agreement, opened up the border to increased truck traffic from Mexico. In response, big Colombian and Mexican cartels shifted their importation routes from the Caribbean to Texas. This meant big opportunities for experienced drug transporters. Juan began to focus almost exclusively on cocaine, his loads grew in size and value, and his primary shipping destination changed from Houston to New York City. Throughout this period Noe was one of his primary drivers. Several times a year Noe drove to a dusty, secluded South Texas ranch in tiny Raymondville or a bright pink produce warehouse in McAllen and picked up between 150 and 700 kilos of cocaine and a "cover load" of vegetables, frozen fruit juice concentrate, or frozen poultry. Noe drove up north for two days, sleeping overnight in the truck. He stopped first at a New Jersey warehouse, to hand the drugs off to Juan's Colombian or Cuban business partners. Next, he dropped by the Hunts Point market in the Bronx to sell off the cover load. On the return trip, Noe brought home boxes of money, as much as five million dollars a load. His own cut: thirty to sixty thousand dollars for six or seven days of work. Once a deal was finished, Juan, Noe, and their friends met in Acapulco or Las Vegas to celebrate.

In January 1999, Juan arranged a megadeal with his partner, Mexican kingpin Nino Valdez: three shipments of cocaine, more than a thousand kilos each, worth a total of five hundred million dollars on the street. Juan arranged for C.R. England, a respected commercial trucking company, to ship frozen cauliflower from Texas to CS Integrated, a commercial warehouse in northern New Jersey. Before C.R. England picked up the first shipment, Juan had his men load it up with cocaine, in specially marked and taped boxes. To make sure the drugs were handed off properly, Juan asked Noe to fly to New Jersey to supervise delivery to his cartel contact, Rigoberto Puga. On January 18, 1999, Noe flew to Newark Airport. One week later the New Jersey State Police seized the first load of twelve hundred kilos, and Noe was in DEA custody.

When Noe finished his story, the agents had him place a "consensually recorded call" to Juan's cell phone, to try to get Juan to incriminate himself. A man answered the call and identified himself as "John." Noe silently nodded to the agents, who were listening in; this was Juan "The Puma" Rodriguez. Noe and Juan had a long, bantering conversation in Spanish, which the agents secretly recorded. Noe told Juan that he was still at the airport, and Juan responded in surprise, "You're still there?" Noe asked when he could get paid, and Juan replied, "As soon as you arrive." Under prompting from the agents, Noe asked Juan if he had been paid yet, and Juan replied that he had not. The two men agreed to meet as soon as Noe got home, and then Juan ended the call. The agents figured they had less than twenty-four hours to arrest Juan before he found out about the seizure. If they delayed even one day, Juan would be in Mexico. So, they decided to get an arrest warrant immediately. That meant they had to get a prosecutor.

———

IN THE NEW YORK CITY Metropolitan Area, there are three U.S. Attorney's Offices: the District of New Jersey, the Southern District of New York, and my own EDNY. All three had venue over this case. Thus Brian and Jimmy were free to choose which office they wanted to work with. The District of New Jersey had the best claim because the cocaine had been shipped to and seized in New Jersey. The SDNY was next in line; Puga and Gutierrez had stayed in a Manhattan hotel, and the controlled delivery to Rojas and Justi had occurred there. The EDNY had the worst claim of all. Our only basis for venue, our only geographical connection to the case, was Noe's car trip to Queens on January 21, when he and Puga drove by, but never entered, a warehouse on Twenty-second Street. This was a thin reed on which to build a case, but Brian and Jimmy did not care; they wanted to work with the EDNY. The reasons for this decision were a little complex.

In the Justice Department, both prosecutors and their offices are assessed by the size and quality of the cases they indict. My boss in Narcotics, Jodi Avergun, wanted to boost the reputation and prestige of her unit, and that meant we had to attract big cases. To accomplish this, Jodi constantly stressed to us that we were in a competitive industry and had to provide exceptional service. "Treat your agents like valued customers. Work with them; help them; try to give them what they want." Most of Jodi's AUSAs imbibed this service ethos. We worked hard to see cases from the agents' perspectives, to help them plan careful and productive investigations, and to gain convictions quickly once they made an arrest. As a result of these efforts, the EDNY had a good reputation among narcotics agents for speed, convenience, and investigative savvy. Jimmy and Brian had worked with my friend Eric Tirschwell in the past, and they had been impressed with the job he did. When it came time to bring the Puma case to one of the three metro districts, they gave Eric a call and asked him to be their AUSA. Eric had a heavy caseload already, but a twelve-hundred-kilo seizure was a relative rarity. Eric checked with Jodi, got approval to take the case, and met with the agents that afternoon.

———

WHEN ERIC OPENED the *Rodriguez* case on Tuesday, January 26, he faced three critical charging decisions. The first was a no-brainer. During the controlled delivery in Manhattan, the DEA had caught Rojas and Justi red-handed. Eric typed up a complaint charging them with violating 21 *United States Code,* Sections 841 and 846, "possession with intent to distribute cocaine" and "conspiracy." Rojas and Justi were arraigned that afternoon. Eventually, after months of legal wrangling, both men pleaded guilty and got long prison terms.

Next, Eric had to find some way to buy off the state of New Jersey. Albonico and his team of New Jersey state troopers had initiated the case and done much of the difficult surveillance work. Now New Jersey state prosecutors wanted a piece of the action. Eric wanted the exact opposite, to keep New Jersey out of the case as much as possible. Though federal and state law enforcement officers generally work well together, having parallel state and federal cases arising from the same criminal transaction can sometimes create a giant mess. If, for example, the two sets of prosecutors disagree on tactics, they might wind up working at cross-purposes. In one case I know, state prosecutors actually indicted a man who the feds had promised would get a free ride in exchange for high-level cooperation. Parallel cases also create discovery problems, for state prosecutors complying with different discovery laws might turn over to defense attorneys information that federal prosecutors want to keep secret.

To prevent these sorts of issues from arising, Eric had to find some way to get New Jersey out of the case. His solution was pretty neat: he threw them Puga. Puga was charged with violating New Jersey state narcotics laws, and in exchange New Jersey prosecutors agreed to keep their noses out of the rest of our case. This was a sound decision, but it came with a cost. Puga was a hardened, experienced drug trafficker. If we had prosecuted him federally, he might have flipped. The New Jersey prosecutors unfortunately took a different approach. They were eager to participate in the case, but they did not care very much whether Puga cooperated or not; they just wanted an easy conviction. They offered him a very light plea deal, without requiring him to testify, a deal he accepted with alacrity. Not only did Puga get out of prison early, but we lost the opportunity to debrief him and use him as a witness. This was a lucky break for Puga and a bad development for law enforcement, but a necessary deal all the same.

Finally, Eric had to decide what to do about Juan "The Puma" Rodriguez. If Eric wanted to arrest him, he had to do it immediately, or Juan would flee to Mexico. Unfortunately, the case against Rodriguez was really weak. The DEA had only two pieces of evidence against him. First, Gutierrez claimed the Puma was his boss, responsible for the twelve hundred kilos of cocaine. Second, the DEA had the tape of the consensual call. The tape should have been great evidence, but it wasn't. Noe and Juan did not explicitly discuss drugs during the call; all that Rodriguez mentioned was payment for unspecified services. Thus, if we arrested Juan, he could claim the payment to Noe mentioned on the tape was for supervising a legal shipment of cauliflower and had nothing to do with drugs. Worse, Rodriguez identified himself only as John when he picked up the phone. This created another useful defense, for Rodriguez could claim that his name was Juan, not John—that Noe had talked to a different person on the call and was now trying to frame him. To rebut that claim, Eric had only one piece of evidence, Noe's word. In short, Eric had a single cooperator case. This was really weak evidence, given the magnitude of the seizure.

Eric struck most people as mild-mannered, polite, quiet-spoken, perhaps a little bit square. He was very tall and slender, with thinning hair and gold-rimmed glasses. When you walked into his office, the first thing you saw was a copy of the Bill of Rights, which he framed and hung on the wall, where his agents could not miss it. Eric did a lot of very big drug cases, and he had on his desk a cassette player that he used to listen to electronic surveillance tapes. Six months before, however, Eric had started dating a classical pianist, and now the tape player was often spewing out Brahms or Chopin. When I gave him a hard time about this, Eric blustered back. "Come on, I have to learn this stuff."

Despite his deliberate manner, Eric was very aggressive when it came to charging decisions. Rodriguez was responsible for a twelve-hundred-kilo shipment of cocaine worth almost two hundred million dollars retail. On the basis of Noe's information, Eric calculated he had probably shipped close to one billion dollars' worth of drugs over the course of his career. Eric recognized that if the agents did not arrest the Puma now, they might never have a chance to bring him to justice. And so, despite the flimsy character of his evidence, Eric went to court and got an arrest warrant. Down in Texas, DEA agents stopped the Puma's truck, placed him under arrest, and flew him up to New York. On February 25, 1999, Eric indicted him on drug trafficking and conspiracy charges. The case was assigned to Judge Nina Gershon. *United States v. Rodriguez* was under way.

———

WHEN RODRIGUEZ ARRIVED in Brooklyn, he was represented by a Texas lawyer named Guy Womack, who flew up to New York for court appearances. Womack was stout, blunt, and pugnacious, with cowboy boots, a buzz haircut, and a slightly affected "country lawyer" manner. At the first status conference in March, Womack's position was crystal-clear. "We do not waive speedy trial," he told Judge Gershon. "Your Honor, we want to go to trial as soon as possible." If a defendant demands a speedy trial, judges tend to defer to them, for that right is guaranteed in the Sixth Amendment. When, however, Judge Gershon set the case down for May, it caused a minor crisis. Eric had no objection to an early trial date, but he had recently gotten engaged to his pianist, and his marriage and honeymoon were scheduled for late May. Some AUSAs would reschedule their weddings to accommodate their trial schedules—it is that intense a profession—but not Eric. Thus he needed what AUSAs call coverage.

In the EDNY, AUSAs with court or trial conflicts are encouraged to work out coverage on their own. One morning in early March 1999 Eric popped into my office and asked me if I would take over *Rodriguez*. My immediate reaction was mixed. The best AUSAs, in my opinion, are those who will fearlessly try weak cases, even total dogs, without any concern for their professional reputations. Alas, I was never like that. I had won all my trials so far, and I had gained a reputation as an excellent trial lawyer. The *Rodriguez* case was weak; whoever tried it might easily lose. Did I want to risk my reputation and my perfect record by taking Eric's case? To be honest, the answer was: not really. On the other hand, I had not been to trial since *Scarpa* the prior fall, and I was dying to get back in front of a jury. A twelve-hundred-kilo cocaine seizure was pretty epic, a major trial by any calculation. Above all, I knew Eric needed a favor. I thought about his proposition for roughly ten seconds, with all these calculations flashing through my head, and then I told him I would be happy to take the case. Jodi blessed the arrangement, and I became lead prosecutor. Two months later, after the trial had been delayed, Eric rejoined the trial team, and we worked the case together as cocounsel, the best of all possible outcomes.

———

FROM THE OUTSET, my goal in the *Rodriguez* case was to get the Puma to cooperate. From Noe's debriefings with the DEA, it was clear that Rodriguez was a major player on the Texas-Mexico border. He was obviously in contact with, or a member of, a major cocaine cartel. If he flipped, we might be able to develop a case of international importance. When, however, I pitched cooperation to Womack after one of our early court appearances, he refused even to consider it. I was not surprised. From a tactical point of view, Womack was in a great position. He was aware that our case—one cooperating witness and one inconclusive tape—was weak. He also knew what I was only slowly discovering: that Noe had major baggage. His drug use, alcoholism, and spousal abuse did not bother me too much. Most cooperators have these or similar problems. We would "front" these issues with the jury and hope it did not get too distracted. The real problem was more salacious. In 1998, Rodriguez had had a torrid sexual affair with Noe's wife, and Noe found out about it. Though they maintained their business relationship, Noe was extremely bitter about Juan's betrayal. Normally, a defense attorney would be worried about a jury's discovering his client had an extramarital affair. In this case, however, Womack was ecstatic, for it gave him the perfect defense: that Noe was falsely accusing Juan of involvement in drug trafficking just to get his revenge. Womack had more than a triable case; he had a winner.

Womack's desire for trial was short-lived. In April he reversed course. The reason was simple: Casas. In my first meetings with Brian and Jimmy, the two DEA agents, I told them that unless they found more evidence, we would probably lose the Rodriguez trial. The agents began to dig around, and in a couple of weeks they discovered important news. On December 31, 1998, roughly a month before our twelve-hundred-kilo cocaine seizure, U.S. Customs had arrested a major Texas drug trafficker named Jorge Casas. By the early spring Casas was spilling his guts, telling Customs about his career in narcotics. Casas told his handling agents he had worked with a dozen major traffickers. One person on the list caught our attention: the Puma. When I got this news, I flew down to Houston with Jimmy and Brian to debrief Casas in person.

Jorge Casas was thirty-five, portly and good-natured, always quick with a laugh or a joke. When I met him for the first time, he was wearing tan prison pants and a white cotton prison T-shirt, with large sweat stains around his armpits and belly. When I asked him questions about his life, to get a feel for his personality, Casas smiled and bragged about his skill with women. "You don't have to look so good. It's all about attitude, the right moves." He was clearly a rogue, but I liked him instantly all the same. Later I asked Jimmy his opinion. Jimmy bluntly responded, "That guy's a fat pig."

Casas was born in Nuevo León in 1965. He immigrated to the United States in his twenties, illegally at first and then, a few years later, with a green card. Casas worked as a migrant farmworker for ten years, picking and packing fruit and vegetables. On one corporate farm, he learned to drive an eighteen-wheeler, and this skill transformed his life. In 1990 he began to work as a drug transporter, driving marijuana and cocaine loads from the Texas border all over the United States. He worked for a bunch of different drug kingpins: Juan Melgosa, Armando Rodriguez, Manuel Garcia, Mario Garcia, Juan Lozano. In that first meeting I asked him about the quantity of drugs he had moved over the course of his career. Casas paused, staring up at the ceiling, trying to calculate the totals. Finally he said with a smug grin: five tons of marijuana, five tons of cocaine. When I asked him how much money he had made in this line of work, he smiled more broadly: two million dollars, tax free. When I showed him a picture of Juan, Casas smiled again. "I've known him since 1992 or 1993. He calls me Guero, 'white man.' I moved four or five shipments for him, always cocaine. Three hundred kilos, four hundred kilos, five hundred kilos, over a thousand kilos on one trip." As Casas talked, I tried to keep a straight face, but inside, I was ecstatic. Got you now, Mr. Puma, I thought. That afternoon I met with Stuart Burns, Casas's prosecutor in Houston. Normally, AUSAs are reluctant to loan out their major cooperators to other offices, but Stuart kindly told me to help myself. A few days later I sent Womack a detailed letter describing Casas's expected testimony.

Casas transformed the case, roughly doubling its strength. One-cooperator cases are very hard to win, unless your corroboration is airtight, and ours, at this point, was flimsy. But having two cooperators gives prosecutors a fighting chance. When I told Womack we intended to add Casas to our witness list, it changed our prospects dramatically. Womack soon told me that Rodriguez wanted to plea. I was glad to hear Womack's new plan. To be honest, I did not want to have to try the case; I still thought we might lose.

THERE WAS ONLY ONE HITCH. When I made inquiries to determine the name of the defense lawyer representing Casas, I discovered, to my immense surprise, that his name was Guy Womack! Womack was, I learned, a hands-off defense attorney. Once Casas started cooperating with the government, Womack didn't pay too much attention to whom he was cooperating against. Womack was momentarily taken aback when Eric and I told him that one of his own clients had ratted out Juan Rodriguez, but he quickly regained his composure. When I asked if he was going to resign from the *Rodriguez* case, he didn't bat an eye. "No, I'll represent 'em both!"

What Womack was proposing was, on its face, astounding. As a general matter, a single defense attorney should not represent two defendants in the same or related cases because of the serious conflict of interest. Every defendant has a right to an unbiased lawyer who is totally devoted to his interests. If, however, a lawyer represents two defendants in the same case, they never really know whether the lawyer's advice is truly in both their best interests or if he is sacrificing one client for the benefit of the other. Womack's representation of both Casas and Rodriguez fell squarely into this dangerous area. When, for example, Womack was recommending that Rodriguez plead guilty, it made me instantly wonder: Does Womack truly think this course of action is in Rodriguez's best interest, or is he trying to make Casas look good, gaining a conviction to Casas's credit so he could get a lighter sentence? The conflict of interest grew even more evident when I thought about the possibility of trial. If I called Casas to the stand to testify against Rodriguez, who was going to cross-examine him? Womack could not, for he would be trapped by his own conflicting duties of loyalty and zealousness to both men, obligated at the same time to protect Casas and to destroy his credibility.

Under Second Circuit case law, I was required to inform Judge Gershon of any potential conflicts of interest as soon as I became aware of them. Accordingly, I sent her a letter describing the situation, and she in turn asked us to come to court. And here I did something I regret.

When judges face a complex legal issue, they typically ask both sides for advice. Judges generally treat advice from defense lawyers with a grain of salt. Defense counsel have a duty to defend their clients zealously, and as a result, many of them "spin" the law in their clients' favor instead of accurately and fairly analyzing it. AUSAs, in contrast, are duty-bound to seek just results. Accordingly, most AUSAs try very hard to give objective, unbiased opinions when judges seek their input. Over the course of my career as a prosecutor, I think I did this very well. When I left the DOJ, several judges told me that when I appeared before them, they always knew they could trust my legal analysis. When, however, Judge Gershon asked for my opinion of Womack's conflict of interest, I did not tell her what I really thought: that Womack must immediately retire from the case. Instead, I fudged. I told the court that there was no "dispositive" case law, that either outcome was defensible, and that the government had no position. This was a true and accurate statement of the law for, under Second Circuit precedent, it was totally unclear whether Womack had to withdraw from the case or not. But my response was tricky and "lawyerly," not honest and straightforward. Though I knew in my gut that the conflict was severe and that Juan should have his own lawyer, I really wanted Womack to remain on the case because that might lead to a very quick plea. In short, I did what a good AUSA must never do: let his desire for one particular outcome affect the objectivity of his legal advice.

When I told Judge Gershon that I had no position, she took off her glasses, rubbed the bridge of her nose, and squinted at me funny. I could tell I had lost some, if not all, of her respect. My position, she told me, was "mystifying." Then she proceeded to do the obvious right thing; she bumped Guy Womack off the case. A few weeks later I received a letter informing me that Rodriguez had a new lawyer, Ivan S. Fisher of Manhattan.

———

IVAN FISHER WAS ONE of the top defense attorneys in the nation. In his mid-fifties, Fisher was tall, corpulent, florid, and graying. He was, without question, a brilliant trial lawyer, famed for his tough cross-examinations and his ability to pick apart a government case piece by piece. Over the last twenty years he had represented defendants in some of the biggest drug cases in the world, like the French Connection and Pizza Connection mafia heroin smuggling cases and the trial of Pastor Parafan, one of Colombia's great cocaine barons. Fisher reputedly charged five hundred thousand dollars a case, and he always had several under way. He had a tony Upper East Side apartment, an art collection, limousines, a country house in the Hamptons. When Rodriguez hired him, I knew we had truly caught a big fish. Jodi Avergun immediately warned me. "Be careful, he's a very good lawyer."

Though Fisher was undeniably talented, he was also controversial. The acclaimed *New York Times* writer Sydney Schanberg (of *The Killing Fields* fame) once attacked Fisher in print for his offensive courtroom tactics: "brazen and jarring, leaving the impression that in his pugilistic vigor, he has thumbed his glove into our eye." He was also personally flawed. In 1989 the EDNY prosecuted him for misdemeanor tax evasion. More recently the U.S. Court of Appeals had criticized him for making false statements to a federal judge. Above all, there was the *Levy* case.

In 1989 a man named Eliahu Levy was arrested on heroin charges, and he hired Ivan to serve as his attorney. Initially, Levy was held in jail awaiting trial, but in October 1989, Ivan got him released, probably on the promise that Levy would cooperate with law enforcement. Levy's co-operation was short-lived. Instead of working for us, he fled to Israel, where he disappeared, never to return. He remains a fugitive today. I was never able to figure out precisely what happened in the *Levy* case, why Levy got released from prison or how he managed to get out of the country. All I do know—all that the DOJ ever publicly stated about the case—is that Fisher was suspected of helping him escape, a serious felony. The EDNY convened a grand jury investigation, and it apparently focused on Fisher, but ultimately, no one was charged.

In the United States, a man is innocent until proven guilty. Maybe Fisher knew nothing about Levy's flight. But the *Levy* case certainly gave me pause. I knew that if Ivan proposed bail for the Puma, I would oppose it. Juan's home in Elsa was only five miles from the Mexican border. Even if we gave him a DEA escort around the clock, it would be easy for Juan to create some diversion—gunfire, perhaps, from his friends or business associates—and slip away to freedom.

The future of the *Rodriguez* case was decided in a short meeting between Fisher and me in late spring 1999. We met at the courthouse on a dark and rainy afternoon. I opened the meeting by proposing our standard disposition: a guilty plea and cooperation. Ivan made a snorting sound, to show his disdain, and dismissed my suggestion with a wave of his hand. Within three minutes our talk had bogged down. Ivan wanted special treatment. I refused to budge. Soon there was nothing to talk about, no common ground.*

During the meeting Ivan got my goat. I hated his dismissive tone, his expensive suit, and his unstated but clear belief that his drug baron and the United States were morally equivalent parties. He represented, I freely admit, everything I dislike about the big-time drug cartel defense bar. As we walked out of the courthouse, I could not resist a challenge. "Ivan, you are welcome to go to trial, but if you do, you are making a big mistake. I guarantee you, your client's going to go to prison for a very long time."

Ivan paused on the courthouse steps, turned, and cocked one of his eyebrows skyward. "If you are so sure he's going to be convicted," he said coyly, "why don't you preview the evidence with me, share what you know?"

In other circumstances, I might have agreed to Ivan's suggestion. Sometimes, if you walk a defense attorney through your case step by step, discussing each piece of evidence with him, he will bring his client in to plead. But in this case I didn't trust Ivan, and I feared him. He was, everyone told me, a very skilled courtroom tactician. I could not afford to give up an advantage by disclosing my trial strategy. I told Ivan, in all honesty, that I could not risk a reverse proffer; he was simply too good a lawyer. But I added a challenge once again, to provoke him. "I'm telling you now, if you go to trial, you're making a big mistake."

Ivan just laughed, a little bit longer than necessary. Then he looked down at me and said, with an incredibly urgent tone in his voice, "I want to have this trial. I'm looking forward to this trial. I've heard you are the very best of the young generation of prosecutors, and I want to beat you. And I am going to beat you." Ivan got into the backseat of a waiting Lincoln Town Car and pulled out toward the Brooklyn Bridge. I walked off in the rain.

As a general matter, I think I am a reasonable prosecutor. I like compromises. If a defendant wants a deal, I will take the easy conviction and move on to other targets. When, however, defendants choose to follow a more confrontational route, I tend to get combative as well. Two weeks

---

*The contents of our discussion have never been publicly disclosed and thus remain confidential. As a result, I cannot repeat what we discussed.

after my meeting with Ivan, Eric and I went to the grand jury and charged Juan Rodriguez with violating CCE, the drug kingpin statute. On the basis of information from Noe and Casas, the indictment alleged that Juan had managed a major cocaine and marijuana business throughout the 1990s. Under the statute and the relevant sentencing guidelines, the Puma faced a minimum, if convicted, of thirty years in prison.

WHEN I TOLD IVAN that his client should plead guilty or face certain conviction, I was not bluffing. Our case was still weak: Noe, Casas, one bad tape. By now, however, I had been a prosecutor for almost two years, and I had run five or six very complex investigations. From these experiences, I had developed a theory. In modern society, I hypothesized, it is almost impossible to commit a complex crime without leaving traces of evidence in your wake: records, documents, phone calls, or seemingly unimportant encounters with ordinary people that turn out to link you to the crime. Thus, if a defendant is truly guilty, you can always find more evidence, if you look carefully enough. If you cannot, that probably means you have got the wrong guy.

How do you prove that a man is a drug kingpin? In *Rodriguez*, we began our investigation by tracking the cocaine shipment backward, from New Jersey to Texas. Albonico talked to the shipping and security managers at CSI in Secaucus and learned that the cauliflower was shipped by a Texas produce company, Fox Foods. The C.R. England truck driver confirmed this information; the load was owned by Fox Foods. I questioned Noe about Fox. He was vague. "It was just something Juan made up to make the shipment look legitimate."

Initially, I thought that investigating Fox would quickly lead back to Rodriguez, but the company turned out to be a well-designed front. Fox's business headquarters, 417 East Coma, Suite 652, Hidalgo, Texas, was an anonymous mail drop at a strip mall mailbox rental store. The company had no active telephones. The Fox bank account was opened in January 1999, right before the drug shipment, and there had been no account activity since the seizure. When Tony Sanchez, our Texas Department of Public Safety investigator down in the valley, asked people working in the produce business about Fox Foods, they all replied, "Never heard of it."

We did not give up. We made a huge list of possible witnesses, and then we talked to each one, to see if anyone could link Fox to Rodriguez. We first interviewed Steve Alberti, the customer service manager of CS Integrated, who told us, "The cauliflower delivery was arranged by a Mr. Pablo Ledezma, of Fox Foods. Never saw him, just talked to him on the phone."

We struck Alberti off the list and moved on to Gus Prevot, the manager of Fresh Freeze Public Cold Storage, Edinburg, Texas. He told us, "I stored a shipment of frozen cauliflower for Mr. Ledezma from January 13 to January 19, 1999, when it was picked up by a driver. I never saw Ledezma, never met him, just talked to him by phone. Ledezma sent me two more shipments of frozen cauliflower on January 19 and January 21, but no one ever came to claim them, and when I tried to call him, he never answered his phone."

Guillermo Nunez, the general manager of Union Fruit and Produce, Hidalgo, Texas: "On January 18, a man named Pablo Ledezma from Fox Foods called to arrange a series of truck-to-truck transfers. We did one transfer on the twentieth, moving pallets of frozen vegetables from a small cargo truck to a commercial carrier, C.R. England. I never met Ledezma. I only spoke to him that one time. He never called back about the other transfers he wanted."

Mauro Gomez, a clerk at Prointer Mail Express, 417 East Coma, Hidalgo, Texas: "On January 4, 1999, Pablo Ledezma called to rent a mailbox for a year. When I asked him to come in person, to provide identification, he faxed me a copy of his Social Security card, number 435-56-6475. I never saw him, and no one ever came in to collect any mail from the box."

A records custodian with the U.S. Social Security Administration told us, "The social security card for Pablo Ledezma, number 435-56-6475, is fake."

After a solid month of digging, we could prove that Fox was a fake company set up by a fake Mr. Ledezma, but we still had no evidence to show that Juan and Ledezma were the same man or that Fox was Juan's creation. I wasn't desperate. On the contrary, I was simply intrigued. Tirschwell's case was turning out to be much more interesting than I thought it would be. I was encouraged too by our first major break.

WHEN ERIC, BRIAN, AND JIMMY reviewed Albonico's surveillance reports for the days prior to the seizure, they noticed that Noe and Puga had gone to a truck stop and a check cashing facility. When they asked Noe about this, he said that he had run short of cash for expenses, so Juan had wired him a fifteen-hundred-dollar comcheck, an electronic money order commonly used by trucking companies to send cash to their drivers on the road. We located the Jersey check cashing facility, subpoenaed its records, and discovered that the comcheck had been sent not by Juan but by F. Garcia Trucking, down in Edcouch, Texas, just two miles from Juan's home in Elsa.

One day Tony Sanchez, our local Texas investigator, dropped by F. Garcia Trucking and questioned Fidencio Garcia, the owner of the firm. When Sanchez called us afterward, the news was electrifying. Garcia told Sanchez that on January 21, 1999, he received a call from Juan Rodriguez, an old business acquaintance from the trucking business. Juan told Garcia that he needed to wire fifteen hundred dollars to one of his drivers, but since he was not a subscriber to the comcheck system, he needed some help. Garcia agreed to wire a comcheck using his own account in return for a fifty-dollar fee. That afternoon Francisco "Pancho" Rodriguez, a member of Juan's family, dropped off the money. Garcia later told me, "I didn't ask him what it was for, and he didn't tell me." When we asked Noe and Casas about Pancho, both told us, "He's Juan's errand boy in the drug trade, helps load, stuff like that."

Garcia's information was not a smoking gun, for Juan could easily provide an innocent explanation. He might claim, for example, that his friend Noe had called him from New York and asked him for fifteen hundred dollars to help him in an emergency, so he sent it to him "no questions asked," as any friend would do. Still, this was an important development, for it showed that Juan was not perfect, and that he might have dropped other clues about his involvement in the shipment if we only knew where to look.

WHEN AN INVESTIGATION IS STALLED, you go to the source, in this case, the Texas Valley. Starting that spring, our team made five trips down to the muggy Texas-Mexico border to investigate every possible lead in person. Together with Tony Sanchez, who served as our guide and Spanish interpreter, we drove a thousand miles across South Texas, from tiny rural towns to modern strip malls, examining every single aspect of the twelve-hundred-kilo transaction. We interviewed bankers, produce brokers, truckers, warehousemen, phone company representatives, local cops, local DEA agents, accountants. I carried a huge stack of subpoenas in my briefcase, and we handed them out at nearly every stop, demanding every record and document that might help our case. We also ate a lot of Mexican food, at tiny roadside dives Sanchez knew from his police work. For me, raised in Houston, this was a bonus, but the constant diet of refritos and tortillas did not sit well with Philly-born Jimmy Duffy. I still remember the disgusted look on his face, one morning over breakfast, when he eyed the menu and asked, in total exasperation, "What the fuck is a breakfast taco?"

We hit many dead ends on our trips. We located, for example, the company that manufactured the customized Fox Foods boxes in which the frozen cauliflower and cocaine had been packed, but we could not discover who had ordered or paid for them. We tracked the cauliflower itself to a Mexican company in Nuevo León, but could not pursue it further; my subpoena power stopped at the border. Fox Foods' bank was a bust as well. Under federal law, you cannot open a bank account over the telephone; you have to appear in person and show identification. Someone claiming to be Pablo Ledezma had opened the Fox account, using the fake Social Security card, but no one at the bank could remember who Ledezma was or what he looked like. I secretly suspected that a bribe had been paid to a bank employee to open the account anonymously, but I had no proof, and we let the issue go. Eventually, however, we caught a break.

ONE MORNING ERIC, JIMMY, BRIAN, and I drove over to Fresh Freeze, the warehouse in Edinburg where "Ledezma" had stored the cauliflower. Gus Prevot, the manager, wanted to help; he thought the drug trafficking epidemic was a major blight on the Valley. Unfortunately, our interview was a bust. All he recalled was the name of the man who called about the shipment: Ledezma, of course. When, however, we reviewed his shipping records, one caught my eye. It stated that the shipment of frozen cauliflower had been released by the warehouse on January 19, 1999, to "driver Francisco Rodriguez." I asked Gus about the entry. He told us that when drivers come to pick up a load of frozen produce, he always examines the trucker's driver's license. "Basically, it's to cover myself. If a company ever says, 'We never got this shipment,' I could say, 'Well, no, you did, here's the name and driver's license number of the driver who picked it up. I checked his ID myself.'" The fact that Pancho had picked up the cauliflower was great evidence for us. Since we already had two witnesses to testify that Pancho ran Juan's drug trafficking errands, this testimony tied Juan more closely to the shipment than ever before. But the proof got even better.

I asked Gus how long it had taken for Francisco Rodriguez to pick up this shipment. Gus thought for a moment and then said, "About forty, forty-five minutes."

"Did you talk to him?"

"Yes, briefly . . ."

"Do you think he was the same person as the Pablo Ledezma who called you on the phone?"

"I don't think so. The driver was, well, a typical truck driver, kind of rough. Ledezma seemed much more educated."

"What did you and Francisco talk about?"

"He was just in a hurry to get going. He told me he was from the area and that he was loading this for his brother."

My eyes lit up. Touchdown!

———

ON THE DAY OF THE SEIZURE Albonico had grabbed a stack of shipping documents from the manager's office at CSI and the cab of the truck carrying the drugs. Several of these documents were written on Fox Foods stationery, listing the company's fake address, 417 East Coma, Hidalgo, Texas. The stationery also listed telephone and fax numbers: (956) 929-6921 for the phone, (956) 929-6867 for the fax. We subpoenaed subscriber information and tolls—the record of inbound and outbound calls—for both these lines, hoping to find something juicy, but quickly hit a dead end. The phone line was activated on January 5; the fax, on

January 8. There were hundreds of inbound and outbound calls on both lines throughout January, and most of those calls were incriminating, to places like Fresh Freeze, CSI, and Noe's personal pager. Unfortunately, there was nothing to tie either phone to Juan Rodriguez. On January 25, the day of the seizure, both telephones went silent.

We sent off another flurry of subpoenas seeking to identify the two subscribers for the phone lines, Alonzo Elizondo and Pedro Mariscal. Both men, we learned, had no driver's licenses, no addresses, no Social Security numbers, no bank accounts, no employment records, and no criminal or driving records. In a modern regulatory society, a real person leaves innumerable paperwork footprints. Maybe these men were undocumented aliens, recently arrived in the United States, but the odds were much greater that they did not exist—that the names were fake. When we went to the Valley, we decided to deepen our inquiry, to see if we could uncover the real man or men behind the names.

The Fox telephone and fax service had been purchased from a Valley telecommunications company called CenturyTel. We went to its headquarters in McAllen and met with George Garza, operations manager, hoping he could tell us something about the two accounts. Garza went into his records storage facility and emerged, fifteen minutes later, with carbon copies of the two phone service contracts. I asked him to examine these two single-page documents and tell us what he could. Garza's analysis was incredibly illuminating.

"These are both what we call easy-go contracts," Garza told us. "In a regular contract, we take all of the subscriber's personal and credit information, run a credit report, and, if the person is creditworthy, we bill them month by month for whatever minutes they use. In an easy-go contract, they pay for all their minutes up front, in advance. Once those minutes are burned off, the phone will go dead."

"Who uses these easy-go contracts?" I asked.

"Well, they are designed for people with bad credit. But they are also used by people who want to hide their identity. Because this is not an ongoing contract, but a single one-time sale of services, we don't run a credit check, and we don't ask for identification. They tell us how much money they want to spend, fill out this form, and we activate their phone."

This seemed a little sketchy to me—they were offering a service that was perfect for criminals—but I let it go. "Can you tell us anything more about these two particular contracts?"

"The only thing I notice right offhand are the customers' addresses. One is 500 West Nolana, McAllen, Texas. The other is 1106 South Seventy-seventh Street, Harlingen. Those are not the customers' real addresses. Those are the addresses of two of our retail stores."

"So when the form asked for the customer's address, these guys put down the addresses of your stores?"

"Yes."

"Is that normal?"

"No, I would say that is highly unusual."

With Garza's help, we were able to identify and track down the two CenturyTel employees who sold the two relevant service contracts. The guy who sold the Fox telephone line was a washout. He had sold hundreds of service contracts over the past year, and he could not remember anything about this particular one. But the second salesclerk was a gem.

When I met Flor Narvaez, she was working behind the counter of a CenturyTel store in McAllen. Flor was twenty-one, attractive, quiet, polite. When we flashed our law enforcement credentials and asked to speak with her, she seemed nervous but kept her composure. We went into a stark little conference room at the back of the store, and I showed her the Fox Foods fax contract. "That's an easy-go, and yes, I sold that service. That's my signature at the bottom." I asked Flor if she remembered anything about this particular transaction with Pedro Mariscal. Flor thought for a moment and then simply replied, "No." My heart sank. Then I took a stab in the dark.

Prior to the trip, I had the agents make up a photo array, six photographs of Latino men, one of them Juan, the other five selected at random from DEA photo files. We showed Flor the array, and she immediately said, "I know this man, Juan Rodriguez." She pointed to his photograph. I was startled, but I tried to remain calm. Keeping my voice as casual as I could—though I am sure I had a slight quaver, I was so excited—I asked her how she knew Juan. She replied, "He is friends with a friend of mine."

"Have you ever talked with him or had any dealings with him, of any kind?"

"Only once. I sold him a phone back in winter."

"Do you remember more precisely when you sold him that phone?"

"No, I just remember it was winter. It was cold."

"Do you remember anything about what happened that day or what kind of service he wanted? Is there anything that sticks in your mind?"

"Yes, there is. It was a prepaid, an easy-go phone. It was weird. He gave me a different name, asked me to put the service in another name. I don't remember what the name was. I just remember he put down a name that was not his own."

I asked her if the name might have been Pedro Mariscal, but she did not recall. She just repeated, "It was odd, he wanted a phone in another name."

Flor's memory never improved, but her testimony was devastating nevertheless. Sometimes evidence is really complex, hard for juries to grasp. In a trial, they might eventually understand that the phone Flor sold to Juan under a fake name was almost certainly the Fox Foods fax line, but maybe they would not. I was certain, however, that they would immediately get one point, which I would hammer home in my closing arguments: that Juan had bought phone service under an assumed name, and honest people don't do that.

I STATED EARLIER that we had no success when we visited the bank where Fox Foods had opened its commercial account. This is largely true—we never figured out who opened the account—but the bank did give us one good lead. To open the account, "Ledezma" was required to prove that Fox Foods was a real company. To accomplish this, he gave the bank a Texas business registration form. Under Texas law, this form had to be notarized. We got a copy of the form from the county courthouse, where it had been placed on file, and then examined the notary stamp. The notary's name was Arturo Trevino, who just happened to be Juan's accountant.

Tony Sanchez, our Texas legman, went to Trevino's office and confronted him with the form. After some prodding, Trevino provided a written and signed statement. He stated that on January 6, 1999, Juan Rodriguez had asked him to notarize a form—he thought it was a business registration form, but he couldn't remember too well—signed by a man named Ledezma, who, Juan claimed, was stuck in Mexico on business. Trevino was not supposed to notarize something for a person not present before him, but he did so because Juan assured him it was okay.

Trevino's information was the smoking gun, tying Juan to both "Ledezma" and Fox Foods. Trevino should have been my star witness, but it didn't turn out that way. When I asked him about the business registration form two months later, on one of my first trips to the Valley, Trevino immediately began to backpedal. He said that he no longer remembered the date he had notarized the form: maybe it was in January, but it could have been earlier. Also, on reflection, he was sure the document he signed had nothing to do with Fox Foods; the form he notarized was concerned with a Mexican land sale. I showed him the business registration form, and he asserted, with a deep flush on his face, that the signature was not his. Or maybe it was. He could not be sure.

When a witness recants his testimony, what do you do? Eric and I had two different reactions. I got tough. "Mr. Trevino, let me make this perfectly clear. See those two guys, Jimmy and Brian? They are federal law enforcement officers. It is a crime, a felony, to lie to federal law enforcement officers. I think you are lying here today, and if I get enough evidence to prove it, I am going to indict you in New York." Then I asked him if he had met with Ivan Fisher or Juan since he first talked to Sanchez. His answer stunned me.

"Oh, yes, Mr. Fisher and his investigators, they came eight or nine times."

"Eight or nine! What did you talk about, this form?"

"Mr. Fisher told me, 'I have news for you, you didn't sign that document.'"

Trevino's statement bowled me over. In every criminal case, the defense attorney has the right, of course, to visit with potential witnesses and see what they know. To visit eight or nine times, however, seemed intimidating to me. And to do what Ivan did—to tell the witness what the lawyer wants the witness to say, instead of asking what the witness knows—well, that seemed to me beyond the pale. Back in New York, I complained to Judge Gershon, but my effort fell flat. Ivan claimed, quite rightly, that he was just doing his job. He had done what a good defense lawyer will do, neutralized a top government witness.*

While I was throwing an ineffectual tantrum, Eric was thinking like a lawyer. That day he began to nose around Trevino's office, talking to his staff, examining records and calendar books, hunting for circumstantial evidence. He soon hit pay dirt. Looking through a receipt book, Eric noticed something crucial. On January 6, 1999, the same day the Fox form was notarized, Juan Rodriguez had paid Trevino twenty dollars.

I hoped at first that this payment was for notary services, but I was soon disappointed. In November 1998, we learned, Trevino was involved in a fund-raiser for the American Cancer Society. Juan agreed to donate twenty dollars. So, on January 6, he dropped off his payment. Still, the payment receipt was, if not a smoking gun, at very least a remarkable piece of circumstantial proof. In the Texas Valley there were thousands of notary publics. Who had notarized Ledezma's Fox Foods business form? Juan's accountant—on a specific day we could prove Juan was in his office.

WHEN JUAN WAS FIRST INDICTED, Eric told Judge Gershon that the trial would last only three days. By the time we got in front of a jury, in fall of 1999, we had found so much additional evidence that the case took us four whole weeks.

My favorite moment in the trial came when Flor Narvaez testified. In most big federal cases, the government turns over its 3500 material—reports containing prior statements of government witnesses—to the defense well before trial. As a result, there are very few surprises in court because the defense generally knows what government witnesses are going to say well ahead of time. But there is one major loophole in this disclosure rule: though the government must disclose all its existing reports, it is under no obligation to create reports in the first place. I knew about this exception, and in Flor's case, I exploited it. When I interviewed Flor, there was no need to generate a report summarizing her statements, for I knew I would remember precisely what she said with-

---

*Ultimately, Ivan was proved right, and I was wrong. At trial, a witness told us that while the notary stamp was Trevino's, the signature was fake, probably that of one of his employees.

out creating a written record. For this reason, I told the agents not to write anything down. As a result, there were no reports or notes to disclose. At trial, Ivan had no advance warning of Flor's likely testimony. He expected, I think, she was going to be a mere telephone records custodian. When Flor got on the stand and said that Juan had purchased an easy-go phone under a fake name, Ivan almost had a heart attack. Red-faced, sputtering, he demanded that Judge Gershon give him more time to prepare his cross-examination. She agreed, but even with a few extra hours, he was unable to dent her story. Desperate, Ivan asked her repeatedly if I or the agents had ever written anything down when we interviewed her, trying to uncover a 3500 disclosure violation. Fortunately, Flor remembered: no writing, just questions. Ultimately, Ivan lost his composure. Near the end of cross, Flor referred to me as John. Ivan jumped all over her, out of simple frustration. "When you and Mr. Kroger speak, you refer to him as John?" he snapped. I loved Flor's response: "No, I call him 'sir.'"

Most trials cause a great deal of anxiety. *Rodriguez* was no different. Ivan was a very skilled attorney, and he shot holes in all the weakest parts of our case: Noe's anger at Juan over the affair with his wife; Casas's long career of crime; the inconclusive nature of the telephone call to "John" the night of the seizure. Despite the constant struggle, I was never really in doubt about the result. Over six months we had converted a single-cooperator case into something much different, a case with so much circumstantial evidence that I told the jury in closing it could convict Rodriguez without even considering the testimony from Noe and Casas. When the jury came back, after several days of deliberation, it found Juan guilty on all counts. On May 18, 2000, Judge Gershon gave him thirty years in prison. That day I looked at Juan to gauge his reaction. He took the blow stoically, emotionless, without even batting an eye. Juan was a very professional drug trafficker. All his life he had known this moment might come. For more than a decade he had taken the rewards of crime gleefully. When the bill arrived, he did not flinch.

THE PUMA TRIAL had an interesting epilogue. In the summer of 1999 Eric sought an arrest warrant for Juan's boss, Nino Valdez, who we assumed had fled the country. Our case against Nino was remarkably weak, even weaker than our original case against Juan. We hoped, however, that if we had someone concrete in custody for Juan to cooperate against, Juan might flip.

When the Puma trial ended, Eric intended to dismiss the complaint against Nino, but in our excitement, we forgot all about it. It didn't really matter; Nino was long gone to Mexico. Six months later, however, Nino, assuming, I guess, that the heat was off, tried to cross back into the United States. U.S. Customs picked him up on our warrant and called Eric. Eric popped into my office one morning, a sly smile on his face. "You are not going to believe this, but they just picked up Nino Valdez on the border. Do you think we should keep him or let him go?"

Eric and I agreed that our case was hopeless, but we thought we should bring Nino to New York anyway. "We'll do the full-court press again, see what evidence we can find. We'll never have a better chance." I fully expected Nino to go to trial. Nino, however, knew all about our successful effort to track down evidence against Juan. We told him that if he wanted a trial, we would do the same thing to him. To our surprise and joy, Nino took a fifteen-year plea. Had we gone to trial, I am pretty certain we would have lost.

CHAPTER THIRTEEN

The Dark Side

The *Rodriguez* case was ethically simple, black and white, not gray. The defendant was a wealthy and powerful drug kingpin, and his crimes caused significant social harm. We offered him a way out, but he chose to fight. After a hard struggle against talented counsel, we got a concrete, positive result, thirty years in prison. Had all narcotics work been so straightforward, I would probably have loved the unit. Unfortunately, that was not the case. As a narcotics prosecutor I was forced to live in a murky world of moral ambiguity.

ONE MORNING I caught the LaGuardia shuttle down to D.C. and took a cab to DEA Headquarters in Arlington, Virginia, just across the Potomac from the capital. The purpose of my trip was to attend a planning session for a major international case. The Colombian National Police had infiltrated a cocaine cartel selling drugs throughout the United States. The CNP had scheduled a date for arrests several months away. Before its takedown, it wanted its American partners to investigate some of the cartel's U.S. drug distribution and money laundering cells. My role was relatively minor. The Colombians had identified two telephone numbers in New York supposedly used by cartel moneymen. I was supposed to wiretap these numbers, gather what evidence I could, and then arrest my targets on the same day the CNP sprang its trap down south.

The meeting was run by a top-ranking member of the Colombian National Police, General Something or Other, a handsome man in a dark gray pin-striped suit. For an hour the General briefed us about his case and the proposed timeline. As a frontline narcotics prosecutor in New York I found his presentation gripping. I had a very limited street view of the war on drugs. Here, in contrast, I got a glimpse of antinarcotics work in all its geopolitical complexity. Battalions of Colombian troops backed by assault helicopters, the General told us, were raiding massive cocaine processing labs. FARC, the Revolutionary Armed Forces of Colombia, a violent guerrilla movement fueled by narcotics profits, was forging a strong alliance with the cartels, trading military protection for cash. Sophisticated U.S. Air Force electronic surveillance aircraft were patrolling the South American airways, pulling narco-trafficking communications out of thin air. Jet boats were moving tons of cocaine up the California coast. Dozens of Colombian judges were being assassinated.

After the General concluded his briefing, he talked with us informally. I asked him, "How many wires do you currently have up on this group? Do you have any specific intel that might be useful in our side of the case?"

He replied, "Over the course of the investigation we have employed two hundred different wiretaps, one hundred of them legal. My DEA colleagues, I believe, have packets ready for you containing transcripts of relevant intercepts that may help you write your own warrant applications." A DEA official at his side nodded in confirmation.

Later that afternoon I picked up my packet. It contained several transcripts of calls placed from my two New York numbers.

At the time I did not give the General's comments much thought. Later that night, however, as I floated in the bathtub, I thought: One hundred of them legal? What is that supposed to mean? Is he telling me he's running hundreds of illegal wiretaps?

In Colombia the police and judiciary are under immense pressure. FARC and the cartels give them a choice: work for us and be millionaires, or investigate us and go to your graves. These threats are very real. Since 1985 more than two hundred judges and investigators, half the Colombian Supreme Court, and twelve hundred police officers have been murdered. Thousands more, fearing the same fate, leak information to the cartels. As a result, there is a very good chance that if the CNP seeks a legal wiretap, authorized by a judge and a top governmental official, it will be disclosed to the drug traffickers before it is up and running. In these circumstances, the CNP, it appears, uses illegal wiretaps, ones that violate Colombian laws requiring judicial screening and oversight, in the hope that its wiretaps will remain secret.

Why did the General tell me this? Why would he admit he was running illegal wiretaps? He was not bragging, flaunting the fact that he was violating Colombian law. On the contrary, he was trying to be helpful. In U.S. courts the admissibility of evidence gathered from foreign wiretaps may depend, in some circumstances, on whether the wiretaps were conducted in accordance with the laws of the host country. I am sure the General knew this. When he told me that half of his wiretaps were "legal," it was his shorthand way of conveying a very relevant fact: because half of his wiretaps complied with Colombian law, roughly half the calls he was intercepting would be admissible in U.S. courts if prosecutors like me needed them to win our cases. When I checked, I discovered, to my relief, that all the call transcripts in my packet came from the "legal" wiretaps.

I felt highly ambivalent about what I learned in that meeting. I understood why the CNP was running illegal wiretaps, and I sympathized with its motives. Drug cartels are tearing Colombia apart. To combat them, the General believed he had to conduct an end run around his own courts. It seemed foolish to hand over all our intelligence to corrupt judges. Still, the news that I was involved, however tangentially, with cops who were violating the laws of their own country was deeply disturbing to me. In our courts the government has to play by the rules, even if it means that a bad guy gets away. We adopt this approach because we believe that keeping government accountable is more important than the results of any one criminal case. Perhaps that was a luxury the Colombians could not afford. But maybe in the long run, I thought, instilling respect for the rule of law was more important to Colombia's future than the results of any one drug case. Nothing is more harmful to the development of democracy than a lawless government. If that is correct, we were hardly doing them a favor when we failed to object to, perhaps even encouraged, their methods.

When I got back to Brooklyn, I investigated my part of the case. Ultimately, we arrested a couple of low-level moneymen. As best as I can recall, I gave them to an eager AUSA in the District of New Jersey to prosecute since that office also had venue. I did not dump the defendants because of the illegal wiretaps. I just wanted to clear something off my docket.

The Colombian government's illegal wiretapping program remained secret for years. In 2006, however, it admitted it was breaking the law and that its illegal wiretapping program extended not just to drug cartel targets but to journalists, opposition political leaders, and government officials, including U.S. government officials working in Colombia. The Colombians have promised to end this abuse. Maybe they will.

———

SOMETIMES ETHICAL PROBLEMS arose even closer to home. For a year I worked with a CI, a confidential informant I will call "Armando." Armando was a former dealer who got arrested by the DEA in a buy-bust in the mid-1990s, before I became an AUSA. To avoid being charged, he flipped. Now he ran a bodega, a low-rent convenience store, in a poor part of New York City. To supplement his income, he supplied information to the DEA and the NYPD: the names, locations, and telephone numbers of dealers working the streets around his store. Armando was held in very high esteem by his DEA handlers, for he was a very productive source, leading us to dozens of seizures and arrests. For this reason, the DEA insisted that I carefully protect his covert status. Whenever I did a case that started with information from Armando, as happened two or three times, I always had to develop completely independent proof of the target's guilt, so the arrest could never be linked back to him. I have no idea how much we paid the guy; that was the DEA's responsibility. But if I had to guess, I would say thirty to fifty thousand dollars over several years.

One day I was interviewing a defendant I will call "Flores" in the Narcotics conference room. Flores was a major cocaine distributor who wanted to cooperate. Our first meeting, several days before, had gone well. Flores seemed honest, displaying few of the telltale physical signs of lying or evasion, and his information was useful. In this second meeting, I planned to discuss his involvement in violence, always a stickier subject. Ten minutes into the proffer, after some routine questions to warm him up, I asked, "Have you ever been involved, in any way, with murder—shot someone, stabbed someone, ordered a murder, helped murder someone, saw someone murdered—anything?"

Flores replied: "Once, about a year ago, one of my customers asked me whether I knew any hitmen. Well, there's this guy Armando, who has a lot of contacts. Armando's got this guy, they call him the Dragon. The Dragon is, like, one of Armando's boys; he's always at his store, does odd jobs for him, delivering, threatening people, stuff like that. So I called Armando, and he brought the Dragon over, and my customer and the Dragon went off to the side and had a conversation. I have no idea what they worked out."

I asked Flores where Armando's store was, and he named a particular street corner, one that rang a clear bell. I asked some more questions about a different topic, so Flores could not sense that I was particularly interested in Armando. Then I declared that I wanted to take a short break. Flores (with an agent for escort) went off to the bathroom, while my lead agent and I went out to the hallway. In a few seconds he confirmed what I already thought: the street corner Flores had mentioned was the precise location of our informant's store.

A few minutes later we resumed the proffer. I asked Flores to tell me more about Armando. "Oh, he's a dealer, cocaine, heroin, some crack. That's really all I know. He moves small amounts, a hundred grams, three hundred grams, stuff like that." At the close of the session we handed Flores a large book of photographs and asked him to identify anyone he knew. He picked out several dealers. One of them was Armando, our informant.

Flores's allegation was serious. Sometimes, in rare cases, the government allows CIs to continue to commit crimes on the street in order to maintain their covers. They are required, however, to disclose all their criminal conduct to their government sponsors. Armando had never been authorized to commit crimes, and he had never told the DEA about ongoing narcotics deals or the fact that he supervised a hitman. Or to be more accurate, no one had ever told me. Maybe someone in the DEA had known it all the time.

Why, you might ask, would Armando double-deal behind our back? One potential motive was greed. We were paying him well, but drug trafficking pays better. Maybe he had decided to return to his original profession after several years of playing things safe. It was also possible, however, that he had been operating in bad faith all along. For years Armando had been ratting out the dealers in his neighborhood. Maybe, I thought, he was using the DEA to eliminate his competitors. It sounds a bit outlandish, but it happens more often than you'd think.

The next day my agent drove to Armando's store and confronted him with Flores's claims. Armando, no surprise, denied everything vehemently. But the meeting served our purpose. If Armando was breaking the law, he would probably stop now, at least temporarily. And if he was telling the truth, no harm, no foul. Our suspicions might keep him on his toes.

When two informants like Flores and Armando provide conflicting information, how do you decide who is telling the truth? Most AUSAs and agents will tell you that they rely on their gut instincts. Usually, however, there is some solid logical basis to explain their intuitive judgments.

In this case, my heart sank the moment Flores told us Armando was dealing, for I believed almost instantly that he was telling the truth. One factor that influenced my reaction was Flores's demeanor. By this point in my career I had conducted more than one hundred proffers, sometimes several a day, and I had noticed certain regular patterns. When witnesses try to incriminate someone who is innocent, they tend to get excited: their voices rise, their gestures become more flamboyant, and when you press them on details, they quickly grow defensive. Flores, in contrast, showed no such signs of emotion or interest. When he talked about Armando, he appeared totally bored.

A second factor was timing. When a defendant wants to implicate an enemy in order to get revenge, he usually talks about that person early and often. Five minutes into a proffer he will blurt out, "I know the guy you want, that guy Miguel. He's a really bad guy, a big dealer." If you fail to take the bait, he will bring up poor Miguel again fifteen minutes later. Flores, in contrast, did not tell me about Armando until our second meeting and then only in response to direct questioning. If he was trying to set Armando up, he was certainly cool about it.

A third factor: my lead DEA agent agreed with my assessment. In criminal investigations, you are constantly making judgments about truth, lies, and credibility. In these circumstances, only a fool relies solely on his own judgment. Over time I had come to trust this particular agent implicitly; his judgment and advice were always sound, mature, and cautious. No agent likes to dig up dirt about his own agency. So when my agent concluded that Armando might be breaking the law, I took that conclusion seriously.

Finally, a decisive factor: corroboration. Though I thought Armando was double-dealing, I did not immediately blow the whistle. Instead, I continued to investigate quietly. Several weeks later a second witness from the same neighborhood ratted out Armando as well. I considered the possibility that Flores and this second witness were colluding together, to frame a common enemy, but rejected it. These two potential witnesses were incarcerated in different prisons, so if they had coordinated their stories, they must have done so before their arrests, a fanciful possibility. The fact that Flores's scoop was now corroborated meant I had to take action; Armando had to be stopped.

The following week I called all the relevant parties together and we met in Jodi's office: Jodi, my case agent, Armando's DEA handler, the handler's supervisor, and I. I quickly presented my evidence that Armando was dealing behind our backs. I knew the DEA would not want to prosecute him, but I expected that it would agree to put Armando out of commission: to cut off his stipend, put him under surveillance, and decline to use him in any further cases. Instead, to my surprise, Armando's handler and his boss angrily refused. They were not interested in the facts. They were not interested in further investigation. They did not want to take any action at all. "Armando's a good man," they insisted. "He's helped us make dozens of good cases. He's brought us huge seizures." They would not put him out to pasture. If we did not want to handle Armando's cases, fine. They would take them across the river to the SDNY.

I was astounded by the DEA's reaction, but I realized later that it was par for the course. In the DEA, agents and supervisors are judged by their "stats." Armando helped these guys boost their seizure counts, and to them, that was all that mattered. Apparently, they were willing to have a drug trafficker on their payroll who might be helping set up paid murder hits behind our backs as long as he kept fingering other dealers. The fact that we are paid to convict dealers, not protect them, seemed to them inconsequential.

If you seize one hundred kilos of cocaine by closing your eyes to the illegal behavior of one informant who deals much smaller quantities, is that trade worth it? To the DEA, the answer was yes. At the time, however, I strongly disagreed, though I was not able to articulate why. Looking back, I see that my reaction was an important indication that after three years as a prosecutor, my ideas about justice were evolving, and I no longer believed that achieving a public policy goal trumped more fundamental concerns about right and wrong.

In the end, the DEA kept Armando on the payroll, but Jodi, thank God, backed me up. The next day she circulated an e-mail throughout the EDNY warning AUSAs not to take any cases in which Armando was involved.

———

WAS ARMANDO WORKING for the DEA, or was the DEA working for Armando? A second case raised that question even more starkly.

One day Jodi called me into her office and asked me to take over a money laundering case from an AUSA who was leaving the office. I tried to object; I thought my plate was already too full. Jodi cut me off. "This won't be much work. The agents don't need supervision. They've been working the case for a couple of years, and they know what they're doing. They are excellent agents. It's a great case." I grudgingly agreed; I knew Jodi would not take no for an answer. But I warned her: "I really don't have much time to spare."

She dismissed my concerns. "They need some subpoenas every once in a while, but that's it. The investigation runs itself. I just have to assign someone to the case officially." She gave me the contact numbers for two U.S. Customs agents. She also told me the name of the case. It was some silly code word like Operation Condor.

At first I did almost no work on Operation Condor. I supplied the agents with two or three subpoenas, but otherwise, I left them on auto-pilot. Within a few weeks, however, I was forced to get a grip on the case. Every quarter Jodi required her AUSAs to file detailed updates on all their cases, so she could monitor our caseloads and ensure that our investigations were moving forward properly. These reports were a great management tool, not just for Jodi but for me as well. As an AUSA I always had a hard time juggling dozens of cases at once. I tended to focus my energy on my one or two most significant matters, those with the greatest public impact or the ones most likely to go to trial. Smaller cases fell through the cracks. Preparing my quarterly report provided a good opportunity to review these lower-priority cases, identify the next investigative steps I needed to take, and push them forward. My next quarterly report was due soon, so I called in the Condor agents to discuss the future of the case.

At first blush, Condor seemed like a great success. The agents had infiltrated a Colombian money shipping business several years earlier and flipped its leader in New York. The organization took "deposits" from Colombian drug dealers in the United States and shipped the money to crooked banks in Colombia and Panama, for a fee. The informant supplied Customs with information on each shipment. We let the majority of the shipments go through to Colombia; we did not want anyone to suspect that we had penetrated the organization. But we intercepted and seized a certain percentage: maybe 10 or 15 percent. To date, the agents had grabbed something like three million dollars, one of the larger money cases in New York.

After this first meeting, I took no action. As Jodi said, the case seemed to run itself. But the more I thought about the facts, the more they bothered me. We were not making any significant arrests in the case. Nor were we generating any useful intelligence about ongoing drug trafficking operations. Thus Condor's value, if any, came from the seizures. Now, three million was a lot of money. When I asked the agents why they thought we should stay the course, they thought the answer was obvious. But to me, it was less clear. Large drug trafficking groups are sophisticated. If your enforcement operations are hurting them, they adjust and adapt. So why, I wondered, would a money laundering organization make no changes to the way it did business after repeated large-scale seizures? Why didn't it change managers, shipping methods, or communication techniques? To me, the answer was clear: its loss rate—our seizure rate—was an acceptable cost of business.

Both drug trafficking and drug enforcement are percentage games. A Colombian drug cartel knows it is going to lose a share of its potential profits at each stage of its business model. The Colombian National Police and the Colombian army will destroy a certain percentage of its product before it leaves the plantation or the lab; more narcotics will be seized at the United States–Mexico border or as a result of internal street enforcement operations; some dealers will fail to pay for the product they receive; and some of the resulting revenue will be lost to seizures or transaction fees before the profits are safely in the hands of the cartel bosses. The cartels' primary goal is to minimize lost profits at each stage, so they can make the largest financial gain possible. The primary goal of U.S. drug enforcement operations, in contrast, is to raise the percentage of lost profits at each step as high as we can, in the hope that this will drive up drug prices on the street.

Given this model, you can see why Operation Condor disturbed me. We were basically laundering the Colombians' money for a 10 or 15 percent fee, and they were letting us do it. That fact was highly suspicious. If we were really hurting them, they would shift their business to a different money broker or put their drug proceeds on the United States' well-established black peso market. The fact that they did not bother but kept on using our informant was a clear sign that laundering money through our informant—through the United States government, in effect—even with its concomitant 10 percent loss, was more cost-effective than the other available alternatives. Indeed, it was possible that our informant's "cooperation" was known in Colombia, perhaps even preapproved. In short, I believed our much-vaunted undercover operation was probably helping the drug traffickers, not hurting them.

Once I had reached this sobering conclusion, I asked the Condor agents to come back in to talk about the status of the case. The resulting meeting, which lasted several hours, was one of the most depressing I ever experienced as an AUSA. At the outset I explained my fears to the agents and proposed that we increase our seizure rate. This might, I admitted, result in the termination of the operation, but that was okay. "If they quit using our broker, that means we are hurting them. Putting this money transmission route out of business will damage them. We should be closing it down, not helping them keep it open." The agents listened coldly and then flatly rejected my argument. They were convinced this was a great operation, and they were incapable of looking at it critically. Like the DEA agents supervising Armando, their professional performance was evaluated primarily in quantitative terms, the number of dollars they seized. Because of Operation Condor, they looked like geniuses without having to do much heavy lifting. Indeed, they got bonuses and awards for this work. When I suggested their work was helping the cartels, not stopping them, they went ballistic.

Eventually we compromised. I agreed to accept the current (low) seizure rate, to keep the operation going in perpetuity. They agreed in turn to let me draft arrest warrants for our informant's Colombian bosses, so that if they ever entered the United States, we could arrest them. From my perspective, this outcome was better than nothing, but it still felt absurd. My job was to fight drug trafficking, not facilitate it. In this position, I felt I had only one morally acceptable option. I went to Jodi and explained that I no longer wanted to work on the case.

I am not sure whether Jodi agreed with my assessment or not. She thought I was smart, but she may have concluded that my analysis was too speculative to act on. Or perhaps she accepted my argument but thought keeping the Customs agents happy was important to our long-term mission, for they were some of our best "customers." Regardless, she did not terminate the case. She simply assigned it to another AUSA. I never checked back to see what happened. Once the case was reassigned, it was no longer my business. I suspect the scheme continued for years.

The Armando and Condor cases were small, localized examples of ways in which some federal law enforcement tactics perpetuate America's drug abuse problem. Federal law enforcement agencies like the DEA and Customs are fighting an elusive and creative enemy. These agencies want to find objective ways to measure success and failure, a commendable goal. So they make seizure counts their primary measure of programmatic success and agent performance. Alas, this metric—like body counts during the Vietnam War—winds up encouraging self-defeating behavior. As my own cases suggest, agents seeking high seizure volumes may avert their eyes when their informants commit crimes or may allow undercover infiltration operations to continue year after year, despite indicators that these operations are helping the cartels, not hurting them.

How common are these problems? Unfortunately, it is impossible for me to say. The fact that I encountered them twice in a relatively brief time, and that agents with very solid professional reputations were reluctant to admit that anything was wrong, suggests that these issues might be occurring systematically. All I know, from my own experience, is that they exist.

———

ONE IMPORTANT WAY in which federal and state criminal cases differ is in the importance of cooperation, of convincing defendants to testify against their peers. In the average state case, there is only one defendant, so there is no one to cooperate against. In federal cases, in contrast, we typically target organized criminal groups with multiple members. In these cases, flipping a defendant so he will incriminate his former friends is often essential to government victory.

When federal agents arrest someone, they bring the defendant to their local headquarters, where they record his or her "pedigree information"—name, address, nationality, and date of birth—and take finger- and handprints. During this process, which usually takes several hours, the agents will try to convince key defendants to cooperate, typically by using a combination of threats and promises. "If you don't come on board now, you are going to rot in prison for the rest of your life. But if you work with us today, we can help you." Sometimes this works, but more often the targets keep their mouths shut; these are, after all, professional criminals. As soon as processing is concluded, the agents bring the defendant to arraignment court. There the defendant gets a defense lawyer. From that point forward, responsibility for flipping the defendant is in the hands of the assigned AUSA. We invite the defendant and his attorney to attend a proffer session. If they agree, we transport the defendant to our office and try to persuade them to confess.

When I first joined the EDNY, no one told me how to flip a target. During my first two weeks I tagged along on two defendant proffers conducted by rookie AUSAs who had started work just a few months before I did. After that, I was on my own. At first I had no idea what to do, but eventually I developed a set of regular protocols that seemed to produce good results. I did not think too deeply about my strategies. My job was to flip people, and that is what I did. In time, however, I grew uncomfortable with my interrogation style. It worked very well, but it was also incredibly manipulative.

"Angel Ramon," as I shall call him, was a drug packager for a Colombian heroin importation ring in Queens: short, squat, ugly, about thirty-five years old. After the FBI arrested him, I quickly identified him as a perfect potential cooperator. My case against him was weak, so getting him to confess and plead guilty was essential. He was central to the conspiracy, so he would have valuable information about my other targets. He had a criminal record, and this prior experience in the criminal justice system might make him easier to flip, for he would understand that our offer to cooperate was not a ruse, but a legitimate way to reduce his sentence. Above all, he was a low man on the food chain, not a boss, so if he ultimately got a low sentence, that would not be a huge injustice.

The agents picked up Angel at the MDC and brought him to my conference room, where we handcuffed him to a chair, to send a message that we remained in total control. Then, instead of starting the meeting, I let him sit for fifteen minutes with his lawyer, stewing. The purpose of this delay was twofold. Waiting makes people nervous, and I wanted him to be tense. It also suggested that I was busy, with lots of cases on my plate, and that he was not a huge priority. I did not want him to feel special.

I finally bustled into the room, apologizing for the delay. I sat with my agents on one side of the table with our interpreter; Angel and his lawyer sat on the opposite side. I spoke first, explaining my goals for the meeting. In this opening speech, I had one primary goal, to strip Angel of any perceived negotiating power.

Most defendants come to their first proffer believing they have leverage because the government wants and needs their cooperation. This perception is often accurate. In Angel's case, for example, I needed his help or my investigation would stall. This fact puts defendants in an empowered position, which they may try to exploit by withholding information or seeking better deals. My opening salvo was designed to disabuse them of this notion. "The purpose of our meeting," I told Angel in a weary, almost bored voice, "is to explore your potential cooperation with the government. To be honest, I couldn't care less whether you cooperate or not. I would just as soon convict you and send you to prison for ten or fifteen years. It makes no difference to me. So if you want to play games today, or lie, or hold back information, we will send you back to the MDC, and you can go to trial. I won't mind. I like trials. As I said, it makes no difference to me."

Defendants hated this speech. You could see their sense of entitlement wither on the spot. I usually concluded with "Do you want to go forward, or do you want to fight the case?" In all the proffers I conducted, somewhere between one and two hundred, every defendant gulped and said he wanted to continue. That put him in the position of a supplicant, someone invested in convincing me to let him sign up. Angel of course told me he wanted to proceed.

Next, I explained to Angel the ground rules for the meeting. Any statements he made would not be used against him in the government's case-in-chief if he went to trial, and that gave him some protection; if cooperation did not work out, he could still fight the case. His statements could be used, however, to cross-examine him if he took the stand at trial. He could terminate the meeting at any time. If he wished to speak to his lawyer alone, all he had to do was ask. If he did not want to answer a question, he need not do so. This speech was important legally, for it would later make it impossible for the defendant and his attorney to claim they did not understand the rules of engagement. But it also played a useful role psychologically. Many of my defendants, like Angel, came from countries like the Dominican Republic or Colombia, where governments are corrupt and torture and abuse by police officials is common. My legal advice was designed to signal that the United States was different, that we played the game straight and cared about the rule of law. It also suggested that we did not care enough about his potential cooperation to trick him.

As soon as these preliminary matters were done, I immediately elevated the stakes. "So, Angel, I don't mean to make you nervous [though of course I did], but the next hour is going to be the most important one in your life. There are two ways this day can end. I am going to listen to you today, and if I think you are telling the truth, I may let you cooperate. As your lawyer will tell you, cooperation may result in a much lower sentence than you would otherwise receive. But you are going to get only one chance. If you start lying or bullshitting me about what you've done, I'll pull the plug. I don't have time to waste. So you get one chance, and if you blow it, you can go to trial."

Then I turned up the pressure even more. "Let's talk for a moment about what happens if you do go to trial. You are welcome to take a shot at it, but I guarantee you, you will lose. I've indicted a hundred people like you, and every single one has been convicted. That's no big deal; it's just how the system works. So if you get convicted, what's going to happen?"

I did not answer the question. Instead, I got up, walked around the table, and sat next to Angel. For some reason, sitting right next to my defendants, so close we could smell each other, made them incredibly tense. I spread the federal sentencing guidelines on the table. "These are the sentencing guidelines. If you go to trial, they will decide what sentence you get, not me or a judge." Then I walked Angel step-by-step through the calculation of his likely sentence, flipping back and forth among the drug quantity tables, the criminal history section, and the sentencing chart. During my analysis I never threatened Angel or raised my voice. I found, through trial and error, that a flat, dispassionate tone, one that reiterated, again, that I did not care about his fate, was more effective. By the time I was finished it was clear to Angel that if he did not cooperate, he was facing a massive jail term.

At this point Angel was sweating heavily, suffering from a borderline anxiety attack. At that precise moment I asked him if he was ready to begin. After my lengthy setup, most defendants recognized or at least believed that this was a solemn moment. Angel nodded. Only at this point, thirty or forty minutes into the meeting, did I begin my questioning.

I started by asking Angel a series of questions about his background: when and where he was born; what his parents did for a living; the names and ages of siblings and his spouse; immigration history; kids; work background; sports. I did this in every proffer. I wanted to get him comfortable talking and answering my questions, and discussing these personal issues made that easy. People like to talk about themselves, and since the answers were generally not incriminating, they did not mind sharing. I also believed that I would be able to control and manipulate the defendant better if I understood his past. For example, I learned from Angel that he had young children. So I referred to them casually from time to time, during breaks in questioning, to remind him that if he played his cards wrong, he would not see them for a long time. "What is your daughter's name? Oh, that's right." Even more important, I was trying to create a personal bond, to make the defendant believe that if he cooperated, I would worry about him and take care of him.

When I saw that Angel was starting to relax, getting comfortable with the proffer, I shifted gears abruptly. "Let's talk a little bit about why you were arrested." Here I changed from open-ended questions to leading ones. "That night you were packaging drugs, correct? It was heroin, right? About a kilo, right?" I adopted this particular strategy for two reasons. First, a defendant usually has trouble incriminating himself, at least at first. By using leading questions, I made it easier to get over that hump. Second, I wanted to make sure that even if the rest of the proffer was a failure, the defendant was locked in and could not claim on the stand at trial that he was innocent. After five minutes Angel was sunk.

Once we were past this hurdle, I asked Angel a series of twenty or thirty very carefully selected questions about his criminal organization: when the group started; whom he reported to; the quantity of drugs it moved; the names of other members; the locations where it stored its drugs. These were my "control questions." Their purpose was not to gain information. Instead, my goal was to discover if the defendant was prepared to be honest. To accomplish this, I asked only questions to which I already knew the answers, from surveillance, wiretaps, or another informant. Some of the time defendants were truthful from the start. Most of them, however, lied at this point, to hide their own culpability or simply see if they could get away with it. Angel, for example, started to bullshit almost immediately. He told me the names of the members of his drug distribution cell, but he lied about the size of their last shipment, the date he began to deal, and the name of his supplier. After three or four blatant lies, I sprang my trap. Sometimes I did this quietly, with mock disgust. Other times I yelled. Angel was sly but dumb, so I thought yelling might be best.

"Angel! Angel! This is such bullshit! You are so full of shit. All you are doing is lying your ass off. The load you received last Wednesday was ten kilos, not two. You've been in business for six months at that location, not two. You get your drugs from Manuel Diego, who you talked to at least six times last week. Everything you've been saying is a lie. What am I supposed to do with you? I already told you I don't need your cooperation. I am not interested in games. We should probably just quit now. I don't have time for this."

Angel's eyes snapped open wide when he heard me repeat very detailed scoop about his crimes. Most defendants go into a meeting believing they hold all the information cards. Now he learned that my investigation had been much more productive and more damaging than he had thought. This had two results. It made him afraid to lie again, because he thought I might know the correct answer. And it made him realize that if we went to trial, he would probably get convicted, for apparently I had a lot of evidence in my back pocket. Of course he did not know that I had shot my bolt and that the information I had repeated to him was everything I knew.

At this point the defense attorney often stepped in. "John, why don't we take a break for a few minutes? I want to talk to Angel alone." I stomped out, pretending to be mad, and my agents followed. The attorney used this opportunity to explain to Angel that if he wanted to cooperate, he should probably play it straight.

When I returned, most defendants assumed I was still mad. Instead, I immediately let up, just to keep them emotionally off guard. "Look, Angel," I said in a soft, kind tone, "I know you are in a tough position. You don't know if you can trust me, and you are taking a big step. I know that. But you have to understand, none of us here has any real stake in this meeting except you. Win, lose, or draw, I am going to go to lunch in an hour, and I won't give this proffer a second thought. My life will go on, and what happens to you won't make any difference. The only person this meeting matters to is you. That's why we are here. If you lie again, just once, I am calling things off, and that's it. No more second chances. Okay? So let's start over from scratch. Are you ready?"

It was only at this point, more than an hour into the meeting, that the true interrogation began. I asked Angel to tell me about the first crime he had committed in the United States, and then we moved forward from there, talking about names, dates, events, and locations. Like many defendants, Angel seemed more sober on this second round, his voice quieter, his manner less confident, his facial expression more pained. Every once in a while I asked him a question to which I knew the answer, just to make sure he was honest, but roughly 95 percent of the information I was learning was new and valuable. Sometimes I got a sense that the defendant was still lying, and we would break off the interview. But most of the time I thought he was honest. I got a sense that many feared to lie again because they believed we were omniscient, that we knew everything already. Of course this was precisely what we wanted them to think.

When you listen to a cooperator, you must search not just for affirmative lies but for the significant gap. Angel told me he first lived in the Bronx, but later moved to Queens. He offered no explanation for this shift, one that is, in New York City terms, as dramatic as changing countries. I thought about this for a while, and then I interrupted. "Angel, what about that thing in the Bronx? You know . . ."

Angel paused. At first he just stared, and then his mouth slowly gaped. His shoulders tensed. Then he whispered, "How did you know?"

I did not answer his question. Instead, I told him, "I'm going to take a five-minute break. Why don't you tell your lawyer about it, and then, when I come back, we can talk about it too, okay? It is going to be all right; we can work with it; you just have to be honest."

When we walked into the hallway, an agent grabbed my arm. "What thing in the Bronx?" I just shrugged. "I don't know. There's always something in the Bronx."

Five minutes later, after I had walked back into the room, Angel confessed to a homicide.

Two comments about my interrogation style are in order. First, it was very successful. I flipped many defendants, and that led to a large number of convictions. Second, it was the product not of some overarching theory but of trial and error. When I started proffering defendants, I knew nothing about interrogation. I wanted results—I was paid to get results—so I experimented, trying different approaches to see what worked. With each passing month, my technique got more elaborate. I added a little pressure here, a little manipulation there. Gradually I morphed into an expert.

At first I was proud of this. In federal law enforcement the ability to flip defendants is a highly valued skill. I even enjoyed what I was doing. Flipping defendants was a challenging game, and I was good at it. When I received an award from the FBI one day, the agents praised my interrogation skills, and I blushed with pleasure. But as time passed, I secretly grew disgusted with what I was doing. My talent, if it could be called that, was to use fear, pressure, and psychological ploys to trick, manipulate, and break defendants down so they would do what I wanted. Sometimes cooperating was in a defendant's best interest, but at others it was a mistake on his part. Angel, for example, might have been better off fighting his original drug case than confessing to a murder.

My supervisors told me my actions were commendable. I could of course see their point. From a utilitarian perspective, my actions were clearly ethical, for they achieved beneficial social results: more killers and drug traffickers off the street. But something about pressuring and manipulating my targets still bothered me, deep in the pit of my stomach. When I was in the Marines, I was a very handy shot with a rifle, but I never wanted to be a sniper. Snipers are useful in combat. But only a total freak, I thought, would want to be an expert at the sixteen-hundred-meter head shot. I had the same sort of qualms about interrogation.

Back in college, I had studied Immanuel Kant's ethical theories. Kant argued that every individual was sacred, deserving of reverence, and should always be treated with respect, not manipulated, tricked, deceived, or abused. For Kant, this rule is not subject to exceptions. Even if abuse or manipulation leads to increased social welfare, it is wrong. At the time I thought this point was valid but trite. Now, however, I had become an interrogator who manipulated other people for a living, and this experience changed my perspective. Gradually I saw what Kant had been driving at. Kant's demand that we treat people with reverence and that we view them as ends in themselves, not as tools to be used to achieve some preferred social outcome, seemed much more relevant than I had thought. Kant's goal was not just to avoid turning persons into victims. He also wanted to protect persons like me. For when an interrogator deceives and manipulates, it does moral damage not just to his target but to himself. Interrogating is corrosive. It dehumanizes everyone concerned.

IF I HAD TRULY BEEN committed to a life of self-reflection, I would have put my growing unease with interrogation under an analytic microscope, to try to understand it better, for it suggested something important: after three years as a prosecutor I was losing my faith in utilitarian moral thinking. At the time, however, I just ignored it. I had a heavy caseload and a job to do. I told myself: no time to get squeamish. In some of my cases, however, this approach was impossible. They raised deep and glaring philosophical questions, ones that jumped up off the table, grabbed me by the throat, and would not let me go.

In 2000, Manuel, my original cooperator in the Bushwick case, came up for sentencing in front of Judge Charles P. Sifton. As part of the process, I gave the judge a detailed letter describing Manuel's cooperation. I informed Judge Sifton that Manuel had worn a recording device at a dozen meetings with violent drug traffickers. These targets routinely engaged in murder, kidnapping, and assault. Manuel had risked his life in my investigation. Accordingly, he deserved a huge reduction in prison term.

My letter was designed to help Manuel, to make sure the judge knew precisely how hard he had worked and how important his contribution had been to the case. But in retrospect, I think I was also engaged in subtle bragging: "Look at me, Judge Sifton! I ran a great investigation!" Maybe the judge sensed this. That might have explained his reaction. He gave Manuel a huge downward departure. Before he did so, however, he took me down a peg. Sifton told me that I had behaved irresponsibly and that I had risked a man's life for nothing. I had arrested a few drug traffickers, he acknowledged, but their places had already been filled back out on the street. The marginal gain I made was simply not worth placing a fellow human being in mortal danger. I was lucky Manuel was still alive.

When Judge Sifton criticized me, I fought back. I pointed out that DEA agents had always been present at these meetings, listening in over a secret transmitter, ready to intervene if a deal turned violent. I also pointed out that because my targets were very dangerous men, it was all the more important to get them off the street. Later, back at the office, I vented to my friends. "What does Sifton want us to do? Just sit here and hand over the streets to murderers? Wiring people up is the only way to make cases. It's the only way to do our jobs. And hell, Manuel knew what he was doing. He knew the risks. He wanted to do this; he wanted the chance for a break in sentence."

Who was right, Sifton or me? Then, as now, I thought my actions were justified. Wiring Manuel up against murderers definitely maximized social welfare. And though I certainly pressured Manuel to cooperate, that coercion was light; ultimately, cooperation was his choice. Thus, from both Kantian and utilitarian perspectives, my actions were probably proper. Nevertheless, Sifton's point was not trivial, a fact I learned the hard way.

One of my early narcotics cases targeted a Colombian drug importation ring sending cocaine couriers through JFK Airport. The law enforcement agency involved—Customs or DEA, I cannot remember which—had an informant down in Bogotá who had infiltrated the ring. Every few months he would give us a tip, the name and flight number of an inbound courier. In return we paid him cash.

One day the agents showed up in my office with bad news. Our informant's phone had gone dead, and their liaison in Colombia could not find him. I asked, "Is it possible he went underground? That he got tired of the risk and decided to disappear?"

The lead agent shook his head. "Look, anything is possible, but I think you have to be realistic. It's almost certain that they caught him."

If an informant is captured by a Colombian or Mexican drug cartel, what happens? Typically, the cartel kidnaps the informant's family and tortures and kills them before his eyes. Wife, children, even infants. Then they start in on the informant. They might saw off his genitalia. Drive spikes into his head. Carve hunks of flesh off with scalpels. When they are finished, they dump his body in the streets to send a message.

During that period of my career, I taught a college seminar on political history at Yale on Thursday evenings. That night I taught the class on Watergate with a savage intensity. I was bitter, angry, cynical, sharp. I could tell I was freaking the students out—their eyes were saucers—but I could not control myself. Finally, at the end of the class, I apologized, and I told them the story about my informant. When I finished, I began to cry.

———

WHEN I FIRST JOINED the Narcotics Unit, fresh from General Crimes, I was still a naive rookie. The *Scarpa* and Badfellas cases had taught me that the line between the good guys and bad guys could easily become blurred, but I was confident that these cases were anomalous, bizarre exceptions, not the rule. I was still convinced that being a federal prosecutor was an ethically simple job. As one of my colleagues liked to say, "We wear the white hats."

In Narcotics, however, I began to realize that the world of federal law enforcement was not so tidy. At first my growing awareness that our war on drugs was morally problematic had little impact on me, emotionally or professionally. I did not analyze my feelings, for I did not have time. Day after day I wrote my wiretaps, proffered my defendants, brought my indictments, and jailed my targets. But no matter how hard I worked, my sense of moral discomfort never went away. Instead, it slowly grew in intensity, like a summer thunderstorm that starts low on the horizon, a distant threat that gradually thrusts its way into your consciousness, until you find yourself dashing for shelter in the rain.

CHAPTER FOURTEEN

How to Win a War on Drugs

The moral ambiguity of narcotics enforcement work would not have bothered me that much if it had achieved a good purpose. Unfortunately, that was not true. Considered individually, my cases were very successful. They certainly garnered me professional praise. But their aggregate contribution to our goal of a drug-free New York was close to nil. I was working thirteen hours a day, seven days a week. But when I got home at night, I knew in my heart that my work was almost meaningless, for the strategy behind the war on drugs was deeply flawed.

———

EVERY YEAR our federal, state, and local governments spend roughly thirty billion dollars on our narcotics control strategy. This strategy, which has not changed in any significant respects since the Reagan presidency, involves three separate kinds of program: foreign source control, drug shipment interdiction, and domestic law enforcement operations. Collectively, these programs are supposed to cut drug supplies on America's streets. As a result, we call our strategy supply management.

Since America spends billions of dollars on our supply management strategy year after year, you might conclude, quite reasonably, that our game plan must be working. Otherwise we'd change it, right? Alas, that is not correct. During my tour in Narcotics, I saw firsthand that the war on drugs was a costly stalemate. Every time we took some dealers or suppliers off the streets, new ones sprang up immediately to take their place, to meet the demand for drugs. We were up against powerful market forces, and those market forces had us beat.

My views were widely shared by the agents and prosecutors with whom I worked. Most frontline personnel working in law enforcement do not talk much about public policy. When we go out to bars after work, we don't debate the issues; we tell "war stories" about our cases. But often, when sitting in the privacy of my office, I prodded my colleagues to share their opinions, and I discovered they all were pessimistic. No one ever told me he thought our drug control strategies worked. On the contrary, every law enforcement professional I talked with—and there were dozens—thought that we were stalled. This view was not unique to New York. In 2006 the National Association of Police Chiefs surveyed thousands of police chiefs and sheriffs. When asked if they believed the war on drugs was successful, only 18 percent said yes.

Of course the personal experiences of law enforcement officials might be misleading. For that reason, policy scholars seeking to assess the success of our drug enforcement programs look for more objective indicators. The principal objective of our drug supply management strategy is to reduce the availability of drugs on the street. Scarcity, we believe, will inevitably drive up drug prices, and we hope that will make using drugs less attractive to the consumer. For this reason, the primary metric we examine to measure the impact of our drug enforcement strategy is price.

In 2005 a team of analysts at the Rand Corporation, an international think tank known for its rigorous, nonpartisan, quantitative research, carefully examined illegal drug prices. The study reached an incredibly somber conclusion:

> *The price record suggests that supply control effects have failed to reduce the use of any established drug . . . The overall trend in cocaine and heroin retail prices during most of the past two decades has been downward (after adjusting for potency). That suggests greater availability of drugs on the streets of the United States, not less. Greater availability and lower price are likely to have made use cheaper and more attractive, thus taking some of the pressure off users to quit or scale back and making it easier for youths to initiate.*

In short, our current strategy is not working. Since 1992 drug use has gone up by one-third. Drug-related emergency room admissions have substantially increased. Perhaps most worrisome, the percentage of kids trying marijuana, cocaine, and hallucinogens has ballooned. We are losing the war on drugs.

The American public clearly understands this. Over the last ten years, polls have consistently revealed that between 70 and 75 percent of Americans believe our drug control policies are failing. In response, politicians have refused to rethink our strategy. Instead, they have simply ratcheted up drug enforcement spending. That approach is, to be blunt, insane.

IMAGINE, FOR A MOMENT, that you were appointed the director of the Office of National Drug Control Policy, the nation's drug czar. Your mission would be to reduce and, if possible, eliminate drug abuse in America. Where would you start? For the last forty years our government has answered: overseas. Over the last several decades the United States has spent tens of billions of dollars trying to reduce foreign drug production, running paramilitary operations and drug eradication programs in countries across the globe, from Colombia to Afghanistan. This effort is politically attractive to both Congress and the White House, for it shifts all blame for our nation's drug problem from the real culprit—our own deep appetite for drugs—to foreign criminals and drug lords. I wish these programs worked. Unfortunately, everyone working in law enforcement, from the frontline prosecutors to the program managers in Washington, recognizes that these costly source control programs are largely futile.

Consider, for example, the most ambitious source control program currently under way, Plan Colombia. Since 2001 the United States has spent more than four billion dollars in that struggling republic trying to cut cocaine production. U.S. military advisers and Pentagon contractors train Colombia's military to fight narcotics traffickers and the revolutionary groups who protect them, while hundreds of U.S.-supplied aircraft spray Roundup herbicide on vast swaths of the Colombian countryside, trying to wipe out coca and poppy plantations. Every year the Bush administration holds press conferences to tout the plan's results. They cite loads of statistics—millions of acres sprayed, hundreds of plantations destroyed—like Vietnam War generals publicizing their body counts. In reality, we have made virtually no progress in Colombia, despite the plan's tremendous costs. The reason for that is simple: the power of markets.

The international market for illegal drugs is huge, somewhere between three hundred and four hundred billion dollars a year, depending on how you measure. In the United States, sixteen million drug users spend sixty billion dollars annually to purchase illegal substances. With such immense amounts of money at stake, producers are not simply going to roll over and die because we spray some herbicides on their crops. Instead, they adjust. When Plan Colombia went into effect, the traffickers responded rationally, as economic actors always do when faced with a change in market conditions. They shifted cultivation to remote, hilly areas that are harder to detect and spray; planted crops in smaller, more fragmented plots; and developed new, more productive coca plant strains, with more leaves per plant and higher, more potent alkaloid levels. The result? Today Colombia provides roughly 50 percent of the heroin and 90 percent of the cocaine imported into the United States, the exact same levels we saw in 2000. Cocaine still sells for twenty thousand dollars a kilo wholesale on the streets of New York, just as it did in 1997, when I started work as an AUSA. And purity levels have remained high. All these indicators suggest that the program has had little positive effect. In the harsh but accurate words of Connie Veillette, an analyst with the Congressional Research Service, "no effect has been seen with regard to price, purity, and availability of cocaine and heroin in the United States."

Recently the Bush administration suggested that we are making progress, only the numbers don't show it yet. No one in law enforcement believes this, in part because the numbers don't lie. Spending billions of dollars on military training and crop eradication in Colombia may be justified for other geopolitical reasons—our massive foreign and military aid, for example, is critical to the Colombian government's political stability and its effort to control FARC, the drug-fueled guerrilla organization—but it doesn't decrease drug use in the United States.

If Plan Colombia is a clear failure, why do we stick with it? One reason is past results. Defenders of the program note that over the past forty years, source control has worked very successfully in other countries like Turkey, Thailand, and Peru. To which I would respond, "Well, sort of." Turkey provides a perfect example. In the 1970s the Turkish government, with the support and assistance of the United States and the United Nations, led a massive effort to eliminate poppy cultivation and opium production. By all measures, the program was incredibly successful. Today Turkey produces virtually no illicit drug crops. Opium, however, is a valuable commodity, just like coffee or oil. As long as demand stays constant, efforts to control production in one country will be futile because the market will respond by shifting production elsewhere. In the case of Turkey, poppy cultivation simply shifted east, to Afghanistan. Today that country produces more than 85 percent of the world supply.

The same thing happened in Peru in the 1980s and Thailand in the 1990s. In both cases, we weaned the targeted source country from drug cultivation only to see the production shift over the border, from Peru to Colombia, from Thailand to Myanmar and Laos. Drugs are big business. If one source dries up, another will pop up to fill the vacuum. As a result, source control is like squeezing a balloon: if you clamp down in one spot, the balloon simply expands in another.

IF THE UNITED STATES cannot cut foreign drug production, we might, as a fallback strategy, try to stop drugs in transit, before they cross our borders, which law enforcement calls interdiction. In the 1980s the Reagan administration began a major drug interdiction effort, deploying significant Navy, Coast Guard, Air Force, and Border Patrol assets to the drug war, hoping to stop the flow of illegal drugs before they entered the United States. At first interdiction was a limited success. Using AWACS planes and fast Coast Guard cutters, we closed down some of the most heavily used drug importation routes, such as the air and sea-lanes between Latin America and southern Florida. The cartels quickly responded, however, by shifting virtually all drug smuggling west to Mexico. Today 65 percent of the cocaine consumed in the United States comes over the Mexican border. There interdiction has largely failed, for our border with Mexico is a sieve.

Since the late 1980s the Latin American drug cartels have developed several basic strategies for sneaking their drugs past American customs officials on the U.S.-Mexican border. One is bribery. Since a kilo of cocaine is worth twenty thousand dollars wholesale in New York or Los Angeles, the cartels can reap huge profits even if they spend five hundred to a thousand dollars a kilo to bribe their way past the border. Over the last twenty years dozens of government officials have been convicted for taking cartel money. Most are frontline border crossing guards. They use cell phones or e-mail to inform drug cartel representatives of the precise vehicle inspection lane they will be manning and then look the other way when a driver behind the wheel of a particular vehicle or possessing a previously selected code word arrives at the border. For two minutes of work, a corrupt guard can make twenty thousand dollars, tax free, two-thirds of his annual salary.

The cartels also use elaborate ruses to distract attention from their smuggling operations. During my stint as a narcotics prosecutor, one of my cooperating witnesses, with more than twenty years of experience moving drugs on the Texas-Mexico border, explained a typical scam. A cartel member, acting with the approval of his bosses, contacted the DEA and volunteered to become a DEA informant for pay. A few weeks later the "informant" reached out to his DEA handlers and told them that a major drug shipment, a million dollars of marijuana, hidden inside a battered blue truck, would be coming across the border at a specified time and place. When H-hour arrived, the blue truck showed up at the border just as the informant said it would, and dozens of agents converged on it. They began to dismantle the truck, and to their glee, they quickly found the stash, hidden in a false fuel tank. That afternoon the government put out a press release touting its most recent drug seizure, and the informant went home happy, with a special government "performance bonus." To all appearances, it looked like a government victory.

In truth, however, the whole event had been staged. The marijuana truck was driven by a stooge, a yokel the cartel had set up to be caught. The marijuana itself was real, but to the cartel, its loss represented a cost-effective trade: one million dollars in lost pot in exchange for a major border distraction. A few minutes after the blue marijuana truck entered the border crossing station, the cartel's real truck, a sleek commercial eighteen-wheeler packed with more than one hundred million dollars of cocaine, entered the same facility five or six lanes away. Normally, the truck would have received close scrutiny, but that was now impossible, for virtually all the inspectors on duty were busy dismantling the decoy marijuana truck and arresting its startled driver, who had probably been told the inspectors would be bribed. The small number of inspectors who remained at their regular posts were totally distracted, watching to see if the lucky agents crawling all over the blue truck would get a bust. When the cartel's truck pulled up in the inspection lane, the inspector took a cursory look. All he saw were boxes of Mexican vegetables, bound for U.S. tables, loaded professionally in a truck that appeared to belong to a respected American carrier. The inspector asked a few routine questions and then waved the truck through.

Bribery and deception are common on the border, but to some cartels, these methods still leave too much to chance; one of my defendants called it border roulette. To improve their odds, the cartels have begun to construct elaborate tunnels that bypass the inspection process altogether. In January 2006, for example, Mexican authorities discovered a tunnel running more than half a mile underground from Tijuana to California. The entrance on the Mexican side was in a warehouse near the Tijuana international airport. Drug shipments could be flown in from Colombia, swept past crooked Mexican customs officials, and unloaded in the warehouse. The drugs would then be lowered down an eighty-five-foot-deep shaft and transported by wheeled gurneys through the tunnel, which had electric lighting, proper ventilation, and a pumping system to keep it dry. On the American side, the tunnel opened up inside what appeared to be an abandoned industrial building, one with several loading bays for tractor trailers. The traffickers would lift the drugs back to ground level by pulley, load them into trucks, and ship them throughout the United States. This particular tunnel was more elaborate than most, but it was not an isolated example. Since 2001 U.S. and Mexican drug authorities have uncovered more than twenty tunnels under the border, some rudimentary, others extraordinarily complex.*

If we could stamp out tunnels and bribery, would our border security strategy work? Unfortunately, the answer is no. The reason is NAFTA, the North American Free Trade Agreement. Launched in 1994

---

*I have not been able to find hard data to back this claim up, but I have a strong sense, from watching the cases charged in court and talking to drug enforcement agents, that bribery has decreased since its peak in the 1990s, while use of tunneling has substantially increased. This may be due to enforcement crackdowns on bribery.

(the paranoid might note that this was the precise time we finished putting the traditional drug importation routes between Latin America and the United States out of business), the agreement opened the border to increased trade and commerce. From an economic perspective, increased trade with Mexico is almost certainly a good thing. But from a law enforcement perspective, it is a disaster. Today roughly a hundred million cars and five million trucks cross this border every year. The trucks carry cheap manufactured goods, tons of fruits and vegetables, and a huge amount of methamphetamine, cocaine, heroin, and marijuana. We want to make NAFTA work, so we cannot stop and search all these vehicles; they would back up all the way to Guatemala. So we search only a tiny percentage of them, far less than 5 percent at most border crossings. The rest are given cursory screenings and waved through.

Drug traffickers don't like our current inspection regime. It is too random and unpredictable. That is why they resort to tunnels and bribes, to make their costs smaller and more predictable. Still, the cartels know that NAFTA has been very good for the drug business. Since we can inspect only a tiny percentage of the trucks crossing the border, they know that a significant percentage of their shipments will pass undetected. I have never seen any solid data on the percentage of drug loads that cross the border undetected, but in the drug prosecution world, experts used to estimate that our success rate was roughly 10 percent. That figure may be a little bit high, it may be a little bit low, but I think it is probably in the ballpark. The fact that roughly 90 percent of the drug shipments to the United States cross the border safely should tell you one thing: in the post-NAFTA environment, drug interdiction, as we currently practice it, simply does not work.

———

BECAUSE WE CANNOT CUT foreign drug production or stop drugs at our borders, the United States winds up fighting the drug war on our own streets, in complex enforcement operations like the ones I describe in this book. Many of these operations are tactically successful. We infiltrate drug distribution rings, lock up dozens of their employees, and put them out of business. Strategically, however, these enforcement operations have little impact. When you bust a cartel's local representative, like Alberto Longas in the Bushwick case, the cartel quickly sends a replacement. And if you take out a whole distribution cell, a new crew will quickly pop up to seize its turf, in order to meet market demand. In short, street enforcement is largely futile because of the power of markets.*

My own Bushwick case is instructive. Our team of agents, cops, and prosecutors took thirty major dealers off the streets between 1997 and 2001, but new groups immediately arrived to replace our defendants. The EDNY busted them too, and then we busted their successors. Eventually this strategy worked. Today, after more than one hundred federal prosecutions against Bushwick wholesale dealers stretching over ten years, plus a major crackdown by the NYPD, Bushwick is significantly safer than it was a decade ago. Because of limited resources, however, the contiguous Brooklyn neighborhood of East New York never got equivalent attention. Today it remains a war zone, in part because traffickers have moved there from Bushwick. This experience teaches us that enforcement can work, but it takes an immense amount of time, money, and energy. Even then success is likely to be local in scope and to last only as long as law enforcement agencies keep up the pressure. In a world of limited resources, that means that the drug problem in many areas will never be addressed or will be addressed only short term. You can plug one finger into a leaky dike, but when the dike has hundreds of holes and you have only ten fingers, that strategy is bound to fail.

Consider one last example. In the 1980s and 1990s we spent billions of dollars successfully destroying Colombia's Cali Cartel, which controlled the Colombian cocaine trade. Law enforcement officials expected this triumph to lead to a significant decline in cocaine importation in the United States. Instead, new Mexican organizations and dozens of lower-profile, hard-to-identify Colombian minicartels immediately rose to fill the Cali vacuum. As a result, the flow of drugs continued unabated.

—————

IF OUR CURRENT DRUG enforcement strategy is not working, should we blindly continue it, or should we try something different? The answer depends of course on the availability of more effective alternatives. So

*As one recent Rand Corporation study put it, "It should not be very surprising that an enforcement-heavy strategy would have only limited success against the established drug markets now prevailing in the United States. Drug markets are fractionated and local in nature. Drug supply chains are networks, not rigid hierarchies. There is no national organization whose local operations can be crippled through arrests made at the top. Also, arrested sellers are easily replaced."

my question should really be rephrased. When we think about drug policy, we should be asking: Is there a more effective way to fight drug consumption and abuse than our current supply control approach? To answer this question, it may be helpful to consider for just a moment our antimafia strategy.

In Chapter Nine I suggested that the reason our antimafia strategy worked so well over the last twenty years is that our enforcement efforts worked in harness with, and not against, market and social forces. When the FBI and the Justice Department went after the mob in the 1980s, the Five Families had already been weakened, perhaps mortally, by the rise of more competitive credit markets, the spread of state lotteries, the decline of organized labor, and the shift of heroin production from the Mediterranean to Latin America. These trends collectively destroyed the mafia's competitive niche, making our enforcement effort much, much easier.

In contrast, we are currently trying to combat drug suppliers in an economic and social environment that is tilted heavily against us. In the United States, sixteen million people are prepared to pay heavily for illegal drugs. Because the demand for dangerous drugs like heroin, cocaine, and meth has been relatively stable over the last decade, and these drugs are incredibly profitable, the economic incentives for people to work in the drug trade remain high. Thus it is no surprise that America hosts an enormous number of dealers willing to meet the demand for illegal drugs, at least 450,000 retail dealers and 50,000 hardened wholesale professionals, many of whom report, directly or indirectly, to cartels that are headquartered in foreign countries. In short, drug trafficking is driven by a powerful economic and social force, the strong market demand for drugs. As long as this is the case, all our enforcement efforts to control supply are hopeless.

For thirty years we have pursued a supply control drug strategy, and that strategy has failed. To reduce drug abuse and all its associated crime, we have to change our approach, from trying to quash supply to reducing the underlying problem, domestic demand. This demand management strategy should involve, among other things, better drug education programs at schools and on television. Above all, it requires drug treatment.

IF THE UNITED STATES really wants to reduce drug abuse, we have to develop a rational, well-funded national drug treatment plan. That plan must include three basic, proven tactics: comprehensive inpatient drug treatment for every serious addict that requests our help, with out-patient programs for those less severely afflicted; mandatory drug treatment in prisons; and diversion programs that send defendants arrested for simple drug possession (as opposed to drug distribution) to manda-tory treatment, not jail. Unlike street enforcement, which simply puts a Band-Aid on a gaping national wound, this national drug treatment scheme would attack the underlying social and economic factors that power the drug trade in the first place.

Expanding drug treatment makes common sense. In the 1990s the Rand Corporation studied the effectiveness of all four major drug con-trol strategies: attacking production in source countries, interdicting drugs before they enter the United States, fighting drug trafficking on American streets, and drug treatment. It found that treatment was by far the cheapest way to control the drug trade effectively: seven times more cost-effective than street enforcement operations like Bushwick; ten times more effective than interdiction; twenty-three times more effec-tive than source control programs in countries like Colombia. This com-prehensive assessment has been backed up by subsequent research and by careful analysis of specific existing programs. One study of New York's diversion program, for example, found that "[n]on-violent drug offenders who complete judge-supervised treatment programs are sig-nificantly less likely to commit crimes again than those who serve prison time." And research conducted by scholars at UCLA calculated that Cal-ifornia saves four dollars for every dollar it spends on its drug treatment program.

The reason drug treatment is so cost-effective compared with sup-ply control strategies is easy to explain. In the United States roughly 90 percent of the demand for the most dangerous drugs—heroin, cocaine, and methamphetamine—comes from roughly 10 percent of the drug-using population, the hardened addicts. Thus even small reductions in addiction can result in huge reductions in drug use and a concomitant reduction of the serious negative social consequences of drug abuse, such as property crimes, child abuse, and medical costs.

As a prosecutor I learned the value of drug treatment firsthand. In 1997, when I was a rookie, I was assigned a very low-level DEA case, *United States v. Jeffrey Gilliam*. Gilliam was arrested on crack charges for "steering," recruiting customers for a neighborhood drug dealer. He was an addict, and he was "paid" for his work with crack to satisfy his own habit. When I first saw him in court at his arraignment, he was a wreck. Though only forty, he looked eighty: undernourished, filthy, shaking, red-eyed, incoherent. All his teeth were missing.

Gilliam had been caught on tape, and he quickly pleaded guilty. Because crack distribution is punished very heavily under the federal sentencing guidelines, he faced a very lengthy prison term. At sentencing, his lawyer asked that he be assigned to a residential drug treatment program instead of jail. I had no idea what position to take in response. So I turned to the probation officer and asked, "Do these programs really work?"

She was scornful. "He's just trying to dodge prison. These addicts never learn."

I opposed the motion, but fortunately, Judge Nina Gershon took the defense counsel's advice, not mine. She delayed Gilliam's sentence and sent him to an inpatient drug treatment center. There, over the next eighteen months, Gilliam was detoxed and received health care, drug treatment counseling, and some serious dental work. Every six months he appeared in court for a status update. Each time he looked significantly better. Finally, after almost two years, he appeared for his sentencing. He looked young, happy, and healthy, up to his normal weight, smiling broadly with a full set of false teeth. He was, probation reported, holding down a steady job at a local video rental store, living in an inexpensive apartment. Above all, he was clean, repeatedly testing negative for drugs. He told the judge that his life was a miracle. I had to agree. When he finally came up for sentencing, I moved for a downward departure, to keep him out of prison.

IF EXPANDED DRUG TREATMENT is obviously needed to get drugs under control, why is it chronically underfunded in the United States? Why, in virtually every major U.S. city, do addicts have to wait for months before a spot at a drug treatment center is available? And why are the available programs run on the cheap, providing less expensive outpatient services instead of more costly, but much more effective, inpatient treatment?

One problem is that we tend to assess drug treatment programs in isolation, without comparing them with the available alternatives. Viewed in this way, treatment programs do not look that attractive. They cost a lot of money, and they achieve mixed results, with large numbers of program graduates eventually returning to drug use. Political leaders look at these facts and conclude that these programs do not work very well. But that is missing the point. Drug treatment is not a perfect solution to our drug problem; it is simply the best one we have. Though drug treatment programs are expensive and have significant failure rates, treatment still remains much more cost-effective than every other available strategy. Though our treatment programs look mediocre in isolation, they look fabulous when compared with interdiction and source control.

The second problem is politics itself. Polls indicate that most Americans strongly prefer spending money on border enforcement and aggressive policing than on drug treatment. This preference is based, in part, on a moral judgment: drug trafficking is wrong and ought to be punished. But pollsters have also found that most Americans are convinced that as a policy matter, enforcement is much more effective than treatment, though the exact opposite is true. Rather than try to educate the voters on this issue, politicians pander to them, in a shortsighted effort to appear "tough on crime." Thus, year after year, we dump more money on enforcement and less on treatment. Back in the 1970s we spent almost 60 percent of our antidrug budget on treatment. Today that figure is down to around 33 percent.

Right now we are fighting the war on drugs with one arm tied behind our back, hitting traffickers as hard as we can, but failing to address the underlying problem of addiction. This is a major strategic error. The social costs associated with serious drug abuse are enormous. To cite just one example, the overwhelming majority of serious child abuse cases in my state of Oregon are linked to methamphetamine addiction. Unless we get serious about treatment, we will never get our drug abuse problem under control.

I do not want to cut domestic narcotics enforcement spending. I think that would be foolish, particularly in the short term. Nor can we ignore border security. In the age of terrorism, we need to be more vigilant, not less. But foreign source control dollars are largely wasted. These programs should be scaled back drastically, with the resulting savings, plus new money as well, plugged into treatment. That is the only way to win a war on drugs. Now, go write your congressman!

CHAPTER FIFTEEN

9/11: Emergency Response

By the summer of 2000 I was fed up with life as a narcotics prosecutor. My discontent was based in part on my growing lack of faith in our narcotics control strategy. Indeed, if you had asked me at the time, I would have blamed my unhappiness on that alone. Looking back, however, I can see that other, more personal factors played a bigger role.

One was simply exhaustion. I worked hard in General Crimes, scrambling to keep up with an ever-expanding docket of cases, but Narcotics was even more demanding. When you run an important investigation or are preparing for a big trial, you have to devote yourself to your case 100 percent. You have to interview every possible witness, pressure every possible cooperator, and explore every possible lead, or you will lose; the margin for error is that small. For me, this basic rule had a corollary. I was convinced that whenever I took a break from work—every baseball game, every dinner out, every lazy morning in bed—I was increasing the odds that a guilty defendant would escape arrest or conviction. Some of my fellow prosecutors thought my conclusion was insane. They claimed that you could do a great job as an AUSA and still have balance in your life. But to me that seemed like wishful thinking. If you want justice, you have to put in the hours. Indeed, you have a professional obligation to do so. If you want to go home at five o'clock, some of your targets will go home free. That is harsh but undeniable.

For two solid years I worked eighty hours a week. I busted a lot of drug dealers, and in return I was accorded a fair amount of professional independence. Jodi, my boss, let me do what I liked. I wore jeans and black Converse high-tops to the office instead of suits, spent tens of thousands of dollars on investigative trips, and dumped cases I did not like on junior, or less favored, colleagues. But I paid in other ways. On weekends you would typically find me at the office, poring over reports or examining evidence. Some afternoons I was so worn out I fell sound asleep in my chair, feet propped up on my desk. Typically, I got through the workday only because I was buzzed out on caffeine—kind of ironic, given my narcotics assignment. I was a good prosecutor but a limited human being.

IN THE EDNY, I was not a rarity; most of us young prosecutors worked like dogs. One result: those of us who were single had pretty stilted emotional lives. When you work all the time, your main chance for romance is with people you meet on the job. In New York City, lots of young lawyers marry other lawyers they meet at work. If, however, the people you interact with professionally are mostly criminals or defense attorneys, that severely limits your options. Most criminal defendants are smelly and wear bright orange federal prison jumpsuits: definitely not hot. The defense bar is not much better. The average defense lawyer in the EDNY is a fifty-year-old male with abundant body hair, a cheap suit, and a paunch. Of course, there were rare exceptions. Ivan Fisher, my opponent in the *Rodriguez* case, had a smart and charming associate in his office whom I would have been happy to date. But the potential conflict of interest was simply too great to contemplate. You cannot date your opponents.

For many single AUSAs, the inevitable fallback position is an office romance. These are often disastrous. Two of my colleagues had a short but steamy affair that ended in bitter tears. They spent the next four years glaring at each other across the conference table at senior management meetings, barely speaking. You also run the risk of mockery. One friend—we'll call her Nancy—got slightly drunk at a party and asked one of our male colleagues if he wanted to come back to her apartment. Her target said he would pass. Nancy probably should have let it drop, but she persisted. "This is your only chance. I'll never ask you again." He deadpanned: "I think I can live with that." Needless to say, the story quickly buzzed around the office. Today that fifteen-second exchange re-mains a defining moment of Nancy's career. When her name comes up among prosecutors and agents, people always tell that story.

A desperate AUSA can also date agents. For a straight guy, the pick-ings are slim, for 90 percent of the agents I worked with were male. For women AUSAs, there are more viable candidates to chose from but even more land mines. Several female AUSA friends dated federal agents they met through work. Most, I think, would report that this was a mistake. The reason for this is simple: agents like to brag. One colleague had a fling with an NYPD detective. They would work late into the night and then go back to her place. Soon clouds of agents were hovering outside her door, inquiring, "Do you have time to prosecute one of my cases?" She once made the mistake of asking an FBI agent why he was so eager to work with her. He replied—to her lasting fury and hurt—"I hear you are a very naughty girl." Needless to say, she is now in private practice.

During my stint as an AUSA, I had a pretty bleak emotional life, and that pushed me to desperate measures. Every year each federal district court judge hires two judicial clerks, recent law school graduates who work as the judge's apprentices, helping him or her decide motions, craft jury instructions, and write opinions. In my second year in Nar-cotics, I was appearing frequently before one particular judge, so I had a chance to check out her clerks, both women that year. One paid me no particular attention, but the other clerk and I exchanged several pointed glances, and I thought she might be interested. Normally, I would not have dated a judicial clerk; if the relationship goes south, you run the risk of alienating a judge. But this clerk was beautiful, tall, lithe, and fair, with long legs and hair the color of wheat. My romantic life was so stunted I could not afford to pass up this chance. I asked around. My friend Ceci Scott, a fellow AUSA, told me her name was Julia.

One day I sucked up some courage, called the judge's chambers, and asked to be connected to Julia. The call went through after ten or fifteen seconds.

"Uh, hi, this is John Kroger. How are you?"

She seemed surprised. "Oh, great. What can I do for you?"

"Well, this is actually a personal call. I was hoping you might have dinner with me one night."

Dead silence for at least five seconds. Then: "Are you kidding?"

"No, I'm not kidding. I am asking you for a date."

[Exasperated] "Is this a prank?"

"No, it's not a prank! I'm serious!"

"I don't even know you."

"Well, yes, but that's sort of the idea behind a date, right? To get to know someone?"

"I don't know. Why don't you drop by chambers sometime and we can talk, get to know one another better?"

I thought about this for a second and then rejected it out of hand. It was sketchy enough for an AUSA to hit on a judge's clerks. But to hover around chambers, trying to land a date, would make me a laughing-stock. What I really wanted at this point was to pretend this call had never occurred. I tried to be noncommittal. "Right, sure, excellent. Well, see you around." Then I quickly hung up the phone.

As you might imagine, I was totally mortified by what happened. Chambers are gossipy places. I imagined that Julia would immediately tell her judge and coclerk about the call and that I would look like what I was, a fool.

Weeks passed. I never heard back from Julia. Fortunately, I had no more appearances in front of her judge. Then, one day, while on arraignment duty in the courthouse, I spotted Julia walking my way. She looked as beautiful as ever. To my surprise, she walked right over to me and said hello. I replied, "Hi, Julia, how are you?" She immediately took a step back, a surprised look on her face, and then blushed lightly. "My name's not Julia. That's my coclerk. I'm Susan!"

My brain almost exploded. Ceci had given me the name of the wrong clerk! I looked at "Julia," now Susan. It was apparent to me that her coclerk had told her about my call and that she had suddenly understood that I had really wanted to go out with her, not her coworker. I started laughing—there was simply no way to save this situation—and then blurted out abruptly, "Well, time to go back to work." I spun around and walked away as quickly as I could. The next time I appeared before that particular judge, she gave me a funny look and I blushed up to my eyebrows, but she was kind enough not to raise the subject. I never talked to Susan—or her coclerk, for that matter—again.

DURING MY FIRST THREE YEARS as an AUSA I never took a vacation; I simply did not have time. By the summer of 2000, I decided it was necessary. I had six weeks of leave built up, and I proposed that I take them all at once. At first the office said no. Margaret Giordano, who had recently replaced Jodi as the head of Narcotics, told me that I could not be spared. I was not satisfied with this answer. Being an AUSA teaches you to use your leverage. When I threatened to resign if I could not take the vacation time to which I was legally entitled, the office quickly backed down. It even gave me a few additional weeks' unpaid leave, an unconventional but much appreciated reward.

If you were suddenly granted two months off, how would you spend it? For me, there were two imperatives. First, I needed an athletic challenge. As a prosecutor I was desk-bound. I needed to get back out-of-doors and do something physically difficult, to get in touch with my inner Marine. My second priority was more complicated. After three straight years of work, I felt psychologically stale, like a machine with gummed-up gears. I needed to alter my daily habits and routine ways of thinking. In fact, I needed an adventure.

Around this time a group of friends who lived out in Portland, Oregon, invited me and AUSA Dwight Holton, my partner on the Bushwick case, to run the Hood-to-Coast Relay. The Hood-to-Coast is one of the most remarkable running events in the nation. One thousand teams of twelve runners each race from the slopes of Oregon's Mount Hood to the Pacific coast, two hundred miles away. When I talked about the race with Dwight, I told him it seemed pretty tough. He just laughed. "Not for you. It'll be a cakewalk. If you want a challenge, you should bike out there."

Dwight was just making a joke, but his comment made me think. When I was young, one of my heroes was T. E. Lawrence, the iconoclastic British soldier and archaeologist. During his student years Lawrence tested his endurance (and tried to find peace) on long-distance bicycle rides across England and France. With Lawrence's example in mind, I developed a plan for my holiday: to bike across the United States. There was only one problem. I had not ridden a bicycle for more than seventeen years, ever since I joined the Marines.

This barrier seemed serious but not insurmountable. When we were children, my brother Bill and I had biked all over Houston on our ten-speeds in search of stores selling baseball cards. Once you learn, you never forget, right? So, in June 2000, I bought a cheap but rugged Trek hybrid, half road bike, half mountain bike, so I could ride off road on trails; a snug one-man tent and a new sleeping bag; some bike tools I did not know how to use; a United States road atlas, which I cut apart with scissors to reduce the bulk; a Patagonia rain jacket; and two pairs of biking shorts. I made one short thirty-five-mile practice ride that left me sore, chafed, and dehydrated. Then, on July 19, I started riding west on country roads, following my maps with a compass strapped to my wrist.

For the next two months all I did was bike under the hot summer sun, fueled by roadhouse cheeseburgers and gallons of sour POWERade Green Squall. At first I was out of shape, and I could ride only sixty miles a day. At night, in my tent, I had troubled sleep. Once, early in the trip, I woke up in a sweat. Judge Raggi, Sung-Hee Suh, and Valerie Caproni had appeared in my dreams, yelling at me for taking time off from work. Most mornings I was so stiff I could barely walk. Sometimes I thought about quitting, about spending the rest of my time off on a beach. After a week, however, I was averaging ninety miles a day, and I rolled swiftly through western New York, Ontario, and Michigan. By day ten I was in a groove. I loved the physical challenge and the feeling of satisfaction when I passed the one-hundred-mile mark for the day. I loved sleeping outdoors and waking up with the sun. I loved the slow but steady sense of progress, watching the land change as I made my way west.

The ride was not a cakewalk. I was attacked by raccoons, froze in my tent at four thousand feet in the Rockies, and tore all the skin off my hands when I had a major wreck, a learning experience from which I deduced that it is a mistake to ride twenty miles an hour and read a map at the same time. But the real adventure was not physical. It was in my head.

Those first few weeks I rediscovered something I seem to have forgotten: that once you get out of downtown Brooklyn, the United States is an incredibly beautiful place. As an AUSA I saw only a very depressing slice of life: crime, murder, prisons, courtrooms. Now I sought and found inspiration. I rode to Seneca Falls, the birthplace of the American feminist movement, where the first convention on women's rights was held in 1848; saw Lake Erie plunge down Niagara Falls; camped on the beach along Lake Michigan; crossed the mighty Mississippi in northern Minnesota, where it is only a small stream; walked the battlefield at Little Bighorn, where Sitting Bull defeated George Custer; biked over the Continental Divide; and hiked onto the ice fields at Glacier National Park. These travels refreshed my soul.

WHEN I STARTED MY TRIP, I made two vows: I would drink less coffee, and I would not read. The first commitment seemed like a medical necessity, for I had become a caffeine junkie, drinking ten or twelve cups a day. My motivation for the second was more complex. I have been a voracious reader since childhood, going through two or three books a week. Now I told myself: You spend way too much time with books. You are reading your life away. You need to live more and read less. So when I began my ride, I did not carry a single volume with me.

I did fine with my promise to reduce my coffee intake. All across the country I limited myself to two cups a day. This was very easy to do, for I was often dozens of miles away from the nearest town. But reading was another matter. Those first few nights, when the sun went down and I was lying wide awake in my tent, I realized literature was essential. I finally gave in at Cheboygan, Michigan. I found a bookstore there and picked up three books: Hemingway's Nick Adams stories, Trollope's *Cousin Henry*, and Joshua Slocum's *Sailing Alone Around the World*, which seemed a fitting choice for a solo continental bike trip. That night I settled into my sleeping bag along the shore of Lake Huron, a headlamp on my head so I had sufficient light to read, and dug into the Trollope. I read for twelve hours straight, until the sun began to come up. Two days later I wrote in my diary:

> *I'm so glad I went to the bookstore. One of the things I have figured out is that you can't completely disrupt your own mental and emotional life even though you are doing something strange. So, for me, the important thing is to read. I finished* Cousin Henry *last night and read one hundred pages of Slocum. When the sun goes down in a campsite and everyone has fires, friends and good food, and you are sitting there with bad food and no fire because you don't want to lug firewood, it can be kind of depressing. But if*

it is beautiful outside, and you've got your light and a good book,
you can read for a couple of hours before you go to bed and it's
awesome. It's not surprising, of course, that what makes me feel
best in the world is reading. But there it is.

When you bike three thousand miles alone, you have plenty of time to think. As I rode along America's beautiful back roads, contemplating my life, I gradually recognized that work as an AUSA had changed me. When I took the job, I was generally pretty optimistic about human nature. People, I thought, were basically good. Now, however, my constant work with cops and criminals had left me with a very different, and much darker, vision of the human condition. My defendants were the worst people in the world: hitmen, drug traffickers, thieves, con artists. Many, like Gregory Scarpa, were sociopaths, totally bereft of any normal moral intuition. Deceit and violence were the basic tools of their trade. Spending every day with these folks had scarred me, for it left me much more cynical about my fellow human beings. After three years as a prosecutor, I expected people to kill; I expected them to lie.

Now, as I rode west, I regained some proper perspective. In every little town friendly strangers stopped to chat or offer help. At first I was truly amazed by this. Later just pleased. One night in Chenango State Park, outside Binghamton, New York, an accountant named Leo Schulz gave me a burger off his grill and a cold Pepsi in exchange for some stories about the mob. In Marquette, on Michigan's Upper Peninsula, Nancy lent me her spare bedroom so I could get in out of the rain. In Walker, Minnesota, Paul Nye of Back Street Bike and Ski retrued both of my wheels and adjusted my brakes and gears. When I tried to pay, he refused. "When people are on long trips, I try to take care of them." George Thorgramson and his daughter, Liberty, gave me a ride in their propane-fueled pickup in eastern Montana when multiple flat tires (and a resulting inner tube shortage) forced me to hitchhike. In Three Forks, Montana, after my wreck, Roger and Roberta Stratton (of the appropriately named Broken Spur Motel) gave me iodine, antibacterial lotion, and bandages for my damaged hands. Roger even offered to drive me twenty miles to the nearest emergency room, but I decided to ride instead, one heavily bandaged hand resting lightly on the handlebars. And at Fact & Fiction, Missoula's great independent bookstore, a salesclerk recommended some great western authors and gave me a little free advice: "If you go up into the Rattlesnake Mountains, your problem won't be with the snakes; it will probably be with the bears." Most Americans, I rediscovered, are really nice people. It sounds corny, but everyone was so kind they restored my faith in humanity.

When I started my trip, I felt weak and exhausted. Now, six weeks later, I felt almost reborn. One evening, camping in a grove of pines at four thousand feet in Montana's Bitterroot Range, I wrote in my diary:

> *This was the best day of my life. Riding up the river valley, there were big mountains on either side going straight up. They are covered with pine. The sun's going down, and everything is cloudy, misty, cool. Words cannot describe it—or they could, if I only had the right ones. I've gone 490 miles in six days. A lot of the fears and anxieties that I was prey to at the beginning of the trip I no longer have. I feel like I am an incredibly strong person. I'm very happy. I've been tasting freedom, which is something I have not had a hell of a lot of lately, and it feels great. I feel like I have my entire life in my own hands.*
>
> *I don't want to start talking about what I have learned from this trip, because it is not over yet, but certainly, certainly, it has been amazing from a personal point of view. Today I felt it. You know, I am not always courageous. Just the other day, I hit a little headwind, and of course that always makes me miserable. But now I have a feeling of great inner security and strength. A feeling that there are a million things in the world I want to do, and that I can do them all.*

I RARELY EXPERIENCE SUDDEN EPIPHANIES. For me, ideas and convictions come slowly, after much reflection. Thus there was no single moment when I realized I wanted to change my life. The process was gradual. But by late August, when I had reached the West, I had undergone a transformation. I was tired of dealing with human frailty, tired of living in New York, tired of putting people in prison. Slowly I began to consider changing my life.

One month later this idea had taken more concrete form, for I had fallen in love with a city. As a child I had never felt at home in Texas. Since then I had lived all over the country, wherever military service, school, or work had taken me: California, Connecticut, Washington, D.C., Arkansas, Massachusetts, West Virginia, New York. I had enjoyed all these places, but I was never tempted to settle down permanently in any of them. I cannot say why. They just never felt right. When, however, I biked into Portland, Oregon, I had one of those rare moments of insight I almost never get. My diary entry speaks for itself:

> *Amazing city. It's got the wildest trees I have ever seen, I think because of the rain.* *Powell's bookstore is by far the best bookstore I've ever visited in my life. It's the most biker-friendly city I've ever been to as well. Trails everywhere. Yield-to-bike signs. More bikers on the road than I could imagine. Totally cool city. I'd like to live in Portland.*

———

WHEN I RETURNED TO BROOKLYN, I scheduled a meeting with Andrew Weissmann, now promoted to chief of the EDNY's Criminal Division. We met in his office on the fifteenth floor, with glorious views of Manhattan. When I sat down, I noticed something new. On the wall above his desk, Andrew had hung a large Jim Dine lithograph of an empty red bathrobe. It was a stunning piece of art and a subtle reference to Andrew's own outstanding career. For decades, Vinny "The Chin" Gigante, the boss of the Genovese mafia family, had wandered the streets of Greenwich Village in his bathrobe, feigning insanity, hoping to escape arrest. Andrew had put an end to this scam, using testimony from a half dozen mob turncoats to portray Gigante at trial as a lucid, rational, and cold-blooded killer. Gigante was now behind bars, and Andrew had a bathrobe on his wall.

At the beginning of our meeting, I told Andrew that I planned to resign from the Justice Department and become a law professor. I figured

---

*These were Douglas firs, the state tree of Oregon, which grow all over the western part of the state, towering into the sky. As a Texas native living in New York who had never been to the Northwest, I had never seen them before.

life as a teacher would give me more time to think, time to write, time for more adventures like my cross-country bike trip. I could still have a positive social impact, training young lawyers, but I would work in a more idealistic, less corrosive environment. I expected Andrew to wish me good luck. Before I could finish my speech, however, he raised his hand and cut me off.

"Before you make a final decision, hear me out. I have an offer for you. You probably don't know this, but the Organized Crime section has been investigating Allie Boy Persico ever since the Scarpa trial ended. We are close to having enough evidence to indict."

I nodded, instantly alert. Persico was the boss of the Colombo Family. Back in 1994, he had used the Scarpa Defense to win acquittal on racketeering and homicide charges, even though the jury found, as a factual matter, that he had ordered at least one murder. Since that time Persico had been rebuilding the Colombo Family, pushing it into new areas like securities fraud. He was smart, rich, good-looking, and vicious, one of the most important federal law enforcement targets in the nation.

Andrew continued. "The case is going to be tough. Allie had a secret apartment on Fifth Avenue in Park Slope. We trailed him there and did a search. The results were incredible; we seized a virtually complete set of financial records for the Colombo Family hidden in a shoebox and on a computer disk hidden in a vent above the stove. We can charge him with RICO, loansharking, and money laundering, maybe extortion. But the search was dicey. They have a reasonably good argument that it was unconstitutional, so we face a serious suppression motion. If we lose the motion, we will have to dismiss; the rest of the evidence is that weak. Amy Walsh is handling the case—"

I interjected, "Amy is great."

Andrew continued. "Yes, she's outstanding, but I want to add another good trial lawyer, someone who already knows the Colombo Family, and that's you. The number of people in history who have busted a mafia boss is pretty small. This is your chance. You can go be a professor later. But right now we need you to do this case. Allie's been acquitted once before. That can't happen again. I want you to do this."

I nodded again, and then I sat quietly for a moment. During my bike trip I had vowed to change my life. I had walked into Andrew's office ready to leave. Now I was being lured back. What was the right choice?

Persico was a repeat killer, and if he got off free, he would undoubtedly kill again. That made winning his case a moral imperative. I also knew Andrew was right about my qualifications. In the years since the Scarpa trial, many of the office's top mafia prosecutors had left for the private sector, like my old trial partner Sung-Hee Suh. As a result, no one but me had the two qualities needed for this task: deep knowledge about the Colombo Family and big-time mafia trial experience. I was the best fit for this case. If that was true, didn't I have a duty to accept? I thought about Andrew's offer for fifteen seconds, and then I agreed. He and I made a deal: I was free to apply for teaching jobs, but I would not leave the office until Allie Persico was convicted.

On January 24, 2001, after months of legal and investigative work, Amy Walsh and I went to a special organized crime grand jury and got a racketeering indictment for Persico. One week later we added twelve more Colombo mobsters to the case. We had no valid murder charges, but we used RICO's permissive joinder rules to charge every other possible crime: securities fraud, drug trafficking, extortion, gambling, money laundering, loansharking. For the next nine months I spent 75 percent of my time on this one case. Amy and I completed our investigation, added more charges, prepared witnesses, flipped some new cooperators, and got ready for our big suppression hearing. But before we could get into court, the case was interrupted.

ON THE MORNING OF September 11, 2001, I was shaving in my Brooklyn Heights apartment when an odd report came over WNYC radio. A small airplane had crashed into the north tower of the World Trade Center, just one mile away from my apartment, across the East River in Manhattan. I put down my razor and craned my neck out the bedroom window. My apartment was southeast of Manhattan, and my view of the north tower was partially blocked, but I could see a thin stream of smoke, no more than that, rising from the top. I knew that small aircraft often used the Hudson River as a flyway, and like many New Yorkers that morning, I assumed a pilot had suffered a heart attack and lost control of his plane. I thought: They'll put it out shortly. Then I went back to dressing, calmly knotting my tie and checking it in the mirror. I wasn't alarmed. I thought the fire was unusual, a curiosity, but not tragic. The smoke just wasn't that thick. If asked, I would have predicted that two or three people had been injured at most. Like most Americans, I was totally oblivious to the threat of a terrorist attack. I had never heard of al Qaeda or Osama bin Laden.

When I got to the street, I started walking east toward the EDNY, up Pierrepont Street. The time was 9:03 a.m. At that precise moment, the second hijacked aircraft hit the south tower. I did not see or hear the impact; my back was turned to Manhattan. But I was immediately aware that something was wrong. All of a sudden hundreds of people poured out of stores and office buildings into the street. Many ran toward the East River Promenade, with its direct view of Manhattan. As I fought through this panicking crowd, I saw that many faces were masks of horror. I bumped—literally—into my colleague Kiyo, the chief of the Civil Division. Kiyo's face was contorted with great emotion: fear, panic. She yelled at me, "Planes are crashing into buildings!" and then she was swept down the street. I heard another person scream, to no one in particular, "We are under attack!" This mayhem left me totally perplexed. I had heard that a plane had crashed into the trade center, but I had seen the smoke plume with my own eyes, and it seemed almost negligible.

When I got to the EDNY, I did not go up to my nineteenth-floor office in the Organized Crime Unit. My windows looked out over South Brooklyn, the Colombo Family heartland, away from the World Trade Center. I headed instead to Andrew's office on fifteen, with its expansive view of Manhattan. As soon as I came through the door, he brought me up-to-date. "It's clearly a major terrorist attack. Jets crashed into both towers."

I shall never forget the next hour. From Andrew's office I could see the scene across the river perfectly. Both World Trade Center towers were wreathed in smoke and flame. From our vantage point I could not see the hole in the north tower, but the impact zone on the south tower was plainly visible, and it was instantly clear that hundreds of persons must have died, for a number of floors had been totally obliterated. Below, we could see tens of thousands of people pushing and shoving their way toward the Brooklyn Bridge, hoping to cross to safety.

I wish that at that moment I had run across the Brooklyn Bridge against the foot traffic and tried to help evacuate the World Trade Center, only a mile away across the river. But in my shock, the thought did not occur to me. I stood instead at the oversize windows with Andrew, stunned, watching the fires grow worse. My friend Kier, who was watching with us, observed in horror that people were jumping from the tops of the towers. To me, Kier's claim seemed unbelievable. Who would jump one hundred floors to certain death? My eyesight is poor, and my glasses' prescription was out-of-date; I had no time, as an AUSA, to visit the optometrist. All I could see were tiny black specks that seemed to be blowing around the sides of the buildings. I could not imagine the ferocious heat of the fire, the flames roasting the men and women trapped in the towers above the impact zones. To calm Kier down, or maybe to reassure myself, I insisted that he was wrong, that it was just falling debris. Later I learned that Kier was right.

Several months before, I had started dating an AUSA in General Crimes named Amanda. She joined us in Andrew's office, and together we watched the tragedy unfold. For ten minutes we were perfectly still, speechless. Then, suddenly, Amanda inhaled sharply and gripped my left biceps so hard it hurt. In what looked like an optical illusion, the whole south tower buckled, and then the cap of the tower, with its giant radio antenna, began shooting straight downward, throwing off rockets of crushed mortar and debris as the lower floors collapsed beneath it. I yelled out, "Oh, my God!" Until that moment, it had never occurred to me that the towers could fall; they were just too big. As we watched in shocked silence, an ominous cloud of gray dust and smoke ballooned into the sky, covering the trade center site, then enveloping all of lower Manhattan. The cloud moved rapidly west through the streets, obscuring block by block everything in its path. Within seconds it had reached the river. Until that moment the significance of the attack had escaped me. Now, in an instant, I knew that the unthinkable had happened: the World Trade Center had been destroyed. As the dust cloud moved across the East River toward Brooklyn, Andrew got a phone call from Main Justice in D.C., with orders to evacuate the building. We all thought the order was silly, but we complied. Before we left, I told Andrew, "If there is anything I can do to help, leave a message on my voice mail."

AMANDA AND I WALKED quickly down Pierrepont Street. The air was filled with bitter-smelling smoke, and a light shower of pale gray ash was falling from the sky, coating our heads and shoulders. The streets were mayhem, already filled with thousands of victims from across the river, many with jury-rigged masks stretched across their mouths, their clothing and faces smeared with ash, coughing, crying. Amanda and I went to my apartment and tried to call family members, to let them know we were okay, but all the circuits were busy. I sat on my bed, stunned. I did not know what to do.

The rest of the day passed in a daze. Looking for some way to help, Amanda and I reported to an emergency blood bank set up in the Brooklyn Marriott Hotel, a few blocks from my home. They needed O-negative blood, my type. After hours of waiting, sitting on the floor of an immense ballroom amid total chaos, I had my arm jabbed by an attendant and my blood slowly collected in a plastic plasma bag. Before my donation was concluded, word came that the blood bank was closing because the facility lacked the proper Red Cross paperwork. The attendant removed the needle from my arm, I was plied with a small paper cup of tepid orange juice, and Amanda and I went back out on the street. Before we left, I asked a medical technician if my blood would be used, but he just shook his head.

Amanda and I reacted very differently to the shock of the attack. She could not sit still; she wanted to be moving, somewhere, anywhere. I, in contrast, wanted to be in a safe, quiet place listening to the developing news. So we compromised. We got into her car, a late-model black Saab, and drove out of Brooklyn to the southeast, as far as we could go, listening to the radio as we drove. We hit the Atlantic Ocean at Rockaway Beach. Even there, in the city's most distant neighborhood, miles away from Manhattan, we could not escape the tragedy. Normally, Rockaway smells like the sea: salt, fish, decaying kelp, a slight sweet hint of tanning oil. Today, however, the wind was sweeping out from the city toward the sea. A giant plume of ash and smoke trailed east from Manhattan, over the harbor, bringing smoke and the acrid smell of a giant electrical fire. Amanda and I sat on the beach and watched Manhattan for hours, saying little. When the sun started to set, we got back in her car and headed toward home.

The drive back into Brooklyn proved more difficult than we expected. All the freeways and major avenues were closed to inbound traffic, to free up passage for evacuees and rescue vehicles, so we were forced to pick our way through Queens and Brooklyn on back streets. We slid past endless lines of boarded-up brownstones and vacant, weed-strewn lots. Most of the streetlights were out. In the shadows, we saw small crowds of people gathering on stoops and at bodegas and liquor stores. On virtually every corner, cops stood alongside fires burning in metal trash barrels, lighting up the night. The drive was quiet but eerie, and we locked our doors.

Eventually we found ourselves in East New York, one of Brooklyn's poorest neighborhoods. For many New Yorkers, being stuck in East New York at night in an expensive car would be nerve-racking, but I was actually relieved. I had never been here before, but I had prosecuted a number of drug cases from this neighborhood, and I knew the streets well from crime scene maps. We quickly reached Pennsylvania Avenue, the neighborhood's main drag, and made our way from there back to Brooklyn Heights. The whole return trip, normally twenty-five minutes on the Gowanus Expressway or Atlantic Avenue, took more than three hours.

Amanda wanted to spend the night at her apartment, a mile or two north of the World Trade Center site. I agreed—Amanda desperately wanted to be in her own bed that night—but getting there was no easy matter. The bridges were closed to traffic, and the Lexington and Seventh Avenue subway lines were out of service. After waiting for almost an hour by ourselves on a lonely subway platform, we finally caught an empty F train to the city. Before we went to bed, we watched an hour of CNN. Prior to this day, I did not have any pressing reason to interest myself in terrorism; I was focused instead on drug rings and mafia families. Thus I knew very little about it. That night, watching the broadcast, I heard, for the first time, the name now so familiar, al Qaeda.

THE NEXT MORNING, around eight, I called Andrew to see if our office would be open. Andrew said we would be closed but that he needed my help. "An investigation into the attack is already under way. We may need emergency search warrants and wiretaps, but the duty judge lives out on Long Island. Can you go see Judge Raggi and ask her to review our applications?" I immediately agreed. Given road closures and traffic, I knew getting out to Long Island would be impossible. Judge Raggi lived close to the courthouse, so she would be a much more speedy and convenient option. Andrew was not, however, solely concerned about speed. "We can't afford to make any mistakes," he told me. "Raggi is such a smart judge. If there are any problems with our warrants, she'll spot them."

I waited until 9:00 a.m., drinking coffee and watching CNN, and then called Raggi's chambers, but I could not get through; the phone lines were still down. I assumed most judges would stay at home this day, but I figured Raggi would come into work. Always controlled, always disciplined, she would view it as her duty, manning her post during a time of tragedy.

I walked to the subway station, but all the trains were down, including the F, so I set out for Brooklyn on foot. Union Square, I saw, was filled with thousands of people, some sitting, crying, others just wandering, their eyes glazed in shock. A few persons, soon to become a flood, were taping homemade MISSING signs to fences and lampposts. By nightfall that evening the whole square had become a shrine, filled with thousands of candles burning in ad hoc memorials.

I cut south to Fourteenth Street and quickly hit a roadblock made of yellow sawhorses and olive-drab sandbags, manned by a national guardsman carrying an M-16. "I'm sorry, sir, I can't let you through. All of lower Manhattan is closed to foot traffic."

I handed the guardsman my law enforcement credentials. "I'm a federal prosecutor. You have to let me through. I'm on official business related to the attack. I have to get to the Brooklyn federal courthouse, across the Brooklyn Bridge." The guardsman conferred with an NCO and then let me pass.

The scene on the far side of the roadblock was sobering. The Lower East Side, normally packed and bustling, was a ghost town: all businesses closed, most of the residents evacuated, stoplights dark, the streets almost totally silent. Convoys of army trucks and armored vehicles rumbled past me, heading south toward the trade center. Every few blocks military police ordered me to halt and inspected my identification. As I walked through Chinatown, I began to notice that the streets were covered in gray cement dust and ash. The closer I got to the attack site, the deeper the ash grew. By the time I got to City Hall, the powdery debris was so thick it felt as if I were walking on a beach, shuffling my feet through thick drifts. Crushed and burned-out cars littered the streets. A burning chemical smell filled the air, making breathing difficult. Part of me wanted to turn west and inspect the attack site, but I knew I would only be in the way of the relief effort, and I felt voyeurism was somehow improper. I turned east instead and walked across the Brooklyn Bridge. Fifteen minutes later, after clearing several more roadblocks, I was at the Brooklyn courthouse.

Judge Raggi was already at work, impeccably dressed as always: black suit, particolored scarf, red hair perfectly coiffed. It may sound bizarre, but I found the judge's appearance oddly reassuring. Terrorists may attack us, she seemed to be saying, but they cannot make us lose our composure. I explained that Andrew wanted to arrange for us to bring emergency applications to her, if the need arose, and Raggi immediately agreed. I got her home address and telephone numbers, and then we exchanged what little news we both had been able to gather. Afterward I called Andrew to let him know that everything was set and asked if there was anything else I could do. He told me to check my voice mail frequently and to meet him the next morning at the office.

———

ON SEPTEMBER 13, 2001, I got into the EDNY at 8:00 a.m. Everything was dead quiet. Because the Gowanus Expressway was closed to normal traffic, no prisoners could be brought from the MDC to the courthouse, and all routine court appearances were canceled. Most attorneys had stayed at home. As soon as I arrived, I went to Andrew's office. Andrew looked tired, with black bags under his eyes. We quickly got to business.

"You probably don't know this, but DOJ had an emergency command center in Manhattan, for use in disasters or terrorist attacks. That command center was right by the trade center, and it was destroyed."

I interrupted. "That was really stupid. Didn't they think about moving it after the 1993 bombing?"

Andrew did not even bother to respond. "We're creating a new command center to coordinate the investigation over on the west side of

Manhattan. Ben and Kelly are over there now. Call Ben as soon as you can. I think you are going to be the night shift."

Ben Campbell was chief of VCE, Violent Criminal Enterprises, the EDNY's gang unit. I called Ben's cell phone and he immediately picked up, saying, "Command post."

"Ben, it's Kroger. Andrew told me to call. How's it going?"

"Well," he replied, "it's kind of a mess, but we're getting things straightened out. We are going to be doing twelve-hour shifts here. Kelly and I will hold the fort till seven. I talked to Andrew. We agreed you and Dwight should take over for the night." He meant Dwight Holton, my colleague on the Bushwick investigation.

Ben gave me the command post's address. He also provided some advice on how to approach it without getting shot, for it was surrounded by an armed security detail. Before we hung up, I asked Ben if there was anything else I could do. Ben paused for a moment. Then he said, "We've got laptops here, but they're not linked to our network in Brooklyn, so we can't access any of our documents." I nodded to myself. For a prosecutor, being cut off from your computer files is a potential disaster when time is of the essence. In any investigation, specific legal documents, following legally prescribed forms, are required to accomplish almost anything. For example, you cannot tap a telephone, plant a bug, subpoena tax or bank records, arrest a suspect, search a house, or force a witness to testify in front of a grand jury without the proper application and authorization forms. Every prosecutor keeps examples of these forms on her computer, which she can call up and modify at a moment's notice, whenever they are needed.

He continued. "I need you to gather exemplars for every kind of form you think we might need. All the basics—arrest warrants, search warrants, every type of subpoena, bank records, tax records, every kind of electronic surveillance, clone beepers, you name it. Put it all on disks and bring it with you tonight. Also, bring two cars with you when you come. I need a way to get home."

For the rest of the day I downloaded onto a set of floppy disks all my own legal exemplars, plus a couple of dozen more exotic items I had never used, which I gathered from Jodi Avergun. Then, at 6:00 p.m., Dwight Holton and I met down in the EDNY's underground parking lot, where two G-cars, reserved for official use, were parked. Using thick

black markers and white poster board, we made giant placards that read
"AUSA" and taped them to our front and side windows. We hoped this
would help get us through checkpoints and keep nervous national
guardsmen from opening fire. I did not think many of the troops had
any idea what an AUSA was, but at least it sounded official.

Dwight and I pulled out onto Cadman Plaza and joined a convoy of
relief trucks and police cruisers slowly crossing the Brooklyn Bridge.
Once we hit Manhattan, we cut over to the West Side. The streets were
total chaos. There were no traffic signals, and tanks, military trucks, and
emergency vehicles were racing everywhere at high speed, many with
sirens blaring, dodging one another, careening the wrong way down
one-way streets, swerving around piles of wreckage from the attack.
Dwight drove remarkably fast, to keep ahead of the armored personnel
carriers that seemed to fill every avenue, and I struggled to keep up, hoping I wouldn't run into a tank. As I drove, I thought: this place feels more
like Beirut than it does lower Manhattan.

The command post was cordoned off from all traffic, so we had to
park five blocks away and approach on foot, passing through several
checkpoints. This was nerve-racking, as the sunlight had started to fade
and all the streetlights were dimmed, the result, I guessed, of a power
shortage. Most of the checkpoints were visible, but not all. At one point
we got hit with a spotlight and a voice rang out in the dark. "Halt! Who
goes there?"

I froze and yelled back, "AUSAs, heading to the command post."

The guards instructed us to lay our credentials on the ground and
then back away. I did it just as I had been taught in the Marines.

A barely visible man in a dark camouflage uniform, M-16 at the
ready, slipped forward out of the shadows. He picked up our creds and
faded back into the night. Then the voice rang out again. "Okay, you can
approach!" We walked slowly forward. As we slipped between the
guards, one grabbed my shoulder and said, "Hey, Kroger." It was a member of the FBI's Lucchese Family Squad, now on security duty.

THE NEW YORK COMMAND POST for the 9/11 terror case, dubbed Operation Pentbomb, was set up in an old government parking garage. Just
two weeks before, I had been to that same garage with a member of the

Colombo Squad whose FBI car got a flat. Now, as we walked up several concrete ramps to the third or fourth level, I saw it had been transformed. In the center of one large parking bay, on dirty gray floors streaked with oil, agents had set up folding tables in the shape of a giant U. Around the tables sat representatives of every relevant agency: FBI, Customs, Immigration, DEA, Secret Service, FAA, Coast Guard, NYPD, plus a dozen others. In front of each person was a telephone, a laptop, and a placard with the name of the agency on it, so if you needed to find someone, you could do so instantly. As I looked around the room, I could see that the situation was tense. Many people looked exhausted. Others looked angry. A phone rang every few seconds. Dozens of agents cycled in and out. People yelled to each other, "Have FBI call Tracom!" "Conference call in fifteen." "I need two agents out at LaGuardia now!" "Where the fuck's the Customs rep?" "No, you will not do that!"

To the left of the U was a small glass-windowed enclosure, the former office, I supposed, of the garage manager. Looking through the grimy windows, I caught a sight of Mary Jo White, the U.S. Attorney for the Southern District of New York. White was sitting at a battered oak desk, her feet propped up, talking on the phone. I could not hear what she was saying—the door was closed—but I saw her gesture forcefully with her free hand.

To the right of the U, on the other side of the room, were two more folding tables, marked "EDNY" and "SDNY." This would be my post. Dwight and I said hello to Ben and Kelly, and then introduced ourselves to the two SDNY prosecutors already on duty. Even in the midst of a major terrorist attack, I noted the immense cultural difference between the two offices. Dwight and I were in khakis, our sleeves rolled up; the SDNY team wore gray suits, striped ties still tight at their collars. I plunked down my laptop, got a large cup of coffee, and started to settle in. All of a sudden Mary Jo White appeared at my side, wearing jeans and a blue Joint Terrorism Task Force T-shirt. "How," she asked calmly, "can we find out the names of the customers of a small bodega out by JFK?"

I looked at the other AUSAs present, but no one said a thing. Mary Jo waited. Suddenly, the answer, a bit of useless information tucked into my brain from a minor General Crimes fraud case, popped into my head. "Have the Department of Agriculture pull all the food stamp records; then interview everyone you find."

Mary Jo nodded. "That's a good idea," she said, and disappeared back into her office.

That night, and on several additional evenings in the coming weeks, I worked alongside hundreds of federal agents, federal prosecutors, and local police officers investigating the attack. This emergency response team pursued two very different investigative tracks. One mission was to follow "undirected leads." All across the country tens of thousands of Americans were calling FBI hotlines and clicking on the FBI website to provide information they thought might help us catch the terrorists. These tips piled up at the rate of more than one thousand per hour right after the attack. Roughly 99.99 percent of these tips were useless, but we had no way of knowing that until each one was checked out. We sent thousands of law enforcement personnel to chase down these wild geese. By the time the investigation terminated, several months later, the government had examined 170,000 different tips.

The other major focus was more crucial and more productive. Everyone suspected that the 9/11 terrorists had received logistical support from other al Qaeda operatives in the country and that additional sleeper cells might be planning further attacks. To identify and neutralize these potential threats, the Justice Department and the FBI began to reconstruct, day by day, the past lives of the nineteen 9/11 suicide terrorists, so we could identify and investigate every single person in the United States with whom they had had significant contact. This part of the investigation progressed with remarkable speed. Within a few weeks the Justice Department had built an incredibly detailed chronology of the terrorists' actions and movements. We knew where they lived and studied, the movies they rented, the clothes they bought, the food they ate, and the books they read. To everyone's relief, we found no signs of additional sleeper or support cells in the United States.

My own role in this effort was minor but necessary: providing legal support to the agents and cops working on the case. The FBI had established a leads desk at the West Side command post where all tips and leads in the New York metro area were funneled. Twenty-four hours a day, exhausted Pentbomb agents and cops checked in at the desk. They turned in the results of their last assignments, grabbed cups of bad coffee or Gatorades out of the cooler, and then picked up new leads to investigate. Sometimes they headed straight back out to the street. Other times they would stop by the AUSA desk, lead forms in hand, and ask for help. One agent needed a bank records subpoena; another, a subpoena for phone records; a third, a telephone pen register. Once an agent had the legal forms she needed, she disappeared, and another agent took her place. I never saw the results of my work; I was just a cog in the legal machine. When I wanted to get the "big picture," I tuned in to CNN, just like everyone else.

Within a few days this work had become routine, but that first night was incredibly chaotic. Though the SDNY prosecutors were terrorism experts, veterans of the Ramzi Yousef and 1993 World Trade Center bombing cases, I knew nothing. At one point I was tasked with determining if the Taliban had an office in Queens. I remember thinking: Uh, what's the Taliban? At that time I had never heard of the governing clique in Afghanistan.

Federal prosecutors pride themselves on their careful, precise legal work. At the command post we took that ethos to a new extreme. We knew that even seemingly trivial leads might produce critical evidence, and we wanted to make sure that if they did, the evidence would not be suppressed in a later trial because of some dumb legal error. So we handled every task with kid gloves. That first night some NYPD cops found an abandoned car parked out by JFK with, reportedly, some potentially interesting evidence inside, visible through the windows.* Normally, I would have told the cops just to search it, for under the 1925 Supreme Court decision *Carroll v. United States*, an old law school chestnut, police can search cars and trucks without warrants. In this case, however, I wanted to be 100 percent sure that if we found good evidence, it would be admissible in court. I got the cops on the phone and warned them, "Don't touch a thing!" Dwight and I then wrote a warrant application. When we finished, we called the cops back and read it to them on the phone, to make sure the facts were 100 percent accurate. Dwight then took our warrant off to a judge, to make sure she agreed we had probable cause to search. As soon as the warrant was signed, Dwight called me, I called the cops, and the vehicle was towed to a nearby NYPD garage. This whole process took less than an hour. Later FBI crime scene

---

*For obvious reasons, I cannot disclose what that evidence was.

experts worked the car over in detail. I never heard whether it produced any relevant evidence. I was already on to the next task.

———

IN OCTOBER 2001 I returned to the *Persico* case. On November 6, Amy and I won our suppression hearing, putting us in a very strong position. For the next month I spent hours on the phone every day, talking with Barry Levin, Persico's lawyer, trying to negotiate a guilty plea. Under the sentencing guidelines, Persico faced only seven or eight years in prison. Amy and I wanted more. Eventually I brought Levin to the table. Pursuant to our deal, Persico got thirteen years in prison and a one-million-dollar fine.

I should have been ecstatic. The elusive Persico had finally been jailed, and I was now free to resign and pursue my teaching career. In truth, however, our victory felt anticlimactic. If you had asked me about *Persico* before 9/11, I would have told you it was one of the most important federal cases in the nation. After the attack, however, it felt trivial. While I had been chasing two-bit mobsters through the streets of Brooklyn, a much more dangerous criminal threat was brewing, one that I—and the whole United States government, it seemed—had totally ignored.

Before the World Trade Center collapsed, I did not feel any obligation to remain with the EDNY. I had served my country, and I had done a good job, but now it was time for me to go, time for me to put my own desire for a new life first. After 9/11, however, I felt differently. Our country had been attacked. To me, it seemed like a horrible time to jump ship. It felt way too close to desertion.

One morning I sent off an e-mail to Alan Vinegrad, our U.S. Attorney, offering to stay with the office. Alan quickly called me back. I told him that with the country at war, I did not feel comfortable leaving government service. Thus, if there was work for me in counterterrorism, I would stay. I expected Alan to accept my offer. The EDNY was converting its gang unit into a counterterrorism team, and I thought he would want to send me there. Alan, however, had other ideas. When I finished General Crimes, Alan had ignored my application to serve in the Organized Crime unit and sent me to Narcotics instead. Now he once again denied my request. He told me that he wanted me to stay with the EDNY, but if I did, I would remain in OC. To me, that offer did not seem compelling. As a mafia prosecutor I had already convicted Scarpa and Persico, and there was no way to top that accomplishment. More to the point, our organized crime strategy was so successful we were running out of top mobsters to prosecute.

At the time I was angry at Alan for his decision. I really wanted to work on terror. In retrospect, however, it worked out for the best. At the time I imagined we would be bringing senior al Qaeda leaders to a criminal trial in New York, as we had done after the 1993 World Trade Center bombing. The Bush administration had other plans. In the years since 2001 we have captured many major terrorism leaders, including some responsible for the 9/11 attacks, but these killers will never face an American jury. They have all been sent to CIA "black detention sites" and our prison at Guantánamo instead.

In President Bush's vision, there is not much room for prosecutors or the rule of law in the war on terror. Instead, his emphasis is on military and paramilitary action alone. This seems like a terrible mistake to me. America gains international credibility when it complies with its own traditional values. When we put people on public trial in fair proceedings, with the right to counsel and the right to object to evidence, we show the world that the United States and al Qaeda are not morally equivalent forces. We also show the terrorists that even massive attacks will not make us abandon the very things that make America great.

———

TRIAL LAWYERS SOMETIMES speak of experiencing the "seamless web," moments in court when suddenly everything fits together and goes your way. In the fall of 2001 I had just such a moment in my professional life. While memories of Oregon were still fresh in my mind, Lewis & Clark Law School in Portland announced a job opening for a professor of criminal law. After interviews and a teaching presentation, the school offered the position to me. I did not hesitate. On January 2, 2002, after Allie Persico's plea, I resigned from the Department of Justice. That same month I moved west to Portland and taught my first class.

During my time as an AUSA I had received many commendations and awards from the DOJ, FBI, DEA, and State Department. Nothing meant more to me, however, than a tribute I received several weeks after I resigned. Jackie DeRoss, the murderous Colombo Family underboss, was in court in Brooklyn facing racketeering charges. Jackie expected to see me there. I was, after all, one of his family's leading nemeses, and I had obtained his indictment. Puzzled, he turned to my successor, AUSA Noah Perlman, and said, "Hey, Noah, where's Kroger?" Noah told Jackie that I had left the office and moved out west, to become a law professor. Jackie smiled and shook his head, as if in mock regret. Then he said, "That Kroger, he's a good lawyer."

PART IV

Enron: White-Collar Crime

CHAPTER SIXTEEN

The Enron Debacle

O n December 2, 2001, just a few months after 9/11, Houston energy giant Enron was forced into bankruptcy after stunning media revelations about insider deals, hidden debts, company looting, and faulty accounting. Five thousand Enron employees in Houston lost their jobs in one swoop. Nationwide, investors, most of them ordinary people with their retirement money invested in Enron through mutual funds and pension plans, lost sixty-one billion dollars. At the time it was the largest bankruptcy in United States history.

Normally a messy corporate bankruptcy does not cause a political firestorm, but Enron was different. Enron chairman of the board Ken Lay was a friend of the Bush family, Enron executives had donated millions to President Bush's 2000 presidential campaign, and company lobbyists had helped craft the administration's energy policy, which favored big oil and gas companies like Enron over conservation or alternative energy. Democrats predicted publicly that the Bush Justice Department would go easy on their cronies. The Republicans denied this charge, but words were useless in this debate. The Bush team knew that if it failed to move aggressively on Enron, there would be a huge political price to pay. Indeed, the Bush administration had no political interest, as some folks on the left have alleged, in going easy on Ken Lay and company. On the contrary, it was motivated to get some scalps quickly.

Investigating the Enron collapse would ordinarily have fallen to the U.S. Attorney's Office for the Southern District of Texas, headquartered in Houston, where Enron was based. Michael Chertoff, the chief of

DOJ's Criminal Division, had other ideas. Most big-city U.S. Attorney's Offices have excellent reputations, but Houston's is mediocre. Right after Enron went bankrupt, the Justice Department announced that since many prosecutors in the Houston office had friends, family, and neighbors who worked for the company, the whole office possessed a conflict of interest and had to be recused. In reality, this was a smoke screen. A senior official at Main Justice told me later that Chertoff was simply worried that SDTX would screw up the case.

With the Texans out of the picture, the next natural candidate to prosecute was the SDNY in Manhattan. The Southern District possessed the nation's most experienced (and arguably most gifted) white-collar crime prosecutors, and it had venue, for Enron had sold its stock on the New York Stock Exchange. But for some reason, Main Justice decided to cut the SDNY out of the loop too. To this day I do not know why for certain, but all of us career prosecutors had our suspicions. Mary Jo White, the outspoken U.S. Attorney in Manhattan, had been appointed to her job by President Clinton, and her relations with the Bush team were tense, for she had been critical, within the Justice Department, of the administration's handling of terrorism. White had a reputation for being completely independent and fiercely strong-willed. She also had immense professional clout, both within the Justice Department and among the media, for she was an almost legendary figure, widely recognized as the top prosecutor of her generation. If White ran the Enron case, Chertoff knew he would not be able to exercise any control over the direction of the investigation. If he even made suggestions, White would tell him not to interfere. White's independence probably scared Chertoff, for like many prosecutors, he is a notorious control freak. It was for this reason, I suspect, that he ordered the SDNY off the case.

Once these decisions were made, DOJ had no option but to create a special task force to investigate Enron. To lead the team, Chertoff chose Leslie Caldwell. Leslie was a veteran of both the EDNY and the U.S. Attorney's Office in San Francisco, and she had dozens of major gang and white-collar cases on her résumé. A former college rower, Leslie is tall and physically imposing. When she walks into a room, people notice. In the courtroom she has undeniable presence.

Chertoff's decision to put the Enron case in Leslie's hands was shrewd. Leslie was a team player with no personal or bureaucratic power base like Mary Jo White's. She would clearly be Chertoff's subordinate. She might not follow all his orders, but she would definitely listen. At the same time, Leslie was not a political hack but an experienced and respected career prosecutor, so his choice could not be criticized on political grounds. Leslie was also very aggressive. Chertoff knew that if a crime had been committed at Enron, she would find it.

Leslie was authorized to hire several assistants. She filled two slots with experienced white-collar fraud prosecutors: Tom Hanusik, the assistant chief of DOJ's Fraud Section in Washington, and Bill Kimball of San Francisco, who had worked big securities cases at both DOJ and the Securities and Exchange Commission. But her two most senior prosecutors were mafia veterans: Sam Buell from Boston and Andrew Weissmann, my old chief at the EDNY.

Leslie's decision to staff the Enron case with mafia prosecutors was made deliberately. In the Justice Department, organized crime work has always been considered the best possible training ground, for this experience produces prosecutors who are tough, aggressive, and creative. They can also handle complexity. As Chertoff, a former mafia prosecutor himself, explained to the *Houston Chronicle*, prosecuting the mob "teaches you not to be daunted by the size of the case. Typically, organized crime cases involve years of criminal activity and a cast of dozens of characters and you learn that by breaking it down a piece at a time you can not only organize your case, but you can present it in a way that is intelligible to a jury."

The decision to hire mafia veterans was also influenced by a second, more controversial factor. Inside DOJ, many senior lawyers believed that the department's white-collar prosecutors were inept: too slow; too cautious; reluctant to charge tough cases; quick to offer light plea deals; overly deferential to the white-collar defense bar. Indeed, many people within the department, including me, blamed our white-collar prosecutors for debacles like Enron. Because the Fraud Section was gun-shy, we believed, the government was not indicting enough fraud defendants, and this underenforcement had created a permissive regulatory atmosphere in which corrupt corporate executives believed they could get away with murder. After Enron went bankrupt, the Justice Department decided to respond aggressively. One way to do that was to transfer successful mafia prosecutors to this new battle against corporate crime.

MY OWN INVOLVEMENT in the case was something of a fluke. On March 7, 2002, Leslie's task force indicted accounting firm Arthur Andersen on one count of obstructing justice, for shredding tons of documents on the eve of Enron's collapse. Leslie assumed that the case would proceed slowly, like most white-collar matters, a year for discovery and trial preparation, with trial, perhaps, in late 2003 or early 2004. Instead, Arthur Andersen demanded its day in court immediately. Sam and Andrew agreed to serve as the trial team, but they wanted to add to the case a third AUSA, someone with good trial skills and some Texas roots, to offset the fact that both Sam and Andrew hailed from the Northeast. Not surprisingly, Andrew thought of me. Leslie and I had never worked together before, but years earlier she had seen me cross-examine Greg Scarpa, and that apparently was sufficient recommendation. On March 19, she sent me an e-mail asking if I was interested in returning to DOJ to try the *Arthur Andersen* case.

I was intrigued by Leslie's proposal, but the idea hit an immediate brick wall. Justice Department ethics regulations prohibit an attorney from participating in a case if he or a family member has a financial stake in the outcome. Back in the 1980s, my sister became an Arthur Andersen accountant, and she was now a partner at the firm. If Andersen lost the case, her partnership would be worthless, giving my family a financial interest in the result of the trial. The idea that I might intentionally sandbag the trial in order to help my sister was preposterous, but rules are rules. The conflict regulation can be waived in extraordinary cases, and Leslie and I briefly considered it, but a waiver would have looked strange. Chertoff had just disqualified the whole Houston office for potential conflicts of interest, and it would be difficult to explain why I was different. Within forty-eight hours Leslie and I agreed that I could not work on the case. A few days later Andersen fired my sister and hundreds of other employees as the company began to implode. When that happened, I knew Leslie and I had dodged a bullet. If I had agreed to work on the trial, Andersen could have alleged that I was acting vindictively because I was angry about my sister's termination.

After I declined to work on the Andersen trial, I did not give the Enron case another thought. I was teaching my first criminal law classes at

Lewis & Clark, and this was challenging enough. Two weeks later, however, Andrew Weissmann sent me an e-mail.

> *John—do you want to work on the Enron case with us? We would love to have you on board and you could work exclusively on the Enron side so there would not be a conflict. What it would require is your joining us after your school year (I assume that is the end of May) and committing for a year (if we finished before then you could of course leave then). Can you take a leave of absence and join us?*

I had resigned from the DOJ just three months before. I had moved all my possessions across the country, rented an apartment in Portland, bought a new car, and started a brand-new career. Did I want to go back? Surprisingly, the answer was yes.

IN *THE INTERPRETATION OF DREAMS*, Freud suggests that some events are "overdetermined," caused by a confusing array of multiple factors, any of which, operating alone, might have been sufficient to make the event happen. Looking back on my decision to join the Enron Task Force, I see that it falls easily into that category, for my motives were definitely complex.

One factor was the sheer size of the case. When I left the EDNY, I believed my career had hit a plateau. I could stay in Brooklyn for another decade, I thought, and never have another case as important as *Scarpa* or *Persico*. Now the most significant white-collar case in history was being offered to me on a plate. That seemed hard to pass up.

I also felt a sense of duty. I was comfortable resigning from the EDNY because I knew I was replaceable. Our Organized Crime Unit had so many good prosecutors and so few major cases I was confident that my departure would not harm the public interest. Enron was different. The company's collapse was not morally equivalent to a terrorist attack, but it was a very serious national disaster, injuring millions of investors. Andrew and Leslie told me that the case was going to be tough and that they needed someone with my investigative talents and trial skills to succeed. This was rank flattery, of course, but I took it to heart nevertheless.

My Marine Corps service had ended years before, but I never really left my Marine values behind. My country was asking for my help, and I did not feel free to say no.

Behind these two rational justifications lurked a third, less palatable one. As an AUSA I had made decisions every day that had a huge impact on people's lives. To give just one measure, by 2002 I had sent more than two hundred people to prison. At the time I thought this power was no big deal. I was used to it, wore it like a second skin. When, however, I resigned from the Justice Department and this power suddenly disappeared, I immediately noted its absence. On my drive out west I got pulled over by a cop for a burned-out headlight. In the past this would not have felt threatening: I was part of the law enforcement team, after all. Now I felt vulnerable, just another civilian.

I also had trouble adjusting to the change of pace. My life as a junior law professor seemed quiet and dull. My telephone never rang. Instead of getting hundreds of e-mails a day, I got two or three. I had no managerial authority, no responsibility whatsoever. No one was going to die because of my judgment; no one was going to go to prison; nothing was going to happen at all.

This newfound sense of insignificance would probably not have bothered me much but for one sad development, the collapse of my relationship with Amanda. When I moved to Oregon, I knew I was putting that relationship at risk. Still, I hoped we would pull through. We had talked about marriage. This would put our commitment to a test.

At first things between us were fine. We agreed to date long distance, I promised to return to New York for my first summer vacation, and we discussed the possibility that she would move west. Within weeks, however, I got nervous. Amanda was not always at home when I called late at night, and when we talked, I picked up verbal cues that something was wrong. As an AUSA I had learned to discern minute traces of deception and deceit in the voices and mannerisms of my defendants. Now, fueled by jealousy, I focused those skills on my girlfriend. This was creepy—I knew it was creepy at the time—but I could not help it. I had been trained to look for dishonesty, and I could not simply flip a switch and turn those skills off, for suspicion was second nature, an occupational hazard. When I talked to Amanda on the phone, I poked and prodded, looking for lies, and when I was confident I knew the truth, I moved in for the kill. Using leading questions, just as in cross-examination, I got her to admit that she was having an affair with a fellow AUSA, a Brooklyn gang prosecutor. The whole experience was awful. Not just because our relationship died, but because I felt like a monster.

Looking back, I now see that my inquisitorial response to Amanda's infidelity was a warning sign, an indication that prosecutorial power had already twisted my personal character. I should have respected that warning, stayed away from prosecuting and stuck to teaching for a while. Instead, I did the opposite. Amanda's decision to cheat left me anxious and sad, my self-esteem in the dumps. When Leslie and Andrew called about Enron, they caught me at a vulnerable moment. They were not just offering me a job but throwing me a lifeline back to a place where I had status, respect, and authority. This was a bad motive to return to public service, but a very human one, I think.

I thought about my options for a day or two and then sent Leslie and Andrew a reply: "I'm in."

IN THE JUSTICE DEPARTMENT we have one cardinal rule: we check our politics at the door. When I was an AUSA, that ideal was beaten into my head: never, ever, under any circumstances let your own political beliefs influence your handling of a case. If you have any doubts, recuse yourself immediately.

Apparently, the new Bush team at DOJ did not get the message. When I agreed to join the Enron Task Force, a senior DOJ prosecutor involved in the case sent me an e-mail: "Better buy some elephant cufflinks if you are coming to DC; certain parts of your resume will not resound well w/the current crowd!" I thought she was joking. A few days later, however, she sent me another e-mail warning. Political appointees, she said, would be vetting my résumé. This was a potential problem, for under "political experience," I had listed all my former jobs in Washington: policy aide to President Bill Clinton, to Speaker of the House Tom Foley, and to Representative, now Senator, Chuck Schumer of New York. My friend suggested that if I wanted to be hired, I might want to "moderate" my résumé a bit. "Seriously, as lame as this sounds, the higher-ups at the department are SUPER right wing."

The idea that career prosecutors would be judged politically, not professionally, sent a shiver of anger down my spine, for that is totally contrary to the DOJ ethic. I thought it would be wrong to cave in to their pressure, so I decided not to edit my past. Instead, I simply moved the description of my Marine Corps service right to the top of the page. Take that, right-wingers! I thought. Apparently, this did the trick, or perhaps no one really cared anyway. All I know is, I got the job. Lewis & Clark Law School graciously granted me a year's leave of absence, a remarkable thing for the school to do, for I had just gotten there. Then, in May 2002, at the end of my first semester of teaching, I loaded up my Honda Civic and drove across the country to Washington. When I got to D.C., I rented a studio apartment next to the zoo, so I could listen to the lions at night. That same day I reported to Leslie and got a desk in our temporary office, on the top floor of a shabby DOJ annex on New York Avenue. I was no longer an AUSA or a law school professor. I was a "Special Attorney, Enron Task Force."

PRIOR TO THE ENRON CASE, I had little white-collar experience. I had handled one major case, involving embezzlement from a cruise ship line, and several criminal tax cases, but for the most part this was new terrain. I was also ignorant about the stock market. As a prosecutor I did not make much money, and living in New York City, where the cost of living is high, I had saved even less. With no skin in the game, I paid Wall Street no attention. Now, however, I felt my ignorance was a serious potential weakness, and it made me nervous. To get up to speed, I read Louis Loss and Joel Seligman's treatise on securities law and studied dozens of recent court opinions. Then I started research on Enron itself.

When you begin a major investigation, your first step is always to gather all the available intelligence about your targets. In most cases, that is easy, for the amount of information is usually limited. In a mafia case you might have a small stack of surveillance reports and a debriefing of an informant; in narcotics work, maybe nothing more than a name and a telephone number. Enron was different. Before the company's bankruptcy, it had been covered closely by the nation's business reporters, and Enron itself had issued hundreds of press releases and earnings reports. After the implosion, dozens of top investigative reporters from the *Houston Chronicle*, *The Wall Street Journal*, *The New York Times*, and other papers began to interview hundreds of former employees, and they were now busy cranking out exposés of the company's culture of corruption. The amount of information in the public domain was immense.

To get a grasp on this huge body of material, I asked Patrick Flanagan, my law school research assistant, to download and print out every news article and press release about Enron since 1990. The result filled fifteen binders. As soon as I got to Washington, I began to read them cover to cover, in chronological order. It took me two weeks.

WHEN I WAS A CHILD growing up in Houston, our local energy utility was Houston Natural Gas. HNG sponsored one of my favorite television shows, *Houston Wrestling*, on Channel 39. When I tuned in on Saturday nights, I would see the HNG commercials. To a ten-year-old, they seemed ominous, featuring a simple, bright blue flame projected over a deep black background.

In 1985, while I was serving in the Marine Corps, Houston Natural Gas was acquired by InterNorth, a large Nebraska-based pipeline company. The InterNorth deal became a legend in Houston business circles. InterNorth thought it was buying HNG, but in truth, it had been suckered by HNG's CEO, a man named Ken Lay. Lay retained all the power in the newly merged company, and it was based in Houston, not Omaha. Soon Lay gave it a new name, Enron. At the time people in Houston rolled their eyes. They thought Lay wanted the company to sound like, perhaps be mistaken for, the giant energy corporation Exxon.

Enron was a company built on deregulation. From the 1930s to the 1980s, natural gas was heavily regulated by the federal government, which set the price for both the sale and transportation of the product. In the mid-1980s, however, the Reagan administration began to eliminate price controls and give gas producers and pipeline companies the ability to contract freely. Some major companies like Columbia Gas Transmission could not adjust to the rapidly changing market and perished. Others thrived, and none more than Enron. Ken Lay understood that the newly deregulated market was grossly inefficient, with large numbers of gas producers struggling to identify and contract with an even greater number of customers. Enron exploited these inefficiencies. It bought huge quantities of gas from producers at steep discounts and then delivered that gas to wholesale customers like power companies through its own nationwide pipeline system. It also offered long-term contracts and futures, a novel idea at the time, so buyers could hedge the risk from future price fluctuations. Soon both producers and users gave up trying to enter the market on their own, preferring simply to deal with Enron. Within a few short years Enron's intermediation strategy, playing the key middleman role between producers and suppliers, had totally transformed the gas sector. The company captured a huge percentage of the market and pocketed substantial profits. By the early 1990s Enron was the leading natural gas company in the United States.

Ironically, Enron's success held the key to the company's ultimate demise. Success built on exploiting a rapidly deregulating market is inevitably short-lived. Other natural gas companies like El Paso and Dynegy watched Enron closely, copied its innovations, and then competed for the same business. Competition stiffened, and Enron's profit margins shrunk.

When the low-hanging fruit in the natural gas market disappeared, Enron's management faced a difficult business strategy decision: it could remain a natural gas company and grow content with smaller profits, or it could diversify into other sectors of the economy and try to replicate its great success in natural gas. Enron was a confident and aggressive company, and its driving force, president Jeff Skilling, was not content to sit still. Instead, he chose to diversify. Over the course of the 1990s Enron rapidly expanded into an enormous array of new businesses in the United States, Europe, and the developing world: energy trading, water, power generation, coal, paper and forest products, telecommunications, retail electricity, and metals. This diversification strategy was costly. Enron paid out approximately $1 billion to construct its Dahbol power plant in India; some $2.4 billion for purchase of the Wessex Water utility in the United Kingdom; $3.2 billion for Portland General Electric in Oregon; $2 billion in cash and debt for the metals trading company MG; $1.3 billion for an electricity company in Brazil; and $300 million for a paper mill in Quebec. The rate of investment was dizzying. In July 1998, Wall Street equity analysts from Donaldson, Lufkin, & Jenrette noted that Enron had spent some $3.5 billion within a few short weeks alone.

Enron hoped to become a world leader in all these new endeavors, but it did not play out that way. Instead of hiring managers with experience in the metal, paper, or water industries to run its new businesses, it decided to rely on its own senior natural gas and energy trading executives, managers, Skilling liked to say, with "Enron DNA." These executives assumed that Enron would succeed in these new areas because "markets are markets," functioning in more or less the same manner. This view proved naive. When Enron's successful gas executives were plugged into new industrial sectors, they failed virtually across the board, often through sheer ignorance, producing massive losses for the company.

Consider, for example, the company's effort to enter the water market in Latin America. In 1999, Azurix, Enron's water subsidiary, made a sealed bid of $439 million to take control of Buenos Aires's water utility. Azurix won the auction, but its bid was nearly three times higher than the next largest offer. Once Azurix took control of its prize, it discovered that the utility was crumbling and that the purchase price did not cover critical assets like the utility's billing system. The bid ultimately resulted in enormous losses. As Texas journalist Robert Bryce later commented, Azurix "didn't burn cash, it incinerated it."

By decade's end virtually every new Enron initiative was failing. To this day no one knows with precision how much money Enron lost—the company's accounting was that hazy—but journalists at *Fortune* magazine have put the cost at "well over $10 billion in cash."

UNDER FEDERAL LAW, publicly traded companies like Enron that sell their stock on the major stock exchanges are required to file quarterly and annual reports with the Securities and Exchange Commission. In these reports, called 10-Qs and 10-Ks, the company must describe all its business operations and provide hard financial data: quarterly revenue, expenses, profits, and debts. That way investors will be able to make sound investment decisions based on accurate, up-to-date information. These quarterly reports are incredibly important in the American business world. If a major company reports bad numbers, its stock price will plummet and credit will dry up. If the numbers don't improve the next quarter, the CEO and his executive team can quickly find themselves fired. In short, the stakes are enormous.

The SEC's quarterly reporting requirement posed a major challenge for Enron. The company's senior executives believed that in the long term, Enron's new business endeavors would succeed. In the short term, however, the company was getting killed. If it admitted, honestly, that its new businesses were struggling, the long-term payoff might never come. Instead, the stock price would plunge. The company might even go bankrupt, and they all would be looking for work.

In most major white-collar cases, the defendants do not begin their careers as criminals. They want to make money in business, and if they succeed and become rich, they never face temptation. If, however, their plans go sour, they are left with only two options: they can be honest and admit their failure, or they can lie and try to fool their investors. At most companies truth prevails. The executives admit their plans have gone awry and take their lumps. At Enron, Skilling opted for plan B.

Throughout the late 1990s Skilling told Wall Street that Enron's diversification strategy was a huge success and that all of its new business units were rapidly gaining market share, reproducing the company's stellar success in natural gas. To back up its claims, Enron's chief financial officer, Andy Fastow, filed financial statements with the Securities and Exchange Commission showing enormous profits and low debt. Wall Street should have treated this tale skeptically, but in the midst of the dot-com boom, when anything seemed possible, most of the brokers, analysts, and reporters covering Enron had lost all perspective. Blinded by Enron's powerful spin, they ate the story up. *Fortune* rated Enron "The Most Innovative Company in America" for five straight years, from 1997 to 2001. Enron traded at a price-to-earnings ratio of fifty-five to one, four times higher than comparable energy and trading firms. And in 2001, when all the dot-com companies collapsed, *Fortune* identified Enron as one of the most reliable "10 Stocks to Last the Decade." Enron executives like Skilling and Fastow became media darlings and walked away with millions in cash, as they sold their inflated Enron stock. By 2000 more than two hundred Enron executives were taking home one million dollars or more a year, and twenty-six made an astounding ten million dollars or more. It was certainly good to be at Enron while it lasted.

Unfortunately for Skilling and Fastow, these blatant lies were hard to sustain. By 2000 the gap between Enron's reported success and its dismal reality had grown enormous. That year, for example, 96 percent of Enron's reported net income was made up, the product of Fastow's fraudulent accounting. At the same time, Enron managed to hide almost twenty-five billion dollars in debts. As the pressure mounted, Skilling cracked. In the summer of 2001 he abruptly resigned to "spend more time with his family." Ken Lay, Enron's former CEO, now the chairman of Enron's board of directors, took Skilling's place at the helm. Lay was informed by his senior staff that the company was on the rocks.* He should have immediately told the truth to Enron's investors. Instead, he continued the cover-up, telling Wall Street that everything was fine. He even met with employees and told them to buy more Enron stock. But quietly, in secret, he began to unload his own Enron holdings.

On Wall Street, Skilling's resignation seemed curious, for few CEOs quit at the top of their game. In response, investigative reporter John Emshwiller at the *The Wall Street Journal* began to look at Enron more closely. At first, he hit a brick wall. Enron's financial statements, he discovered, were incredibly abstruse, filled with hard-to-decipher legalese and Byzantine financial jargon that seemed designed to hide more than it disclosed. Slowly, however, Emshwiller began to piece together and report the truth—not all of it, not even most of it, but enough to prove that Enron was not the successful company Skilling claimed.

When the *Journal* began to uncover Skilling's and Fastow's lies, Enron's stock price started to slump. In response, the company tried to clean up its act. On October 16, 2001, Lay announced for the first time that Enron was losing money and that some of its reported financial numbers were inaccurate, though he did not admit the true extent of the problem. He hoped this limited concession to reality would boost Enron's credibility and quiet the market, but it only added fuel to the fire. On November 8, 2001, under massive pressure from stockholders and the media, Lay conceded that all of Enron's financial statements going back to 1997 were inaccurate, though again he failed to disclose the true extent of the debacle. This time, however, Wall Street had had enough. When Enron executives told the market that none of the company's stellar revenue, debt, and cash flow numbers were accurate and admitted in

---

*To this day I think it is difficult to assert with any certainty how much knowledge Lay had about Skilling's and Fastow's crimes prior to replacing Skilling as CEO. After that point it is clear he knew precisely what was happening.

a private meeting with bankers in New York that more than twenty billion dollars in debt had been kept off Enron's financial statements, investor confidence evaporated. Enron's stock price declined to zero and the bankers cut off credit, leaving Enron unable to pay its bills. On December 2, Enron filed for bankruptcy. Lay walked away with more than a hundred million dollars; Skilling, fifty million; and Fastow thirty million. Investors got stuck with the cost, losses of more than sixty-one billion dollars.

WHEN LESLIE RECRUITED ME to join the Enron Task Force in the spring of 2002, I asked her how long the case would take. She replied by e-mail: "I'm estimating one year for the whole ball of wax." On the basis of this e-mail, I assumed that the task force was almost finished with the investigation and ready to charge top defendants. This turned out to be totally inaccurate. The controversial Arthur Andersen prosecution had absorbed all of the task force's time and attention throughout the spring without providing any significant leads to the larger Enron case. As a result, the investigation had not really started.* I had expected to spend the summer in court. Instead, I spent most of June and July meeting with the other AUSAs and the FBI, plotting investigative strategy.

In theory, the Enron investigation was simple. We would first obtain all of Enron's public statements: its quarterly and annual financial reports; press releases; and transcripts of presentations to Wall Street stock and bond analysts. Then we would compare those glowing public statements with the company's true financial condition. If we found a gap between reality and public spin—a gap between what the senior executives knew about Enron and what they told the public—then we could charge those executives with a crime, securities fraud.

Sometimes proving securities fraud is easy. In the *WorldCom* case, for example, the fraud was massive but childishly simple. Faced with huge losses they did not want to reveal, executives at the giant telecommunications and telephone company doctored its balance sheet, labeling $3 billion in short-term costs as capital expenditures—long-term invest-

---

*Four years later, when Jeff Skilling and Ken Lay were convicted at trial, I jokingly sent Leslie a copy of her e-mail: "one year for the whole ball of wax." She replied: "That was just a recruiting tool!"

ments. Since capital expenditures, unlike operating expenses, are not subtracted from revenue when a company calculates and reports its earnings, this sleight of hand transformed a $662 million loss in 2001 into a reported $2.4 billion profit. Unfortunately for CEO Bernie Ebbers, this rudimentary accounting manipulation was very easy for auditors to detect and easy for a jury to understand. Ebbers is now serving a twenty-five-year prison term.

Enron was different, quantum mechanics to WorldCom's basic math. One problem was the sheer bulk of the evidence. Enron was the seventh-largest company in America, with twenty thousand employees and business operations all over the world. To get a grip on possible crimes and to assess possible defenses, we would have to identify and interview thousands of witnesses. When the FBI searched Enron headquarters for evidence at the start of the case, it seized more than ten million documents. Wading through this haul to see what we had was a monumental task.

A second problem was the lack of whistle-blowers. Sherron Watkins, a former Enron executive, testified before Congress about Enron's problems, and she volunteered to help, but she was not a senior executive, and her knowledge of the company's true financial position was limited. What we needed was a high-level inside informant who had worked closely with Skilling and Fastow, but no one came forward voluntarily. We faced, in essence, a corporate code of silence.

Finally, there was Enron's bizarre financial structure. During the company's last few years in existence, it had entered into thirty-five hundred separate complex transactions with banks and investment funds designed to doctor its financial statements. Some of these transactions were intended to provide Enron with undisclosed cash, the twenty-five billion dollars it secretly borrowed to stay in business. Others were designed to manufacture imaginary but reportable revenue. Each of these transactions had its own bizarre Enron code name: Chewco, Grayhawk, Braveheart. Enron's executives insisted to Congress and the media that all these deals were legal because they complied with all the relevant accounting rules. If that was correct, then Enron's crooks might be able to escape conviction. Our job was to sort out the truth. The only way to do that, we believed, was to examine each transaction in detail, looking for signs of fraud.

Unfortunately, I quickly discovered that analyzing these deals was tough. On my first day of work I examined one, and my heart sank. Looking at a transaction diagram, I saw a confusing swirl of boxes and arrows, to me a meaningless maze. I counted twelve different "special purpose entities," shell companies that existed purely on paper, each with a different financial purpose. The diagram was annotated with opaque comments like "3% equity stake," "unwind swap sub hedge," and "3.1 million post-split shares from LJM I through swap sub." I thought: I am never going to be able to understand all this.

I did not feel any better when I asked Tom Hanusik, our resident fraud expert, to explain what I was looking at. "Oh, well, you see," he said, pointing at some of the boxes on my chart, "Enron executives bought some Natwest and CSFB investments that were held in SwapSub and then dumped the proceeds into an off-balance sheet SPE called Southampton Place LLP, which was funded by a loan from Chewco and a charitable trust, with three percent equity ostensibly at risk, before paying the funds back out to the investors." Ah. Right.

The sheer complexity of this mess drove our investigative strategy. Most white-collar prosecutors try to build document cases, based primarily on incriminating business records. These cases may be dull, but they have one great advantage: documents don't lie. In contrast, we decided from the outset that we would try to construct a cooperator case, built primarily on the testimony of witnesses. To some extent, this strategic choice reflected our professional experience. Leslie, Sam, Andrew and I were used to trying mob, gang, and narcotics cases, in which the only evidence comes from the mouths of cooperating conspirators, so it felt natural for us to follow that model. But we also thought we had no other option. The Enron business records were so voluminous and hard to decode we thought it could take years to determine what evidence was relevant. Moreover, they were so dense, packed with so much complex finance jargon and legalese, we thought jurors might really struggle to understand them. To fix these problems, we needed key Enron insiders to flip and cooperate, to help us understand how the deceptive financing schemes worked and then explain the case to a jury.

The complexity of the case also forced us to prioritize our investigative efforts. After a few weeks of work we realized that we lacked the time and resources to conduct a comprehensive forensic analysis of Enron's financial condition. I calculated, for example, that if we tried to analyze each one of Enron's thirty-five hundred potentially fraudulent financial transactions, it would take the six of us more than a decade. So we were forced to pick and choose. Leslie and Andrew carefully studied the voluminous press coverage of Enron's collapse and the Powers Report, Enron's own internal investigation of fraud at the company, which had been released in early 2002. Then, on July 9, 2002, Leslie circulated a memo dividing the most promising areas of the case among her five prosecutors. Bill and Sam took the Chewco and Grayhawk transactions; Tom took NatWest and RADR; Andrew took Southampton and LJM. My own assignment was a little different. Leslie did not ask me to examine any specific transactions. Instead, she asked me to investigate an entire business unit, Enron's telecommunications division, Enron Broadband Services.

CHAPTER SEVENTEEN

The Broadband Scam

In 1998, Jeff Skilling pushed Enron into the telecommunications business as part of the company's diversification strategy. The new division, dubbed Enron Broadband Services, or EBS, was supposed to be a cash cow. In 2000 and early 2001, Skilling and other executives told investors it was a major success. In the summer of 2001, however, Enron laid off or transferred virtually all of EBS's employees, and the new company was quietly shuttered. Investigators and journalists learned later that EBS had lost some two billion dollars, a business disaster.

My marching orders from Leslie for the Broadband investigation were vague. "EBS was Skilling's baby, and I hear it was really messed up. Take a look and see if there's anything there." She did not tell me to target any particular suspects. She did not need to. EBS had been run by CEO Ken Rice and his deputy, Chief Operating Officer Kevin Hannon. Rice, a boyish multimillionaire playboy with a racing stable of Ferraris, was one of Jeff Skilling's closest friends. Hannon, Rice's smart, hatchet-faced enforcer, had worked closely with Skilling for years. If we could jam these two men up and flip them, they might help us make a case against their boss. To make this happen, the FBI assigned eight experienced agents to the case.

———

IN MOST CRIMINAL INVESTIGATIONS, including white-collar cases, agents and prosecutors typically start with clear proof of a crime. My prior cases, for instance, had always begun with huge drug seizures, a dead body, or a pile of stolen money. The Broadband investigation was different. When Leslie tasked me with examining EBS, we had no idea if a crime had been committed there at all.

Under federal law, lying to investors is not a crime unless the lies are "material," or important. If a CEO lies about the color of his new office carpet, that is not securities fraud. But if he lies about the size of his company's quarterly profits, it is. For this reason, the agents and I began the Broadband case by asking: What public statements did Enron executives make about their telecommunications business that, if false, would really have deceived investors? FBI Special Agent Jeff Jenson, who served from the outset as our lead case agent, did an initial assessment of EBS's public presentations. He quickly identified two events on which we decided to focus.

On January 20, 2000, less than two years before its bankruptcy, Enron held a conference in Houston for several hundred Wall Street stock analysts. The highlight of the presentation came in the afternoon. Prior to this date, Enron had kept relatively quiet about its Broadband unit. Now Ken Rice and other EBS executives made a startling announcement. Enron, they told the analysts, had developed unique proprietary telecommunications network software that gave Enron's "intelligent network" advanced capabilities far exceeding those of all its competitors. This software, they claimed, would revolutionize the Internet, providing hitherto unimagined quality control. To back up this claim, Enron ran a demonstration at its headquarters. It took a distorted Internet video image and, with the flick of a switch, converted it to picture-perfect clarity. The announcement hit the market like a bomb. By the close of the next business day Enron's stock price had shot up from fifty-four to seventy-two dollars on the strength of its "technology play."

The next year, in January 2001, Rice and Hannon repeated this performance. Enron's intelligent network control software was now a full-fledged "operating system," analogous to Microsoft Windows, allowing customers moving data on Enron's network to schedule telecommunication services from their desktop computers, pay for various degrees of guaranteed quality control, and be billed automatically for just the broadband capacity they had used, things no other telecommunications company in the world could offer. Rice also claimed that there was tremendous market demand for EBS's products and services. At the end of the presentation Jeff Skilling told the analysts that EBS was worth thirty-six billion dollars.

These two presentations were incredibly rosy, portraying EBS as a thriving business with a unique product. Within a few short months, however, EBS had been shut down. These facts raised one basic question. When Rice and other executives portrayed EBS as a huge success, had they simply been wrong about the facts, or had they intentionally lied? My job was to figure that out.

Our investigative strategy was simple. The FBI transcribed the two analyst presentations. Then we took these transcripts on the road. We showed them to former EBS executives and asked, "Is there anything here that is inaccurate?" We hoped that if we interviewed enough people, eventually the truth would emerge.

AT ITS PEAK EBS had employed more than five hundred people. Whom should we interview first? I had no clue. Fortunately, Greg Rupert, one of our agents, did. In one of our early planning sessions, Greg mentioned that a major law firm involved in the Enron civil litigation had been looking closely at EBS. "Most of the firm's investigators are former bureau types. Let me go up to New York and see what they have." When Greg returned, he handed me reports from interviews with numerous former EBS employees who claimed that the company was a sham: no customers, no software, and a network that barely functioned. As I looked at this impressive haul, Greg told me, "I think we better go see this Bill Collins first."

On a hot day in August 2002, I sat down with Bill Collins in a sleek high-tech conference room at the U.S. Attorney's Office in Portland, Oregon. Collins was in his forties, a little portly, with sandy hair and large, owl-like glasses. He had been hired by Enron to help develop its telecommunications business model, and he had had close and frequent contact with most of EBS's top executives. At first our interview went poorly. Collins was a veteran tech executive, and his speech ran thick with acronyms and technical terms: "IP on glass," "EIN API," "automatic provisioning," "beta test," "QOS." After a few minutes I stopped him. "Bill, I don't understand a single thing you are telling me. And I don't know anything about your industry. So assume I am a total idiot, okay?

Start over again, and this time explain the EBS business model to me from scratch, in the simplest terms you can."

For the next five hours Bill gave me a primer on the telecommunications business. The Internet, he told me, was awesome but flawed. Every minute hundreds of millions of people dumped vast amounts of information on the same networks, and because of this traffic, lots of "data packets" were lost or scrambled. Some simple applications, like e-mail, worked fine. Others did not. For example, you could not transmit DVD-quality video and television images over the Internet because of all the distortion. The solution was to build a high-tech software-driven "intelligent network" that could control information flows in a much more sophisticated manner and then sell and trade access to this network like a commodity. Bill told me that writing the software to accomplish this vision was "like going to the moon," an extremely difficult task. "Even Microsoft," he said, "would have trouble doing it." But if you could do it, it would revolutionize the industry and generate billions of dollars in revenue. That, he told me, was what Enron wanted to do.

The next day I handed Bill a pen and a copy of the transcript of the January 2000 stock analyst conference. I made a simple request: "Read through these materials, and mark every claim you think is false." For the next hour, while I paced up and down the hallway, Bill sat quietly at our conference table, making hundreds of check marks.

When he was done, I asked him his impression. "Look," he said, with an edge in his voice, "all of this is bullshit. We wanted to build an intelligent network. We wanted to be able to control quality of service. We wanted to have network control software. But we never got close. We never had any of this stuff. That's why I quit before the 2000 analyst conference. I knew we were going to lie to everyone, and I didn't want to be there when it happened. I thought no one was going to believe us, our lies were so blatant. What if they asked us to prove it, to prove we had a network like this? Where were the customers? Where was the revenue? I thought the stock price was going to collapse, so I sold every share I had the month before and left. Then what happens? Wall Street buys the whole story! I wound up leaving millions on the table."

"Who knew all this?"

"Everyone knew it. It was no big secret."

For the next several hours Collins talked us through the analyst conference transcript paragraph by paragraph, explaining why Enron's claims were false. He told a compelling story, but to be honest, I really did not believe him. Come on, I thought, the seventh-largest corporation in America isn't going to lie about something tangible like the existence of software. It would get caught too easily. I thought Bill might simply be a disgruntled ex-employee who was mad that he had lost out on the chance to be a millionaire. So when he finished, I pushed him a little.

"Look, Bill, your story is amazing, but it is pretty hard to believe. Guys like Rice, they are going to claim you are lying. So, how can you prove your story is true?"

Bill did not get huffy or defensive, the way most witnesses do when they are making something up. Instead, he calmly replied, "Go ask any former engineer at that company."

"Like who?"

He rattled off a list of five or six names. Then he said, "They'll tell you the exact same thing. But I have an even better test. If this network control software existed, it would totally transform the telecom industry. Any major networking or software company would pay billions for it. So where is it? If Enron has it, where is it? Just ask them for it. Software code is a physical thing. So where is it?"

I asked Bill why the other telecom companies did not cry foul. His response was fascinating. "I think they thought we were making it up, and that the truth would come out when we tried to sign up customers. But maybe they feared us. Maybe they thought we had pulled it off. I don't know."

A few days later I flew to Silicon Valley to meet with Shawna Meyer, whose name Bill Collins had supplied. Meyer had been EBS's director of product engineering, working directly with the Enron network, and she was thus a crucial witness. I expected her to tell a very different story from Collins. Instead, she confirmed every one of Collins's facts, and then some. "The company was a disaster," Meyer told me. "All the engineers used to joke about the so-called intelligent network software because it didn't exist. We called it secret sauce or pixie dust. You just sprinkle a little of it around, and like magic, you have the world's best network. When we met with potential customers, we had to tap-dance around the facts, like the little frog with the cane and the top hat you see on TV."

I asked Meyer how they convinced outsiders that the software really existed. "We had a demonstration. We showed a picture that was heavily distorted, and then we flipped a switch, and presto!, the picture became perfectly clear. But it was totally misleading. We could do that on a free-standing PC, but it would never work on a network. The challenge is simply too great. That's why I quit. When you get up in the morning, you have to look yourself in the mirror and feel good about what you do. I didn't anymore, so I left."

I interrupted. "Did you have an exit interview?"

"Yes." She named a senior executive.

"What happened?"

"I told him that I didn't want to work at Enron anymore, that the people I worked for were unethical and that I didn't trust them. He asked me to stay. I had a lot of stock options that I would lose if I resigned. If I left, it would cost me between four hundred and five hundred thousand dollars. He told me to stick around and 'vest in peace.'"

"What does that mean, 'vest in peace'?"

"Just hang out, don't do anything controversial, and get my next set of options."

OUR NEXT STEP was to find some documentary evidence that confirmed Collins and Meyer were telling the truth. At the outset of the case the FBI had seized ten million documents from Enron's Houston headquarters, and most of this evidence had been scanned into a searchable database. In addition, we had seized a number of computer backup tapes from Enron's information technology department. Using these tapes, forensic computer specialists had been able to restore tens of thousands of old Enron internal e-mail messages. Starting in August, all of the agents and my colleague Deb Tarasevich, a talented lawyer at the SEC, worked around the clock digging through this material, looking for documents and messages that might help our case. Much of the material we found was highly technical, so technical I thought its value in a future jury trial would be limited. But two items caught my eye.

In December 1999, just before the 2000 conference, EBS executives had compiled a series of PowerPoint slides they intended to show to investment analysts. Someone on our team—I cannot remember who, though I suspect it was Deb—went back and found all the early drafts of these slides and compared them with the final draft. This examination showed that initially Enron planned to describe its software as "under development." By the time the conference arrived, however, those two critical words had been edited out, so that the final slides suggested that the software existed. This was clear, powerful evidence that sometime during those months the senior executives had decided to lie about their progress in order to make a more powerful splash.

The second piece of evidence was even more damning. In late December 1999 a group of senior EBS executives were conversing by e-mail about the impending analyst conference. One guy wrote that the Broadband Operating System, Enron's planned "intelligent software," would not be successful unless it was ubiquitous, adopted widely in the industry, like Microsoft's Windows. Bill Collins fired back:

> *The BOS dreams of being ubiquitous. But as long as it's not doing anything in our network and isn't ready and doesn't work, the analogy to other industry technologies is not quite apropos. We are not in much of a position, since today BOS and EIN and API* has zero market share, zero customers, zero installed base. I don't care what lipstick and rouge you paint that bitch up with, she's still just dead meat lying on the sofa just threatening to stand up and steal the show.*

This one e-mail convinced me, more than any other single item, that Collins and Meyer were telling the truth. None of the recipients sent responses like "What do you mean? The software is installed everywhere, and it is running great." Instead, they simply let Collins's comment stand.

Later I asked Collins what he meant when he said the failed software might "steal the show." He looked at me blankly. "The show, the show. You know, the analyst conference."

---

*EIN was the acronym for Enron's planned software-driven network, the Enron Intelligent Network. An API is an application programming interface, a critical feature that would allow programmers to design new applications that could run on Enron's software.

AT THIS STAGE in the Broadband investigation, I had two good witnesses, several strong pieces of documentary evidence, and a promising list of other persons to interview. If I had been wise, I would have quietly continued to beef up my case, interviewing more witnesses and finding more incriminating documents. Instead, I made a huge mistake.

By August of 2002 the Enron Task Force had existed for eight months, and the pressure on us for results was growing. We were working very hard, in my case, more than one hundred hours per week. We were also making progress. To the public and the media, however, it looked as if we were stalled. Every day on television CNN's Lou Dobbs closed his *Moneyline* show by displaying his sardonic "Enron Corporate Fraud Scoreboard." The scoreboard showed the number of days since the company's bankruptcy and the total number of Enron arrests, a number that seemed permanently fixed at zero. I cannot speak for anyone else, but Dobbs's smug and biting criticism got on my nerves— unprofessional, but true.

More significant, there was a growing sense inside the task force itself that we were spinning our wheels. The size and complexity of the case were overwhelming, and some promising paths had turned into dead ends after thousands of hours of work. No senior Enron executives would talk to us, and we had no way to breach this wall of silence. When we talked about the case over lunch—the only time we could slow down and assess our progress—all the prosecutors agreed that we needed a big break. That desire made me greedy.

I should have spent August and September building my case. Instead, I shot the moon. I contacted a senior Broadband executive—let's call him Executive X—and tried to flip him. My motive was simple. I thought that if we could get a quick guilty plea and the promise of cooperation, it might break the case wide open.

Going into my meeting with Executive X, I was extremely confident. I was, after all, the interrogator with the golden touch, flipping defendants left and right back in Brooklyn. In the meeting, I used all my proven pressure tactics. I announced that an indictment in the case was likely, previewed some of my best evidence, walked the defendant through the prison sentence he would get if he were convicted, and explained the benefits of cooperation. I expected these methods to work, just as they had in the past. Instead, my confidence—call it clueless arrogance if you will—was horribly misplaced. The reaction of the lead defense attorney, a distinguished lawyer in his sixties, said it all. When I finished my presentation, his face was flushed with anger. "I think this is a bunch of bullshit. I think you are just trying to scare us." Needless to say, my target did not flip.

At the time I thought I had hit a particularly stubborn defendant, a man in denial. Over the next six months, however, I tried to flip several other senior Broadband executives, and I failed across the board. No one cooperated. No one offered to help. What went wrong?

There were some clear benefits to staffing the Enron case with mafia prosecutors. We were aggressive, tough, and decisive. But there was also a serious cost, at least in my own case. I was used to interrogating professional drug dealers and mafia killers, and my tactical sense was shaped by those experiences. When I transplanted my skills to the white-collar world, they were much less successful. The reason for this was so obvious I should have realized it before I made a fool of myself. Corporate executives, even crooked ones, are very different from professional street criminals. They have more money and are better educated than most criminals, and their sense of empowerment makes them less susceptible to government tricks and coercion. They also fear prison. Most professional drug traffickers know that at some point in their lives they are going to jail. If pleading guilty and agreeing to spend some time in the can are the price they have to pay to escape longer sentences, they are prepared to pay it. For wealthy executives, in contrast, the idea of incarceration is terrifying. They will do anything to avoid it. So getting them to admit their guilt is extremely difficult.

There is also the problem of cognitive dissonance. Most white-collar criminals go to church or synagogue, make donations to charities, and enjoy good reputations, not just in their communities, but in their own minds. As a result, admitting guilt always involves a huge blow to their self-image. Many executives are so convinced that they are good people they simply cannot accept the fact that they broke the law. In many cases, this psychological barrier makes cooperation not just unlikely but impossible.

Finally, all these difficulties are exacerbated by the white-collar defense bar. Defense attorneys know that if they tell their clients they are crooks and recommend cooperation, they risk losing their giant fees, for an offended executive will probably hire a new lawyer—one who accepts and reinforces the executive's saintly self-image. They also know that if a case goes to trial, rather than ending early in a plea, their fees will be much higher. As a result, defense lawyers are much more likely to recommend a stonewall in white-collar scandals than in cases in which they represent less well-heeled clients. Many lawyers convince their desperate clients that the government is on a witch hunt and laugh all the way to the bank. To give just one example, *The New York Times* has reported that O'Melveny and Myers, the firm that represented Jeff Skilling, ultimately billed him fifty-four million dollars for his defense.

IF I HAD BEEN a more experienced white-collar prosecutor prior to the Enron case, I would have understood that flipping corrupt executives can be very tough. Unfortunately, I did not, and that proved costly. Prior to my meeting with Executive X, my EBS investigation was flying under the radar screen. No one outside the task force knew what we were doing. This was a definite advantage, for it ensured that we could get to witnesses and interview them first, prior to any defense interference. When, however, I disclosed the existence of our investigation to Executive X, we lost this ability to control the pace of the case. When rich executives know they are targets, they do not sit back and wait for indictment; they take proactive steps to shape the evidence in their favor. At this early stage, they know the facts and potential witnesses better than the government, for they worked at the company, and the prosecutors and agents did not. They use this superior knowledge to generate a comprehensive list of potentially important witnesses. Then they deploy their immense financial resources—in the Enron case, tens of millions of dollars—to hire teams of lawyers and investigators to meet with and debrief those witnesses before the government does. In the Broadband case, for example, Executive X's lawyers started calling witnesses like Shawna Meyer and requesting meetings within forty-eight hours of our interview. This convinced me I was on the right track, for I had never even mentioned Meyer when I tried to flip Mr. X. But it also scared me.

When the government and the defense interview witnesses, they have very different motives. Assuming the government prosecutor is ethical, the government simply wants to learn the truth, whether that is good or bad for its case. Indeed, prosecutors typically want to know all the "bad news" up front, before making a virtually irreversible charging decision. Big-time white-collar defense lawyers, in contrast, are paid not to discover the truth but to win. For this reason, their witness interviews are not dispassionate inquiries into the facts but loaded efforts designed to neutralize the government. This typically involves a very destructive tactic, one prosecutors call poisoning the well.

Most persons working in business today are remarkably ignorant about criminal law. For example, they rarely understand precisely what kinds of acts violate the securities fraud laws. Like most nonlawyer witnesses, they are also easy for a trained lawyer to manipulate. A smart defense attorney exploits these facts. His opening pitch might sound something like this:

LAWYER: Look, the government is on a witch hunt, and they are going to indict people at EBS whether they committed any crimes or not. Now, you were not a criminal, were you?
WITNESS [shocked]: No, of course not.
LAWYER: I know that. I am sure you are a very honest person. But I worry about the government prosecutor. It's a felony, you know, to fail to report a crime if you know about one in your workplace. [This is technically correct, though the government rarely charges the arcane crime of misprision of felony, 18 *United States Code*, Section 4. For example, I never charged it once in my whole time as a prosecutor, and I was certainly on the aggressive side of the charging spectrum.] So, if there was crime all over EBS, and everyone knew about it, like the government says, you were required to report it, and if you didn't, the government can come after you and indict you. Now, I know you never reported any crimes; no one did. So let me ask you: Is that because you were part of a giant criminal conspiracy, covering things up, like the government says?

WITNESS [worried now that maybe he too will be targeted]:
No!

LAWYER: Of course not. The government is out of control
here, insisting everyone at EBS was a crook. You didn't
commit any crimes, did you?

WITNESS: Of course not.

LAWYER: And you never saw anyone else commit a crime
there, did you? Because if you had, I am sure you would
have reported it to the SEC.

WITNESS: Uh, well, no, not a crime. I mean, maybe there was
stuff that wasn't perfect, ethically, but, uh . . .

LAWYER: And if you were not aware of any crimes, that means,
I guess, that you never thought Bob [the lawyer's client] was
committing crimes, right?

WITNESS: Uh, no, none that I knew of.

LAWYER: He was a good man, right?

WITNESS: Uh, sure.

LAWYER: Great, that's what I thought.

From this hypothetical exchange, you can see why this defense strategy
is called poisoning the well. If the defendants can reach a white-collar witness first, they can use leading questions, subtle misrepresentation about
the government's intentions, and a little fear to get most witnesses to say
that they never saw a particular executive commit a crime. This makes
that witness totally unusable as a government witness at trial, even if it
turns out that the witness did in fact see and hear vitally important evidence. For if the government calls the witness to say, for example, that the
EBS network did not work properly or that certain accounting rules were
broken—the "ethical" concerns the witness brought up in the interview
with the defense lawyer—the defense can respond with a devastating cross.

LAWYER: Ms. Stevens, isn't it true that before you talked with
the government in this case, you met with me?

WITNESS [gulping]: Yes.

LAWYER: And is it not a fact that you told me that to your
knowledge, not a single crime had been committed at EBS?

WITNESS: Yes.

LAWYER: In fact you told me that you did not believe my client ever broke the law, correct?

WITNESS [voice barely audible]: Yes.

LAWYER: You told me Bob is a good man.

WITNESS: Yes.

LAWYER: No further questions.

From this short analysis, I hope you can see why my premature interview with Executive X was a disaster. When I tipped off the defense attorneys that we were on their trail, they immediately leaped into action, contacting potential witnesses. Not all defense attorneys are willing to poison the well; some play their interviews straight. But an appreciable number believe it is a legitimate tactic. I knew that if we did not move fast, our target's lawyers would hit every possible witness first, and our investigation would fail. The agents and I discussed this fact, and we decided not to give up. Instead, we opted to race.

For the next few months I worked harder than I ever have in my life. I felt bad that my strategy had backfired, that I had let my agents down. I wanted to make it up to them. I also wanted to make sure that justice would be done.

WHEN I FIRST JOINED the Enron Task Force, all the prosecutors were based in Washington, D.C. This choice had nothing to do with investigative efficiency; most of them were from the Northeast, and they simply hated being in Houston. Houston, however, was my hometown. More to the point, our grand jury, much of our evidence, and most of the agents were there. After my failed interview with Executive X, I decided to move.

My new office in Houston was located in an innocuous-looking glass-and-steel building right off the 610 Loop, about ten minutes from downtown. One of my walls was covered by an enormous erasable whiteboard, ten feet wide and four feet high. That whiteboard became my primary management tool. Using a black marking pen, I drew a giant three-month calendar on it. Then the agents and I made a comprehensive master list of witnesses we thought we should interview. The agents then worked the phones, locating witnesses. As soon as they had an interview scheduled, we put it up on the board. Soon the entire calendar was filled.

During the next sixty days the Broadband agents and I met more than seventy witnesses. Some weeks we stayed in Houston, interviewing locals, but most of the time we were on the road. EBS was a telecommunications company, and after it went bankrupt, its employees relocated all over the country. One week we hit Seattle on Monday, Portland on Tuesday, San Francisco on Wednesday, Denver on Thursday, and Phoenix on Friday. This frenetic pace was tiring but necessary. One night I was sitting in an FBI office in Denver, interviewing a former EBS network engineer. As we talked, his cell phone rang. He apologized and took the call. Within ten seconds his face had turned red, and I heard him say, "I'm with them right now. I'll call you back." After he hung up, he turned and said, "What a coincidence. That was Executive Y"—one of my targets.

When the agents were not traveling, they continued to dig through Enron documents and e-mail, looking for useful evidence. Every week they put one or two boxes of exhibits in my office, which I placed into binders and took on the road. At night, when I settled into my hotel room after a long day of interviews, I put on ESPN, got out the documents, and hunted for gems.

The most powerful items I reviewed were our targets' brokerage records. At the same time that Rice and Hannon were hyping Enron's telecommunications business, they and three of their senior executive colleagues dumped over $225 million worth of their inflated Enron shares on the open market. Rice's sales were typical. Between the January 2000 analyst conference and July 2001, when the business unit collapsed, he sold more than $53 million. These records made the case much more clear. If you are looking for a motive to lie about the company's success, I said to myself, there it is.

Our race with the defendants was exhausting. By the end I had caught a bad spell of bronchitis that took me almost a month to shake. The workload and lack of sleep also made me irritable and prone to argue. The defense attorneys on the case thought I was an insufferable jerk. Even the agents told me bluntly that I drove them crazy with my incessant demands. Our efforts, however, were incredibly successful. By the end of October we had identified over a dozen solid witnesses who told us that the Enron network was not "intelligent," that the much-hyped software never worked, and that the presentations Enron made to stock analysts were false. Some of them had discussed these facts directly with Ken Rice and other senior EBS executives. This was crucial, for it would help us prove that Enron's misrepresentations were intentional, not the result of sloppiness or ignorance.

BEING IN HOUSTON was not just good for the case; it was good for me personally. During the twenty years since 1983, when I left home to join the Marines, I had spent less than twenty days back at home. I had flown in for weddings and a few holidays, but my relationship with my parents seemed permanently damaged. When we met, our interactions were strained and artificial. I talked with my father about the weather, with my mother about books, but our conversations were brief, cold, and forced. Even time with my brothers and sisters was difficult. Being back at home made me uncomfortable, raising ghosts from my childhood that I preferred to keep repressed. I usually followed what I called the forty-eight-hour rule: never stay in Houston for more than two days.

Now, however, I was present in Houston for weeks on end, and slowly relations began to thaw. Though my two sisters had moved away, one to Chicago, the other to Boston, my three brothers still lived in our old neighborhood. All three were successful lawyers, married with kids, living in nice houses. Slowly, shyly, I started to drop in on them. Bill and I would go to a baseball game, Richard and I to dinner. Some nights we stayed up late, talking about our lives, our careers, and our childhoods. I saw my nephew Ben play basketball, my niece Rebecca Francis play soccer. I got to know my sisters-in-law. Soon it felt normal to see them. For the first time in my adult life I began to feel as if I had a family.

To my surprise, even things with my mother and father improved. My father is a history and public policy buff, constantly reading books about past and current events. Now we sat talking for hours, arguing about politics and the state of the world. We did not agree on much: my father thought the world economy was about to collapse, a financial panic just around the corner, and Chinese world domination inevitable, while I was much more optimistic about America's future prospects. Politically, we were worlds apart. My father thought Franklin Roosevelt a deceitful warmonger and Bill Clinton an incompetent cad. But strangely, these differences did not matter. After all these years we were talking.

———

THROUGHOUT THIS PERIOD the Broadband investigative team and I always kept our eyes on our major strategic goal, gathering as much evidence as possible against Ken Rice and Kevin Hannon, so they would flip against Jeff Skilling. Jamming up Hannon proved relatively easy. Though many Enron executives were incompetent, Hannon knew his job. When he joined EBS in the first quarter of 2000, at Skilling's request, he quickly realized the unit was a disorganized mess. To gain control over the business, Hannon created a weekly reporting system to track costs and revenue. These reports were called dashboards, because they displayed all the relevant financial data graphically, in charts, on one well-organized page. In the late fall we uncovered a complete set of these weekly dashboard reports, a priceless find. I admired Hannon's management talent. In a company full of con artists, he demanded concrete data. Alas, that data flow was his downfall, for it proved he knew the precise truth about EBS at the exact time that he, Rice, and Skilling were lying to Wall Street. The nail in the coffin was a detailed report by McKinsey & Company, the respected management consultants, that concluded that EBS was in almost hopeless condition. Hannon's lawyers told the Securities and Exchange Commission that Hannon got this report after the rosy January 25, 2001, analyst conference. I went back to check the dates, and I discovered that this was untrue. Hannon had received the report the week before. Hannon had been one of the primary architects of the 2001 conference. This proved he knew the whole presentation was false.

Strengthening our case against Rice was more challenging. Rice was potentially a very important witness, for he was not just a top Skilling subordinate but one of Skilling's closest friends and confidants. He was also, unfortunately, a notoriously sloppy manager, spending more time with his race cars than reviewing data and reports. This worried me, for I thought it gave him a good defense: "I had no idea what was going on;

I was too busy goofing off." To foil this ploy, we needed to find a smoking gun.

One of the most outrageous assertions made during the 2001 analyst conference was Skilling's claim that EBS, which was more or less worthless, was actually worth thirty-six billion dollars. Special Agents Jeff Jenson and Raju Bhatia dug through countless Enron e-mails trying to determine who had prepared this estimate. Ultimately they tracked it to a small team of EBS financial experts. When we interviewed these men, we heard a remarkable tale. Late in 2000 Rice had tasked them with calculating the value of the Broadband unit. They knew he wanted a highball figure, so they developed an econometric model that ultimately produced an inflated figure, something like eighteen billion dollars. Several members of this team told me that they thought this estimate was absurdly high, given EBS's lack of customers, but that was the Enron way. When they presented their analysis to Rice and Hannon, however, it did not go over well. Rice just shook his head. "Go back and make it higher. It has to be higher than last year."

The prior year, the team learned, Jeff Skilling had boasted to Wall Street that EBS was worth thirty billion dollars. There was no legitimate way to reach this high an estimate; EBS simply wasn't worth that much, even under the rosiest of scenarios. So the finance team simply decided to make things up. They took Skilling's thirty-billion-dollar number and lobbed on an extra 20 percent for good measure, producing a total of thirty-six billion dollars. Rice accepted this falsified figure and passed it on to Skilling—and to all of America's investors.

When we finished this series of interviews, I was ecstatic, for I knew this story put Rice in a wringer. It proved, in a very graphic manner, that Rice had not told investors the truth. He was guilty of securities fraud.

———

IN ALMOST EVERY SERIOUS SECURITIES FRAUD CASE, prosecutors find that the corrupt executives did not just make false statements to investors or analysts; they also manipulated the data on their corporation's financial reports. The reason for this should be obvious. You can boast all you want about your company's success, but if your financial statements do not show strong earnings, no one will believe you.

In the summer of 2002, at the start of our investigation, I began to look closely at EBS's financial data. The inspiration for this, as in other parts of the case, was Bill Collins, the Enron executive who first told us about the fraud. When, early in the case, I told Collins I was skeptical that things at EBS were as bad as he said, he told me, "The proof is in the pudding. If Enron really had the world's most advanced telecommunications network, they would have had paying customers lining up at the door. So check their deal flow."

I took his advice. When I studied Hannon's weekly dashboard business reports, I saw that Collins was right. In 2000 and 2001, EBS had virtually no paying customers. This was intriguing information, for when I looked at Enron's publicly filed financial statements, I saw that EBS reported at least fifty million dollars in new revenue per quarter. This raised an obvious question. If EBS had no customers, where did all its revenue come from? The answer was fraud.

In the spring of 2000, Enron executives realized that they would never generate enough legitimate revenue to substantiate their claim that the Enron Intelligent Network was up and running, so they began to look for shortcuts. In the end they used two illegal deals to plug their "earnings hole." The first was code-named Backbone. As part of its effort to build a network, EBS had acquired thousands of miles of unusable dark fiber—fiber-optic cable that had been strung along the ground but could not transmit any data because it was not attached to any network hardware, like routers or servers. If Enron could sell off some of this useless fiber, it could generate badly needed earnings. When, however, Enron went into the market, no one was interested in buying, for every telecommunications company had a similar glut of dark fiber on its hands. To fix this problem, Enron turned to the only potential buyer, itself. Andy Fastow, Enron's chief financial officer, created a special Wall Street–financed investment fund called LJM, named for his wife, Lea, and his two sons, Jeffrey and Matthew. In the summer of 2000, Fastow's LJM fund snapped up a huge quantity of Enron's dark fiber for a cool hundred million dollars. Enron in turn immediately reported this revenue on its publicly disclosed financial statements.

When I first began to examine the Backbone deal, I knew Fastow was involved in some pretty sharp practices, but I was still perplexed. Why, I wondered, would Fastow buy a close to worthless asset from his own company? I got my answer on August 30, 2002, when I interviewed Chris Loehr. Loehr was only twenty-four when he went to work for Enron in 1999. His job was to do Fastow's administrative scut work. That day, as we sat in the task force's Washington conference room, Loehr told me, "Backbone was crooked from start to finish. EBS needed revenue, and so LJM bought a hundred million dollars' worth of dark fiber. But LJM wasn't really buying this stuff. Enron promised Fastow that the deal would be temporary. As soon as Enron could afford to, the deals would be unwound. Enron would buy the fiber back from LJM, or arrange for someone else to do so, at a guaranteed higher price, one that ensured LJM would receive a huge profit. In the end everyone was happy. Enron reported a hundred million dollars in EBS revenue on its financial statements, LJM investors got a risk-free return, and Fastow pocketed a fortune in transactions fees." No one got the shaft but Enron's investors, who believed Enron's financial statements were accurate.

Years later Ken Rice, the Broadband CEO, called Backbone and similar frauds crack cocaine. The deals generated massive amounts of reportable revenue, but the pleasure was short-lived. The quarter after Backbone was completed, EBS found itself in the same jam, with no customers and no reportable revenue. The solution of course was more fraud.

IN 2000, EBS and Blockbuster, the video and DVD rental chain, entered a long-term contract to develop a home video on demand business. Blockbuster would go to Hollywood studios and get the right to broadcast top movies over the Internet. Enron would then transmit these movies to home consumers over its advanced intelligent network. When the deal was announced, analysts predicted that Enron would make a fortune. In truth the plan hit the skids almost immediately. Blockbuster failed to obtain quality movie rights from the studios, leaving Enron trying to market films like *The Care Bears* and *Black Mama, White Mama*. Enron in turn was never able to develop a cost-effective way to deliver these films to its customers' television sets, for of course its own high-tech network did not work. Ultimately Enron jury-rigged a special video delivery network, but it cost a fortune and was never hooked up to more than a thousand homes. Even then, it worked really poorly. The set-top boxes, for instance, tended to catch on fire. As a result, the whole Blockbuster project never generated more than a couple of thousand dollars in income. According to Bethany McLean and Peter Elkind, two reporters for *Fortune* magazine, one sardonic Enron executive handed project manager David Cox a five-dollar bill and said, "I just doubled your revenue."

The Blockbuster deal was a flop, but at Enron even failures were expected to generate reportable revenue. The result was Project Braveheart, a complex deal orchestrated by an executive I will call "Steve Woolf." The Braveheart transaction was designed to get around the accounting rules applicable to contracts like the one with Blockbuster. Under those rules, Enron was not allowed to "recognize" revenue from the contract—report it to investors—until the cash actually arrived at its door. That was a problem, since the Blockbuster deal did not actually generate any earnings. Woolf realized, however, that if the contract was owned by a joint venture, a new business owned and controlled by both Enron and another company, then the new business itself could be sold, and that revenue reported immediately. This left him with two hurdles: he needed to find one company that was willing to create a joint venture with Enron and a second that was willing to buy it.

Woolf was not daunted. First, he convinced nCube, a small Oregon video technology company, to join his new venture, called EBS Content Systems LLC. Then he "assigned" the Blockbuster contract to the joint venture, so that the new company had a plausible source of revenue. Finally, he sold Content Systems' "future revenue" to the Canadian Imperial Bank of Commerce (CIBC) for $110 million. This $110 million was reported as revenue on Enron's financial statements in the fourth quarter of 2000 and the first quarter of 2001, making EBS look as if it were generating substantial new business. Steve Woolf was an Enron hero, rewarded with a $350,000 bonus.

Braveheart looked extremely fishy, so FBI agents Jenson and Bhatia put the deal under a microscope. Together, the three of us interviewed witnesses from nCube, CIBC, and Arthur Andersen, examined complex transaction documents, and found and read hundreds of e-mails. Soon we concluded that EBS had broken the law.

One problem related to the joint venture, EBS Content Systems

LLC. Under the accounting rules, this company had to be a real, long-term business. We discovered, however, that it was a shell, a mere box on a piece of paper, created for the sole purpose of avoiding the accounting rules for contracts. It had no office and no employees. Moreover, nCube was not a true partner. Enron had simply asked it to lend its company name to the deal for a few months—long enough for Enron to record its $110 million in revenue—in return for a fixed, guaranteed fee of $100,000. This guarantee violated all the applicable accounting rules, so Woolf and his team never disclosed it to Arthur Andersen, their auditor. They kept it secret, and that is accounting fraud.

The second step of the deal was equally sketchy. Banks are in the business of lending, not buying, so why would a Canadian bank buy the potential revenue from a highly speculative video business? The answer, once again, was fraud. Enron secretly told the bank that no matter what happened, Enron would ensure that the bank got its money back plus interest, whether the video business made any money in the future or not. The bank agreed, because from its perspective, the deal was not really a sale at all but a loan: it gave Enron $110 million, and Enron agreed to pay the money back with interest. Indeed, the bank even booked the deal as a loan on its own financial statements. Enron, however, treated the loan as an asset sale and reported the proceeds as revenue. Once again, the true structure of the deal was hidden from Andersen's auditors.

To us, this looked illegal.* Unfortunately, I thought that would be very hard to prove. The documentary evidence was damning, but only if you understood accounting and had the skill and patience needed to read highly complex business records. Most juries, I thought, would find this impossible. To win, we needed a live witness, an Enron insider who could explain the transaction in ordinary language and tell the jury why it was a crime.

Steve Woolf worked closely with four subordinates on the Braveheart deal. That gave us four shots to get the witness we needed. Given those odds, I was confident I could get several people to tell the truth. Af-

---

*CIBC routinely did deals like Braveheart with Enron because they were highly profitable—at least until Enron went bankrupt and defaulted. CIBC was ultimately sued by defrauded Enron investors for its role in the Enron collapse. The bank settled for a whopping $2.4 billion—without admitting any wrongdoing!

ter all, my interviews with Enron's network and software engineers had gone extremely well. Alas, this calculation turned out to be wrong. The engineers I had debriefed were not really Enron types but telecom industry veterans hired away from companies like GE and ATT, with very different corporate cultures. The team that worked on Braveheart, in contrast, was composed of classic Enron products, young graduates of prestigious business and accounting programs, steeped in Enron "values," reporting to Andy Fastow. These guys turned out to be much more tricky customers.

Our first witness, "Bob," was a handsome, dark-haired guy in his late twenties. After Enron had collapsed, he moved on to another good job. At his request, we met in the Admirals Club, a frequent flier business lounge at a major international airport. We sat in leather chairs around a polished wooden table. Every few minutes airline employees would enter to top off our coffee.

I asked Bob about the secret guarantees Enron made to nCube. Bob looked troubled, then vehemently denied that any had been made. "That would have blown the accounting. We all knew that. We would never have done that." In response, I opened one of my black binders and removed five or six different documents Bob had written or received while at Enron. All the documents mentioned the secret guarantees. My witness grew pale and stuttered, but he was not able to come up with a coherent explanation. "I guess we made these guarantees, but I don't remember them. I don't understand it." No matter how hard we tried, Jeff, Raju, and I could not get anything else out of him. We tried every tactic we knew: confronting him with documents, joking with him, threatening, warning, good cop/bad cop. Eventually we gave up. Bob was clearly not our witness.

Our next interview was with "Dave," whom we met at the FBI office in Houston. At the beginning I told Dave and his lawyer that if he had violated the law in the Braveheart deal, we would immunize him from prosecution as long as he told the truth. In Brooklyn my word was respected, but Dave's lawyers did not know me, and I do not think they believed me. For most of the interview Dave was tense but composed, and I thought he was telling me the truth. When, however, I asked about the secret agreement with nCube, the whole tenor of the discussion changed. Sweating heavily—he knew this was the crux of the issue—

Dave told me he was not aware of any guarantees or promises. As he talked, I looked closely at his hands. A few moments before, they had been flat on the table. Now they were shaking badly. Strike two.

My third interview took place at a defense lawyer's office in a major midwestern city. After a little prodding, "Sharon" told me that Enron had violated the relevant accounting rules. Jeff, Raju, and I were elated, but our joy was short-lived. Two weeks later, when I met with Sharon in Houston to prepare her grand jury testimony, she reversed course. Maybe there were guarantees, she said; she really did not know; she was confused; she had played only a small part in the deal. Her defense lawyer then intervened. "Last time you surprised us with your questions. We were not ready, not prepared to answer. I feel you tricked us. We are willing to answer questions, but only after you turn over all your documents to us first."

When the defense attorney alleged that I had tricked his client— apparently by asking her to tell the truth—I almost exploded. I got up abruptly and walked straight out of the room. During my prior years as a prosecutor I was never judgmental about my defendants, even the mobsters. I understood why they became criminals and why they might lie in proffers. I even liked some of them. But to me, these Enron folks were different. They seemed privileged, dishonest, and unethical, smart enough to game the legal system and sleazy enough to do it. Some of them were lying to avoid indictment. Others had good jobs and worried that if they told me the truth, they might have to testify at a well-publicized trial, which might damage their careers. I found their behavior very disturbing, for it seemed as if they had learned nothing from Enron's collapse. I walked around the FBI office for five minutes, trying to calm down and regain my equilibrium. Then I picked up Jeff Jenson's telephone and called the attorney for a woman named Luitgard Fischer.

LUITGARD "LOUIE" FISCHER had been Steve Woolf's primary deputy on the Braveheart deal, one of the persons, I believed, most responsible for the fraud. I had not contacted her earlier because I thought I might want to indict her. Now, however, I was running out of options. I told her lawyer there might be a chance for Louie to cooperate but that the door was closing fast. He invited me to meet her the next morning.

I told him, "She may have to take a plea. She was in this deal up to her elbows."

He responded, "Before you make any charging decisions, wait till you hear her story."

The next morning Raju, Jeff, and I drove to a sleek glass office tower in downtown Houston. We first met briefly with Fischer's attorney and signed a proffer agreement. Then he left us alone with his client in a conference room, a bold way to signal that she had nothing to hide. Louie was a fashion plate in her late twenties or early thirties. She wore a stylish black pinstripe suit, expensive black leather shoes with high, clunky heels, and a pair of funky, heavy-framed glasses. Born in Germany, she spoke with a breathy Continental accent. Our interview began bizarrely. "Professor Kroger," she said, "I've read all about you on the Internet, and I've seen your law review articles. I hear you are very smart. I've been waiting for you to contact me. I've wanted to tell the truth about this deal for months."

I was totally surprised by this opening salvo. No one calls me Professor, even at my own law school, and I had never been researched by my own targets before. I have to say, it felt creepy. But I was pleased by her offer to tell the truth, a commodity in short supply. To prevent any more bizarre personal comments, I started to ask Louie questions. The result was equally odd, the most rapid confession I have ever heard.*

"Did you work on the Braveheart transaction?"

"Yes."

"Was it legitimate, or a fraud?"

"It was fraudulent."

"What made it fraudulent?"

"Oh, it was fraudulent in five or six ways."

"Like what?"

"The joint venture was not a real joint venture. We never shared control with nCube. They were not a long-term partner. The business was not worth one hundred ten million dollars. The nCube equity was never at risk. We lied to Arthur Andersen. The money should never have been reported as income."

---

*One possible competitor: in 2001, mafia killer Frankie Smith admitted four or five murders in the first thirty minutes of a first proffer with AUSA Patricia Notopoulos and me.

"Did you know what you were doing was wrong?"

"Yes, I knew it violated the accounting rules."

"Who else knew?"

"Steve Woolf, several others."

This whole exchange took less than three minutes. By the time it was over, I had to fight hard to keep from grinning. The agents continued the debriefing, asking more detailed questions, but I barely paid attention. I had heard all I needed to know. We had our witness.

Fischer's bold strategy worked in her favor. Later that week I agreed to write her a nonprosecution agreement, immunizing her for any crimes she might have committed at Enron. Defense lawyers would claim that my decision was disgusting, that I rewarded a criminal with a sweetheart deal because she told me what I wanted to hear. I viewed it differently. I trusted Fischer, and I believed her, for her claims were backed up by the documents. I wanted to send a signal to other potential Enron witnesses. We are not engaged in a witch hunt, nor are we interested in prosecuting low-level executives. It might be a paradox, but the best way to stay out of jail is to admit everything you did. If you take responsibility for your actions and tell us the truth, instead of giving us the stonewall, you will be rewarded.

———

WHEN WE TALKED to former EBS employees, they rarely mentioned Enron's chairman, Ken Lay. He was, we gradually realized, completely uninvolved with Broadband's day-to-day operations. In contrast, Jeff Skilling came up all the time. Skilling, we were told, had pushed Enron into the telecommunications industry in the first place because he wanted some "dot-com sizzle" in Enron's stock price. He was also a micromanager, closely monitoring EBS's progress. It quickly became apparent that if we played our cards right, we might develop a good case against Skilling for lying about the Broadband debacle, even without help from Rice and Hannon. Once we completed the Braveheart investigation, Jeff and Raju shifted their attention to Skilling. They quickly found a smoking gun.

In the first three months of 2001, Enron's stock price had dropped precipitously from the high eighties to fifty-nine dollars. One reason for the decline was a rumor on Wall Street—an accurate one, it turned out—that Enron's ballyhooed Broadband business was failing. To stanch the bleeding, Skilling scheduled a conference call with all the major Wall Street analysts on March 23, 2001. During the call, which Enron tape-recorded, Skilling flatly declared that all the rumors were false. Enron, he said, was "having a great quarter" selling bandwidth capacity and had "an enormous lead over other players" in the industry. Indeed, everything was great, "ahead of plan," "very positive." Skilling denied there were any layoffs at EBS whatsoever. Enron was, he stated, just moving people around within the unit. He insisted that EBS was "coming along fine. In fact, I'm pretty optimistic about it." Skilling deflected every skeptical question, insisting the company was doing fine.*

Examined in isolation, the March 23 tape was meaningless, for it did not prove Skilling was a crook. Perhaps, I thought, Skilling honestly believed his own spin. Or maybe Rice and Hannon were lying to Skilling to cover up their own failure. In January 2003, however, we learned these scenarios were impossible, for we found incontrovertible evidence that proved Skilling had lied.

When we interviewed witnesses who worked in EBS's Portland, Oregon, office, several of them told us that in the early spring of 2001, Skilling and Rice had come to Portland to announce a round of layoffs. Miraculously, the meeting had been videotaped, and Jeff and Raju found the tape, buried in an Enron video archive. When we first played the tape at our task force office in Houston, I almost fell out of my chair. The Portland layoff meeting had been held on March 15, only eight days before Skilling's optimistic conference call with Wall Street. At the start, Ken Rice announced that EBS's business was in an "absolute meltdown," with much lower revenues than projected. Skilling then leaped in. He told his employees that "the whole revenue opportunity that we saw in this marketplace is gone or it's shrunk significantly." He continued. "The revenues are gone. I mean, it . . . it's . . . it's . . . it's bad . . . I mean, it . . . it's a bad situation." Skilling then informed the stunned employees, in direct contradiction to his statements to Wall Street, that 240 jobs were being cut. The huge gap between Skilling's negative internal assessment and the glowing report he gave to investors just eight days later was clear

---

*Three months later Skilling showed how he would respond when pressed. When one analyst on a conference call expressed reservations about Enron's financial position, Skilling publicly called him an asshole.

proof that he was a crook, willing to lie to pump up the Enron stock price. When we screened the tape for Leslie Caldwell, she almost purred with pleasure.

BY JANUARY 2003, the Broadband team had developed good evidence against eight Enron executives, including Skilling, Rice, Hannon, and Woolf. In an ordinary criminal case, involving drugs or violence, we would have moved directly to the charging phase, analyzing our evidence, deciding whom we were going to indict, and then putting our targets under arrest. By tradition, however, the department acts very differently in white-collar cases. Instead of swooping in on our surprised defendants, we first send target letters to all those we think we might indict, to give them notice of the impending charges. Then we give their attorneys—and the putative defendants themselves, if they wish—an opportunity to come in, meet with us, and try to persuade us not to indict. This provides white-collar criminals two big advantages other defendants do not get: a chance to head off a case privately before the defendants are publicly charged and the ability to prepare themselves and their families, financially and emotionally, for the consequences of arrest.

When I was a mafia and drug prosecutor, the fact that white collar defendants got special treatment always bugged me. In the American criminal justice system, rich people already have immense advantages, for they can afford to pay for an aggressive, resource-intensive investigation and defense, an option poor defendants—even those who win the "legal aid lottery" and are represented by excellent public defenders— simply do not have. The fact that money affects the quality of justice is undeniable. Why make things worse by giving wealthy people additional procedural advantages as well?

When I joined the Enron team, I complained about this practice to Leslie Caldwell. To her credit, she took time to explain why it exists. White-collar cases, she told me, are often incredibly complex, and this complexity boosts the odds that even the most careful prosecutor will make an error. In the Enron case, for example, the evidence included ten million documents. We did not have the time or resources to review all this evidence, and thus there was a real risk that we might overlook important exculpatory material, something that showed a defendant was not guilty. The defendants, in contrast, often know the documentary record better than the government, because they have inside scoop, from their time working for the target company. As a result, they may possess information we desperately need in order to make a wise and just charging decision. To encourage them to share their knowledge instead of hoarding it until trial, we give them a chance to block an indictment up front.

On January 6, 2003, Leslie and I sat down with Bruce Hiler, attorney for our top target, Jeff Skilling. Because our own Enron Task Force conference room was small and unimpressive, with blank white walls and a stained carpet, we borrowed one from another DOJ division with a highly polished wooden conference table and paneled walls. Hiler was one of the most respected members of the Washington securities bar, a former top lawyer at the Securities and Exchange Commission. He wore a beautiful, well-cut dark gray wool suit, a pale blue shirt with white French collar and cuffs, and what I guessed was a Hermès tie. His hair was well coiffed and heavily sprayed, with no strands out of place. I recall manicured nails, but that could be my imagination. Of course Hiler could afford to look rich. At this point Skilling had already set aside more than twenty million dollars for his defense.

When the meeting began, I was very anxious. In Brooklyn I faced some good lawyers, but guys like Hiler were, I thought, in another category altogether. They could charge millions for their work because they were the smartest lawyers in the world. I half expected Hiler to whip out some bombshell piece of evidence that would transform the case and make me look like a fool. This concern dissipated almost immediately. Hiler talked for ninety minutes, but his whole message could be boiled down to one sentence: "Jeff believed everything he said." Later that night I recorded in my diary: "They don't know anything we don't know. They've got no hidden secret weapon. Their presentation ignored basic, incontrovertible facts. So we have, at worst, a triable case."

Over the next two months I met with many more defense teams. A couple presented a version of the Skilling defense. "Everything my client said was accurate, and even if it wasn't, he had no reason to think his statements were false." The rest tried out variations. One defense attorney told me, "Our client did nothing wrong, but if you decided not to prosecute, he could be a good witness for you." Another said, "John, gentlemen settle these things civilly, with a fine." He did not mean that I should be more polite, though that was probably in the back of his mind, but that I should let him deal exclusively with the SEC. A third said: "Look, everyone in Silicon Valley was lying about their technical capabilities." Only one guy was really creative: "My client is an engineer, and engineers talk differently than ordinary people. So when he said that Enron 'had' software that 'possessed' certain capabilities, what he meant was that Enron 'would have software in the future' and that it 'would have those capabilities.'" I almost laughed out loud. Joe Ford, the lead FBI supervisor on the whole Enron case, interrupted that proffer, incredulous. "Are you telling me that engineers don't know the difference between the present and the future tense?" Only one attorney really impressed me: Bill Dolan, an experienced and gracious old hand who represented Ken Rice. Dolan did not try to bullshit or spin. Nor did he suggest that if the price were right, his client would rat out the rest of the pack. Instead, he kept things simple: "We are still trying to learn the case. We hope to keep in close contact with you. If there are any important developments coming down the pike, please let us know."

In the end nothing the defense attorneys told us had much impact; they batted zero for eight. This failure was due in part to the strength of our case; the defense attorneys appeared to have no exculpatory evidence to present. But it was also a failure of technique. I was outraged about what happened at Enron, and I was convinced that the defendants had broken the law. Thus the "we did nothing wrong" speech left me totally exasperated. Indeed, it made me even more likely to dig in my heels, for it seemed to me that none of the defendants had learned a single lesson from Enron's demise—or any humility, for that matter. If, in contrast, a defendant had been willing to admit some wrongdoing, to take some responsibility, I would probably have been more conciliatory. I might even have offered immunity, as I did with Louie Fischer. But no one did, so the point was moot.

Why, you might wonder, were the best attorneys in the world so tone-deaf? In some cases, their clients probably insisted that they not give up an inch. As I noted earlier, lots of attorneys agree to take a tough position even though it is counterproductive, because it solidifies the relationship between them and their rich, fee-paying clients. But I think another dynamic was at work as well.

If you want to negotiate with a prosecutor, it helps if your lawyer is a former prosecutor as well, who knows how the government thinks. That is one reason smart executives in real trouble hire legendary former U.S. Attorneys like Bob Fiske (or Mary Jo White, who resigned from the Justice Department in 2002 and is now in private practice) to defend them. In the Enron case, in contrast, many of the lead attorneys at this stage—Hiler, for example—were not criminal defense lawyers at all, let alone former AUSAs, but experts in civil securities fraud. These lawyers spent most of their careers beating up the hapless SEC, denying all wrongdoing, stonewalling, delaying, and then walking away with small fines. They thought the same thing would happen here. Instead, they walked into a buzz saw. We were not just prosecutors but former gang and mafia prosecutors, convinced that DOJ had gone too easy on white-collar defendants in the past. When these attorneys used their standard tactics, they backfired.

ONCE WE COMPLETED OUR MEETINGS with defense attorneys, it was time to make charging decisions. By this time in my career I had indicted and put in jail some two hundred defendants, so I brought significant experience to this task. Still, I was very anxious about my own potential bias. In a case like Broadband, involving a long and challenging investigation, the investigators (both agents and prosecutors alike) are often so invested in building their case that they lose objectivity, and that can result in reckless or baseless indictments. To help combat that possibility, I requested that Leslie assign a second prosecutor to the case. To my delight, Leslie proposed the EDNY's Ben Campbell, my former boss on the 9/11 investigation. Ben looked like the young Ron Howard, with red hair, freckles, and a boyish smile. At first people called him Opie. After, however, he had won some major trials, his nickname got modified. Now agents called him the killer Opie. Over the course of his career Ben had supervised hundreds of prosecutors and reviewed thousands of indictments. He was moderate, cautious, and deliberate, the perfect complement to my own more impetuous style.

Together, Ben and I discussed the evidence with the Broadband agents until we all reached a consensus. Then we reviewed our recommendations with Leslie, to make sure they made sense. Ultimately, we agreed to seek indictments against seven EBS executives: our two major targets, Ken Rice and Kevin Hannon, for lying to investors about Broadband's technology, customer base, and finances; Steve Woolf and an Enron accountant for the notorious Braveheart deal; and three other senior executives for planning the deceptive 2000 analyst conference and then selling their pumped-up stock. We decided not to indict about a half dozen additional men and women because their crimes were minor or our proof was too weak.

The biggest question was: What do we do with Skilling? Everyone on the Broadband team wanted to indict him for lying to Wall Street about EBS. We had a sound reason for this. Typically, it is easier to flip your targets if a bigger fish, whom they can cooperate against, is already under indictment. Thus we thought indicting Skilling might help us recruit other targets to the witness table. But to be honest, our desire was mostly about ego. We were proud that the Broadband team had put together the first viable criminal case against Enron's CEO, and we wanted to make that fact public. When, however, I discussed a possible indictment with Leslie, she wisely shot me down.

"Look, you have great ammunition, but the case is half baked. Skilling was CEO of the whole company. We can't indict him just for lying about one business unit. We need to give a jury the big picture. Your investigation is way out in front. It's going to take another six months or a year before we really know what he was doing with EES, with Wholesale, with LJM, and with the international assets. Be patient. We'll get there eventually." This advice was obviously correct, and we set Skilling aside. His time had not yet come.

On May 1, 2003, Ben and I presented a proposed indictment to the grand jury charging our seven EBS targets with 221 counts of fraud, insider trading, and money laundering. After the grand jury had voted in favor, we retired to the courthouse steps for a televised press conference. I hate press conferences—to be honest, I think prosecutors should try to avoid the media, even in big cases—so I frowned into the camera. That afternoon a friend called. "Kroger, I saw you live on CNN. You looked fierce." Later I saw the same clip. I think I looked mean.

That afternoon all the prosecutors and agents on the case met upstairs in our courtroom office. The atmosphere in the room was festive.

Though a charge is only an accusation, the beginning of a case, not the end, we all thought we had passed a milestone. The Enron debacle had been hard to investigate, and we were moving more slowly than we initially anticipated. It felt good, as one agent put it, to "finally have something up on the board."

CHAPTER EIGHTEEN

Getting Away with Fraud

W
hen I joined the Enron Task Force and began to debrief Enron witnesses, I was shocked by the degree of
corruption we uncovered. At first, I thought Enron
must be unique. Over the course of 2002, however,
we learned that Enron was not an aberration. At the same time Enron
was filing false financial statements, other huge corporations like Tyco,
WorldCom, Qwest, Adelphia, and HealthSouth were engaged in similar
schemes designed to pump up their stock prices. As Enron defense
lawyers constantly told me during our investigation, "We were just doing
what everyone else was doing."

How is this possible? I remember asking myself. How can America's
largest corporations get away with such extensive lies for years? As I investigated the Broadband case, I tried to answer this question. It was not
essential to my criminal case. I simply wanted to understand how America really works. In the end, I reached some chilling conclusions.

THE STOCK MARKET is an essential tool of our economy. To thrive in a
competitive marketplace, companies need constant access to capital to
pay for research, development, worker training, new equipment, and
other strategic investments. For the economy to work efficiently, producing the maximum amount of new jobs and societal wealth, this capital must to flow toward the most innovative and valuable companies,
not to poorly managed ones offering worthless products or services. To
achieve this efficient allocation of resources, we allow corporations to

compete for our money. All publicly held companies report facts about their financial condition and business performance to the SEC, and then investors back the ones that sound like winners.

The stakes in this competition are huge. If a company reports that it is struggling, the price it must pay to raise necessary capital will go up, making success even harder to achieve. If the bad reports continue, funding will dry up altogether, resulting in bankruptcy. To avoid this calamity, some executives cheat by hiding their companies' flaws. That is what happened at Enron.

There is no simple solution to the problem of securities fraud, no easy way to manipulate the social and economic playing field to reduce the threat. This makes it very different from problems like drug trafficking or organized crime. Dangerous drugs like heroin or methamphetamine have no useful social purpose. If we drastically reduce the demand for these drugs, through tough enforcement and a national drug treatment program, there will be no downside. In contrast, heavy-handed regulation to reshape the securities market, the kind of regulation that might reduce fraud, would hurt the nation more than help.

One certain way to decrease radically the amount of fraud, for example, would be to prohibit companies from releasing any financial information that had not been reviewed and authenticated first by on-site government auditors. This would improve the accuracy of available financial data but at an unacceptable price. The free market for capital, the engine that powers our economy, cannot work properly unless investors have access to massive amounts of timely information. If regulators delay or reduce the volume of available information, through imposition of stringent government requirements, investment decisions will suffer and capital will flow arbitrarily, causing serious economic harm: lost jobs, decreased competitiveness, and decreased national wealth. It would also create a brand-new criminal problem, an illegal black market for timely corporate financial data. The solution, in short, would be worse than the problem it was designed to address.

Attempting to improve corporate ethics is probably hopeless as well. Business schools should provide more ethics training, and Congress should require senior officers of publicly traded companies to take ethics refresher courses, but I doubt this will reduce the incidence of fraud. The reason is simple: moral self-selection. In the United States, people are free to choose whatever careers they want. Those who care little about money become soldiers, teachers, artists, and librarians. Those who desire personal wealth are drawn to business. As a result, our large corporations are staffed almost entirely by people who are more vulnerable to the lure of money, and potentially more at risk of committing fraud to achieve it, than ordinary Americans.

In October 2002, Jeff, Raju, and I interviewed "Charles," a young former Enron executive who had worked on an illegal transaction. At first Charles denied that Enron had violated any accounting principles. Eventually, however, he grudgingly conceded that yes, "in retrospect," Enron's financial reporting was not accurate. Still, we could not get him to admit that this was wrong, either legally or morally. The gap between his ethical understanding and ours was simply too immense. Instead, he kept insisting, "This was cutting-edge stuff." Raju was so disgusted he walked out of the meeting.

After Enron's collapse, Charles jumped straight to another large company, and he is now busy, I presume, climbing this new corporate ladder. Enron's collapse did not affect him one whit, personally, financially, or professionally. His moral blinders remain firmly in place.

After our meeting I thought about Charles's background, and I recalled that he had attended elite Jesuit institutions for both college and business school. As a result, he had been forced to take several serious, comprehensive courses on ethics, for training in moral theory is a basic (and commendable) element of Jesuit education. This fact still makes me shake my head. If six years of Jesuit education cannot produce more honest business executives, nothing will.

To me, Charles was the representative Enron employee. He was not a bad person, but his moral compass was weak. The fact that he wound up at Enron was not an accident, for he was attracted to Enron's "get rich quick" culture precisely because his ethical sensibilities were limited. Companies like Enron are a honeypot for the ethically challenged, and I do not see how we can change that. Indeed, I'm not sure we want to. When people create valuable new products or new services in order to get rich, we all benefit, with new jobs, a more vibrant economy, and a deeper tax base. Greed may not be inherently good, but it does have its uses.

In the end, we are stuck with the risk of fraud, for it is hardwired into the free market economy. All we can do is try to limit its frequency and impact, through early detection and swift, proportionate punishment.

IN THE UNITED STATES we rely on five institutional players to detect and punish fraud: independent auditors, boards of directors, Wall Street stock analysts, the SEC, and federal prosecutors. These five groups provide our primary line of defense. If they fail, fraud will flourish. Unfortunately, all five are seriously flawed. If you want to know why Enron and other companies could get away with fraud for years without being caught, the answer is simple: our watchdogs failed to do their jobs.

TO HELP ENSURE that corporations report accurate information to the SEC, federal securities law requires that their financial statements be audited by independent certified public accountants. The auditor examines the corporation's books and determines if the financial reports have been prepared in compliance with all relevant accounting rules. The auditor then issues an opinion on whether the financial statement fairly presents the financial position and operations of the corporation.

Auditors hold a position of unique responsibility. As the Supreme Court has explained:

> By certifying the public reports that collectively depict a corporation's financial status, the independent auditor assumes a public responsibility transcending any employment relationship with the client. The independent public accountant performing this special function owes ultimate allegiance to the corporation's creditors and stockholders, as well as to the investing public. This "public watchdog" function demands that the accountant maintain total independence from the client at all times and requires complete fidelity to the public trust.

Enron of course employed the now-defunct Arthur Andersen accounting firm to perform this vital function. If Andersen had done its job properly, Enron would never have been able to deceive the investing public. Unfortunately, Andersen failed. Enron's financial statements were completely misleading, but Andersen approved them year after year without qualification. It did this at times because of deception: in deals like Braveheart, Enron executives lied to their auditor just as they lied to everyone else. But Andersen was hardly blameless. Neil Batson, the court-appointed Enron bankruptcy examiner, closely scrutinized Andersen's role in Enron's demise. Batson concluded that Andersen auditors gave "substantial assistance" to Enron's crooked executives. They helped design some of Enron's most egregious accounting manipulation schemes, failed to bring unusual transactions and controversial accounting decisions to the attention of its board of directors, and did not insist on disclosure of the real facts about the company to investors and the SEC, even though they knew that the financial statements were fabrications. In sum, Andersen's failure was comprehensive and decisive.*

Why would a respected firm like Arthur Andersen help a client commit fraud? Not surprisingly, part of the answer is greed. In the late 1990s competition was tough in the accounting business, and Arthur Andersen was struggling. Of the Big Five accounting firms, Andersen had the smallest auditing business and slowest rate of growth. It had also lost its lucrative business consulting practice, which had spun off from the parent company and become independent. This competitive decline hit each Andersen partner directly in the pocketbook. As a result, Andersen was desperate to keep their fee-paying clients happy, even if its clients wanted to cook the books. Barbara Ley Toffler was a former professor at the Harvard and Columbia business schools who worked at Andersen from 1995 to 1999. When Andersen began to struggle, Toffler later wrote, clients became "too valuable to defy." As a result, Andersen was transformed into "a place where the mad scramble for fees had trumped good judgment."

Enron was Andersen's largest client in 1999, paying more than fifty-two million dollars in auditing and consulting fees, and this clearly affected the way Andersen audited Enron's books. Consider the case of Carl Bass. An Andersen partner and a member of its elite Professional

---

*Andersen's poor performance at Enron was not an aberration. Andersen was also the auditor for Waste Management, the trash conglomerate, which improperly inflated its earnings by $1 billion, and McKesson HBOC (earnings inflated by $300 million), Qwest (earnings inflated by $1.2 billion), and WorldCom (earnings inflated by $9 billion). This pattern suggests that Andersen's failures in the Enron case were not the action of one or two rogue auditors, but the result of a pervasive firm culture that placed management's interest in positive financial reports and its own interest in large auditing fees before the investors' interest in accuracy.

Standards Group, Bass opposed Enron's proposed accounting treatment of a controversial scheme called the Raptors, which transformed one billion dollars in losses into a billion dollars in apparent gains. Bass's judgment was right—the Raptors transactions were criminal—but that did not matter. When Enron complained to Andersen headquarters about Bass's "temperament," Andersen removed him from the Enron audit, and the deceptive Raptors scheme sailed through unchallenged.

Andersen also cheated because it thought the potential costs of doing so were low. In the past, auditors played by the rules because they feared being sued by angry investors. In 1994, however, in a landmark case called *Central Bank of Denver v. First Interstate Bank of Denver*, the Supreme Court reversed long-standing practice and precedent in eleven federal circuits and held that auditors could not be sued in private lawsuits for aiding and abetting—assisting—securities fraud.* Congress made things worse. In 1995, after extensive lobbying by the accounting profession, Congress passed (over President Clinton's wise veto) the Private Securities Litigation Reform Act, which made it much harder for investors to sue crooked companies and their professional advisers. Together, these actions by Congress and the Supreme Court provided accountants with virtual immunity from investors' lawsuits. As a result, Andersen knew there was very little risk that it would be held accountable for its corrupt actions.

THE AMERICAN PUBLIC generally thinks of the chief executive officer as the ultimate authority within a corporation, but in truth the law imposes this duty on the corporation's board of directors. Corporate boards of major companies like Enron are composed primarily of senior business leaders. They are charged with monitoring the company's performance on behalf of its investors. They are supposed as part of this duty to help detect and disclose fraud. In practice, however, that rarely happens. In the Enron case, for example, the directors were out of touch.

---

*The *Central Bank* case was part of a clear historical trend. Though the Rehnquist Court was generally hostile to the rights of criminal defendants, it worked hard to protect big corporations and white-collar criminals by interpreting federal fraud statutes as narrowly as possible. This provoked Justice Stevens to question in one case "why a Court that has not been particularly receptive to the rights of criminal defendants in recent years has acted so dramatically to protect the elite class of powerful individuals who will benefit from this decision." *McNally v. United States*, 483 U.S. 350, 376 (1987) (Stevens, J., dissenting).

They had no idea that the company's financial statements were fraudulent and made little effort to find out.

Consider the LJM affair. In 1997, Enron CFO Andy Fastow decided to create his own personal investment company to buy assets from Enron in shady deals like Backbone. His proposal should have set off alarm bells. It involved a massive conflict of interest, for Fastow was seeking to profit personally by making sharp deals with his own parent company. It was also bizarre. Why would Enron need to do deals with its own CFO?

The LJM proposal violated Enron's code of ethics, which prohibited "self-dealing" between the corporation and key insiders, so Skilling and Fastow were required to present the idea to Enron's board of directors. The board should have rejected the idea immediately. As one Arthur Andersen partner commented in a 1999 e-mail, "Why would any director in his or her right mind ever approve such a scheme?" Failing blanket rejection, the board should have given the idea careful scrutiny. Had it done so, it might have discovered that Fastow's motives, to doctor Enron's financial statements and enrich himself at the shareholder's expense, were criminal.* Unfortunately, the board simply rubber-stamped the proposal without trying to understand it.

Why did Enron's board fail so completely? Some commentators have suggested that it was particularly incompetent, a collection of Ken Lay cronies more interested in picking up fat checks and flying to exotic locales than looking out for investors. There is a grain of truth to this view. Each director received approximately $350,000 per year for their very limited service, and they all did, in fact, fly for some board meetings to nice resorts, where they dined on delicacies and drank expensive wine. But this conclusion overstates the case against the Enron board and, paradoxically, understates the ultimate significance of the problem. In truth the Enron board failed not because it was incompetent but because of a broader, more systemic problem: even good boards are bad at catching fraud.

---

*Because its diversification strategy was failing, Enron possessed numerous worthless or underperforming assets. It wanted to sell these assets, to cut its losses, but if it sold them on the open market, the company would take huge losses and be forced to admit that the diversification strategy was failing. To get around this problem, Enron sold these assets to Fastow's LJM investment firm. In return for buying borderline worthless assets, Fastow received roughly thirty million dollars in fees. Enron also promised that it would eventually buy back every single asset at an inflated price, so Fastow and his investors were never at financial risk. In short, it was the ultimate sweetheart deal. It was also a crime.

Boards of directors of major corporations like Enron have a very difficult task, mastering the operations of a complex company with thousands of employees, complicated financing, and multiple product and service lines. To do this properly, they would need to work full-time. In America, however, most boards devote only five or ten days a year to the task. As a result, they are under extreme time pressure. At Enron these problems were particularly acute. Given the company's size and complexity, as well as the huge number and range of issues put forward for its approval, the board usually devoted less than one hour to review even the most complicated issues, like the LJM scheme. When Fastow's proposal came to a vote, the directors had no time to give the idea independent consideration. They listened to a brief summary that downplayed both the size of the conflict of interest and its risks, approved the proposal quickly, and moved on. I am sure none of the board members had any idea that they were putting the entire company in jeopardy.

To make matters worse, boards are captive audiences. Though directors have the right and duty to ask searching questions, the information they receive is carefully screened by the corporation's senior executives. If men like Skilling and Fastow want to hide explosive issues rather than disclose them, they can usually get away with it.

Finally, there is a question of trust. The board of directors hires the CEO, and it selects of course a person it trusts. Once it has made that judgment, it is unlikely to reconsider it, particularly in cases like Enron, in which the company's stock price is shooting through the roof and Wall Street labels its CEO a star.

The Enron board might have paid closer attention to Skilling and Fastow if it had seen clear warning signs that the company was in trouble. If, for example, Wall Street stock analysts had warned investors about the risky LJM deals, the board might have taken notice. But that did not happen. Wall Street was not an Enron critic, it was Enron's most exuberant cheerleader. That raises a new question: While Skilling and Fastow were engaging in massive fraud, where were the analysts?

EVERY MAJOR WALL STREET BROKERAGE FIRM and investment bank employs a team of stock analysts to monitor the performance of major companies and report on their potential investment value. These analysts issue reports and make investment recommendations: buy, sell, or hold. Millions of investors throughout the country rely on this advice because they believe these recommendations represent a more sophisticated and informed view than they can reach on their own.

From an analyst's perspective, Enron posed an interesting challenge. On the one hand, there was a powerful reason to recommend the stock to investors; Enron consistently reported strong revenue and low debt. At the same time, analysts had good reason to worry. A company's financial statements should be straightforward, clearly describing the company's business and financial position. Enron's were incomprehensible.

When Enron compiled its annual financial data, it employed an accounting technique called mark-to-market accounting, in which a company's assets are "marked," or valued on the books, not at their purchase price but at their current market value. As a result, its financial statements failed to distinguish between paper revenue attributable to estimated changes in the market value of assets and real revenue paid by actual customers. Mark-to-market accounting made it impossible for analysts to judge Enron's actual business performance accurately. It also allowed Enron to report imaginary revenue to the SEC simply by estimating that its own assets had increased in value.*

Enron also renamed its business divisions every year or two and shifted its business operations among those divisions constantly, making

---

*Under traditional accrual accounting, a company typically records revenue when cash comes in the door from its customers in return for delivered goods and services. Under mark-to-market, or MTM, accounting, in contrast, a company's assets are carried on the books not at purchase price but at "fair value." Each quarter companies using MTM value their assets and record quarterly changes in the fair value of those assets as gains or losses. So, for instance, if a company using MTM originally bought ten units of a commodity at a unit price of $1, and the price of the commodity shot up to $2 in a particular quarter, the company would record $10 in revenue in that quarter, even though it had not sold the commodity in question. If the price subsequently dropped back to $1, and the company still owned the commodity, the company would report a $10 loss. Companies that are engaged almost exclusively in the trading of stocks, commodities, or their derivatives often use MTM accounting because it arguably provides a more accurate picture of their true financial position. Unfortunately, the Enron case shows that in the wrong hands, MTM can be severely misused. Many of Enron's physical and contractual assets were unique and nonfungible or had value based on necessarily speculative assumptions about the long-term price of commodities. Since there was no clear and definitive market price for these assets, Enron was forced to "estimate" fair market value for MTM purposes. Inevitably, it crookedly "estimated" that its assets were rising in value. This allowed it to report the subsequent "gain" in estimated fair value as revenue on its financial statements even though that gain was purely imaginary. For example, Enron marked up its investment in Mariner Energy, a private oil and gas exploration company, from $185 million in 1996 to $367 million in 2001 and reported the difference as revenue. Later, after bankruptcy, Enron conceded that this figure was inflated by some $256 million.

it impossible for analysts to follow the financial performance of any given product or service line on a consistent basis. Even worse, the company's reports were filled with incomprehensible legalese, designed to confuse and mislead. Sometimes incredibly important information was buried deep in dense, highly technical footnotes that even securities lawyers could not decode. As a result, Enron's earnings statements were, one expert later testified before Congress, "inscrutable," not just to laypeople but to sophisticated analysts as well. This fact was not a secret. Early in 2001, ten months before the company collapsed, *Fortune* ran a story calling Enron's financial statements "impenetrable." Nevertheless, Wall Street praised Enron to the skies. As *The Wall Street Journal* later commented, "Rarely have so many analysts liked a stock they concede they know so little about."

The baffling character of Enron's financial statements was a major red flag. As one financial expert later testified before the Senate Governmental Affairs Committee, "for any analyst to say there were no warning signs in the public filings, they could not have read the same public filings I did." Many major institutional investors like Janus, Fidelity, and American Express clearly got the signal. In early 2001 they began to dump millions of Enron shares on the market. In contrast, the major Wall Street analysts remained totally bullish on Enron. In the fall of 2001 all fifteen of the largest Wall Street firms had buy recommendations in place. By late October 2001 ten of the fifteen were still recommending Enron, though by this point both Skilling and Fastow had resigned, the SEC had announced a public investigation, and *The Wall Street Journal* was running almost daily stories about Enron's earnings manipulation.

Why, you might wonder, did sophisticated Wall Street analysts fail to react to warning signs so evident to other major financial players? The answer is depressing. Banks and brokerage firms fund stock research and provide it free to investors not as a public service but because it helps the banks and brokerages make money. Stock research reports stimulate the trading of stocks. When, for example, an influential bank or broker recommends that investors buy a particular stock, transactions in that stock increase, generating brokerage transaction fees and commissions for the firm. Since, however, there are always more potential buyers for a particular stock than there are potential sellers of the same stock, buy recommendations, on average, generate much larger fees and commissions than recommendations to sell. As a result, brokerage firms have a direct financial incentive to rate companies favorably. The result is not surprising. In 2002, right after Enron went bankrupt, Wall Street analysts rated 66 percent of all stocks as "strong buys" or "buys," compared with only 1 percent rated as "strong sells" or "sells."

This inherent bias is heightened by a second problem, corporate coercion. If a bank tells investors to dump the stock of a large company like Enron, the company may retaliate by withholding corporate business. As a result of this dynamic, banks have a direct financial interest in keeping the big companies happy by issuing overly rosy reports. Investigators have discovered, for example, that in 1992, Morgan Stanley's managing director of corporate finance secretly instructed his firm's analysts to make "no negative comments about our clients." More recently investigators discovered that Merrill Lynch was publicly touting client stocks in positive research reports even though its analysts privately described the same companies in internal e-mails as "junk," "shit," and "crap." If an analyst bucks this trend and issues an honest negative report, he places his career in jeopardy. One Wall Street survey found that 61 percent of analysts have suffered retaliation for writing a negative stock report at some time in their careers.

Enron was a major banking customer, burning through some $230 million in banking fees in 1999 alone. This gave it a lot of clout, and every major bank wanted to curry favor. So instead of telling the truth about Enron, the banks issued positive reports repeating Enron's lies.

Only one major analyst put integrity before greed: a man named John Olson, who worked for Merrill Lynch. Olson's fate is instructive. In 1997 he wrote a research report raising concerns with Enron's performance and changed his short-term Enron recommendation from "buy" to "neutral." Note that point: not "sell," just "neutral." In reaction, Enron executives went berserk, threatening to withhold all future banking fees unless Merrill upgraded the rating. Merrill Lynch in turn forced Olson out of the firm and replaced him. Not surprisingly, its new Enron analyst quickly changed Enron's rating to "buy." Olson later commented that "analysts had to be very encouraging, or provide strong buy recommendations for current or prospective banking clients, so the firm-wide bonus would be unusually generous. And if you didn't do that, you'd get whacked."

THE SEC is the primary government agency responsible for preventing securities fraud and protecting stock investors. When auditors, boards of directors, and Wall Street analysts fail to prevent fraud, because of greed, incompetence, or conflicts of interest, the commission is supposed to step up to the plate. When, for example, Enron filed its incomprehensible financial statements, the SEC should have taken action, requesting clarification or opening an investigation. Instead, it did nothing. The negligence that led to this disastrous inaction is easy to describe, for the facts are stark. From 1998 to 2001 the SEC staff did not review any of Enron's quarterly or annual financial statements.

The commission has an explanation for failing to read Enron's reports, and at first blush, it appears plausible. Throughout the 1990s the number of publicly traded companies increased dramatically, while SEC resources grew at a much more modest rate. As a result, the SEC claims, it was forced to prioritize, and it chose to devote its time and resources to reviewing initial public offerings, not the filings of supposedly reliable blue-chip firms like Enron.

Most commentators have accepted the SEC's excuse. If you actually do the math, however, you quickly see that it will not hold water. It takes about a week for a lawyer or accountant to review carefully the financial statement of a large company, even a complex one like Enron. That means that an SEC staff member could review fifty such forms per year, if she worked on nothing else. Since the Fortune 500 companies submit five hundred annual reports, ten SEC accountants or lawyers could clearly handle the load. Since the SEC has more than three thousand employees, more than fifteen hundred of them lawyers or accountants, it certainly has enough staff for this task. The SEC's problem was not lack of resources; it was poor management.

After Enron went bankrupt, the SEC hired the business consulting firm McKinsey & Company to study its operations. McKinsey's report has not been released publicly, but portions were leaked to *The Wall Street Journal*. Those excerpts confirm that mismanagement at the SEC led directly to its failure to examine Enron's financial statements. The study revealed, for example, that SEC supervisors gave their employees numerical targets for reviewing corporation filings. In response, the employees began to game the system, choosing to examine "smaller, easier-to-review filings rather than more complex ones," so it was easier to meet their targets. With this system in place, it is no surprise that the SEC staff decided not to review Enron's long, turgid financial statements.

Even if the SEC had carefully monitored Enron's performance, however, it might not have done much good because the commission is notoriously ineffective in court. The SEC has adopted a litigation strategy called file-and-settle, which is designed to avoid the risks of trial, including both the costs of protracted litigation and the potential embarrassment of losing. Under this paradigm, the SEC typically works out a deal with a malefactor before filing a lawsuit and then files and settles the civil complaint on the very same day. Wall Street defense lawyers know that the SEC is eager to arrange a settlement up front, and they use this fact as leverage, threatening to go to trial unless they get sweetheart deals. Not surprisingly, SEC fines are invariably small.

To see how file-and-settle strategy works in practice, consider the SEC's record with Arthur Andersen. Before the Enron case, the SEC had caught Andersen cooking the books of major companies on two prior occasions. Both times the firm settled with the SEC and paid small fines without admitting any wrongdoing. These ineffective SEC enforcement actions had no impact on Andersen's sloppy auditing practices or dangerous firm culture. Instead, Andersen kept plugging along at companies like Enron, rubber-stamping false financial statements. The firm clearly assumed that if it got caught once again, it could easily get out of the jam one more time by paying a small fine. Because of SEC mismanagement, getting caught violating the law was just one more cost of doing business—and a minor cost at that.

WHEN ALL THE OTHER FRAUD WATCHDOGS FAIL, federal prosecutors with the United States Justice Department are responsible for cleaning up the mess. DOJ's white-collar crime mission is straightforward: to catch and punish as many corrupt executives as it can, so their peers will be scared straight. Unfortunately, the Justice Department's record in this area over the last fifty years has been poor. The title of a 2003 *Wall*

Street Journal article tells the whole story: A RARE HEADLINE: WALL STREETER COULD FACE JAIL.

The Justice Department has never emphasized white-collar crime for one basic reason: fraud cases are very difficult to prove. Prosecutors have to devote massive amounts of time and energy to bring a major white-collar case to court. Even then prosecutors run a high risk of losing, for upper-middle-class white-collar defendants tend to have much greater jury appeal than the average drug dealer or robber, and their high-priced white-collar defense lawyers, often former federal prosecutors themselves, are usually excellent advocates in court. Given these "high entry costs," many U.S. Attorneys' Offices charge only slam dunks. They leave more challenging cases to the SEC, and the defendants get off with fines.

Even when, however, prosecutors do their job aggressively and obtain important convictions, white-collar cases often fizzle at sentencing. Though judges routinely hand down ten- or twenty-year prison sentences to drug traffickers, they have traditionally declined to treat guilty corporation executives with equal severity, even though the social costs of white-collar crime, measured in lost jobs and retirement savings, are often enormous. The reasons for this are complex, but the main cause is social bias. When our overwhelmingly white federal judges sentence a young Latino drug trafficker, they see an alien threat. But when they encounter a white-collar crook who looks and talks like them, with an elite education, a stable middle-class family, and significant financial assets, they see not an "other" but themselves, not a true criminal but a man who "made some bad choices."

The classic example of this bias at work comes from the Enron case itself. James Brown was a wealthy Merrill Lynch banker from New York who lied to the Enron grand jury and to FBI agents about his role in the Nigerian barge deal, a fraudulent transaction designed to pump up Enron's reported earnings artifically. He was convicted of conspiracy, fraud, and obstruction of justice. Under the relevant sentencing guidelines, he should have been hammered at sentencing. Indeed, the Probation Department for the Southern District of Texas recommended a sentence of thirty-two years—overkill, I admit, but that gives you some sense of the enormity of the crime.

Judge Ewing Werlein saw the situation differently. Werlein is a former corporate lawyer and he clearly had deep sympathy for Brown's fall from grace. Before imposing sentence, Werlein told a crowded courtroom that white-collar defendants can be adequately deterred by low prison sentences, an outrageous claim refuted by the Enron debacle itself, which proved, if nothing else, that the light sentences imposed in past white-collar cases had not been sufficient to deter other executives from committing similar crimes. Werlein described Brown's fraud as "rather small and benign," a remarkable assertion, for the deal cost investors some $43 million and produced more than $1.4 million in illegal gains for Merrill Lynch. Finally, Werlein revealed his true colors. White-collar defendants, he stated, simply cannot "tolerate" the long sentences given to other types of defendants. He concluded by giving Brown a three-year sentence in a low-security prison.

Judges like Werlein undercut deterrence and chill prosecutorial effort. We are never going to get white-collar crime under control until judges start sentencing corporate defendants to substantial prison terms for their crimes.

SINCE 2002 political leaders and regulators have tried to fix many of the problems I have discussed in this chapter. Congress increased the SEC's budget; passed the Sarbanes-Oxley Act, requiring corporations to meet more rigorous auditing standards; and subjected accounting firms to tighter regulation. The SEC started to review the financial filings of the Fortune 500 companies. The United States Sentencing Commission amended the federal sentencing guidelines to increase white-collar jail sentences. And New York Attorney General (now Governor) Eliot Spitzer eliminated some of the more blatant conflicts of interest that render Wall Street stock reports worthless. These were positive steps, but they left many critical issues unaddressed. Boards of directors continue to struggle to detect fraud in their own companies. Wall Street stock analysis remains driven more by greed than integrity. Executives still face huge temptations to fudge their financial data. And despite increased funding, the SEC remains largely toothless.

In 2004, I wrote a law review article proposing a series of reforms to address these remaining issues, including a major overhaul of the SEC, changes in accounting practices, and a new, more stringent criminal fraud statute. At the time I hoped we might see more progress. Now, however, I know it is hopeless. Right after Enron, politicians were highly motivated to try to stop corporate crime. Today, however, the corporate reform movement has run out of gas.

If you look back at recent American business history, you see that white-collar crime occurs in boom-bust cycles. In the 1970s we saw a major wave of big accounting fraud cases; in the 1980s, the savings and loan debacle, insider trading, and junk bond fraud; in the 1990s, rampant Enron-style earnings manipulation. With each new crisis, political leaders called for tough new rules and the Department of Justice indicted a few high-profile cases. Then attention lagged, regulators got lazy, and enforcement budgets were cut once again. Soon the incentives for executives to cheat returned. Today, this cycle continues.

Consider the performance of the Bush administration. In 2002, after Enron collapsed, the president held a press conference to unveil a new Corporate Crime Task Force. He promised that from that moment on, holding white-collar criminals accountable for their crimes would be a major emphasis of his administration. In 2003, however, our nation went to war in Iraq, and public attention shifted away from corporate crime. When this happened, the Justice Department returned to business as usual. Since 2003 the number of indicted federal white-collar cases has declined sharply. Indeed, the number of fraud prosecutions today is substantially lower than under President Clinton. This is not because fraud has been eliminated. The Justice Department has simply walked away from the problem, leaving securities fraud enforcement to the SEC once again.

Our much-ballyhooed crackdown on corporate crime has been mostly smoke, not fire. In the post-Enron environment, major companies were scared, and that helped keep large-scale fraud in check. But even as we speak, things are returning to normal. Another wave of white-collar fraud is inevitable.

CHAPTER NINETEEN

The Fastow Dilemma

The Broadband case was important, but it paled in significance compared with the Enron Task Force's main effort, to bust Enron chief financial officer Andy Fastow. When we began our investigation, we had no concrete evidence that Fastow had committed a crime, but we felt sure he held the keys to the case. As the CFO he was the person most responsible for Enron's financial statements. If anyone had broken the law at Enron, it was likely to have been Fastow. He also occupied a strategic position in the firm hierarchy, high enough to share close counsel with Ken Lay and Jeff Skilling, but not so lofty that we could not use him as a witness. In mafia cases, you flip capos against bosses. Fastow, we believed, was an Enron capo.

Andy Fastow was born in 1961 and raised in Washington, D.C. He went to college at Tufts, where he studied Chinese. There he met Lea Weingarten, the heiress to Houston's Weingarten supermarket fortune. Lea and Andy married and moved to Chicago, where they got M.B.A.'s at Northwestern. Fastow served a stint as a banker, and then, in 1990, he and Lea moved to Houston, where both took jobs at Enron. Lea became a fixture in Houston society, donating widely to charities and collecting art. Andy became Enron's award-winning CFO. The couple had two sons. In the fall of 2001, Fastow resigned under a cloud, amid rumors of large-scale fraud. Now he was waiting to see what we would do.

Our Fastow probe began in spring of 2002, during the Arthur Andersen trial. Most of the task force lawyers were in Houston, helping Andrew and Sam, but Tom Hanusik was left back in Washington with authority to investigate whatever part of the Enron case he thought would be most productive. Tom read the Powers Report, Enron's internal study of the company's collapse, and he decided to concentrate on one single transaction, code-named Southampton. Later I asked Tom what had drawn him to this particular deal. He replied with typical understatement, "I chose Southampton because, quite frankly, it looked suspicious to me that people would 'invest' $5,000 and get back $1 million six weeks later." Within a couple of weeks Tom had put together a solid fraud case against a former Enron executive named Michael Kopper. His choice of targets could not have been more auspicious. Kopper was Fastow's principal deputy. He was also a weak link.

Throughout the Enron case it was very hard to flip senior Enron executives. They had all "drunk the Kool-Aid," insisting in interviews that Enron was the best-run corporation on earth. Kopper was different. He was gay, a relative rarity in Enron's stripper-obsessed heterosexual upper circles, and perhaps that made him feel like an outsider. Whatever the reason, he was more honest, more realistic, and more objective about his own conduct and his likely fate if he refused to cooperate. When Tom threatened an indictment, Kopper quickly capitulated.

When Kopper agreed to be interviewed, it gave our fledgling case a huge boost. Fastow, he told us, was the principal architect of a vast criminal scheme to doctor Enron's financial statements and boost his own personal wealth. Kopper helped us understand Enron's organization and culture, explained dozens of dirty transactions, and identified incriminating documents. When we digested all this intelligence, we knew we had sufficient evidence to indict Fastow for fraud. Leslie assigned the *Fastow* case to Andrew Weissmann, her top deputy. Andrew quickly put together a case, and he was ready to charge by late September. That left us with an important question: Should we do a perp walk?

———

TRADITIONALLY, FEDERAL PROSECUTORS and agents have followed a double standard in arrests. We bust most defendants at their homes or workplaces, put them in handcuffs, fingerprint and photograph them at a law enforcement agency office, and then transport them in custody to the courthouse for arraignment. We treat high-level white-collar defendants differently. They do not get arrested at home and dragged to court in cuffs. Instead, we give them advance notice of the arrest date and allow them to report to court under their own power, walking through the front door with as much dignity as they can muster, accompanied by their lawyers. The ostensible justification for this discrepancy is tactical: white-collar defendants, the argument goes, are unlikely to flee the jurisdiction and can be trusted to show up for their court dates, while other kinds of defendants cannot. This is not a frivolous argument. A guy like Fastow is much less likely to run than a drug dealer or armed robber. But the double standard remains troubling. Rich people get much better treatment in the criminal justice system: better lawyers; greater chances of acquittal; nicer treatment in prison. It seems horrible to me to institutionalize that preferential system from the moment of arrest.

In 1987, Manhattan U.S. Attorney Rudy Giuliani tried to change this practice. Giuliani developed an insider trading case against a Kidder, Peabody broker named Richard Wigton. Instead of allowing Wigton to surrender at court, Giuliani sent agents to arrest and frisk Wigton on the Kidder, Peabody trading floor and then marched him out the front door in cuffs, before hosts of waiting media. Giuliani's goal was legitimate. Faced with rampant securities fraud on Wall Street, he wanted to send a graphic signal that the era of leniency for white-collar criminals was over and that persons who cheated would be held accountable. He also wanted to ensure that all charged defendants were treated alike. Unfortunately, Giuliani's aggressive tactics gave the white-collar perp walk a permanent bad name. His case against Wigton was weak, and a few months later, after Wigton had been thoroughly dragged through the mud, it had to be dismissed, a very bad precedent.

In the weeks before Fastow's arrest, all the agents and prosecutors discussed whether a perp walk was appropriate or not. Most, including me, wanted to arrest him at home. I was not worried that Fastow would flee. I simply wanted to ensure that he was treated just like any other criminal defendant, with no special privileges. Leslie Caldwell disagreed—wisely. One of Leslie's great strengths as a prosecutor was her moderation. She was aggressive in court, but she did not pick unnecessary fights. Here she decided to compromise. Fastow, she told the defense lawyers, could surrender at FBI Headquarters under his own power. Then, after booking, the FBI would transport him to arraignment in government custody. Both sides got part of what they wanted.

Fastow retained a little dignity; the government got photographs of a high-profile defendant in cuffs.

———

I WAS IN HOUSTON the day Fastow was arrested, questioning witnesses before the grand jury, so I popped down to the courtroom to see his arraignment. That night I told a friend, "Fastow looked flush and a little red in the face, a little grim. He looks like a guy who will cooperate." This judgment proved hopelessly optimistic. Fastow hired John Keker of San Francisco to represent him. Keker, a former Marine Corps combat officer in Vietnam, is one of the most talented and aggressive defense attorneys in the country. His office is filled with busts and portraits of Napoleon. When you hire Keker, you send a signal: we are going to trial. With Fastow digging in, we clearly needed more leverage. We found it in a 1997 transaction called RADR.

The RADR deal was a classic example of Enron corruption. Enron owned windmills in California that collected substantial government subsidies for generating "alternative energy." When Enron bought the Oregon utility Portland General Electric in 1997, it became a public utility holding company, and under the law it was no longer legally eligible to collect these subsidies. To get around this problem, Enron sold the wind farms to an investment partnership called RADR. RADR was ostensibly an independent company, but in fact it was merely a shell, created by Fastow and secretly controlled by its parent company, Enron. Enron provided RADR with 97 percent of the financing needed for the purchase, and in return it got to keep most of the wind farm subsidies. Fastow provided most of the remaining 3 percent, a "fig leaf" amount designed, ludicrously, to make it look as if Enron did not totally control the RADR partnership. In return for that $419,000 investment, Fastow got a guaranteed profit of over $200,000. This was tiny by Fastow's later standards, when he plundered some $30 million from Enron stockholders. But at the time he was happy to have it.

Fastow's deal was totally sleazy, so he decided to keep it secret. That caused a new problem. Under securities laws designed to prevent corporate looting, Enron was required to disclose on its financial statements any company transactions with "related parties," top corporate insiders like Fastow. If Fastow complied with these disclosure rules, energy regulators would discover his scam. For this reason, he decided to hide his crime by committing a new one. He gave the $419,000 to his wife, Lea, and instructed her to "loan" it to his deputy, Michael Kopper, a more junior Enron employee not covered by the related party rules. Kopper was then listed as the actual investor on RADR transaction documents, even though this was not really true. Fastow also hid his profits. They were not paid to him directly. Instead, they were paid from the RADR trust to close Fastow friends, who then wrote checks to Lea and Andy's kids. When it came time to pay their taxes, the Fastows claimed that these checks were gifts, not investment income. To avoid triggering the requirement that gifts in excess of $10,000 be reported to the Internal Revenue Service, most of these checks were written for smaller amounts, an illegal tactic called smurfing. Ultimately, the Fastows kept some $208,000 off their tax returns. In sum, Fastow achieved a criminal law trifecta: he committed tax fraud to hide the securities fraud he committed to cover up his violation of the energy laws.

When Andrew Weissmann indicted Fastow in late 2002, he included RADR in the charges, but he did not charge Fastow's wife or the other minor participants in the scheme. At the time we viewed this as a straightforward case for prosecutorial discretion. Lea Fastow had knowingly signed the Fastow's fraudulent joint tax returns, but it was clear that the moving force behind the crime was her husband. Moreover, tax evasion cases of this size are almost never charged criminally. Instead, they are typically settled civilly by the IRS, with tax cheats paying back taxes plus a fine. There was also a question of resources. During the Enron investigation we uncovered a huge number of small crimes at the company. If we had indicted every trivial case we stumbled across, we would get tied up in the courts indefinitely, fighting minor defendants when we needed to be focusing on their chiefs. So we left Lea Fastow alone.

By the spring of 2003, however, our calculation had shifted. Our case was stalled. We desperately needed Fastow to cooperate. That meant we had to pressure him. In a meeting with John Keker, Fastow's attorney, Leslie made a threat: if Andy Fastow did not flip, the task force would indict his wife. This tactic was legal. Several federal courts of appeals have held explicitly that the government can threaten to indict a defendant's spouse if the defendant refuses to plead guilty, as long as there is probable cause to support the charge.* But it was definitely hardball.

Leslie believed her threat would do the trick. Most men, after all, would do anything to keep their spouses out of prison. Fastow, however, told us to pound sand. Apparently, he liked his money and his freedom more than his wife. That left us with an ethical quandary: Should we charge Lea Fastow or not?

Leslie raised the Lea Fastow issue in a special, prosecutors-only meeting held in our conference room in Washington. Most of the AUSAs in the room thought the issue was clear-cut: we should indict her immediately. "Lea was not an unsophisticated dupe," one of my colleagues insisted. "She had a very strong finance background, with an M.B.A. and work experience as a banker and Enron assistant treasurer. When she agreed to fake her taxes to hide her husband's crime, she knew exactly what she was doing. She broke the law, and that makes her fair game."

I was not so sure. On the one hand, I knew instantly that the correct "prosecutorial answer" was to indict. Leslie made the threat, and we had to follow through. Otherwise, our credibility in negotiations with other Enron targets would be nil. I also believed that indicting Lea was justified as a matter of public policy. Convicting Ken Lay and Jeff Skilling was critical, for if we failed, it might encourage other corporate executives to commit similar crimes. If winning required indicting Lea Fastow, so be it. The alternative—letting Skilling and Lay escape—was simply too costly.

There was also my own history. Back in 1999, during the Bushwick case, I had arrested drug trafficker Nelson Aguirre's young wife, Marysol, in order to gain leverage over him. Then I had proposed a deal, her freedom for his guilty plea. At the time I had done this without compunction. It seemed both necessary and proper. How was this any different? Were my qualms the result of a double standard? Was I guilty of the bias in favor of the rich that plagues the criminal justice system? Was I proposing that we treat a rich banker's wife differently from a drug dealer's just because she is white and wealthy?

---

*See, e.g., *United States v. Marquez*, 909 F.2d 738, 741 (2d Cir. 1990) (government may threaten to prosecute defendant's wife if defendant does not accept plea bargain).

Still, something about the idea of indicting Lea Fastow really troubled me. As Leslie and the other prosecutors talked, I suddenly recognized what it was—the kids. The Fastows had two small sons. If we indicted Andy and Lea, their kids faced the prospect of growing up with both parents in jail. What we were proposing, in essence, was to take those two kids hostage, a very ugly exercise of brute government power. One of my fellow prosecutors made this clear at our meeting. He said, "Let's see how Fastow feels about going to trial when his children are in fucking foster care."

AS AN AUSA I rarely applied formal ethical theory to prosecutorial problems. I had decided early in my career that it was simply too abstract to help. When faced with a tough decision, I tended to follow standard prosecutorial practices and my own gut instincts instead. Now, however, I felt different. I am not sure why. Perhaps my six-month break as a law professor had changed my perspective. As I sat at the conference table, I found myself thinking: What would the philosophers John Stuart Mill and Immanuel Kant think about this?

Mill, I thought, would indict. For a utilitarian, an act is morally justified if it is likely to produce positive social consequences. Here the end—the ultimate convictions of Ken Lay and Jeff Skilling—appeared to justify our questionable tactics.

Kant, in contrast, would have been horrified. According to Kant, people should be treated as individuals and given their just deserts. To use them as tools—to sacrifice them simply to achieve a social goal—violated our prime ethical commandment to treat every person with reverence and respect. If Lea Fastow truly deserved to be indicted, then fine. But if, as seemed to be the case here, we were treating her differently from other tax cheats simply to pressure her husband, then that was morally out of bounds.

When I first became an AUSA, I was a utilitarian. Over time, as I interrogated dozens of defendants and bent them to my will, I began to see Kant's point about the sanctity of human dignity. Now I was simply confused. We appeared to have a true ethical quandary on our hands, a problem with no cost-free outcome. Filled with conflicting emotions, I did something rare for me. Instead of taking a position at the meeting,

I kept my mouth shut. Leslie noticed this, and perhaps it troubled her. A few days later she pulled me aside and asked me point-blank, "Do you think we should indict Lea Fastow or not?"

I did not share any of my theoretical musings with my boss. Prosecutors are not philosophers. She would have thought I was crazy if I had told her that this problem showed the limitations in utilitarian reasoning or suggested that Kantian ethics should guide our charging decisions. Nor did I tell her what was in my heart: that our proposed use of government power—our threat to destroy a family if a defendant did not do our bidding—struck me as brutal and callous. Leslie would, I thought, write this off as rank sentimentalism. Instead, I sought an easy way out. Leslie, I knew, might not value a philosophical objection, but she would certainly consider a pragmatic one. So I told her, "If we indict Lea Fastow just to squeeze her husband, I think we are going to get crucified in the press." Leslie nodded—she knew that was a risk—but I could tell she was not convinced. And she was right not to be. In the Justice Department, our job is justice. If that requires us to anger the media, so be it.

ON MAY 1, 2003, the same day as the arrests of our seven Broadband defendants, we arrested Lea Fastow for fraud and tax evasion. The timing was not accidental. We hoped that if we arrested Lea at the same time as many other persons, it would not look as if she were being treated unfairly. I expected that the press would go berserk. In fact no one cared. Enron was such a symbol of evil we could probably have shipped Lea to Guantánamo and no one would have objected. A quote in the *Houston Chronicle* from one commentator, an attorney not involved in the case, said it all: "Under normal circumstances the public may consider that type of leverage reprehensible. But in this current market where the public is looking for blood, such common prosecutorial tactics used to leverage pleas would not likely be met with public derision."

That afternoon Joe Ford, the lead FBI agent on the task force, gathered all the agents and prosecutors together in our courthouse and thanked us for all our work. "You should all be very proud. We did really good today." Then he looked at me and frowned. A few of Joe's agents had been critical of the Lea Fastow indictment. On one conference call to discuss her case, one agent blurted out, "We should focus more efforts and resources on putting Enron executives in jail rather than orphaning more children." Joe blamed me for this. He thought, incorrectly, that I was going behind his back, stirring up opposition among his agents. Now he made his feelings known. Staring right at me, he said pointedly, "No thanks to the critics who don't believe in our case."

Leslie was kinder. She could sense, perhaps, that after ten months of nonstop work, I was at the end of my tether, so she gave me a little morale booster. "John," she said, in a voice loud enough for virtually everyone in the room to overhear, "you should really be proud of your work today. The Broadband case would never have happened if you hadn't pushed so hard. You and the agents have really done an amazing job. I hope you feel great."

Jeff Jenson, the lead FBI agent on the Broadband case, was listening closely. As soon as Leslie finished, he jumped in. "Oh, he doesn't give a shit," he said in his sardonic manner. "All he wants to do is get back to his hippie, dope-smoking law school." I looked up at Jeff and smiled.

One week later Leslie and I sat down in Washington to discuss my future. Leslie opened the meeting on a positive note. "You've done a great job this year. Don't even think about going back to Lewis & Clark." She then laid an attractive offer on the table: I could hand off the in-dicted Broadband case to Ben Campbell and work full-time investigat-ing Skilling and Lay. It would, she said, be "the trial of the century."

Leslie's proposal was obviously very appealing. In the Broadband in-vestigation, we had uncovered strong evidence that Skilling had inten-tionally lied to investors. I was confident that if we dug aggressively into other areas of the company, we would find a similar pattern. I was inter-ested in Lay too. Back in March, Sam Buell and I had developed a legal strategy for charging Lay with fraud on the basis of his secret Enron stock sales in fall of 2001, and though we all agreed such a charge was premature and based on too little evidence, I was convinced that suffi-cient evidence would eventually fall into place.

Back in the old days—say, 1999—I would have accepted Leslie's of-fer with alacrity. No trial lawyer likes to pass up a big case. Now, however, I was quick to decline. "When I joined the task force," I told Leslie, "I promised my colleagues at Lewis & Clark that I would be gone for only a year and that I intended to return to Oregon and teaching. I have to keep that promise." Leslie nodded, and then we dropped the subject. In the Justice Department, people value personal integrity. Leslie understood that if I made a commitment, I needed to keep it.

My answer to Leslie was true, but a little beside the point. I am sure that if I had asked for another year of leave, Lewis & Clark Law School would have granted it. My real reason for wanting to leave was more basic. I was proud to have worked on the Enron case and glad that I had completed my part of the investigation. But to put it bluntly, I did not want to be a federal prosecutor anymore.

MY DECISION TO LEAVE the Justice Department was motivated in part by a conversation I had one day with my colleague Sam Buell. Sam and I spent several hours discussing legal strategies for charging Ken Lay. When we finished and I started to leave his office, Sam commented, "You are working amazingly hard. I could not work the hours you do. It doesn't seem sustainable." I just shrugged. I had always worked long hours, both in politics and as a prosecutor. I told Sam, "I think it's necessary for the case." But later that night, as I sat in my studio apartment, I thought more deeply about what Sam had said.

I had always believed that hard work was a prosecutorial imperative. Indeed, I looked down scornfully on AUSAs who did not "get it," who failed to emulate my work ethic. If you fail to put in the hours, I told myself (and the rookie prosecutors I supervised in Brooklyn toward the end of my time there), you take a huge risk that your defendants will go free and that justice will not be done. Rationally, however, I could not take that position with Sam Buell. Sam was one of the best prosecutors in the Justice Department, with a huge list of big cases to his credit. I had no doubt he was a better prosecutor than I was. If Sam thought I was overdoing it, that required some thought.

That evening I asked myself bluntly: Why do you work such long hours? If, as Sam suggested, my brutal pace was not professionally necessary, perhaps professionally unsustainable, why did I do it? Was hard work truly an ethical requirement? A function of my commitment to help others? Or was I driven by other, less justifiable forces?

I sat in my armchair for hours, considering this problem, and I recognized, for the first time ever, what was probably obvious to my friends all along, that my whole adult life I had been using work as an emotional crutch. My childhood had been traumatic in important respects, leaving me feeling vulnerable and unloved, and I had tried to fill that void with long hours on the job and professional success. I understood too that ever since my days as a philosophy student at college, I had been searching for the wrong thing. For almost twenty years I had asked myself daily: What does it mean to be a good human being? This question had served its purpose. Though I was not raised with any particular ethical orientation and had struggled badly as a teen, I had gradually learned to be a reasonably good human being. I did not cause anyone unnecessary grief or pain, I was self-critical and reflective, I had learned the value of honesty, and I made a reasonable contribution to the welfare of my community. Now, though, I concluded that I needed to shift focus. Being a good person was no longer sufficient. I had to try to be a happy one as well. And if that was my goal, then working ninety hours a week on the *Enron* case was not the right path.

MY DECISION TO RESIGN was also grounded in deep discomfort with the *Lea Fastow* case. When I joined the Justice Department, I had expected my professional life to be morally simple. People broke the law, and I would hold them accountable. I did not expect to make tough judgments about right and wrong. I thought the law would do that for me. As I gained experience as a prosecutor, however, I gradually came to understand that this expectation was naive. Federal prosecutors, I discovered, have broad discretionary powers. When they decide whether to charge someone with a crime or not, they have to make judgments about the person's innate worth and future prospects, judgments that no human being can make with any confidence. I also learned that even well-intentioned prosecutors can present false testimony at trial, that a just process and a just result cannot always be obtained at the same time, that informants are both necessary and deceitful, that a certain small percentage of agents are corrupt, that our law enforcement policies often encourage crime rather than prevent it, and that successful interrogation requires the ethically questionable manipulation of other human beings. As this evidence began to pile up, I should have paused and asked myself: Is this job really simple at all? Or is it an ethical quagmire? But I did not. I was so busy and so convinced that my work was both necessary and useful that I repressed my concerns.

The *Lea Fastow* case changed all that. I knew that from a law enforcement perspective—and from a utilitarian perspective—we were right to indict her. I knew it was good for the case. I knew the public would want us to do it. Nevertheless, it troubled me deeply, for I worried that when we singled her out for special treatment, we had made the wrong decision—had done something unjust.

I had always believed that to be a good AUSA, you had to be decisive, aggressive, and unemotional. For years I had been confident in my judgment. Now I felt doubts. Suddenly all the concerns I had suppressed over the years came flooding out. I asked myself, for the very first time, a very serious question: What happens if being a good prosecutor requires you to do something you find morally repugnant?

I did not try to answer this question. I knew that I could not answer it in the middle of a case, working eighty or ninety hours a week. But I suspected that if I gave it a great deal of thought, I might be able to understand both myself and my job better. Sitting in my Washington apartment, a thought dawned on me: If I go back to teaching, I will have plenty of time to try to understand the moral complexities of life as an AUSA. I might even be able to write about it.

WHEN WE DECIDED TO INDICT Lea Fastow, did we do the right thing? If you polled all the former Enron prosecutors, they would insist, I think, that we clearly made the correct call. Andy Fastow was the one essential witness against both Ken Lay and Jeff Skilling. Without his testimony, we could not make our case. As a result, we had to take every legal step in our power to try to bring him to the table. Prosecutors don't think in philosophical terms, but they are generally utilitarian in their orientation. In this case, they would argue, the end justified the means.

Unfortunately, I do not think the world is so simple. Both utilitarianism and Kantianism reflect powerful human intuitions about the nature of ethics. We believe that every human being is entitled to be treated with dignity and not used or manipulated. At the same time, we recognize that the needs of the many must, at least in some circumstances, trump the needs of the few. If these two values clash, we face a moral dilemma. Do we respect the individual, or do we sacrifice him or her to the public good?

In the vast majority of criminal cases, this conflict does not arise, for most of the time these two powerful ethical urges work in tandem. But as an AUSA I learned that there are some cases, like Lea Fastow's, where these two moral drives do collide. These situations pose real ethical challenges. Is it okay to arrest several low-level mopes, persons we would not ordinarily charge, just to increase the odds of getting someone to flip against our more culpable targets? Is it morally acceptable to pressure a defendant to become an informant on the street even though this might cost the informant his life? Is it proper to trick, manipulate, and pressure defendants in the interrogation room so we can use their testimony to convict others? Should we threaten to indict a wife just to get her husband to plead guilty?

Some legal scholars believe resolution of these philosophical conflicts is easy: in government the utilitarian answer must always prevail. On April 21, 2005, for example, Berkeley law professor John Yoo addressed this precise issue in a debate at Columbia Law School. Talking about the conflict between Kantian and utilitarian thinking, Yoo stated:

> *You could be a consequentialist [another name used to describe utilitarians like Mill, who believe actions should be judged by their consequences]. In government, most people are. I think it would be very difficult to be a Kantian and have any responsibility in government . . . Most people in government have to be consequentialists because you are constantly making trade-offs, not just in this area, but in all kinds of areas. Your mental computer would shut down if you were a Kantian and you had to make these kinds of decisions.*

Yoo may be right; maybe in government, the ends always do justify the means. But suppressing our Kantian values, our belief in the sanctity of the individual, may be dangerous. Yoo's own career provides a powerful warning, for he is not just an academic; he was the primary legal architect of the Bush administration's controversial war on terror.

On August 1, 2002, Yoo sent a memo to the CIA to provide legal guidance on a fundamental question of values, the use of torture in CIA interrogations. Historically the United States has opposed torture outright. Now Yoo sought to change this approach. He argued that international law does not ban all torture, but only "the most extreme acts." Physical violence was fine as long as it did not cause organ failure or death. Psychological coercion was acceptable too if it did not cause permanent or long-term harm. Even if these narrow prohibitions were violated, Yoo told the CIA that its interrogators could not be held accountable because prosecution "would represent an unconstitutional infringement of the President's authority to conduct war." This gave interrogators who crossed ethical and legal boundaries a virtual get-out-of-jail-free card. Later, in 2005, he summarized his position in a telephone interview with *The New Yorker* reporter Jane Mayer: "They can't prevent the President from ordering torture."*

Why did Yoo adopt such morally and legally obtuse positions? The answer, I think, lies in his outright rejection of Kantian ethics in the governmental context. Because he believes that persons in power must suppress their Kantian values, he wound up ignoring Kant's most vital teaching, that all human beings should be treated with dignity and respect.

Yoo's position is horribly wrong, if only because it is too simplistic. When we exercise power over the lives of others, we cannot simply be either utilitarians or Kantians; we must be both.

The human condition is tragic precisely because it is complex. Like the character of Antigone in Sophocles's great drama, we face, on rare occasions, the conflicting pull of contradictory moral claims.† These moral dilemmas can occur in ordinary daily life, but they are much more common in government, for it is there that we mediate and resolve

---

*On January 9, 2002, Yoo sent a separate memo to the Department of Defense discussing the treatment of al Qaeda and Taliban fighters. He stated that these detainees were not protected by the Geneva Convention, which bans torture, cruelty, and degrading and humiliating treatment, or our nation's own War Crimes Act. They were, on the contrary, fair game, unprotected by domestic or international law. These extreme positions have been repudiated by the Bush administration, under pressure from both public opinion and the U.S. Supreme Court.

†In the play, Creon, the king of Thebes, decrees that the body of the dead rebel Polynices must be left unburied, without customary rites and honors. Antigone, Polynices's sister, is caught between two conflicting moral duties: Should she follow Creon's binding law and leave her brother's body to carrion or obey "the unwritten and unfailing statutes of heaven"? She decides to bury her brother's body but pays the price, death, for disobeying the king's orders.

the conflicting demands of the many and the few. If we pretend these dilemmas do not exist or that utilitarian calculations must trump all other concerns, then we risk ending up like Yoo, morally blind.

Back in 1973, political theorist Michael Walzer wrote a famous article addressing this precise issue. It is entitled "Political Action: The Problem of Dirty Hands." I first read it in a college ethics course, but by the time I was working on Enron, fifteen years later, I did not remember it well. After we indicted Lea Fastow, I got a copy from the library. It was, as lawyers like to say, directly on point.

In the essay, Walzer suggests that in public life, moral dilemmas are inevitable. There is no way out of this jam. Whatever course of action you take, no matter how moral you try to be, you will emerge with dirty hands. As Walzer candidly admits, "I don't think I could govern innocently."

When put in these positions, Walzer argues, we have to employ utilitarian reasoning, for in the end government officials bear "a considerable responsibility for consequences and outcomes." Any other approach, he says, would violate the official's public responsibilities, his duty to those whom she serves. To return to the *Lea Fastow* case, Walzer seems to counsel that if the public good demands it, we should indict her even if it seems unfair.

Walzer insists, however, that we recognize the high moral costs of this choice. When government actors pursue outcomes that are good for society as a whole, they often commit serious moral wrongs against individuals caught in their web. We should not, like Professor Yoo, sweep this fact under a rug. Instead, we should acknowledge that we have done something which, however necessary, was also grossly unjust. These moments are not to be celebrated. We should not boast that we like to play hardball, as prosecutors often do. Instead, we should confess that in our effort to achieve justice, we have done something atrocious, used another person like a pawn. This expression of remorse is the only way to remind ourselves that utilitarianism has its costs and that the moral stakes, in Walzer's words, are "very high."

———

THE LEA FASTOW STRATEGY worked precisely as Leslie hoped. Though it took months to work out a deal, Andy Fastow pleaded guilty in January 2004 and agreed to cooperate against Jeff Skilling and Ken Lay. In return we let his wife plead guilty to a misdemeanor, not a felony. We also agreed that she and Andy could serve their prison terms one at a time, so their kids would never be without a parent. Lea Fastow ultimately served one year in prison for tax evasion. She would never have been sentenced at all if her husband had seen the light earlier and agreed to help us before we had to indict her.

From a strategic point of view, the Broadband case was a huge success as well. In the summer of 2004, both Ken Rice and Kevin Hannon pleaded guilty to securities fraud. Both admitted that they and other EBS executives had repeatedly lied to investors about the Broadband unit's technological capabilities, finances, and customer base. Rice forfeited $14 million. Hannon coughed up another $3.2 million. Then they flipped, just as I had hoped.

In the late spring of 2006, almost three years after I left the Enron case, Rice and Hannon joined Andy Fastow (and a handful of other convicted Enron executives) as government witnesses at the trial of Skilling and Lay. The three men testified that Skilling and Lay lied to investors rather than admit that Enron was a bankrupt shell. Skilling was convicted on sixteen criminal counts, several of them related to his lies about EBS. He was sentenced to twenty-four years in jail, one of the longest white-collar sentences ever imposed in the United States. He is now serving time in a low-security federal prison in rural Minnesota. Lay was convicted on six counts. Before he could be sentenced, he died of a massive heart attack.

I expected the remainder of the Broadband case to end on an equally successful note. Instead, the ride has proved very bumpy. In the Braveheart trial, the man I have called Steve Woolf was convicted on five criminal counts for accounting and securities fraud. After his trial, however, the Fifth Circuit Court of Appeals ruled that the jury instructions defining fraud used in a separate Enron trial, involving the Nigerian barge scam, were improper. Since the judge in the Braveheart case had used the same jury instructions, she decided to throw out all five of Woolf's convictions. Now his case is up on appeal, to see if any of the convictions are valid and, if not, whether he can be retried.*

---

*In the same trial, junior Enron accountant Michael Krautz was acquitted of all charges.

The three other Broadband defendants went to trial in July 2005. The result was a fiasco: three months of very dull and confusing testimony, accompanied by inflammatory defense charges of government deceit. When the dust cleared, the jury acquitted on some counts and deadlocked on the remaining 90 percent. Today, in late 2007, we are all still waiting for the retrial.

I am very proud of the work I did on the Enron case. If I had not pushed so hard, Ken Rice and Kevin Hannon would never have been forced to answer for their crimes, and Jeff Skilling might have escaped conviction. But I have struggled emotionally as I watched my successors try to wrap up the remaining defendants. Prior to Enron, I had convicted 99 percent of the persons I charged.* When I handed off the Broadband case, I expected us to win it easily. Instead, we have seen years of expensive and time-consuming litigation.

At times I second-guess myself. Maybe, I think, my charging decisions were too aggressive, the cases too difficult to win. At other times I feel guilty. I have huge confidence in my skills in the courtroom. Maybe if I had stayed with the case, instead of returning to Oregon, it would have ended more quickly. Today all I can do is sit back and watch. The remaining Enron defendants have a right to their day in court, and they are innocent until proved guilty. I have faith in juries, and I respect their decisions. We shall see.

---

*In 1999, as part of the *Persico* mafia case, Amy Walsh and I charged a mobbed-up Long Island businessman with extortion. He went to trial against two of my colleagues in the spring of 2002, while I was teaching at Lewis & Clark Law School, and won. I also lost a murder-for-hire conspiracy case. The defendant pleaded guilty and went to prison, but afterward his case was dismissed and he was released because the crime did not have a sufficient interstate connection to support federal jurisdiction.

New Beginnings

One hot afternoon in June 2003 I loaded up my Honda Civic and started driving west. My career as an AUSA was finished. That fall I returned to the classroom at Portland's Lewis & Clark Law School. I also began to write this book. My goal was in part quite personal: to try to understand my own life. I also had a broader purpose in mind. AUSAs wield immense authority, but we operate in the shadows, with little public oversight. To me that seems dangerous, for in a democracy the use of power should never go unexamined. People, I thought, should have a better understanding of what AUSAs do.

In the ancient Roman Republic, magistrates leaving public office were required to justify their actions and account for their conduct before the public. I think the Romans had the right idea. Scrutiny helps keep people honest. To that end I decided to put my own career under a microscope.

WHEN I THINK BACK on my time as a federal prosecutor, I feel an immense amount of nostalgia. I miss chatting with Mario Parlagreco about Shakespeare; arguing trial strategy with Eric Tirschwell and Sung-Hee Suh late at night; digging through boxes of evidence, looking for hidden gems; standing up to close a trial and looking the jury in the eye; working with the agents who became my close friends. Above all, I miss a simple thrill that never grew old, no matter how many times I experienced it: the opportunity to say, at the beginning of every court appearance, "John Kroger for the United States." The quality of your professional life as a lawyer depends, to a great degree, on the nature of your clients. Back in the old days I did not sufficiently appreciate what I now recognize. No matter how long I practice law, I shall never have a client as great as the U.S.A. I represented our country in court over a thousand times, and I am very thankful to have had that chance.

Still, I am glad I left when I did. Being an AUSA is a great job, but a harsh one, with a very high burnout rate. In big-city offices most AUSAs move on to other jobs after four or five years. This is partly a function of economics. Once you have been an AUSA, it is easy to make a lot of money as a private corporate litigator. But it is also the result of moral stress. Being an AUSA is tough. We want to be idealistic, but in the end we accomplish our jobs through threats. You threaten to send your targets to prison for life unless they cooperate; you threaten to send your witnesses to prison if they don't tell the truth; you threaten your defendants' spouses with indictment unless your defendants plead. And when your threats do not work, you have to back them up. Over time the suffering you witness and the suffering you cause begin to change you. Some prosecutors grow callous, and they forget that their defendants are human beings. "These people are all animals," I have heard career prosecutors say. Others like me lose their innocence. As time goes on, we grow increasingly aware of the nature and extent of our power, and that makes us more anxious, more hesitant, and more cautious. Eventually, either we grow numb or we resign.

There is also a personal cost to the job. In big-city offices, the caseloads are so huge, the demands of the job so intense, and the stress so severe that it takes a toll on personal and family life. A good AUSA in the middle of a major trial must be obsessed with his or her case. To win, it takes total focus. Unfortunately, your family and friends pay the price. Today virtually all my AUSA friends from the EDNY and the Enron case are in private practice. Their new jobs demand a lot of time, but the stress level is different. As Eric Tirschwell, my trial partner on the Puma drug kingpin trial, told me just the other day, "In a civil case no one is going to go to prison. That changes everything."

THE ESSENCE OF LIFE as an AUSA is judgment. Every day you get up and you judge other human beings. You determine what they did, how evil they are, how likely they are to obey the law's commands in the future. Then, when you have as much information as you can gather, you decide their fate. You send some to prison, and you let others go free. It is an important job and a necessary one, but dangerous as well.

The Bible tells us: "Judge not, lest you be judged. For with what judgment you judge, you shall be judged: and with what measure you mete, it shall be measured to you again." I take that biblical passage to heart. I loved being a federal prosecutor. I loved the responsibility and the power to do good. But ultimately I am glad I passed that power to someone else. All of us desire to live a good life, but that does not happen automatically. The risk of moral failure is very real. If we handle our responsibilities poorly, without proper care and concern, we can do more damage in the world than good. The more time we spend pointing the finger at others, the less we spend assessing ourselves. In this way, prosecution can lead to moral blindness. Putting people in prison for a living can be bad for the soul.

———

FOR THE LAST FIVE YEARS I have been a law professor in Oregon. These years have been, without question, the happiest of my life. I love teaching. In my criminal law classes, I train the next generation of lawyers to be good prosecutors and defense attorneys, a very important and useful task. But my true passion is teaching jurisprudence, or legal philosophy. Together my students and I read Aristotle, Kant, and the utilitarians, trying to understand the nature of justice. I approach this reading with the same enthusiasm I had years ago as a college freshman. I still want to understand what justice is, still hunger for insight into how to be a good human being. Every year I listen closely to my students. Every year they teach me something new.

The real source of my contentment, however, is not my professional life. Today I work forty hours a week, not eighty, and that gives me room to enjoy a richer life. I spend lots of time outdoors, running, hiking, and snowboarding, enjoying Oregon's amazing natural beauty. I have managed to save money for the first time in my life, and I have been able to buy my first house. My parents and I are reconciled. Above all, I have fallen in love. In short, I seem to have grown up. Life is good.

Having found peace and fulfillment, a wise man would undoubtedly hesitate to change his course in life. Some days I definitely feel that way. I tell myself that I want to teach for the rest of my professional life. But on others I yearn to return to public service. That desire is in my blood.

Three weeks ago Oregon's attorney general announced that he would not seek another term in office, and I have decided to announce my candidacy to take his place. My motive is simple. Oregon is a unique state, offering a very high quality of life, but we face great challenges. Mexican drug cartels are flooding the state with methamphetamine, and our high addiction rate is causing massive child abuse. Polluters routinely violate our environmental laws. Crooked mortgage brokers, scam artists, and identity thieves prey on consumers, particularly senior citizens. The attorney general of Oregon has immense powers to tackle these problems. As the state's chief legal officer he can file civil lawsuits, supervise criminal investigations, and use the office's bully pulpit to help shape the state's crime and enforcement policies. If he does his job right, he can make a real difference in the lives of the citizens of the state.

To be honest, I am nervous about running for political office. In an age of spin, lies, and attack ads, I am not sure that conviction and experience are enough to win an election. I worry about the inevitable ethical compromises of political life. I worry about raising the money needed to win. Nevertheless, I think I have to try. I want to take polluters and white-collar criminals to court and hold them accountable for the harm they cause; improve child support enforcement, so single parents get the money they need to raise their kids; and fight for a new drug treatment program, to cut the demand for meth and other narcotics. I know how to do these things, and I believe I can do them well.

My campaign is going be a long, hard struggle. I am definitely a political underdog. To be blunt, there are some powerful corporations in the state that are not thrilled at the idea of a former Enron prosecutor as their next attorney general. But I am going to enter this battle with every ounce of energy I have. In this life, I have learned, there are some things so important they are worth fighting for.

Sources

Throughout this book I have tried to describe my experiences as honestly as possible. I have made nothing up. On occasion I have altered the identity of a lawyer or informant, and in some cases the underlying facts of a case, to protect privacy or safety. Where I have done this, I have generally noted it in the text or the source notes included below. Where I repeat statements made in court, those quotations come directly from official court transcripts, unless otherwise indicated. When I repeat statements made out of court, from my conversations with witnesses, agents, or other lawyers, those statements come from memory. As a trial lawyer I know that memory is a faulty tool, deceptive, often self-serving. I have tried to be as accurate as I can.

This is not a tell-all book. Federal Rule of Criminal Procedure 6(e) prevents government attorneys from disclosing any matters occurring before a grand jury. Accordingly, I have not described any grand jury proceedings, and I have not disclosed any information originally presented to a grand jury that was not later disclosed by the government in court.

Lawyers also owe a duty of confidentiality to their clients. Normally, this rule is very easy to apply. If an attorney wants to write about a case, he must first seek permission from his client. Application of this rule is more complex for government prosecutors. Our client is the public, and there is no practical way to obtain such consent from the citizens of the United States. Though scholars have called for a new rule to address this unique situation, the bar has not done so. Accordingly, I have done my best to use commonsense judgment. I have not disclosed the contents of meetings with Attorney General Janet Reno and Michael Chertoff, then the chief of DOJ's Criminal Division, because I believe senior Justice Department officials have a right to discuss issues openly with their subordinates without worrying that their comments will be repeated in public. In countless instances, I have not disclosed information about a particular case because that information was never publicly disclosed. I have also left two cases out of this book entirely, one because it raised potential national security concerns, the other, involving possible corruption in a foreign government, because of its potential to harm (or at least to complicate) U.S. foreign relations. Though I have discussed law enforcement tactics, I have not given away any tactical secrets, and I have not discussed particular law enforcement technologies.

All the cases discussed in this book are completed, with one exception, Enron, which may drag on for years. To avoid prejudicing any defendants involved in that case whose matters are still pending, I have not discussed any evidence that has not been made public in prior Enron trials, and I have used pseudonyms more broadly in that section of the book than elsewhere.

PROLOGUE: WAITING FOR A VERDICT

The *Scarpa* verdict colloquy comes from the transcript of *United States v. Scarpa*, Cr. No. 94-1119 (RR) (EDNY), which was publicly filed as an appendix in the Scarpa appeal, *United States v. Sessa*, United States Court of Appeals for the Second Circuit, Docket No. 99-1312(L), 99-1366 (XAP), 99-1509 (CON). The quote from Justice Jackson is taken from Robert H. Jackson, "The Federal Prosecutor," 24 *Journal of the American Judicature Society* 18, 18 (1940). The quote from Judge Gerald Lynch is from "Panel Discussion, The Expanding Prosecutorial Role from Trial Counsel to Investigator and Administrator," 26 *Fordham Urban Law Journal* 679, 682 (1999), which provides an excellent overview of the ways in which prosecutorial function has changed since the 1960s. The classic discussion of the ways in which prosecutorial power has been enhanced in American society is Bennett L. Gershman, "The New Prosecutors," 53 *University of Pittsburgh Law Review* 393 (1992). I have altered the name and identity of "Jimmy," the courtroom security officer. To help ensure accuracy, AUSA Dwight Holton reviewed the text.

CHAPTER 1: THE MAKING OF A PROSECUTOR

I have altered the name of the friend I identify as "Bob." The Gopnik quote on humanism is from Adam Gopnik, "Read It and Weep," *New Yorker*, August 28, 2006. The "beep-me-at-home" quote is from Christopher Georges, "Clinton's Young Staff, Resigned to Reality," *Washington Post*, April 25, 1994. The "How old would that make" quote is from an editorial, "The White House Kindergarten, Etc.," *Washington Times*, April 30, 1994.

CHAPTER 2: THE CODE OF SILENCE MURDERS

I previously wrote about the Charlestown Code of Silence Murders case and its legal implications in John R. Kroger, "The Confrontation Waiver Rule," 76 *Boston U. Law Review* 835 (1996). The facts and judicial analysis of legal issues in the case can also be found in several judicial opinions: *United States v. Houlihan*, 201 F.3d 427, 1999 WL 1319197 (1st Cir. 1999); *United States v. Houlihan*, 92 F.3d 1271 (1st Cir. 1996); *United States v. Houlihan*, 887 F. Supp. 352 (D. Mass. 1995); and *United States v. Houlihan*, 871 F.Supp. 1495 (D. Mass. 1994). My account of my own involvement is based primarily on my own recollections. To check facts and dates, I referred to the fabulous *Boston Globe* coverage of the case, led by reporter Judy Rakowsky, which included but was not limited to: Kevin Cullen, "The Code of Silence Is Cracked in Charlestown," October 29, 1993; John Ellement and Shelley Murphy, "Handgun Sought in Slaying Is Believed Found; Informant Is Said to Break Charlestown Code of Silence," April 16, 1994; Judy Rakowsky, "Indictment Hits Alleged Murder, Cocaine Dealing in Charlestown," May 19, 1994; Judy Rakowsky, "'Code of Silence' Target of Charlestown Arrests," June 23, 1994; Judy Rakowsky, "After 2 Years, Arrests Give Charlestown Fresh Hope," July 25, 1994; Judy Rakowsky, "6 More Indicted on Slay Charges; Father, Son Died in Charlestown," July 27, 1994; Judy Rakowsky, "Prosecutors Prepare Case Against 8 from Charlestown," October 6, 1994; Judy Rakowsky, "Prosecutor: Witnesses in Charlestown Threatened," October 9, 1994; Matthew Brelis, "Car of Man in Charlestown Case Bombed," November 4, 1994; Judy Rakowsky, "'They've Been Playing God for Years'; Trial to Test Charlestown Code of Silence," November 5, 1994; Judy Rakowsky, "Charlestown Drug Ring Case Outlined in Court; 6 Accused of Deadly 'Silence' Conspiracy," November 9, 1994; Judy Rakowsky, "Charlestown Native Testifies, Breaks Area's 'Code of Silence,'" November 17, 1994; Judy Rakowsky, "'Code of Silence' Case Is a Theatrical Affair," November 25, 1994; Judy Rakowsky, "'Code of Silence' Witness Testifies Detective Ignored Drug Evidence," November 30, 1994; Judy Rakowsky, "'Code of Silence' Witness Says Defendants Were Her Friends," December 9, 1994; Judy Rakowsky, "Crucial Link Is the Goal in 'Code of Silence' Trial; At Midpoint, Prosecutors Confident," December 27, 1994; Judy Rakowsky, "'Code of Silence' Witness Tells of Hit List; Testifies He Helped Defendant Kill Man," January 18, 1995; Judy Rakowsky, "'Code' Judge's Ruling Raises Eyebrows," January 30, 1995; Judy Rakowsky, "Witness Testifies He Sold Drugs for 'Code of Silence' Defendant," February 4, 1995; Judy Rakowsky, "'Code of Silence' Defendant Pleads Guilty," February 23, 1995; Judy Rakowsky, "Final Arguments Heard in 'Code of Silence' Case," March 8, 1995; Judy Rakowsky, "3 Convicted in 'Code of Silence' Trial," March 23, 1995; Judy Rakowsky, "Another Bullet to Dodge; 'Code of Silence' Defendant to Face New Trial," May 21, 1995; Paul Langer, "Last Defendant Pleads Guilty in Code of Silence Case," June 17, 1995.

The Markovits quote on the duty of zealousness is from Daniel Markovits, "Further Thoughts About Legal Ethics from the Lawyer's Point of View," 16 *Yale Journal of Law and the Humanities* (Winter 2004), 85. The quote from a "top attorney" on the same topic is from Steve C. Briggs, "The Myth and Mischief of Zealous Advocacy," Colorado Bar Association President's Message to Members, *Colorado Lawyer* (January 2005). The quote from Justice Sutherland is taken from *Berger v. United States*, 295 U.S. 78, 88 (1935). The quote from Justice Douglas is from *Donnelly v. DeChristoforo*, 416 U.S. 637, 648–49 (Douglas, J., dissenting). My estimate of the number of criminal AUSAs is derived from the *United States Attorneys' Annual Statistical Report for FY 2004* (2005), 3, which reported that there were that year, 5,412 Assistant United States Attorneys, 78 percent of whom did criminal work and 22 percent civil cases. My estimate of the number of state prosecutors comes from the *Sourcebook of Criminal Justice Statistics, 2003*, which reported that in 2001, the last date for which such statistics have been collected, state and local prosecutors' offices employed 79,436 people, 33.5 percent of whom were prosecuting attorneys or chief prosecutors. I have changed the names of the prosecutor who helped me with my interview hypothetical questions and the senior supervisor who flashed me her underpants for what are, I hope, obvious reasons. Polling information about the public reputation of lawyers can be found at www.galluppoll.com/content/default.aspx?ci=1654.

CHAPTER 3: THE TEDDY BEAR BURGLARY

This chapter is based on the trial transcript from *United States v. Ancel Elcock*, Cr. No. 97-992 (DGT) (EDNY) and my own recollections of the case. The text of Elcock's letter to Claudia Pelz, which was used as evidence in the trial, comes from a copy that I have kept in my personal files. A summary of the facts can be found in Judge Trager's extradition opinion, *Ancel Vincent Elcock v. United States of America*, 80 F. Supp.2d 70 (EDNY 2000). The U.S. Court of Appeals' decision upholding Elcock's conviction and sentence may be found in *United States v. Elcock*, 173 F.3d 846, 1999 WL 147035 (2d Cir. 1999).

CHAPTER 4: OPERATION BADFELLAS

This chapter is based on the trial transcript from *United States v. Anthony Martinez*, Cr. No. 97-725 (FB) (EDNY), the government's brief in *United States v. Anthony Martinez*, U.S. Court of Appeals for the Second Circuit, No. 00-1767, and my own recollections. A summary of the facts of both the underlying case and Saladino's perjury can be found in *United States v. Anthony Martinez*, 26 Fed. Appx. 40 (2d Cir. 2001). The PRISON GUARDS PROBE TAINTED headline ran above a story by Jerry Capeci in the New York *Daily News* on August 16, 1999.

CHAPTER 5: THE HUMAN FACTOR

Most of this chapter is based on my own recollections. The facts of the Sullivan perjury and suicide may be found in the government's letter to Judge Raggi, dated March 9, 2000, from the file in *United States v. Stanford Francis*, Criminal Docket No. 99-1106 (RR) (EDNY), as well as in William K. Rashbaum, "Officer Accused of False Testimony Kills Himself, Police Say," *New York Times*, March 15, 2000. I have also discussed that case at length with the lead prosecutor, former AUSA Eric Tirschwell, who has reviewed that portion of my text for accuracy. I have changed the name of the attorney whom I have called "Charles Mears" in the Secret Service counterfeiting case and altered the identity of "Dora" in the money smuggling case. To refresh my memory of the facts in the *Zorina-Burmagina* case, I referred to the judgments, *United States v. Olga Zorina*, Cr. No. 98-064-02 (JG) (EDNY), and *United States v. Lyudmila Burmagina*, Cr. No. 98-064-01 (JG) (EDNY). The quote from Judge Gleeson comes from my memory, not a transcript.

CHAPTER 6: THE SCARPA CREW AND THE FBI

My brief history of the Scarpa Crew and its criminal activities is based on personal knowledge and the trial transcript from *United States v. Scarpa*, Cr. No. 94-1119 (RR) (EDNY), which was publicly filed as an appendix in the *Scarpa* appeal, *United States v.*

Sessa, United States Court of Appeals for the Second Circuit, Docket No. 99-1312(L), 99-1366 (XAP), 99-1509 (CON). A summary of the facts of the case can be found in the Court of Appeals' decision upholding Scarpa's conviction and sentence: *United States v. Scarpa*, 4 Fed. Appx. 115 (2d Cir. 2001). A summary of the facts relating to Scarpa's 1980s drug trafficking business can be found in *United States v. Scarpa*, 913 F.2d 993 (2d Cir. 1990). My discussion of the DeVecchio scandal is based on the exhaustive multi-volume appendix filed publicly by Ellen Corcella and Sung-Hee Suh in the *Scarpa* case, which is part of the official record. The quote describing the defense as "bizarre, but not entirely implausible," is from *Orena v. United States*, 956 F. Supp. 1071 (EDNY 1997) (Weinstein, J.), which also contains an excellent summary of the relevant facts about Scarpa Senior and DeVecchio. To help ensure accuracy, Sung-Hee Suh reviewed Chapters Six through Nine. I also discussed the *Scarpa* case with Valerie Caproni, who provided her recollections about the case's bizarre procedural history.

My brief history of the mafia and the FBI's mafia enforcement efforts is based on extensive reading and research over the years, as well as hundreds of discussions with FBI agents, defense attorneys, and fellow prosecutors. The best single-volume history of organized crime in America is *New York Times* investigative reporter Selwyn Raab's *Five Families*, St. Martin's Press (2005). For readers interested in the story of the government's assault on the mafia, a great source is Professor James B. Jacobs's *Busting the Mob, United States v. Cosa Nostra*, New York University Press (1994). As a mafia prosecutor I always kept a copy of Carl Sifakis's *Mafia Encyclopedia*, 2d ed., Checkmark Books (1999), at my desk. The quote from James B. Jacobs regarding J. Edgar Hoover is from Jacobs, *Mobsters, Unions, and Feds*, New York University Press (2006), 10–11. The estimate that 350 FBI agents were assigned to organized crime work is from Raab, 264. Readers interested in keeping up-to-date on the mafia world should turn to Jerry Capeci's website Gang Land, at www.ganglandnews.com. Gang Land is a remarkable source, functioning as a small-town newspaper for everyone in the mafia world: prosecutors, agents, wiseguys, inmates. Capeci is also the author of *The Complete Idiot's Guide to the Mafia*, 2d ed., a comprehensive 444-page treatise.

CHAPTER 7: HITMEN
For information on the Cathy Palmer incident, see Judy Keen, "Prosecutor Undaunted by Booby-Trap Threat," *USA Today*, January 31, 1990. For the contract on Greg Andres, see Robert F. Worth, "Mob Boss's Lawyer Charged with Aiding Murder Plot," *New York Times*, June 25, 2005, and William K. Rashbaum, "Mob Trial for a Man Who Wears His Attitude," *New York Times*, February 21, 2006. For the Tom Wales case, see Paul Shukovsky, "FBI Cuts Agents Looking into Murder of Tom Wales," *Seattle Post-Intelligencer*, June 3, 2006. For the Aronwald case, see William Glaberson, "Mob Figure Admits Roles in Murders, Including Judge's," *New York Times*, August 14, 2004. The balance of this chapter is based on my own recollections.

CHAPTER 8: A MAFIA MURDER TRIAL
My account of the Scarpa trial is based on the trial transcript from *United States v. Scarpa*, Cr. No. 94-1119 (RR) (EDNY), which was publicly filed as an appendix in the Scarpa appeal, *United States v. Sessa*, United States Court of Appeals for the Second Circuit, Docket No. 99-1312(L), 99-1366 (XAP), 99-1509 (CON), as well as my own recollections. For the Gerry Shargel incident, see Jerry Capeci, "This Week in Gangland," www.ganglandnews.com, November 14, 2002. For the Slotnick assault, see Anthony M.

DeStefano and T. J. Collins, "Slotnick Deems Assault a Mere Mugging," *Newsday*, July 17, 1987, and Peg Tyre, "Judge Bats Slotnick off Persico Case," *Newsday*, January 28, 1994. In my account of Billy Meli's cross-examination, I have altered the last line slightly, because the official record does not match my strong memory of his precise choice of words. I do not recall the name of the Virginia prosecutor who taught me cross-examination and so have used the name Thompson.

CHAPTER 9: HOW WE BEAT THE MOB

This chapter, like Chapter Five, is based on my personal experience as well as extensive reading and conversations with organized crime agents and prosecutors dating back to my time as a mafia prosecutor and continuing to the present. I should note a particular (and broad) debt to Professor Jacobs of NYU, particularly in my discussion of the mafia and organized labor. The Gleeson quotes regarding the value of accomplice testimony and the sentencing guidelines are from John C. Jeffries and John Gleeson, "The Federalization of Organized Crime: Advantages of Federal Prosecution," 46 *Hasting Law Journal* 1095 (1995). For the Local 560 case, see Jacobs (2006), 19, and Jacobs (1994), 31–78. My data on consumer credit cards are from Thomas A. Durkin, "Credit Cards: Use and Consumer Attitudes, 1970–2000," *Federal Reserve Bulletin* (September 2000), 623–26. Information on lending by the SBA and Accion USA comes from those two organizations' websites.

CHAPTER 10: WIRETAPS

My calculation that 500,000 Americans work in the drug trade is undoubtedly conservative, since there were 319,500 arrests in the United States for sale or manufacture of illegal drugs in the United States in 2004 alone. See U.S. Department of Justice Bureau of Justice Statistics, Drug Law Violations—Enforcement (2005 version), at www.ojp .usdoj.gov/bjs/dcf/tables/salespos.html. For the number of DEA agents and "federalized" local law enforcement officers working on drugs, see Bureau of Justice Statistics, Drugs and Crime Facts, available at www.ojp.usdoj.gov/bjs/dcf/enforce.html. For 16 million American drug users, see Jonathan P. Caulkins, Peter Reuter, Martin Y. Iguchi, and James Chiesa, "How Goes the 'War on Drugs,' an Assessment of U.S. Drug Problems and Policy," Rand Corporation (2005), 1. My discussion of the Garcia wiretapping case is based on my own recollections and on publicly filed documents from the case, captioned *United States v. Nicolas Garcia et al.*, CR-00-425 (EDNY) (CBA), including the docket sheet, the multiple affidavits in support of arrest warrants, indictments, judgments, and the government response to the defense motion to suppress, July 14, 2000.

CHAPTER 11: BUSHWICK

My discussion of the Bushwick case is based on my own recollections as well as the complaint in *United States v. Lora*, M-99-0781; the complaint in *United States v. Granados-Rienan and Longas*, M-99-0982; the complaint in *United States v. Castellano et al.*, M-99-0966; the sentencing minutes for *United States v. Diaz*, 99-CR-580 (ARR), May 28, 2002; the sentencing minutes in *United States v. Castellano*, 99-CR-580 (ARR), May 27, 2004; and the docket sheet and judgments filed against the various defendants. My decision to discuss Oscar's cooperation in this book is a bit unusual because cooperation is typically kept secret. I have done so, however, because Oscar's cooperation has been publicly acknowledged by the United States in open court and in publicly filed documents. Cooperation by "Manuel" has never been publicly acknowledged, so I have altered his identity and my description of his conduct in material respects. I have slightly edited Paul Nalven's remarks at Oscar's sentencing, adding a couple of words and cutting a few, for Paul is an articulate guy, and I suspect that the somewhat incoherent official transcript reflects the court reporter's limitations rather than Paul's exact phrasing, but I have changed nothing of substance. My discussion of the Correa prosecution is based on my own recollections and the public docket sheet, CR-01-1117 (ARR). My discussion of the Aguirre case is based on my own recollections and the docket sheet, CR-01-706 (ARR). My discussion of the Boston Crew case is based on my own recollections plus publicly filed documents from *United States v. Medina et al.*, CR-00-1034 (RR), including the judgments, docket sheet, indictment and superseding indictment, the letter to the court dated December 19, 2000, the government response to defense motions dated January 30, 2001, the sentencing minutes for Jesus Medina dated October 4, 2001, and various defense motions, as well as the docket sheet publicly filed in *United States v. Matos*, CR-01-679 (RR). For information about the Bushwick initiative since 2001, see, e.g., press release, "Fourteen Defendants Indicted on Drug Trafficking and Firearms Charges," U.S. Attorney, Eastern District of New York, June 28, 2006, available on the EDNY website. For Bushwick today, see Jeff Vandam, "Living in Bushwick, Brooklyn; Bargain Hunting? Stay on the L Train a Little Longer," *New York Times*, June 11, 2006. For the 1990 and 1995 Bushwick crime statistics, see the New York Police Department website for its "Compstat" reporting for the Eighty-third Precinct.

CHAPTER 12: HUNTING "THE PUMA"

The chapter is based primarily on the trial and court transcripts from *United States v. Juan Jose Rodriguez*, Cr. No. 99-166 (NG) (EDNY) and my own recollections of the case. The Guy Womack conflict of interest was discussed extensively in open court on April 15, 1999. The Manhattan controlled delivery was the subject of extensive testimony in a public suppression hearing on June 4, 1999. The Arturo Trevino affair was discussed in open court both during the trial and in a status conference on June 16, 1999. For background on attorney Ivan Fisher's suspected involvement in the flight of a former client and his misrepresentations to the EDNY bench, see *United States v. Levy*, 25 F.3d 146 (2d Cir. 1994). For Sydney Schanberg's views of Fisher's courtroom tactics, see Sydney Schanberg, "New York: What Price a Waiter's Life," *New York Times*, June 22, 1982. For Fisher's tax fraud, see Pete Bowles, "Probation for Lawyer in $1M Tax Case," *Newsday*, November 21, 1989, and "Lawyer Pleads Guilty in Income-Tax Case," *New York Times*, August 22, 1989. For Fisher's $500,000 fee, see, e.g., Walter Goodman, "Books of the Times: A Truly Tangled Web," *New York Times*, September 5, 1988, and Ry Siegel, "Subpoenaed on Fees: Has U.S. Put Lawyers on the Defensive?," *Los Angeles Times*, June 14, 1985. To help ensure accuracy, Eric Tirschwell reviewed a draft of this chapter.

CHAPTER 13: THE DARK SIDE

This chapter is based primarily on my own recollections. I have changed several names in order to protect privacy and, in some cases, safety. I have also altered the facts of some cases to maintain confidentiality. For the statistics on violence against judges and police in Colombia, see Rafael Pardo, "Colombia's Two-Front War," *Foreign Affairs* (July–August 2000). For information on Colombia's illegal wiretapping program, see

Juan Forero, "Wiretaps Raise New Problems for Colombia's Uribe," *Washington Post*, May 16, 2007; Chris Kaul, "Wiretap Scandal Grows in Colombia," *Los Angeles Times*, May 16, 2007.

CHAPTER 14: HOW TO WIN A WAR ON DRUGS

My discussion of narcotics enforcement strategy is based on personal knowledge gained as a narcotics prosecutor, extensive reading, and my study of narcotics strategy as a law professor. My views have been heavily influenced by the Rand Corporation studies noted below, which provide, I think, the very best analysis of America's war on drugs. I wish more people would read them. For the 2006 poll conducted by the National Association of Chiefs of Police, see Jim Kouri, "2006 Police Chiefs Poll: Terrorism, Gun Control, Drugs," March 2, 2006, in www.americanchronicle.com. For the quotation from the Rand study regarding U.S. drug prices, see Jonathan P. Caulkins, Peter Reuter, Martin Y. Iguchi, and James Cihesa, *How Goes "The War on Drugs"?: An Assessment of U.S. Drug Problems and Policy*, Rand Corporation (2005), 7. For facts that drug use has increased by one-third since 1992 and that the greatest social burden comes from addicts, not casual drug users, see *Research Brief: Assessing U.S. Drug Problems and Policy*, Rand Corporation (2005), 1. For increased drug use by kids, see Caulkins et al., 5, 15. For drug-related emergency room admissions, see ibid., 7. For polls of ordinary citizens, see ibid., 27. For Plan Colombia, see Joel Brinkley, "Anti-Drug Gains Don't Reduce Flow to U.S.," *New York Times*, April 28, 2005; Juan Forero, "Congress Approves Doubling U.S. Troops in Colombia to 800," *New York Times*, October 11, 2004; Juan Forero, "Letter from the Americas: Hide and Seek Among the Coca Leaves," *New York Times*, June 9, 2004; Indira A. R. Lakshmanan, "$4b Later, Drugs Still Flow in Colombia," *Boston Globe*, May 21, 2006. For the size of the international drug market, see *2005 World Drug Report*, v. 1: *Analysis*, issued by the United Nations Office of Drugs and Crime (2005), 127. The figures for numbers of U.S. drug users and total money spent come from Caulkins et al., 1. For the Veillette quote, see Connie Veillette, "Plan Colombia: A Progress Report," CRS, Library of Congress (2005), at "summary." For a discussion of the way in which source control efforts have simply pushed narcotics production to other countries, see Mattea Falco, "Passing Grades," *Foreign Affairs* (Fall 1995). For the fact that 65 percent of cocaine comes across the U.S.-Mexico border, see "Drug Trafficking in the United States," 2006 version, published by the DEA, available at www.dea.gov/pubs/state_factsheets.html. For bribery, see David Johnston and Sam Howe Verhovek, "Bribery on the Border," *New York Times*, March 24, 1997. For the tunnel, see Randal C. Archibold, "Officials Find Drug Tunnel with Surprising Amenities," *New York Times*, January 27, 2006. For the quotation from the Rand study regarding the limited effectiveness of our enforcement strategy in the United States, see Caulkins et al., 16. For the 1990s Rand study on effectiveness of treatment versus other strategies, see C. Peter Rydell and Susan S. Everingham, *Controlling Cocaine: Supply versus Demand Programs*, Rand Corporation (1994). For the New York diversion program, see Paul von Zielbauer, "Court Treatment System Is Found to Help Drug Offenders Stay Clean," *New York Times*, November 9, 2003. For treatment in California and the UCLA study, see "A Victory for California," *New York Times*, April 10, 2006, and "Jail Won't Cure Drug Users," *Los Angeles Times*, July 17, 2006.

CHAPTER 15: 9/11

This chapter is based on my own recollections of September 2001 and the diary of my 2000 bike trip. To help ensure accuracy, Dwight Holton, with whom I worked on the

9/11 emergency response, reviewed the text. On November 2, 2001, FBI Director Robert Mueller stated in a White House press briefing that law enforcement had investigated 170,000 tips from ordinary citizens since 9/11. I have altered material facts about the car search warrant described in this chapter.

CHAPTER 16: THE ENRON DEBACLE

This chapter is based on my own recollections, my personal copies of e-mails sent to me at Lewis & Clark Law School prior to my joining the Enron Task Force, and a copy of the July 9, 2002, Caldwell memo, which I retained in my files. This chapter and Chapter Eighteen also reflect very broad reading about Enron and its finances. For a complete list of the hundreds of works about Enron I have relied upon and a more comprehensive discussion of Enron's business strategy and financial fraud, see the references in my article "Enron, Fraud, and Securities Reform," 76 *Colorado Law Review* 57 (2005). For Chertoff's comments about mafia prosecutors, see Michael Hedges, "Tough Trio Assembled for Probe," *Houston Chronicle*, September 9, 2002. The Bryce quote is from Robert Bryce, *Pipe Dreams* (2002), 176. The McLean and Elkind estimate of losses is from Bethany McLean and Peter Elkind, *The Smartest Guys in the Room* (2003), 412. To help ensure accuracy, Andrew Weissmann reviewed a draft of my Enron chapters.

CHAPTER 17: THE BROADBAND SCAM

This chapter is based on my own recollections and the indictment in *United States v. Rice et al.*, criminal docket no. H-03-93-04 (S.D.Tx. 2004); the trial transcript from *United States v. Joseph Hirko et al.*, criminal docket no. H-03-93-05 (S.D.Tx. 2005); the trial transcript from *United States v. Jeffrey K. Skilling and Kenneth L. Lay*, criminal docket no. H-04-025 (S.D.Tx. 2006); the trial transcript from *United States v. Kevin Howard and Michael Krautz*, criminal docket no. H-03-0093 (S.D.Tx. 2006); and the transcripts of Skilling's March 23, 2001, conference call with Wall Street analysts and March 15, 2001, meeting with Portland employees, which were posted publicly on the Justice Department website during the Skilling and Lay trial. For Skilling's legal fees, see Alexei Barrionuevo, "U.S. Wants Ex-Enron Chief to Pay Lay's Share, Too," *New York Times*, August 15, 2006. I have reconstructed the Loehr, Collins, and Meyer interviews from memory. The quote about Cox and "doubled revenue" is from McLean and Elkind at 293.

CHAPTER 18: GETTING AWAY WITH FRAUD

Many of the ideas and basic analysis contained in this chapter were presented in much greater detail, with scholarly support, in my article "Enron, Fraud, and Securities Reform," 76 *Colorado Law Review* 57 (2005). For more information, I refer you to that source. For the quote from the Supreme Court regarding the responsibility of an auditor, see *United States v. Arthur Young & Co.*, 465 U.S. 805, 817–18 (1984). For the Batson quote regarding Andersen's "substantial assistance" see *Final Report of Neal Batson, Court-Appointed Examiner*, In re Enron Corp., No. 01-16034 (AJG)(Bankr. S.D.N.Y. Nov. 4, 2003), 46–47. For the Toffler quotes, see Barbara Ley Toffler, *Final Accounting: Ambition, Greed, and the Fall of Arthur Andersen* (2003), 62, 6. For the Andersen partner e-mail regarding the Enron directors and LJM, see Rebecca Smith and John R. Emshwiller, *24 Days* (2003), 293. For the quote stating that Enron's financial statements were "inscrutable," see testimony of Charles L. Hill, director of research, Thomson Financial/First Call, in *Enron Collapse: Impact on Investors and Financial Markets, Joint Hearing Before the House Subcommittee on Capital Markets, Insurance, & Government*

Sponsored Enterprises, and the House Subcommittee on Oversight & Investigations of the Committee on Financial Services, 107th Congress (2001), 128. For the *Fortune* story regarding Enron's financial statements, see Bethany McLean, "Is Enron Overpriced?" *Fortune* (March 5, 2001), 123. For the quote from *The Wall Street Journal* discussing analysts liking a stock they knew so little about, see Rebecca Smith and John Emshwiller, *24 Days* (2003), 173. The quote from a financial expert before the Senate Governmental Affairs Committee can be found at Staff of the Senate Committee on Governmental Affairs, 107th Congress, *Financial Oversight of Enron: The SEC and Private-Sector Watchdogs* (Committee Print 2002), 60. The data regarding "buy ratings" on Enron stock in 2001 and retaliation against analysts are from the same source at 5 and 6. Morgan Stanley's "no negative comments" policy is discussed in "The Rohrbach Memo: 'No Negative Comments,'" *Wall Street Journal*, July 14, 1992. The "junk," "shit," and "crap" quotes are from the Governmental Affairs Committee report cited above at 62. The Olson quote is from Robert Price, *Pipe Dreams: Greed, Ego, and the Death of Enron* (2002), 252. Quotes from the McKinsey study of the SEC are from Mark Maremont and Deborah Solomon, "Missed Chances: Behind SEC's Failings: Caution, Tight Budget, '90s Exuberance," *Wall Street Journal*, December 24, 2003, at 228. The "Rare Headline" quote is from "A Rare Headline: Wall Streeter Could Face Jail," *Wall Street Journal*, April 24, 2003. For the sentencing of James Brown, see Mary Flood, "Former Merrill Lynch Executives Get Less Prison than Requested," *Houston Chronicle*, April 23, 2005, 11:16 p.m. (online edition). For statistics on federal white-collar prosecutions, see, e.g., "Timely New Justice Department Data Show Prosecutions Climb During Bush Years," Transactional Records Access Clearinghouse, Syracuse University, at trac.syr.edu, posted September 28, 2005. These 2005 data have been reconfirmed by data from the first half of 2006, the most recent available.

CHAPTER 19: THE FASTOW DILEMMA

This chapter is based primarily on my own recollections. The quote from Tom Hanusik comes from a 2006 e-mail exchange between us discussing the origins of his investigation into Michael Kopper and the Southampton deal. For the Wigton case, see James Sterngold, "Figure in Insider Case Might Return to Kidder," *New York Times*, August 7, 1987, and Geraldine Fabrikant, "Inquiry's Surprising Targets; Richard B. Wigton," *New York Times*, February 13, 1987. For the facts of the Lea Fastow RADR case, see indictment dated April 30, 2003, and first plea agreement dated January 14, 2004, from the file in *United States v. Lea W. Fastow*, criminal docket no. H-03-150 (S.D.Tx.). The quote from a legal commentator on the arrest of Lea Fastow is by former federal prosecutor Jacob Frankel, in Mary Flood and Tom Fowler, "Fastow May Have to Plea Bargain to Protect His Wife," *Houston Chronicle*, June 9, 2003. John Yoo's comments regarding consequentialism in government service can be found at www.law.columbia.edu/law_school/education_tech/streaming?#rtregion:main. Yoo's two "torture memos" are available from a number of different sources online. The first is entitled "Memorandum for William J. Haynes II, Re: Application of Treaties and Laws to al Qaeda and Taliban Detainees," January 9, 2002. The second: "Memorandum for Alberto Gonzalez, Re: Standards of Conduct for Interrogation Under 18 U.S.C. Sections 2340-2340A," dated August 1, 2002. For an excellent discussion of the memos and their significance, see Jane Mayer, "The Memo," *New Yorker* (February 27, 2006). Michael Walzer's essay "Political Action: The Problem of Dirty Hands," is from *Philosophy and Public Affairs* v. 2, no. 2 (Winter 1973), 160.

Acknowledgments

I owe an enormous debt to Katie Roiphe, Jan Mieszkowski, Katharine Mieszkowski, and Laura Rosenbury, who read early drafts of this book and encouraged me to continue to write about my life as a prosecutor. Elyse Cheney has been the perfect agent, helping me to define the book and improve the quality of the writing. This book would not exist if not for her faith in me and my project. Courtney Hodell at Farrar, Straus and Giroux has been an amazing editor. Having Courtney edit the work of a first-time author is like asking Barry Bonds to play Little League. I thank her for the care she has devoted to the manuscript.

Many present and former federal prosecutors and agents reviewed parts of this book, including Matt Segal, Eric Tirschwell, Sung-Hee Suh, Valerie Caproni, Dwight Holton, Jeff Jenson, Andrew Weissmann, and Leslie Caldwell. Paralegal Tereva Soto of the EDNY helped me gather public documents relevant to the Bushwick case. Elizabeth Reichoff provided excellent proofreading and made numerous helpful suggestions. I am deeply grateful for their help and assistance. Needless to say, I am responsible for any errors that remain in the text.

The research and writing of this book was supported by several summer faculty research grants provided by Lewis & Clark Law School. Lewis & Clark has been a great intellectual home for me. I am very grateful to the dean and faculty for their support. I would also like to thank my outstanding Lewis & Clark research assistants, who helped improve the book in many ways: Patrick Flanagan, Amanda Austin, Erin Kollar, Frank Lupo, Micah Steinhilb, Charles Marr, Alicia Cobb, Emily Jackson, and Mark Ahlemeyer.

I have dedicated this book to my parents, who put me on the path to law school. But special thanks must go to Michele Toppe and Isaiah Freier, who provide love and support when I need it most.

A Note About the Author

JOHN KROGER is a former federal prosecutor who served on the Justice Department's Enron Task Force. He was also the deputy policy director of Bill Clinton's 1992 presidential campaign. He now teaches law at Lewis & Clark Law School in Portland, Oregon.